W9-BNZ-525

# The Man Who Owns the News

ALSO BY MICHAEL WOLFF

*Autumn of the Moguls*

*Burn Rate*

*Where We Stand*
(with Peter Rutten and Chip Bayers)

*White Kids*

# The Man Who
# Owns the News

**MICHAEL WOLFF** | Inside the Secret World of Rupert Murdoch

Broadway Books | *New York*

*For my mother*
*the first newspaper person in our family*

BROADWAY

Copyright © 2008, 2010 by Michael Wolff

All rights reserved.
Published in the United States by Broadway Books, an imprint of the Crown Publishing
Group, a division of Random House, Inc., New York.
www.crownpublishing.com

BROADWAY BOOKS and the Broadway Books colophon are trademarks of
Random House, Inc.

Originally published in hardcover in the United States by Broadway Books in 2008.

Cataloging-in-Publication Data is on file with the Library of Congress.

ISBN 978-0-7679-2952-3

Printed in the United States of America

10 9 8 7 6 5 4 3 2 1

First Paperback Edition

ACC LIBRARY SERVICES
AUSTIN, TX

CONTENTS

## ACKNOWLEDGMENTS

It's important to get lucky when you write a book. My first stroke of good fortune happened when my daughter Elizabeth introduced me to her colleague Leela de Kretser, a reporter at the *New York Post*. My next stroke was that Leela was extremely pregnant and looking for a job with more flexible hours for after her baby's birth. My next was that before the *Post*, Leela had been a reporter at the *Herald Sun*, Murdoch's paper in Melbourne, where she grew up. An Aussie who's worked for two Murdoch papers to help with the research for a book about Murdoch—that's striking gold. My good luck has again and again been compounded by her keen perceptiveness about all things Murdoch, her fine-tuned interviewing skills, her in-the-trenches knowledge of the news business, and her unflagging humor. In twelve months we have done more than 120 interviews together, crossed Australia, and sat for more than fifty hours with the book's subject. It may take an Australian to know one. Leela has talked out every aspect of the book with me, been as acute an analyst of News Corp.'s customs as anyone I've consulted, and somehow made all the trains of this project run on time. This book rests as much on her shoulders as my own—the mistakes will have undoubtedly come in those instances where I ignored her warnings and advice.

My friend of twenty years, Christopher Silvester, a Fleet Street diarist of long standing, helped track down old Murdoch hands in London, convince a wide assortment of Murdoch's current British friends and foes to chat about him, assemble the surprisingly large body of Murdoch literature, skillfully conduct some of the notable background interviews for the book, and read the manuscript with patience and a keen eye.

Simon Dumenco, who may well have edited as many words of mine as any editor has for any writer, read this manuscript with the greatest care and offered the wisest of counsel, saving me from countless instances of excess and embarrassment.

This project began in the summer of 2007 in a column I wrote for *Vanity Fair* about the Dow Jones takeover. My *VF* colleague Doug Stumpf was the first to see the possibilities for this material as the basis of a book and urged me forward. *VF*'s editor, Graydon Carter, provided some of the initial insights that form the portrait of a new and evolving Murdoch. All of my colleagues at the magazine have been extraordinarily supportive of the project—and tolerant of my obsession with KRM.

My editor at Random House, Phyllis Grann, and her colleagues Steve Rubin, Bill Thomas, David Drake, Kathy Trager, and Jackeline Montalvo have been enthusiastic, discerning, and smart publishers—and fast, too, turning around a complicated manuscript on a relative dime. Their colleagues in London, Gail Rebuck and Dan Hind, have also worked with speed and good humor. Dan deserves special thanks for helping me through that most galling, pernicious, and absurd literary process: a British libel read.

And then there is Andrew Wylie, my agent. I called Andrew about the possibility of doing a book involving Murdoch and Dow Jones on a Friday afternoon in August 2007. Before the following

Friday he had helped shape a proposal, conducted an auction, and scored me a publisher. Watching him work that week was one of the most awesome things I've seen in thirty years of trying to find someone who knows what they're doing in the book business.

This book, in its twelve months from inception to completion, has depended on many hands. That includes Danit Lidor, Jackie Cook, Mark Bowker, Lisa Payton, Kim Carollo, Kate Hammer, Rehaneh de Kretser, Jennifer Fishbein, Sheldon Gravesande, and Genevieve Gorta, who did the transcribing of hundreds of hours of interviews. It also includes Michelle Memran, my *Vanity Fair* colleague, who with Marni Hanel, Joanne Gerber, Danit Lidor, and Althea Chang fact-checked the manuscript.

None of this would have been possible without the singular cooperation of this book's subject, who not only was (mostly) a patient and convivial interviewee but also opened every door I asked him to open. He has been as helpful in facilitating this book as I can imagine any CEO ever being with a writer who owes him nothing. Indeed, he asked for nothing in return for his openness and cooperation. Likewise, News Corp. executives in New York, Los Angeles, London, Melbourne, and Sydney have been as generous and expansive in discussing their boss as I might have hoped—all of them being as fascinated by him as I am. Members of the Murdoch family—wife Wendi, daughters Prudence and Elisabeth, sons Lachlan and James, sons-in-law Matthew Freud and Alasdair MacLeod, sisters Janet Calvert Jones and Ann Kantor, nephew Matt Handbury, and mother, the remarkable Dame Elisabeth—have made the time to help me and each has been thoughtful, straightforward, and in almost every case uncommonly perceptive about their family, the family business, and, not least of all, the subject at hand. In the end, however, only Dot Wyndoe, Rupert Murdoch's personal assistant for more than forty years, could be reliably counted on to schedule a meeting, supply a specific piece of information, or locate an address—she's made everything so much easier.

Gary Ginsberg, News Corp.'s executive vice president, global marketing and corporate affairs, has been unfailingly helpful throughout this process. And while I have—rather often, I'm afraid—deviated from his guidance, disagreed with his views, and, I suspect, undermined his interests, he has been, and I hope will remain, a good friend.

Andrew Butcher, who joined News Corp. as a copyboy straight out of high school and rose to be a longtime spokesman for the company, has been an invaluable guide into the News Corp. culture. He has in too many instances to count made sense of what at News has not seemed to make any sense at all. This book is vastly smarter for his having shared his insights.

Dow Jones executives, both past and present, along with many *Wall Street Journal* staffers have been extremely forthcoming with time and information. Members of the Bancroft family, all of whom have spoken off the record, have been keen to have me understand the complicated currents and diverse characters within the family, as well as the real story of the takeover, so often very different from the way it was told, not least of all by their own paper.

Everybody in my family has not just lived all the details of my year with Rupert Murdoch, but has offered some pretty good advice (unsolicited or not).

And it is not just my family who has endured this book and pitched in when needed. Janon Fisher, Leela's husband and a newspaper reporter, has shared insights and extended great patience. Chris de Kretser, in Melbourne, Leela's father and a newspaperman for more than forty years, sat up over many nights reading the manuscript with an eagle eye, catching all sorts of errors of fact and carelessness.

The following people have been interviewed for this book, have shared valuable information about its subject, or have offered useful advice about its creation. I owe them, as well as numerous others who have asked to remain anonymous, a great debt:

Col Allan, editor in chief, *New York Post;* Jesse Angelo, managing editor, *New York Post;* Ken Auletta, *New Yorker* staff writer;

Vicky Barnsley, CEO, HarperCollins UK; Richard Beattie, attorney for Simpson, Thacher and Bartlett, LLP; Emily Bell, director of digital content for Guardian News and Media; Simon Bax, former chief financial officer of Fox Filmed Entertainment; Tony Blair, former prime minister of the United Kingdom; Mark Booth, former CEO, BSkyB; Maggie Brown, British journalist; Charlie Burgess, Fleet Street editor; Peter Chernin, president and COO of News Corp.; Michael Costa, media banker, Merrill Lynch; Gordon Crovitz, former publisher of the *Wall Street Journal;* Gary Davey, former CEO, Star TV; Barry Diller, chairman and CEO of IAC/InterActive Corp.; Matthew d'Ancona, editor, *Spectator* magazine; Jeremy Deedes, former managing director of the Telegraph Group; John Dolgen, former chairman, Paramount Pictures; Sir Rod Eddington, director of News Corp.; Karen Elliott House, former publisher of the *Wall Street Journal*; Edward Jay Epstein, author; David Faber, CNBC chief correspondent; Philip Falcone, senior managing director, Harbinger Capital Partners; Ivan Fallon, chief executive, Independent News and Media UK; Steve Fishman, *New York* magazine writer; Jonathan Foreman, former *New York Post* reporter; Michael Fuchs, former head of HBO; Michael Garin, a founder of Lorimar Telepictures; Stephen Glover, British journalist and one of the founders of the *Independent*; Roy Greenslade, media columnist and commentator, the *Guardian*; Richard Greenfield, Wall Street media analyst at Pali Research; James C. Goodale, former general counsel and vice chairman of the New York Times Company; James Harding, editor in chief, *Times* of London; Bert Hardy, former chief of News International; John Hartigan, chairman and CEO of News Limited; Tony Hendra, author and humorist; Les Hinton, CEO of Dow Jones; Alan Howe, former *Sunday Herald Sun* editor; John Huey, editor in chief, Time, Inc.; Arianna Huffington, co-founder and editor in chief of the Huffington Post; Sir Bernard Ingham, Margaret Thatcher's former press secretary; Richard Ingrams, co-founder and former editor of *Private Eye*; Jay Itzkowitz, former senior corporate lawyer at Fox Entertainment; Michael Jackson, television and news media executive; Sir Simon Jenkins, columnist, the *Guardian*, former editor of the *Times* of London and the *Evening Standard*; Lon Jacobs, News Corp. general counsel; Michael Jones, former political editor of the *Sunday Times*; Peter Kann, former CEO, Dow Jones; Trevor Kavanagh, former political editor of the *Sun*; Sir Chips Keswick, former Murdoch banker at Hambros Bank; Robert Kindler, vice chairman for investment banking at Morgan Stanley; Jonathan Knee, Wall Street banker; Andrew Knight, director of News Corp.; Phillip Knightley, author of *The First Casualty* and former *Sunday Times* reporter; Ed Kosner, former editor of *New York* magazine; Dominic Lawson, former editor of the *Sunday Telegraph*; James B. Lee Jr., vice chairman, JPMorgan Chase; Joanne Lipman, former *Wall Street Journal* editor; Sir Nick Lloyd, former editor of *News of the World*; Frank Luntz, political consultant; Brian MacArthur, former editor at the *Times* of London and the *Sunday Times*; Stephen Mayne, Crikey founder; Tom McGrath, entertainment and media executive, former chief operating officer of the Viacom Entertainment Group; Bill Mechanic, former CEO and chairman of Fox Studios; John Micklethwait, editor of the *Economist*; Kelvin MacKenzie, former editor in chief of the *Sun*; Piers Morgan, former editor in chief of the *News of the World* and the *Daily Mirror*; John Motavalli, author of *Bamboozled at the Revolution*; John Nallen, News Corp. deputy CFO; Andrew Neil, former editor in chief, *Sunday Times*; Mark Oliver, media consultant, CEO, Oliver and Ohlbaum Associates; Norm Pearlstine, chief content officer at Bloomberg; M. Peter McPherson, former chairman of the board of Dow Jones; David Penberthy, Sydney *Daily Telegraph* editor; Chapman Pincher, *Daily Express* reporter; Mario Platero, U.S. editor, *Il Sole 24 Ore*; Joyce Purnick, reporter for the *New York Times* and reporter at the *New York Post* at the time of the Murdoch takeover; Jeff Randall, business reporter for the *Daily Telegraph* and former editor at the *Sunday Times*; Jane Reed, director of Times Newspapers Limited; William Rees-Mogg, former editor of the *Times* of

London; Arthur Siskind, former News Corp. general counsel; Andrew Ross Sorkin, business reporter for the *New York Times*; Roger Smith, Wall Street analyst and former Warner Communications executive; Michael Schrage, former *Washington Post* media business reporter; Malcolm Schmidtke, former editor of the *Sunday Age*; Stanley Shuman, managing director of Allen and Company LLC; Anne Spackman, editor in chief, Times Online, *Times* of London; Patrick Spain, CEO of HighBeam Research; Rob Spatt, attorney for Simpson, Thacher and Bartlett, LLP; Paul Steiger, former managing editor of the *Wall Street Journal*; Irwin Stelzer, economist and Murdoch confidant; Cita Stelzer, research associate, Hudson Institute; Andrew Steginsky, fund manager; Peter Stoddard, former editor of the *Times* of London; Robert Thomson, editor in chief, the *Wall Street Journal*, former editor in chief, the *Times* of London; Richard Tofel, former *Dow Jones* senior executive; Donald Trelford, former editor in chief of the *Observer*; Rebekah Wade, editor in chief, the *Sun*; Jonathan Wald, senior vice president for business news, CNBC; Lord Wakeham, former British MP; Jann Wenner, founder of *Rolling Stone*; Francis Wheen, *Private Eye*; Robert Wiesenthal, executive vice president and chief financial officer, Sony Corporation of America; Charlie Wilson, former editor of the *Times* of London; Petronella Wyatt, reporter for the *Daily Mail*, daughter of Murdoch confidant Woodrow Wyatt; David Yelland, former editor of the *Sun*; Richard Zannino, former CEO, Dow Jones; Mortimer Zuckerman, proprietor of the New York *Daily News*.

Lastly, my appreciation to Claridge's in London, where so many of the interviews for this book took place. Claridge's, a hotel possessed of virtues of a prior age, actually has a fondness for writers and has, on my many trips to London for this book, cosseted me in style, looked after me with care and interest, provided me with a home away from home (far better than my actual home), and demonstrated over and over again that old saw that, given the choice, a civilized man might well prefer to go Claridge's rather than to heaven.

The question with which I began this book was still the question when it ended, becoming ever more insistent in the ensuing months after publication: Why did Murdoch allow me into his office and his family?

One of the executives who has worked most closely with Murdoch over the past dozen years or so told me, "The answer lies in the egotism of two men." That is, Murdoch and Gary Ginsberg, his powerful and ever present public relations assistant, who would pay a heavy price for his involvement with this book.

Murdoch believes he is going to do nothing less than save—and control—the newspaper business. His faith in newspapers and his astute bet on them are key parts of the legacy I was meant to enshrine. As for Ginsberg, my book, according to those familiar with the court politics of News Corporation, was meant to elevate him in direct proportion to how much it pleased Murdoch and therefore give him greater political standing to resist the two other factions vying most hotly for influence over

Murdoch: Roger Ailes, head of Fox News, and the Murdoch children.

In News Corporation's perfect ad hoc character, neither Murdoch nor Ginsberg had read much of what I had previously written (this might be an information company, but they like their information in the short version). Hence, when they did read the book, they were not just angry but profoundly bewildered.

"It's all about him," said Ginsberg.

"Well, it is a biography," I said, reasonably.

"But it's so *personal.*"

What he meant, I believe, and what Murdoch's ire was about, is that I had diverged from their fixed and traditional idea of a biography, particularly one that had the cooperation of the subject: something dignified and formal, a self-serious compendium of chronology and details. (They were particularly keen on the details of deals, of who had bested whom.) By way of comparison, Ginsberg referenced the biography of Warren Buffett, *The Snowball: Warren Buffett and the Business of Life*, by Alice Schroeder, which had just been published, as the kind they had expected from me (although it is unlikely either man had read that book).

It is worth noting that the Buffett biography was elaborately stage-managed by Buffett and his staff. I was chosen largely on impulse (partly because I asked, partly because I knew Ginsberg, and partly because I was one of the few journalists not appalled by the mere idea of Murdoch's takeover of the *Wall Street Journal*), and then nobody at News Corp. could quite be bothered to pay attention to what I was doing. Once in the door, I became an afterthought. Murdoch talked to me in his rambling fashion (Ginsberg was often in the room but always engrossed in his BlackBerry) without, in News Corp. character, apparent plan, preparation, or direction—posterity clearly bored him. This allowed me, I believe, to write a book that caught him more in mid-sentence than in a carefully reflective mood—more about what he was actually thinking than what he might want to be thought of as thinking.

Eight or nine weeks before the book appeared, Murdoch and Ginsberg got a purloined copy of the manuscript. Other than the copy in the hands of the book's publisher, there were, in London, only three copies, each with one of the newspapers that were considering serialization: the *Guardian*, which ultimately won the serial; the *Telegraph;* and the *Mail*, with each paper signing a nondisclosure agreement. Murdoch's son-in-law, Matthew Freud, as well connected as anyone within British newspapers—partly because, in spite of his father-in-law's frequent disdain for him, he represents himself (not inaccurately) as a prime mover within the highest reaches of the Murdoch organization—obtained one of the copies and passed it to New York.

In the course of a day, Murdoch, as though suddenly panicked about posterity, personally left me more than a dozen increasingly insistent and irate voice-mail messages, saying he had read four of the book's seventeen chapters and had "grave concerns about the facts."

The things he seemed to object to most—beyond hotly disputing details such as the circulation of the *Daily Mirror* in 1968—were some of the things in our discussions he had taken most delight in: his steady jabs at Peter Chernin, the company's then COO, whom he would force out in the summer of 2009; his ridiculing of Roger Ailes ("Well, the man's insane"), who, as Fox News became ever more profitable, became ever more powerful within News Corp.; and his plans for buying or leveling the *New York Times*.

I believe that Murdoch somehow thought Ginsberg would sanitize these aspects of the book. At the same time, I believe that Murdoch was trying to slip them in and then would blame Ginsberg when they were not sanitized. And, indeed, although the book is from the horse's mouth, Ginsberg would suffer for it. In November 2009, Ginsberg lost his job, purged both because of this book and because liberal Ginsberg had run more and more afoul of Fox News' Roger Ailes, who threatened to quit over Murdoch's casual disparagements of him and Fox News (which he blamed on Ginsberg) in the book (and who ended up with a big raise because of it) and because James Murdoch was trying to assume more control of his father's day-to-day affairs.

But ultimately, Murdoch's willingness to cooperate with this book, on top of being an act of ego, was, I believe, in Murdoch fashion, together with his decision to buy the *Wall Street Journal,* a backhanded sort of strategy:

He *was* sending a message, it just wasn't for posterity. Rather he was letting off steam. He was bored with where his company was going; he was feeling out of the loop and he wanted back in; he wanted to reaffirm his own job and mission. Whatever the world might think about how he did his job (which was ultimately of little concern to him), he was, like his father before him, a newspaperman. He wasn't a vendor of the crummy television shows and movies that he never watches—even if that's how he made most of his money. He was the proprietor of the greatest news empire in the world. That's what News Corp. was, and no one should forget it. Damn it.

Since Murdoch's acquisition of Dow Jones and the *Wall Street Journal* and the completion of this book, the newspaper industry in the United States has entered what is undoubtedly the most dramatic downturn in its history—by all accounts a structural rather than cyclical decline. News Corporation's share price suffered the steepest decline of any of the major media holding companies, and it took a $3 billion write-off associated with the Dow Jones acquisition. At the same time, Rupert Murdoch became the world's most public defender of newspapers, continuing to strategize and fantasize about how he might take over the *New York Times*—while baldly denying that's what he was doing. Publicly he would call my descriptions of his designs on the *Times* nonsense—but it is a subject that he discussed in almost every one of our interviews. (At one point in our discussions, Murdoch said that he thought I was writing this book too early, that the real story was not just his takeover of the *Wall Street Journal* but when he capped his plan with the acquisition of the *Times*.)

Murdoch's desire to own the *Times* is, I would continue to argue, at the heart of the transformation of the company that began with his acquisition of the *Journal.*

That's his dream plan: First the *Journal,* which at $5.6 billion was almost double what he would have paid if he had waited only six months, and probably five times more than he would have had to pay if he'd waited a year (making the Bancroft family, Dow Jones's controlling shareholders, the luckiest or savviest newspaper owners to have ever walked the earth), but no matter. He would not only prove his mettle as a respectable and tough-minded publisher—for a man who cares little about what people think of him, he still understands the tactical value of being able to appear respectable—but he'd also have a cost-efficient infrastructure for quality newspaper publishing in the U.S. Hence, he'd be ready to pounce on the *Times* when it became available.

This was to the mounting consternation of Peter Chernin. Chernin saw himself as the most important executive in the company—not least of all because many people on Wall Street saw him that way. He, not Murdoch, ran the company's U.S. entertainment, television, and interactive businesses, which contributed the lion's share of News Corp.'s revenue and profits. These were businesses—including Fox Studio, Fox Network, and the owned-and-operated television stations around the country—that Murdoch had little or nothing to do with. Murdoch's province, largely in partnership with his son James, was the complicated initiatives of pay television in foreign markets—which included the highly profitable Sky satellite television network in the U.K., a successful venture in Italy, and other more problematic ventures in Asia and Eastern Europe—and the company's legacy newspaper business.

Most of Murdoch's time was spent on the increasingly less profitable newspaper business. This could be as granular as overseeing the redesign of the *New York Post*'s Sunday paper (a failed initiative). Such preoccupation on Murdoch's part was good for Chernin—it meant he was left alone.

But Chernin, having carved an independent fiefdom within News Corporation, increasingly rankled Murdoch. On the one hand he needed Chernin to run the parts of the business that didn't interest him at all; on the other hand he certainly didn't want someone to get credit for his company, nor anybody to rain on his parade if he wanted, for instance, to buy a newspaper, nor for there to be a contender to his children's primacy at the company. In other words, Chernin had to go. In their negotiation over a new contract, Murdoch simply refused to renew the understanding they had come to during the last contract agreement: If Murdoch left the company during the term of Chernin's contract, Chernin would get the CEO job. So Chernin, whom Murdoch had made a wealthy man, left in the summer of 2009. (At one point in my discussions with Murdoch, when Hillary Clinton, whom Chernin actively supported as one of her most significant fund-raisers, was still in the race, Murdoch and Ginsberg speculated on what job Chernin might get in a Clinton administration. Ginsberg, even more loyal to Chernin than to Murdoch, said treasury secretary; Murdoch, scowling, said commerce at best.)

I do not think it has yet become clear how much Murdoch has altered the direction of News Corp., or really bet the farm, with the acquisition of Dow Jones. Investors, selling down News Corp. shares, surely suspect something is up—and aren't happy about it. But News Corp., unlike most other major public companies, does not try to make its ultimate strategy clear. More consistently, it tries to succeed in one area (even though such success may not be its main reason for being) to compensate for its failure in another area (which might well be Murdoch's main area of interest).

Simply, Rupert Murdoch wants to use the resources of News Corp., its vast entertainment assets, to save and to dominate the news business. His fronts are newspapers, which every other sentient being but him believes are in terminal decline; online distribution, a medium about which he, not using a computer, has no firsthand knowledge, but which he believes by sheer force of will and jawboning he can turn into a fee-making and profitable outlet for news (or at least so frustrate his online customers that they will return to the printed paper); and developing international markets, where, in the Murdoch manner of making many simultaneous bets, he might well succeed in being the newsman of the future.

Notably, too, he has succeeded in an almost complete remaking of the *Wall Street Journal* with an entirely counterintuitive business strategy. In a world where specialized business information has increasing value, and generalized, commodified information has decreasing worth, he has changed the *Wall Street Journal* from the leading business-focused brand to a brand that, denuded of its distinctive look and feel, has been refocused on broad, top-headline, general-interest international and national news coverage—oh, yes, and with a sports page.

A company that, when he bought it, was making $50 million a year in profits—already a woeful historical decline—will have lost, during his second year of ownership, close to $100 million. And yet, having remade it more and more in his image—a faster, stronger, snappier, more dramatic, less fussy, less snobby paper—he is a happy man.

And that is the point I have tried to make again and again in this book: News Corporation is about letting Rupert Murdoch have what he wants—the man, however wrongheaded, will not be denied.

I must add here perhaps the most fitting coda—which is my experience with the empire striking back.

Toward the end of my interviews with Murdoch—which at times focused on his relationship with Wendi Deng, the young woman for whom he broke up his thirty-two-year marriage—Gary Ginsberg pleaded with me, on what he said were instructions from the boss, to fudge the date when Murdoch first met Deng. Murdoch wanted it moved from before the end of his marriage to his second wife, Anna, until after. Now, as it happens, I was thinking about how to blur a similar time line in my own life and knew exactly why Murdoch was squirming. Nevertheless, I demurred, pointing out that, at any rate, many people knew the real date. "Then," Ginsberg said, "you won't have his support. Count on the opposite."

For three months after its publication, my book was not mentioned in any of the Murdoch media outlets anywhere in the world, until, in early March 2009, the *New York Post*, under a full-page headline worthy of a louche sports star or major celebrity, spelled out the details of my personal life.

Gossip was one of the consistent themes in my conversation with Murdoch. If I brought him gossip, that made him much happier than when I did not. Sometimes I made up the gossip—that kept him just as happy. Gossip, for Murdoch, is partly business intelligence—who is saying what to whom; who might be buying what; who has less money than he says he has; who is fighting with Murdoch's enemies or allies—but Murdoch also likes simply to know who is sleeping with whom. He especially likes to know which liberals are sleeping around (but he will take conservatives too). It is a prurient interest, but it is also leverage. He refers to having pictures and reports and files—though this may be as much what he imagines a powerful person like himself should have, whereas the reality is, as often as not, that all that his much vaunted files contain is the casual speculation of sycophantic reporters feeding him what he wants to hear.

In February, Col Allan, the editor of the *New York Post*, had come to him with a rumor about me. This was both as an offering to his boss and an effort by Allan to suit his own purposes. Allan was annoyed by what I had written about him in this book, and further annoyed that I had been outspoken about the *Post*'s publication of a cartoon that equated Barack Obama with a chimpanzee. (In this regard, Allan was on the hot seat with Murdoch—after an outpouring of anger about the cartoon, Murdoch, for the first time in his career, had to offer a personal apology for something one of his papers had published.)

Murdoch, I am told, listened to Allan's version of the details of my personal life, asked the age of the woman I was seeing, asked about her background, and told Allan to do what he wanted to do if he had the story.

Allan didn't, as it happens, have the story—although a *Post* reporter spent a week or so calling my friends and colleagues. The *Post*'s rules are quite specific on this issue: You cannot say two people are having sex unless one of the parties says they are, or unless there are photos, legal papers, or other irrefutable proof—or if there is another published source that says it's so.

The first report about me came from a Web site I had never heard of, a one-man operation about New York gossip, run by someone who also wrote items for the *Post*'s Page Six. The site had little traffic, and a story about me was unlikely to get it much more. The site's owner and writer was not someone I knew (or even knew of), nor, as far as I can figure, did he know anyone I knew, and yet it was written with a type of anger and venom that sounded, to say the least, out of context. (The change in my personal life is, as far as I can tell, the only scoop, as it were, the site has ever broken.)

The *Post* took up the coverage from there, its headlines following me for weeks thereafter, its reporters staking out my house.

Planning this foreword, I called up Richard Johnson, the longtime editor of the *Post*'s Page Six, to say I wanted to interview him about the episode: "Ahhh . . . hmmm . . . oh boy . . . well . . . I can't be interviewed because that's not the way we do things," said Johnson.

But Johnson has always been an oddly transparent character with a curious desire to be liked (or not to be blamed), and I knew to persist.

"Did you leak it for the initial Internet hit?"

"We're not that enterprising," said Johnson. But then he added, "It wasn't me. It was Col."

"Col had this leaked so you guys could republish?"

"If the shoe fits."

The *Post* even got onto a lawsuit involving various members of my wife's family (part of this suit involved my wife's efforts to move her eighty-six-year-old mother from an apartment we owned into an assisted-living facility or more suitable arrangement— which, in the *Post*'s translation, made me a granny basher), and sent photographers to chase my wife and daughter down a courtroom hall after a hearing. (The *Post*'s campaign stopped after I sent an e-mail to Ginsberg asking if there would be any reservations about me posting online the fifty or sixty hours of unedited interviews I had done with Murdoch.)

This is, in the end, age-old newspaper behavior (and part of the reason Murdoch loves newspapers so much) and the News Corp. formula: gossip, enforcement, a culture that instinctively protects itself, and that, above all else, seeks to do what it believes the boss wants done.

**FALL 2007–WINTER 2008**

Rupert Murdoch, a man without discernible hubris—or at least conventional grandiosity—had nevertheless begun to believe that his takeover of Dow Jones and the *Wall Street Journal*, something he'd dreamt about for most of his career, might actually indicate that he and his company, News Corporation, had a certain destiny, a higher purpose of which the world should be made aware.

He'd started to think that his triumph in the quest for Dow Jones was an opportunity to rebrand—the kind of marketing frippery he usually disdained. He was even toying with the idea of changing the name of News Corp., that oddly boring, generic-sounding throwback to the company's earliest days—his first paper in Adelaide, Australia, was the *News*—to something that could better indicate his and News Corp.'s philosophical reason for being.

What that reason for being exactly was . . . well, um . . . that was still hard to actually put into words. But it had something to do with . . . well, look at these:

He had mock-ups of full-page ads that, he was thinking, should run in all the *Wall Street Journal*'s competitors—particularly the *New York Times* and the *Financial Times*—on the day he took over the paper.

One of the ads had the big headline "Agent Provocateur." Another pursued the idea of pirates—the notion being that for more than fifty years the company had been . . . well, if not exactly outlaws . . . not *literally*, still . . .

When, after many hours of conversation with Murdoch, I despaired of ever getting an introspective word out of him, his son-in-law Matthew Freud, the PR man from London, advised me to ask him about "being a change agent."

This conversational gambit prompted Murdoch's enthusiastic unfurling of these ads and eager, if far from concrete, ideas— "We're change agents," he kept repeating, as though new to the notion—about the meaning of News Corp. and, by extension, himself. It also prompted dubious looks from some of the executives closest to him. Murdoch's sudden search for an ennobling and guiding idea was a vexation not just because it called attention to exactly what News Corp. executives often despaired of—that image of run-amok ruthlessness that the battle for Dow Jones had stirred up all over again—but also because it was distinctly out of character.

Soul-searching wasn't, to say the least, a part of the News Corp. culture. So it was curious, and unsettling, to have the veritable soul of the company trying to figure out why he'd gotten where he'd gotten, and for what good reason.

Such a statement about his fundamental righteousness (and even, perhaps, relative coolness) was, significantly, being urged on him by his son James, a Harvard dropout who had started a music label and then spearheaded News Corp.'s new-media initiatives in the 1990s, and who had become the CEO of British Sky Broadcasting (BSkyB), the News Corp.–controlled company that operates the Sky satellite TV network in the United Kingdom. Not long before, Murdoch had favored his older son, Lachlan, and before that his daughter Elisabeth, to eventually run News Corp. But now it was James. In fact, unbeknownst to the rest of News Corp., James was about to be given responsibility for the U.K., Europe, and Asia by his father—who wanted to spend more of his time at the *Wall Street Journal* and, in addition, wanted to use the opportunity to put James in reach of the top spot in the company (without having to actually turn over the top spot).

James had been, much more so than his father, particularly aggravated by the terrible press heaped on his dad and on the company because of the Dow Jones bid. Alternately aggressive and defensive, James was looking for a way to fight back. In fact, it was not entirely clear that the father's sudden enthusiasm for brand development wasn't about pleasing his son, clearly the apple of his eye at this moment. (He was very excited about showing off BSkyB's annual report, for which his son was responsible and which he thought was the kind of thing they could be doing at News Corp.—every employee, he said, as though new to the novelty of an expensively produced annual report, could get one!) There was enough triumphalism around News Corp. to please everybody.

Gary Ginsberg, News Corp.'s executive vice president for global marketing and corporate affairs and one of the executives most frequently attending Murdoch, while worried about the particular branding initiative of the ads, had his own brand idea that he was pushing. He had, of late, vastly expanded his portfolio beyond just being the company's PR guy to include, among other things, big-concept brand-awareness thinking. In this role, he was helping spearhead the bid News Corp. was making with the Related Companies, a major Manhattan real estate developer, for the rights to build a massive complex (larger than Rockefeller Center) on the biggest undeveloped piece of land in Manhattan. News Corp., with its naming rights to News Corp. Center (unless they changed the name of the whole company), would become the anchor and one of the main brand names of midtown.

In light of the fact that Rupert Murdoch now owned the most important—all right, the second most important—newspaper in the world, not to mention having created the world's most successful media company and being quite possibly the most influential businessman of the age (certainly the most influential for the longest time), why wouldn't he want to figure out just how he'd done what he did and claim credit for it? (Of course, another reasonable view, one that Murdoch—for so long a deal-a-minute guy—also seemed to subscribe to, was about how little meaning or calculated direction or vision there had been in the growth of News Corp. But no matter.)

Murdoch was, frankly, impressed with himself. Delighted. Giddy. He couldn't believe how exhausted he felt once the deal was done. He'd held his anticipation and excitement "all inside," and as soon as he could relax, he felt "wiped out." Perhaps more than any other accomplishment, getting the *Wall Street Journal* was, in and of itself, the big one, and not just a next step toward something else.

And there was the other stuff. Legacy stuff. There were his two young children—Grace, six, and her sister Chloe, four—and how they would think of him in, well . . . the future. There were his older children and the importance of defining the meaning of the company he would be leaving them. That was James' point. That was also what he was always hearing from Matthew Freud, the Svengali-ish marketer, who was now married to the family. Brand was legacy. The bigger the brand message, the bigger the legacy.

Plus there was Murdoch's wife, Wendi, thirty-nine. Her energy, her sense of possibilities, her urge to take over the world, to leave her mark, might be as great as his own. Perhaps they were competing.

Not to mention that at nearly seventy-seven, even a man without hubris should get a chance to make a statement. If not now, when?

On the other hand, it also seemed a potentially great mistake to attribute too much sentiment or craving for positive recognition to his motivations.

For one thing, the branding statements toward which Murdoch seemed to gravitate were not so much about News Corp.'s greatness or vision as they were about kicking dirt in people's faces. His true message about his acquisition of the *Wall Street Journal* was that he was the winner.

A month or so after the Bancroft family voted to sell him their great-great-grandfather's company, Murdoch invited the *Journal*'s fifteen top editors to lunch at the Ritz-Carlton downtown and brought along as the featured guest Col Allan, the profane, hard-drinking and foul-tempered editor of the *New York Post*. (Not too long after the sale went through, Allan was dressing down a subordinate so heatedly that he slammed his hand on the desk and cracked his cuff link—a gift from the police commissioner.) In journalistic terms, Allan might be as different from a *Wall Street Journal* editor as, say, a pit bull from a spaniel. Allan's very presence at the lunch announced that the *Wall Street Journal* had been taken over by News Corp. (Not to mention that it was just delightfully evil of ol' Rupe to bring ol' Col along to scare the bejesus out of his new charges.)

Murdoch's march into the *Wall Street Journal* newsroom with his two lieutenants—loyal Les Hinton, who ran News Corp.'s U.K. operation and who would be coming to run the Dow Jones business, and inscrutable Robert Thomson, the London *Times* editor, who would be taking over the *Journal*'s newsroom—was not the arrival of someone who wanted his great purpose and historic destiny to be roundly applauded. Rather, with the back of his hand, he let it be known that the *Wall Street Journal* was his most recently conquered nation—the staff at the *Journal*, many of whom were soon to be displaced persons, were merely history's flotsam and jetsam. They were the impediments to change. He was the change agent. "We might," he said one afternoon as he considered his new conquest, "have to let people go just to make a point." He summarily replaced Dow Jones' top executive, Richard Zannino, and the *Journal*'s publisher, L. Gordon Crovitz. He was purposely brutal with the sitting editor, Marcus Brauchli—who was, in theory, protected by the editorial agreement Murdoch had entered into with the Bancroft family in order to buy the paper. Doing an easy end run around the agreement that precluded him from unilaterally firing the existing editor, Murdoch had brought in his own editor of choice, Thomson, an Australian, and called him the publisher. The News Corp. people were bemused that people didn't immediately understand that Thomson's arrival as publisher was a demotion of Brauchli. The News Corp. people did not even let Brauchli speak at Murdoch's first meeting with the entire newsroom.

"Doesn't he understand it's our paper now?" said one of the executives closest to Murdoch, smacking his head. And if publicly disregarding (and dissing) Brauchli didn't make the point, "the fact that Rupert will stop speaking to him will," the executive chuckled. Although Murdoch offered some begrudging words about working together when he spoke to the staff, what he actually meant, News Corp. people were explaining, was that if you had a problem, leave. There was work to do, a paper to put out. A Murdoch paper.

For many journalists, hatred of Murdoch had come to define the profession. As the Dow Jones takeover progressed, both Bill Keller, the executive editor of the *New York Times*, and his boss, Arthur Sulzberger Jr., the paper's publisher, were busy characterizing Murdoch in cocktail party conversations as the worst thing that had ever happened to journalism. That's how Keller earlier confronted Ginsberg: "How can you work for the Antichrist?" The *New York Times* more and more defined itself as "not a Murdoch paper."

That characterization paralleled how Murdoch defined the profession too: there were the elites, whose contempt for him encouraged him to regard *them* as all the more contemptible, and there were those who worked for him, who were, necessarily, true believers in him.

Of note, the journalists most unhappy about Murdoch taking over the *Wall Street Journal* were often unhappy themselves. Unhappy because their jobs were insecure—the *Journal*, itself, had had waves of layoffs—their influence waning, workload increasing, and paychecks going down, indeed unhappy always knowing that they had to worry about Murdoch taking over. The people who worked for Murdoch were, arguably, among the happier people in the media business. As a newsman at News Corp., your influence increased rather than dimmed. Both Fox News and the *New York Post* took a manic delight in their influence. And Murdoch himself was fiercely loyal—even if you talked dirty to underlings, as the Fox News commentator Bill O'Reilly had, or took money from sources, as *New York Post* "Page Six" editor Richard Johnson had.

Murdoch's intention, which he began to announce everywhere with something like a sadistic glint, was to use the *Wall Street Journal* to go to war against the *New York Times*, not least of all because the *Times* was ground zero for the journalists who held him in contempt.

He'd acquired one of the two best papers in the world—which every journalist who didn't work for him assumed he would ruin—in order to destroy the other. It was a kind of personal revenge as well as, possibly, a viable business strategy.

It would be a true, and perhaps final, newspaper war.

A few weeks into the writing of this book, when news of Murdoch's willingness to sit for a series of interviews with me had spread—suggesting that I might have sold my soul or that I was in danger of losing it—I ran into Jonathan Alter, *Newsweek*'s lead writer and a figure of doubtless journalistic rectitude, in a television studio in Manhattan.

"I hope you're going to use your access to Murdoch," he said without preamble, "to really screw him."

"So *that's* how we do this job," I said—mordantly, I hoped.

Alter was not to be dissuaded. "You've got to ask yourself, is it good for the country or bad for the country? And Murdoch is bad for the country."

Tina Brown, who like Murdoch had achieved media renown in New York by way of London's Fleet Street, offered me the unsolicited counsel to avoid certain seduction, advising that my job was to educate readers about Murdoch's "cynical amorality" (a journalistic sin she is often said to be no stranger to herself).

When the former Murdoch executive Judith Regan—as much an avatar of Murdoch methods and values as anyone, and, to boot, quite a nut—sued News Corp. in the fall of 2007 for all manner of alleged conspiracies and slights, she was suddenly taken very seriously by anti-Murdoch journalists, regardless of her own operatic tabloidism. His enemies were automatically an honorable journalist's friends.

If he was demonized by one side, it was not easier to get a more rounded portrait from the other side—the people who worked for him. Pressed in an interview for his estimation of Murdoch, Col Allan, the editor of the *New York Post,* pronounced him a "gifted journalist," who could do any newspaperman's job in the world. Rebekah Wade, the editor of the *Sun* in London, told me with great intensity one evening that she had really considered from all angles what made Murdoch Murdoch, and her conclusion was that he was "a genius!"

There was a curious and stark divide among journalists as the Dow Jones battle progressed: overt hostility on the front page—the *New York Times* launched a major investigation against him—and palpable fascination on the business pages, an eager, breathless, gossipy interest in all things Murdoch.

At the *Journal* itself, as the deal proceeded, reporters became not just chroniclers of the moods and inclinations of Dow Jones' owners—the Bancroft family—but also the propagandists influencing those moods and inclinations. The *Journal's* reporters were waging, in effect, a proxy fight against Murdoch.

As soon as the takeover was sealed there was another, reflexive response: an attempt to calm the waters, curry favor, and even discover an admiration for the man heretofore the Antichrist. *New York Times* media writer David Carr censoriously opined during the takeover that Murdoch "has demonstrated a habit over time of using his media properties to advance the business interests of his organization." Then, with the takeover completed, Carr pronounced him one of the most admired figures of the new media class precisely because he integrated all his business interests. *New York* magazine elevated Murdoch in one of its emblematic best-of lists to one of the best things about New York. Marcus Brauchli, the editor who somehow wasn't getting the message that he wasn't wanted, was telling people how positively he thought the Murdoch experience was going to turn out. Part of the antipathy to Murdoch is created when people go out of their way to swallow their pride and suppress their better judgment in an effort to love him—and then he brushes them away like so much dust.

It was not without cause for some concern or self-scrutiny that Murdoch was willing to sit for extensive interviews for this book, something he had done only in a begrudging and limited fashion in the past with would-be biographers.

Possibly his willingness had something to do with his perception that I regarded many of his enemies—particularly the journalistic priesthood—with some of the same contempt with which he regarded them. Uncomfortable talking about himself, he was nevertheless immediately animated when it came to talking about his various nemeses. To the extent that I had written about what had long seemed to me a fatal flaw among many anti-Murdoch journalists—namely, that they were increasingly part of an anemic and dwindling business, that they had lost the ability to make people want to read what they had written—I was, he seemed to think, on his side.

I might also have been perceived as having a family connection. News Corp. is, as they often say, a family company. They mean that in an atavistic as well as sentimental sense. If you or yours have been part of News Corp., you are more trustworthy than those who haven't been. You've crossed some line, undergone some self-selection.

My wife's first job out of law school, more than thirty years ago, was as an associate in the law firm Squadron, Ellenoff, Plesent, and Lehrer, which represented Murdoch from the time he came to the United States. And while she was there for only two years three decades ago, several of the people who were her colleagues back then still have major roles at News Corp. now. In any ordinary corporate enterprise, most connections and relationships are fleeting. At News Corp. they can last for generations. You gain permanent citizenship in Murdochland. You've married the mob.

When my daughter Elizabeth graduated from college in 2006, Vicky Ward, a colleague of mine at *Vanity Fair* and a former editor at the *New York Post*, walked her résumé into the *Post*, where she was hired as a junior reporter—a job she has since left. (Murdoch and I have the same bias in this regard: We believe our children should work for newspapers—that to be a newspaper reporter, as long as it is still possible to be one, is the world's best job.)

Having been in the journalism business in New York for more than thirty years, I have inevitably been an anti-Murdochian too.

During the dot-com era, I had a public spat with Murdoch's son James, then running the not-too-successful News Corp. Internet businesses. I ridiculed his messianic pronouncements, and he called me (in an interview in *GQ* magazine), much to my then-eight-year-old son's delight, "an obnoxious dickhead." (When, writing this book, I reminded James of this, he felt it necessary to insist he'd been misquoted, saying that he had only called me a "jerk.")

When I became the media columnist at *New York* magazine, in 1998, my first column was about Murdoch's imminent divorce from Anna, his wife of thirty-two years. I found it a delightful possibility that marital acrimony—especially in California, a community property state, where the Murdochs then resided—might fracture the empire (I was wrong). Not too long after this, I wrote a column not just attacking the *New York Post* but analyzing its vast business failures and concluding that, by any logic, Murdoch must shut it down (wrong again). This resulted in a vendetta by the *New York Post*—not, as it happened, against me but, with greater effectiveness, against *New York* magazine's then parent company, Primedia.

During the 2004 presidential campaign, I found myself, as the result of some idle cocktail party chatter, in a room of determined left-wing types considering how to counter Fox News with a campaign to demonize Murdoch, who was not only the very personification of Big Media but a thrice-married foreigner (with an Aussie accent so thick no one in the foreigner-hating heartland would ever mistake him for anything but a foreigner) with a Chinese wife. You couldn't have a better villain.

On the other hand, covering the media industry, I had an increasing interest in who was succeeding and who was failing. Also, I was curious about someone who so obviously did what he enjoyed doing, rather than someone who rushed, willy-nilly, to do what all the other boys did. Indeed, Murdoch was, with a little critical interpretation, the man to blame for the idiotic hodgepodge we call a modern media company—because everybody had followed Rupert. As much as you might detest him, he had been, over so many years, an original and unstoppable force—in addition to having had great fun doing it. (Of course, this is also true of many con men and despots.)

And then too, I had started to think that he was somehow . . . less threatening. He was, after all . . . old. There weren't too many public companies being run by men in their seventies. The end was, had to be, near—didn't it?

Now, it is true that William Shawcross, whose biography of Murdoch was published in 1992, clearly thought Murdoch was in a wind-down phase (Murdoch's second wife, Anna, thought this too, frequently telling people that he had assured her of his imminent retirement—"And she believed him!" said Prudence, his daughter from his first marriage), when, in fact, News Corp. was only then entering the most significant phase of its growth. Still, there *had* to be an end. How much longer could he reasonably impose himself?

I ran into Murdoch in 2002 at a technology conference in California. He'd seemed hapless-looking, holding on to a stuffed animal he'd gotten in a swag bag and planned to give to his new daughter—but also, it seemed, holding on for dear life. In wise-guy fashion, a few of us—fellow conference attendees—asked him if he wanted to go for a drink. He accepted our invitation with great alacrity and, finding the bartender at this particular establishment in Monterey lackadaisically AWOL, commandeered the bar himself. Here was an appealing man, puckish, easygoing, unpretentious, in a Wal-Mart flannel shirt. He seemed like someone's grandfather—indeed, he bore a strange resemblance to my own. We ended up having dinner and chatting for several hours. When I recounted this story in a column in *New York* magazine, Murdoch's only response was to complain about the comparison of him to my grandfather.

This is the background of my prior relationship with Rupert Murdoch and of his unexpected willingness to be interviewed by me. I assume this book is part of his branding and legacy strategy—but if so, it has lacked most usual marketing or PR controls. There was no approval of the manuscript or agreement to provide News Corp. with a prior look. There were no restrictions on what I might ask about.

My interviews with Murdoch, over nine months, took place either in his office at News Corp.'s headquarters at 1211 Sixth Avenue in midtown Manhattan, over lunch in a private News Corp.

dining room, where we shared his health food drinks, or at his Manhattan home on Park Avenue—his temporary home while his new apartment on Fifth Avenue is being refurbished—when his wife was away and he was looking after his children. (An ordinary Manhattan scene of nannies, dogs, play dates, and a father picking up after all of them.)

On several occasions I was alone with him, but most other times I was accompanied by my research assistant, Leela de Kretser, a former reporter at the *New York Post* (and, before that, at Murdoch's paper, the *Herald Sun*, in Melbourne, Australia, where she grew up). Gary Ginsberg also was often present, occasionally participating in the discussion, but most often just listening.

Murdoch is a game but difficult interview subject. He trails off before finishing sentences; he speaks in what is frequently just a low mumble; his Australian accent is still thick and his Australianisms often opaque; he sometimes dips into an alarming reverie in which he is either carefully weighing his words or napping.

He's not good at explaining himself and gets annoyed and frustrated when he's asked to do so. He rarely has patience or interest in talking about the past, and he has a tenuous grasp on dates, to the point of sometimes transposing decades; he has little capacity or even language for talking about his own motivations and character. But any issue that was on his mind at the moment of the conversation he seemed always willing to explore. His thinking was, in fact, remarkably transparent—often almost guileless. His narrative of that day's events is detailed, sharp, amusing, and revealing. I certainly came to look forward to these interviews, and perhaps he did too.

He also arranged access, with only the gentlest prodding, to his top executives, all famously reticent and tight-lipped (and quite unpracticed in just exactly how they ought to be talking about him), and to all his family members—mother, sisters, wife, and children—in New York, London, Melbourne, and Sydney. "Just say anything you want to say—the worst you can think of," he told his daughter Prudence, in Sydney, who seemed to take him at his word.

One question I asked most everyone: "Why do you think he's doing this?"

Nobody had a very good answer.

# ONE

# The Butterfly Effect

**THE EARLY 1970S**

Without any firm plans and only some old family contacts, forty-two-year-old Rupert Murdoch, an Australian publishing entrepreneur relocated to Britain—not the most savory one either; reports of the "Page 3" bare-breasted pin-ups in his London newspaper precede him—starts traveling regularly to New York in 1973, looking for business opportunities. He cuts a certain sixties-ish figure: the pretty slick media executive. With his double-breasted blazer, longish dark hair starting to thin (the beginnings of a seventies comb-over), a frequent cigarette (he'll stop smoking within the year), and satisfied, plumpish figure, he's more the Madison Avenue or Mayfair type—an artful combination of diffidence and intensity—than a casual or scruffy Fleet Street guy.

His father was the most powerful newspaper publisher in Australia. Some twenty years after Sir Keith Murdoch's death, his son has made his own name—in Australia, he's *almost* as famous as his father was—and has now branched out, aggressively and noisily, to the United Kingdom. But if he's known for anything in the United States, it's that two years before, in London, he was the main character in a bizarre incident that got international attention: he's the rich guy whose wife was targeted by kidnappers who instead snatched and then murdered the wife of one of his executives who'd had the misfortune of borrowing the Murdoch family car (a Rolls-Royce, which added nicely to the story). He's the disreputable tabloid publisher at the heart of a macabre tabloid tale. The subtext of the kidnapping as it's been reported in the London papers is that it surely has something to do with, and confirms, his notorious character. (Not to mention what it says about the perils of working for him.) That's Murdoch: He's shady and alarming and dangerous.

So New York, in addition to its business potential, is something of an escape from what the Brits feel for him, and he for them. New York, he senses, is his kind of town—a place where he'll be more welcomed than disdained for his bit of notoriety.

He's a workaholic when this is not yet a popular thing to be. He's got no friends—has really never had any. "Too busy, to tell you the truth," he will explain decades later in one of our interviews. At the age of seventy-five, he'll say to his third wife, Wendi Murdoch, when she presses him on the issue, that he could have had them if he'd wanted to. He has no interests outside of his work: not sport (he may be the only Australian man not interested in sports), not culture, not reading, not movies. He has no social aspirations either. Money itself isn't even that compelling to him. He's eerie, or scary, in his lack of lifestyle desires and need for approval. There's almost a sort of autism or fanaticism to his focus. He's a new sort of business guy—"married to the business," as he will characterize himself many years later, not without some ruefulness. Working isn't the means to an end; it's the end. It's one man's war—a relentless, nasty, inch-by-inch campaign.

For the past twenty years, he's been focused almost solely on newspapers. He perhaps knows as much about the various aspects of putting out a newspaper—paper, printing, distribution, advertising, reporting, editing, headline writing, promotion—as anyone in the world. When he hasn't been working at one of his papers—eight in Australia, as much as two thousand miles apart; two more, twenty-five hours away, in London—he's been traveling between them. It's a kind of monomania that, from an early age, fascinates and disturbs other people.

He's aloof, contained, preoccupied. "Shyness," Simon Jenkins, a former editor of Murdoch's *Times* of London, will write in his 1986 study of newspaper owners, is "a characteristic shared by most second-generation proprietors, growing up under dominant fathers." In 1984, Harry Evans, another editor of the *Times*—whom Murdoch would rancorously fire—will recall the Rupert he first met in 1969 as being socially "crippled by shyness." "He shuffled, smiled and left sentences in mid-air. He seemed too diffident to be a tycoon and too inarticulate to be a journalist. This was as appealing as it was surprising."

Still, he can be disarming—if he cares to. He's not a great conversationalist, but he's a decent listener. He can even appear to be self-effacing—though this would hardly be the case. He asks good questions, and he's witty in an understated way (it's a sort of hangman's wit—he's most entertaining and caustic on the subject of other people's lapses, losses, and screwups). He's a good gossip—he'll offer information and he's appreciative of the information you give him; he's hungry for it, often rewarding the people who give it to him with sudden, surprising openness and easy, almost giggling laughter.

On the other hand, he's often disconcertingly direct or abrupt—cutting to the chase, breaking the social flow. It's a tic. It's unsocialized. Lacking any depth of self-awareness (and being impatient with what that implies), he's not all that interesting when it comes to talking about himself; he can't tell you why he does what he does, and has never been all that interested in the question. But he can be trenchant about other people—he's got a snap sense of their weaknesses. He can apply this to their spouses, their bank accounts, their ambitions (he's an expert on overreaching); he's always filing away telling, or damaging, personal details.

He's without flamboyance or personal exaggeration—he's rather buttoned-down, in fact. His occasional excesses—the Rolls-Royce in London, for instance—are guilty ones. (Later, even when he's much richer, he'll continue to be awkward about anything that suggests personal vanity or indulgence—the face-lift he'll get in the late eighties, which he will remain embarrassed about, and which will later fall, or the fretful decision to finally get himself a private plane after he buys Twentieth Century Fox and feels he has to match his status with that of the Hollywood people.) He certainly does not seem like a tabloid publisher—or what you would think a tabloid publisher might seem like.

To his employees—the people who, apart from his wife, know him best—he can be cold, impatient, all business, even cruel. And yet among them there's a sense of excitement and opportunity about working for him—and this at a time before he's done much to suggest great excitement or opportunity. He tends to hire people who are grateful for the chance, who feel they're getting more from life because of him than they would have without him. Outsiders tend to view his little band as not ready for prime time. It's one of the reasons he will, in his career, be so regularly underestimated: he never seems to be surrounded by the brightest bulbs, the A-team. Still, they are a devoted, or at least dependent, group.

Certainly the little gang that comes with him to New York in 1973 and 1974, none of whom has done any business here before, fails to impress anyone—in fact, he sends them all back and recruits other, soon-to-be-dependent, not exactly top-of-the-class people.

Those who work for him are all, in their way, followers and hangers-on—he is careful to cultivate no partners.

Bert Hardy, an advertising sales executive Murdoch recruited in London in 1972—and whom Murdoch will fire eleven years later—will later regard the Murdoch years as the most amazing and satisfying of his career. (This sense of awe or wonder is a theme of Murdoch lieutenants.) Hardy senses early on that Murdoch is different from other businessmen. But what makes him different, what motivates him to be different, remains for Hardy enigmatic.

Hardy cannot say, for instance, why Murdoch, a publisher from Australia and London, in 1973 buys a local newspaper company in San Antonio, Texas, except that it is for sale and he can afford it—which, in fact, *are* Murdoch's reasons. And that he has to begin somewhere. (As Hardy will recount years later, the two lieutenants whom Murdoch sent to do the deal initially returned empty-handed because the price had gone up. "I didn't send you to negotiate; I sent you to buy the paper," said Murdoch, and sent them back.)

With his odd beachhead in San Antonio, and his plan to start an American tabloid, the *National Star*, he moves his wife and four children—who, five years before (then with two children), he moved from Sydney to London—to Manhattan, where the Murdochs rent a place on East 72nd Street.

The reputation that will form around Murdoch derives not least of all from the impression that there is something uninvited about him—and his failure to recognize that he's not welcome, or, conversely, his enjoyment of that fact.

The single most vital, most complex element of business is, arguably, entrée. Whom you know is the basis not just of your credibility but of what information you have, and hence your success. This is also called access to the deal flow: If you don't know the people who know the people, the first time you hear about an opportunity will be when you read about it in the *Wall Street Journal* or the *New York Times* because someone else has already acted on it. Hence, too late for you.

One of the reasons all but the most well-financed entrepreneurs remain mostly local phenomena—even Kerry Packer, the richest man in Australia, and one of Murdoch's primary competitors, stays in Australia—is that part of the skill you need as an entrepreneur is knowing your own turf and market. Assuming you can re-create it elsewhere involves an amount of recklessness and grandiosity.

And there's something shifty about people who try.

It's a literary staple, the hustler's tale: the nobody from somewhere else arriving in a new place and convincing people that he or she is somebody. The characteristics of this kind of person—the charm, the plasticity, the calculated generosity—are suspect ones. He's likely escaping something, or trying to reinvent himself. That story, most often, has an unfortunate end.

Murdoch in 1974 is only qualitatively different from that hustler. He's legitimate, but the legitimacy isn't worth all that much. His company, News Ltd., has a relatively modest value of $44 million (inflation-adjusted, that would be about $200 million in 2008—not even a midsize publisher). He's got nothing that would make anyone particularly notice him. He's starting in New York pretty much from scratch.

He actually seems like someone New Yorkers might easily take advantage of: a wannabe. There are always new wannabes—foreign wannabes are the best—ripe for the picking in New York.

He doesn't, however, make the wannabe's mistake of presumptuousness, demanding attention he doesn't deserve. James Goodale, the general counsel and executive vice president of the New York Times Company, a figure of great hauteur and authority in the New York media business of the 1970s, is involved with the Columbia University Media and Society Seminars, gatherings of media eminences, when he first meets Murdoch. Goodale, a proper host, goes out of his way to chat with Murdoch at a gathering because Murdoch isn't talking to anyone. In a group of people who have known each other for years, Murdoch is content to be the odd man out, not forcing himself on anyone, not asking for attention—or too shy to seek it out. "Placid, modest, unassuming, alone," is how Goodale will recall the new man in town many years later. At first blush, there's no reason not to like him—no reason to be on your guard at all.

His slate isn't actually blank. For what it's worth—and it's a marginal boast—his family is one of the leading newspaper families in Australia. When he was nineteen and visiting America, he spent a Sunday at Hillandale, the country home of the Sulzberger family, the controlling shareholders of the *New York Times*, in Connecticut. On that same trip, he and his father visited Truman in the White House. He would later see both Kennedy and Johnson. His family entertained Katharine (Kay) Graham, the publisher of the *Washington Post*, in Australia; she returned the favor when he arrived in the United States, hosting a dinner party for him full of Johnson administration officials. He knows Leonard Goldenson, the head of ABC, who has sold him programming for his one television station in Australia.

Still, he's got to be incredibly crafty or particularly foolish to think he can re-create his business in New York. Either he's going to need a preposterous amount of luck to succeed here, or capital (which he doesn't have), or he has a preternatural vision of what's going to happen in the worldwide media industry.

Certainly in hindsight it will seem like vision. The great change that is about to come to the media business—evident nowhere in 1974—will make Murdoch possible and transform him as well. But to assume he sees this now is, practically speaking, a dramatic fallacy.

In 1974 it is almost impossible even to articulate the vision he will later get credit for: that the media business is going to go global. For one thing, the word *media* hardly exists. There is just a set of unrelated publishing, entertainment, and distribution industries. The word *global* isn't used to indicate a market. All he can sense is that the United States is big. That its media market may someday be like its automobile market—and have that kind of effect in the world. But this is also pretty far-fetched.

There isn't a model, in 1974, for turning your media business into a movable feast. Media businesses, more than most any other businesses, are local.

What's more, the media business in the United States is fixed—"not just monopolistic but growing ever more boring" is his first impression. There hasn't been any real movement in the media in years. It's locked in place by regulation, audience habits, and aging technology.

The business is dominated by the three television broadcast networks, each of which has made the leap from a dominant radio network. If there's a media kingpin, it's Bill Paley, who founded and controls CBS. There is NBC, controlled by RCA. And ABC, run by Leonard Goldenson.

There are the eight major movie studios, whose ownership is largely controlled by Hollywood insiders.

The publishing world—books, magazines, newspapers—consists largely of independent companies: old-line publishing houses in books, single-title companies in magazines, local ownership in newspapers. Only in newspapers is there some shift: the first stage of significant chain consolidation.

Other than the network evening news shows and the news-weeklies—*Time* and *Newsweek*—there are no real national news outlets. The *New York Times* is a metropolitan paper. The *Wall Street Journal* is a specialty business publication. *USA Today* does not exist. CNN does not exist. Cable television and cable news do not exist.

The fact that Murdoch will become the dominant player in each of these media categories, those that exist when he arrives in the United States and those yet to exist, is beyond rational explanation. Even the most obvious explanation—that he has no baggage, that he's the first modern media man—is untrue. He's a newspaperman—the most retro of all the media disciplines.

He's a foreigner; he's got limited resources; he's never done business in the United States before. What's more, as a newspaperman, his style of journalism—the workingman's tabloid—has been out of fashion for a generation.

What, then, is his special advantage? It may be that of the confidence man for sussing out the new environment, for absorbing information, for insinuation, and then for tricking people. Or that he enjoys what he does more than anybody else. Or that he has created for himself a bubble world—one in which he can be unmindful of other people's doubts and conventions, one in which he's able to view life in terms of only his own needs and desires. Or that he is able to subjugate his own ego to the job at hand, what the people around Murdoch call, with great respect, his natural curiosity, but which is really an extreme, killed-the-cat kind of curiosity, the curiosity of a thief; he's not just interested but covetous, not just covetous but insatiable.

Well, yes. All true enough. But still fantastic. Empires like the one Murdoch will create are most commonly built on some structural advantage: a monopoly, a financing strategy, a technology, a unique idea, some marketing genius. He has none of these.

At the end of the day, it may be just freakish relentlessness and opportunism. He tends to create a disturbance, or pick up the tremulous motion of a disturbance, that in the chaotic motion of the atmosphere becomes amplified, eventually leading to large-scale atmospheric changes . . . or some such. Or it's the business equivalent of superb hand-eye coordination—of knowing when the opportunity presents itself and how to snatch it.

**1997**

The opportunity Rupert Murdoch will act on in 2007, more than three decades after arriving in New York, actually begins its slow unfolding ten years before. It's an opportunity that comes as the result of a large and old family's inability to express its desires, not least of all because it can't quite figure out what those desires are. It's a muddle that a lot of people have had a vested interest in encouraging.

Dow Jones, publisher of the *Wall Street Journal*, which Murdoch has fantasized about owning almost since his arrival in the United States, is controlled by descendants of Clarence Barron's wife, Jessie Waldron—with whose money Barron acquired Dow Jones in 1902. This is the Bancroft family, named for Hugh Bancroft, a Boston Brahmin who married Jessie's daughter and Barron's stepdaughter, Jane Barron, and who killed himself in 1933.

The Bancrofts are a totemic American newspaper family not least of all because they have owned their paper without having much to do with it other than on a ceremonial basis. They leave the paper to be run by its editors—and have been militant (or, depending on your point of view, negligent) in guaranteeing this independence, though some of the younger generation of Bancrofts might argue they've been tricked into granting it.

When Joseph P. Kennedy tried to buy the paper after Jane Bancroft's death in 1949, Jane's daughter, Jessie Bancroft Cox, pronounced the oath: Grandfather's company is not for sale to anybody, at any time, at any price. This was not only an oath but a commandment: If A (an inquiry about the possibility of the family selling the company) happens, B ("no way") is the response. The paper's very identity has been derived from that implacable guarantee of independence and freedom.

As it turns out, the Bancrofts have been as protected from reality as they are virtuous, idealistic, or committed.

Indeed, the managers of the paper believe the Bancrofts have granted them a sort of trust to run the paper for the paper's sake. In many ways, they believe that it is their right to run the paper as they see fit—and their right to take advantage of the curious situation that has let them. After all, among the famous names associated with the paper's excellence, none is Bancroft. The Bancrofts are merely a fluke of trust and estate law—a rather happy fluke.

Such happiness has not been taken for granted by the people running Dow Jones. The Bancrofts are never to feel need (the paper has always paid a king's dividend) or anxiety—the family is never to be presented with a quandary or an alternative to their continued passive stewardship.

In the 1980s and 1990s, as the media business came to be more and more about roll-ups and acquisitions (particularly of superior brand names) and as the business of business information exploded, it became increasingly anomalous that Dow Jones was neither acquirer (which it would be hard-pressed to be, paying out so much of its earnings in dividends) nor acquiree.

This irregular, or quaint, situation has been largely the product of one man's conduct—his tone, touch, bearing, and demeanor. Mien is as valuable to him in his job as it would be to, say, a funeral director in his.

Everybody gets along with Peter Kann, the Pulitzer Prize–winning foreign correspondent at the *Wall Street Journal,* who in 1989 became the *Journal*'s publisher, and in 1991 the CEO, and subsequently chairman and CEO, of Dow Jones. He is unfailingly soft-spoken, eminently reasonable, pleasantly self-effacing, even charmingly bashful. That is Peter Kann's ultimate skill, or his most brilliant tactic: being liked so much that nobody wants to disappoint him, wound him, or confront him. He is a principled conservative, a cultured New Englander, and a man of some ineffable sadness—his first wife, Francesca Mayer, died in 1983. His demeanor also serves to hold people at arm's length, to keep them from pressing him. It is perhaps noble that he puts his sadness or diffidence or ability to deflect in the service of maintaining a great journalistic organization.

Kann's mandate as the CEO of Dow Jones is taken from the family's historic instruction not to sell; the mandate he takes from the *Wall Street Journal* is not to have the mandate not to sell revoked or modified. He has to be so dignified, so pained, so reasonable that the Bancrofts, and specifically the older Bancrofts in control of the family's money and ethos, will continue to want to protect him in the same way that they believe he is protecting them and their company. Still, if the older generation might be aghast at the thought of having to deal with something related to *business*, the young generation might be less so. But if there is no issue, nothing to deal with, then no foul.

Kann has decided that if nobody makes an offer to buy Dow Jones, then there will be nothing to discuss with the company's controlling shareholders. An expression of interest without a number, Kann and Dow Jones' lawyers long ago concluded, is not an offer. What's more, Dow Jones being a public company, they have constructed a rationale about insider information—they don't tell the family what they have to know to make reasonable decisions about the company because, well, they aren't allowed to tell; keeping information from the family has become a cherished legal obligation.

Protecting the family like this, cosseting them (or keeping them in the dark), has produced not just a docile controlling shareholder group but a remarkably sanguine and unified one. Indeed, to appear otherwise—to ask questions, for instance—is a gaucherie of high order and, too, might possibly be construed by Peter Kann as an affront, a break in propriety and politesse, which would be quite horrifying to the Bancrofts.

This holds true even as the company has been bypassed by so many business opportunities that might have not just helped the company but profited the family. There was Bloomberg, for instance, and the new market for financial data, a business that might seem a natural one for Dow Jones. Or cable television, in which it briefly dabbled. Or a business news channel—which it bid for but lost to NBC.

Dow Jones instead banked on something called Telerate, which it first invested in and then bought outright. Telerate might have competed with Bloomberg, except for the fact that it didn't. At Dow Jones itself you could find executives and reporters consulting their Bloomberg terminals, while the Telerate machines weren't even turned on. Where Bloomberg was clever and fast and satisfying, slicing and dicing data in all sorts of new ways, Telerate was kludgy and slow and so often infuriating.

In the fall of 1996, Dow Jones baldly and innocently confessed to the market (the company was not only bad at technology but bad at PR) that its big electronic media bet would need vast new investment—and thereby tanked its stock. It was the biggest dive in the company's history as a public corporation.

And it *took* the biggest dive to raise the Bancroft family's eyebrows. But even here, the family has remained mostly understanding. In fact, if there are some grumblings inside Dow Jones about Kann, he knows he has the nonjudgmental support of the Bancrofts. And if there are some Bancrofts who might feel some vague frustration over the way things are going, there is the weight of the rest of the family to buffer any expression that might be seen as ungenerous.

The exception is Billy Cox III, from the Cox-Hill branch of the family. Billy's grandmother is Jessie Bancroft Cox, the daughter of Jane Barron and Hugh Bancroft. His father is Bill Cox Jr. His father's sister is Jane Cox Hill MacElree. Of the three branches of the Bancroft family, the Cox-Hills are famously the most difficult—although, in their fashion, nobody in the Bancroft family quite acknowledges that anyone can be difficult.

Billy Cox—forty-one in 1997—and his father, Bill Cox Jr., and grandfather, William C. Cox, are the only Bancrofts to have actually worked at Dow Jones since Hugh Bancroft's suicide. Bill Cox Jr.—whom everybody in the company tends to call Bill Cox Sr.— has with equanimity worked out a middle-manager position for himself in the company. He has become a kind of affable mascot. His charm is in the constant assertion of his insignificance.

His son, Billy, hasn't been so deft or submissive. Genteelly put (at least by management), he hasn't been able to do what his father did: find the right role. Less genteelly put (also by management), he is a disgruntled employee.

Telerate, whose failure he thinks he understands from his view inside the company, becomes Billy's opportunity to express his anger. In a series of letters to Kann and to the Dow Jones board, he becomes an annoyance and, although no one will admit this, an unsettling reminder of ultimate accountability.

He is joined in his agitating by his second cousin Lizzie Goth—thirty-two in 1997. Lizzie Goth is the daughter of Bettina Bancroft, who is the only child from Hugh Bancroft Jr.'s (the son of Jane and Hugh Bancroft, from whom everyone in this tale is descended) first marriage, to Bettina Gray.

Lizzie's mother, Bettina Bancroft, died in 1996, at the age of fifty-five, leaving all her holdings to Lizzie, the first member of the younger generation to receive a direct stake in the company—hence her sudden and uncharacteristic (for a Bancroft) activism: It is her money.

Together, Billy and Lizzie start asking advice of investment bankers (among them Nancy Peretsman at Allen and Company, Murdoch's longtime banking firm) and—most noxiously to the rest of the family—going to the press. Such media attention, notably an article in *Fortune* by Joe Nocera for which Cox and Goth were obviously the source—draws a parade of suitors to the *Journal*'s office. These include Arthur Sulzberger Jr., chairman of the New York Times Company; Donald Graham, chairman of the Washington Post Company; Marjorie Scardino, chairman of Pearson; Michael Bloomberg, chairman of Bloomberg LP; and Rupert Murdoch. (Ten years later, though, Murdoch won't remember that it was the Cox-Goth contretemps that caught his attention. His visit will blend with all the other times he thought about how much he'd like to buy Dow Jones.)

All suitors are given the prescribed response: "No way!"

But neither Billy Cox nor Lizzie Goth nor any other members of the family, including those on the Dow Jones board, are informed that the company has suitors—not a peep. So the possibility that the family might convert its holdings into cash is not broached, nor is the possibility that it might create with the *Times, Post,* or *Financial Times* a quality publishing powerhouse, with the scale, brand, and cash flow that might dominate the information industry.

After they blab to *Fortune,* Cox and Goth are, for all practical purposes, shunned by the rest of the family. Shortly after the article appears, Cox is forced out at Dow Jones. Both Cox and Goth will move overseas. While other younger Bancrofts—those in their thirties and forties—are also full of questions about their odd inheritance and enforced stewardship, they are all rich enough and passive enough not to want to deal with the cold shoulder that would greet them if they voiced too many complaints within the family. What's more, in 2000, with the bull market surging and technology advertising at its peak, Dow Jones will reach $75 a share—its pinnacle.

And yet 1997 leaves the family and its trustees jittery—the Bancroft trustees, at the family's ancestral (well, since 1940s) trusts and estates firm of Hemenway and Barnes, in Boston, now ask for and get a position on the board alongside the three seats reserved for the three branches of the Bancroft family. Since the trustees control the trusts that control the company, "ask" can well be read as "demand." There is a regular effort now to deal with the obvious fact that Dow Jones isn't the best investment in the world. On the advice of its trustees and advisors, the family sells down as many shares as it can while still keeping control.

But in the fashion of a family that dislikes overt conflict, nothing happens. And nothing changes either. Except that everybody gets older, including Kann, including the Bancroft cousins, including Murdoch—moving everything toward . . . something. Nothing—even nothing itself—goes on forever. A lack of movement is itself odd and disturbing, and if you are finely attuned to these sorts of things—stasis where there should be progress—it suggests its own sort of opportunity.

Which falls to the person who plays the longest game.

# TWO

# Around the Corner

## LATE 2004

There are two events at the end of 2004 that might have raised questions about Rupert Murdoch among his closest advisors—if doubting him or having any skepticism at all about him was an option, which it was not.

This is not just because he surrounds himself with particularly compliant lieutenants—or, as they tend to call one another, henchmen. But because the men (all men) who surround him—and many have been with him for decades—have come to believe that he has special powers, that he can "see around corners." They not only believe this but *need* to believe this. Where, in other companies, other executives wait for the top executive to falter, count on it even, here any sign of faltering or error is adjusted or rationalized or made part of the plan by the people around him. They believe in him—if not as an omnipotent person, then as the closest version of one they ever expect to come upon. His near omnipotence is their meal ticket;

his near omnipotence is their brand. What is News Corp. but a company built around the instincts, impulses, and gambles of its leader?

Both of the troubling events that occur at the end of this year involve Murdoch's family, which is the central governing principle of News Corp. Fostering the well-being, power, and present and future opportunities of the Murdoch family, in its multiple iterations, is, after only Rupert's interests (which he judges—for the most part anyway—as part and parcel of his family's interests), the reason for the company's existence. Inside News Corp., you treat the Murdochs like they are the royal family—or the way the British royal family was regarded before Rupert Murdoch's tabloids came along and destroyed their mystique.

Murdoch sees himself, and hence everybody at News Corp. sees him, as first and foremost a good family man—even if he has three of them.

There is the early, left-behind family: former wife Patricia Booker, whom he continued to support through her many travails after their divorce until her death in 1998, and their daughter, Prudence, born in 1958, who moved in with her father when she was nine. Then there's the dominant middle family: former wife Anna, to whom he was married for thirty-two years, with their daughter, Elisabeth, born in 1968, son Lachlan three years later, and son James fourteen months after that. And now the new family: wife Wendi and daughters Grace, born in 2001, and Chloe, born in 2003. There is also his centenarian mother. And then his three sisters and their families and their various involvements with News Corp. Murdoch, the most famous lone gun in the age of business lone guns, is an extremely encumbered one.

This can be difficult for the executives closest to him. They are often caught between their responsibility to keep the greater Murdoch family happy and his not-infrequent tendency to make his family quite unhappy.

The consternation he is causing in late 2004 is related to what is perhaps the most confounding and dramatic moment in the history of News Corp. and of the Murdoch family: the fact that, against all indications, character, and personal beliefs, one day in 1998 he upped and left his wife for a woman thirty-eight years his junior—Wendi Deng, from Shandong Province in China. Within every other company, indeed with regard to every other powerful man, this surely would have been treated for what it was, a leveling human weakness, or even great comedy. At News Corp., his breakup and remarriage were treated with a level of sensitivity, graciousness, and respect as hardly exists in human nature and certainly does not exist on the gossip pages of his own newspapers. Indeed, several of his closest executives shortly followed suit and left their wives.

Although there is nothing stylish about him, nothing young (except his wife), nothing particularly lifestyle-oriented about his lifestyle, he had, after the breakup, curiously moved to SoHo, Manhattan's most chic-ishly aspirational neighborhood. His sons, Lachlan and James, both exceedingly fashionable, lived nearby.

But as peculiar as downtown Rupert is, it is not nearly so jarring and out of character as what he does next: impulsively agreeing to pay $44 million for the most expensive apartment in New York.

To his executives, this is *not* Rupert Murdoch, and certainly for his adult children, it is *not* their father.

Rupert Murdoch doesn't show off. What you see is what you get. He is an old man, with a crevassed face, in inauspicious suits, with an ever-present singlet under his white shirt. He might be worth $10 billion, give or take, but the money has never been the thing.

His wife, Wendi, as she will tell me in an interview in 2007— as she was finishing decorating the apartment—finds his tightness particularly laughable and, in a sense, endearing. "His whole family like this. They so cheap. When he ordered the boat"—the 183-foot sailboat *Rosehearty*—"he worried," she will relate in a Chinese accent as pronounced as his Australian one, "people think it's too extravagant, too much money. I said, 'Rupert, don't worry.

All our friends like Tom Perkins or David Geffen, they have like this huge ship. I don't think you're extravagant. Your boat is not as spectacular.'"

His penuriousness, his aversion to pretense, his disdain for grandness or affectation or—his worst, most damning word—elitism, is the DNA of his company.

But in a real-estate-mad city, it is hard not to give the most expensive apartment pretty glaring meaning. Real estate is the art of the obvious. Real estate defines the man. Murdoch *is* surely saying something pretty unsubtle and, it would seem, against his very nature.

He might in fact be more appealing and less threatening as a slightly foolish rich man. If on one end of the rich scale there is Donald Trump, all mouth and affect, calling attention to himself, on the other end is Rupert Murdoch, shadowy and scowling, all head and no affect, his personality largely hidden from view. We actually seem, counterintuitively, to like it when the rich buy what they want—it brings them down to size, their needs. But it is hard to fit Murdoch into this ordinary and fallible role. Even though he is among the most gilded men in a gilded age, he is not characteristically associated with stuff, with the personal symbols of wealth—the houses, the boats, the planes. He has them (as many as seven homes—in Los Angeles; London; Beijing; Canberra, Australia; Carmel, California; Long Island; as well as Manhattan) but, partly because he works all the time (with an OCD level of attention), and partly because he comes across as rather less than human—ruthless as well as remote—the normal human pleasures and pride of being rich don't seem to define him or leaven him. He's Nixonian in that sense—enjoyment does not seem to be a priority. He is just so clearly more interested in power than in things. He understands that the symbols of power—and this is not something necessarily so well understood by the rich and powerful—aren't power; they are distractions.

What's more, he always seems to be on the run. Disconnected, physically as well as emotionally. Everywhere but nowhere. Not

part of anything. Just a man with a phone. He seems abstract, dis-
embodied, puzzling. Not like you and me. Not susceptible to the
ego enhancements we'd be susceptible to. When his second marriage ended, nobody, but *nobody,* thought there might be another
woman.

The most logical reason for a rich man to break up his longtime
marriage was not even considered—not even by the great gossips
and analysts who closely follow him (and a divorce when you're one
of the richest men in the world—a resident, at that time, of California, a community property state—is followed very closely). He
is just too remote, unfeeling, preoccupied, old (he is a man who
seems permanently old—his singlet is his symbol).

Unlike so many of his peers, he has never become a familiar
part of the social comedy. The media, for one, has not brought him
down to size because he owns it—or owns enough of it to effectively inhibit its natural derisiveness. His public relations man of
thirty years, Howard Rubenstein, even negotiated a truce with the
other New York tabloid, Mortimer Zuckerman's *Daily News:*
Neither man's paper will truck in the other's personal life.

Indeed, the hatred that people bear him and the fear they have
of him have much to do with the sense that he has no weakness, no
vanity, no need. He does not need to be liked—does not, it seems,
even like to be liked.

And yet here he is, wanting something so transparent, so
human. Why would he want to start showing off at his age?
Preening. Making a lifestyle statement.

Oddly, Murdoch has lived here in this exact same building once
before (though in a much less imperial apartment—one that cost
$350,000 in the 1970s), with his second wife, Anna, steely and gra-
cious, who had been nicely attuned to the world's grandest neighborhood. Now Murdoch is moving back into the building with
Wendi. He is being reborn as nouveau riche.

The once-and-future-wife aspects of the dwelling (in all of
these buildings you have *ancien régime* neighbors and great atten-

tive staffs with vast historical memories) have to be figured into his statement. Either the current wife wants what the former wife was entitled to and Murdoch is giving it to her, or Murdoch himself wants to show that he is powerful enough not to have to go down a separate tangent, live *downtown*, just because he has a new wife.

He noticed it first in the *New York Times:* Laurance Rockefeller had kicked the bucket. It's that old New York truism—the way to find an apartment is to read the obituaries. He'd glimpsed the place once. When he lived here with Anna, in a duplex, he went to a building meeting in the Rockefeller triplex. Seeing that Laurance was dead and gone, that the place might be available, he started calling everybody he knew so he could be the first one to make an offer when it came on the market. He had Dick Parsons, then the CEO of Time Warner and a former banker, write a letter to David Rockefeller, the former head of Chase Manhattan Bank and one of the grandest of the city's grandees as well as the late Laurance's brother.

Overlooking the zoo in Central Park, it is, at eight thousand square feet, with twenty rooms and four terraces and eleven and a half bathrooms over three floors, an "incomparably imperial apartment," as the *New York Observer*, the preeminent chronicler of the city's imperial apartments, gushes.

Except Wendi, for one, hardly thinks so.

"We go there, the walls are falling apart," she'll tell me. "It's very WASPy. I didn't understand. It's not me. There was a hole in the floor . . . Awful. I think they live there all their lives. They hadn't done anything for forty-five years. Everything is falling apart. The art was fantastic. I said to Rupert, 'Isn't that a great Monet?' But we didn't buy those. They're gone and the carpet is old."

Other than the view over Central Park, she finds it hard to make sense of the threadbare and dowdy place—especially at $44 million. She says to Rupert that they'll have to tear the whole thing down—and he says no way! And she says, well, negotiate, definitely don't agree to the asking price. But he tells her to let him handle it—and immediately offers the whole $44 million.

By now, his family is used to (if also slightly embarrassed by) his not very convincing efforts to be young. The hair dyed obviously and vainly orange—or, occasionally, aubergine—the same color used by Sumner Redstone and Donald Trump (they seem too proud to go out and get an expensive dye job, but too vain not to have a dye job at all). And his exercise regimen and his new diets. And, of course, the new children.

But his family—new and old—worries that the $44 million apartment doesn't seem like him trying to be young; it seems more like trying to do something, make a statement, before it's too late. To say forget the Rockefellers—he is the man of the moment. The man who sits on top of the city, which is arguably true, but so unlike him to say. To have what he wants while he can still get it.

His executives, not at all used to having to deal with issues of Murdoch's self, or identity, or vanity, retreat into the customary safety of assuming that he knows absolutely what he's doing. Hence, after a day or two of exchanging puzzled and worried looks and dealing with the press (ultimately, the most difficult press inquiry is about who is going to pay the $50,000 a month for the temporary place while the new one is being renovated—Murdoch doesn't understand, at least not until the PR people and accountants explain otherwise, why the company shouldn't be paying the tab), they merely treat the new apartment with the same tact and gravitas with which they treated his remarriage.

His older children—curious, to say the very least, on edge, really, sometimes in a cold fury, or cold sweat, about *their* place in the Murdoch world—are holding their breath while they wait to find out what it means that their cheapskate father, suspicious of most airs and vanities, now clearly seems to want people to know he has arrived.

What does it mean? Is this a final statement? Some biological urge to make physical his presence before it's too late? A valedictory piece of real estate?

And then there is a second distressing event, occurring also at the end of 2004: Murdoch makes a mistake. The man who never takes his eye off the ball takes his eye off the ball. And in doing so, possibly imperils just about everything—his leadership of the company as well as his family's future hold on it.

In a move that the company's bankers and its CFO, Dave DeVoe, think will help raise the price of News Corp. shares, the company, after long debate, decides to formally transform itself from an Australian company to an American one, and to transfer from the Australian Stock Exchange to the New York Stock Exchange. When that happens—and News Corp. and its bankers are well aware of this—all the News Corp. stock that is held by index funds in Australia (that is, the funds benchmarked to the Australian market) will automatically be put up for sale by their institutional holders. This happens on November 2, Election Day in the United States, which ought to find Murdoch directing the repurchase of his News Corp. shares, but instead finds him flying from L.A. to New York on the phone getting exit numbers that are then showing John Kerry on his way to becoming president. Arriving in New York, Murdoch heads to Fox News. He gets glummer through the evening and has more and more to drink, until, sitting with Roger Ailes in the control room as the raw data comes in, the results begin to turn toward George W. Bush's reelection and he and Ailes become more and more elated. Murdoch doesn't go home until 3 A.M.

This election day also finds John Malone, the great cable television pioneer, longtime Murdoch rival, sometime Murdoch partner, and cold, calculating, disruptive, opportunistic, brilliant son of a bitch, out at his home base in Denver, buying up the News Corp. shares as they come onto the market.

By the end of Election Day, George Bush is once again president, and John Malone has a menacing 19 percent voting stake in
News Corp.—a stake second only to the Murdoch family's 30
percent.

Almost immediately the calls start going out to the Murdoch
circle. It is a breach of all systems. The walls have been stormed.
Malone's options for wreaking havoc in the company are now wide-
ranging. He could become an activist shareholder—an entirely foreign notion at News Corp., where the only man of action has been
Murdoch himself. He might demand seats on the News Corp.
board, a heretofore famously compliant body. He could continue to
buy more shares until he goes head to head with Murdoch himself.
He could begin a long siege, a war of nerves and lawsuits, to desta-
bilize News Corp. and weaken the Murdoch family's control.
Malone's presence is no less threatening given his reassurances that
he does not mean to be a threat. It is most of all threatening
because Murdoch is a man in his mid-seventies.

Malone's intent is likely to wait out Murdoch. In a world, without Murdoch he'd have maximum leverage. He could stand clearly
in the door and prevent Murdoch's children from running the company that was started by their grandfather and built by their father.

Within days a poison pill is put in place at News Corp., making
it impossible for Malone to up his stake from 19 percent and for any
other outsider to amass a stake larger than 15 percent. But, in turn,
that provokes shareholder suits, particularly by obstreperous
investors in Australia.

He's handled worse than this—much worse. And yet the very
fact that it has happened, that he didn't do the simple thing of buying the company's shares, is another indicator of News Corp.'s perhaps mortal flaw: that a $40 billion company is always waiting on
one man to do what needs to be done.

But don't go there—nobody goes there.

Murdoch himself is perfectly straightforward about what has
happened. He messed up. It is his fault. He's kicked himself for it.

"I was asleep or something," he will tell me three years later. But everybody around him is terrifically eager, desperate even, to put the blame somewhere else: on the banks, on the Australian regulators, on the index funds.

They can't let it be the old man's fault. They can't let that be suggested, because if it's the old man's fault it might mean . . .

The single largest factor in News Corp's future is almost never discussed. He thinks it embarrasses everybody else when he brings it up. And everybody else thinks it embarrasses him.

Other people's old age is a perfectly acceptable topic. His former wife Anna—the mother of three of his children—married "a nice old man." He gets a particular kick out of telling stories about Sumner Redstone, the eighty-five-year-old not-always-composmentis chairman of Viacom, one of News Corp.'s chief competitors. And then there is his longtime banker and former board member, Stan Shuman, with him since 1976, who, he feels, is past his sell-by date (Shuman will become a board member "emeritus"). John Kluge, the former head of Metromedia, "must be a hundred or ninety or something—and looks it," Murdoch happily will note, recalling the man from whom he bought his first American television stations.

It is not just his age that is a verboten topic for the people around him but all other suggestions of his vulnerability as well. This is out of an old-fashioned sort of respect due the patriarch. And it is out of a pervasive sense that he *isn't* vulnerable (indeed, as to his age, his ninety-nine-year-old mother is still alive and well in Australia, as everyone regularly repeats and reminds themselves). And the fear that he is.

Nobody mentions his obvious hearing problems. If an outsider brings it up, the insiders are careful to downplay it—"No! Why do you say that? He hears fine." If he loses his train of thought, this is just a sign of his deeper concentration. And his prostate cancer—a carefully controlled story in 2000—is now, when it's mentioned, and it's rarely mentioned, a further demonstration of his indomitability, isn't it? He's recovered, hasn't he? And never missed a day of work.

They can and will continue to rationalize. No one around him, for instance, would say, or even consciously think (or if they did they'd suppress it in a hurry), "You old fool, why are you buying such a vanity apartment?" Or "You senile turkey, how could you miss something so basic as a mother lode of voting shares coming on the market?"

Perhaps the apartment is a new phase of his personal development: The outsider has taken over the inside. Possibly Murdoch and News Corp. are about to transition from their perpetual not-of-our-class status into the elites. As for Malone, that son of a bitch, people at News Corp. understand that sometimes Murdoch has to put himself into a corner in order to get out of a larger mess—he functions well when it's do-or-die.

And yet existential dread is existential dread—there will be an end. Sometime. Which they know. Sort of.

## SPRING AND SUMMER 2005

Actually, Malone's stake isn't the only thing threatening his family's future. Murdoch has, by early 2005, more immediate problems. His two key executives—Peter Chernin, the COO and president of News Corp., and Roger Ailes, the head of Fox News—are ganging up on Lachlan.

It is Murdoch's deepest and most atavistic desire that one of his own will run the company in the future. This is problematic for a number of reasons, not least of all that none of his children is remotely qualified. Unless he himself appoints one of his children CEO—that is, uses his power and influence to supersede himself, which for him would be a kind of suicide, no more likely than the Queen of England turning over the throne—the Murdoch family, with him out of the picture, doesn't necessarily have enough control over the company to dictate succession. Post-Rupert, the board of News Corp.—even though its members are abjectly loyal to Rupert—would have other issues to consider, like shareholder suits. Such a succession plan—from the grave, as it were—is going to take a great deal more finesse on Murdoch's part. It isn't helping that Chernin and Ailes are agitating against Lachlan, who, after a mostly successful chapter running News Corp.'s Australian operation, has come back to the United States as the company's number three executive, behind Chernin.

News Corp. has been, for most of its history, distinguished by its self-effacing, if not weak, executives. What you understand as a member of the News Corp. family—even as a well-loved member—is that there is one father who is sui generis and irreplaceable. Without the father there is no family. It is a company without competing power centers. Without, strangely, even competing egos. All power and personality and even need exist in relation to the greater power and personality and need. Everybody is in the service of what Murdoch wants. This is almost freakishly out of the norm of any large organization—all of which are most characterized by their political intrigues and plots and competing power centers.

Not News Corp. The only time an executive ever really tried to insist on his value independent from Murdoch himself was in the early nineties, when Barry Diller, then the head of Fox Studio and the Fox network, suggested he ought to receive a meaningful stake in the company. Murdoch and Diller, acknowledging the insuperable conflict, worked out the terms of Diller's departure.

Chernin has succeeded at News Corp. precisely because he never wanted to succeed in the terms in which he seems to have now succeeded. He has been a man content making many millions a year. But suddenly Chernin's affable Everyman style has become all the rage.

In an industry that was dominated for a generation by extreme figures and megalomaniacs, Chernin is suddenly a major relief and the new role model. There is the sense of a whole new generation of nice, reasonable, and, well, normal guys ready to run outsized media businesses: Chernin at News; Jeffrey Bewkes, the number two at Time Warner; Bob Iger, the number two at Disney. It's the age of the number two.

Chernin looks like an actor, but he's too pretty, too bland, to be a star. A lack of distinction envelops Chernin. He's frictionless. Smooth. He is by nature and temperament not quite even a number two, just a supernumerary. That's how he's described by virtually everybody—or, at least, that's how he was described until he became many people's candidate for number one at other companies.

Chernin had cemented his power at News Corp. months before the Malone problem. For six months the rumors had been everywhere—not least of all because of Chernin's own deft promotion of the story—that he was a candidate to replace Disney's embattled and unpopular CEO, Michael Eisner, who had pushed up his retirement.

Disney's feelers to Chernin (whether or not it was an outright offer or great poker playing on Chernin's part) had put Murdoch on the spot. His departure would have left News Corp. without even the appearance of a successor—except for Lachlan, and that's precipitous (not to mention highly presumptuous, if not downright obnoxious and ridiculous, for many shareholders, least of all John Malone). It would have meant that Murdoch, at seventy-four, would lose the person he'd come to rely on most—from a certain point of view, although not Murdoch's, his co-CEO—and it would have cost the company dearly in market value. Billions, possibly. News Corp. would not just lose Chernin but have to compete against him as well.

Chernin's ascendancy to the COO spot at News in 1996 has helped normalize the company. The most significant divisions of the company report directly to Chernin, leaving Murdoch free to play the role of wide-ranging, visionary-ish CEO. That's the way it's done. Let the CEO think great thoughts, let the operator keep the lid on. Under Chernin, News Corp. has become less omnivorous, less restless, less unpredictable—less Murdoch.

Chernin would certainly argue that this has been good for the company and good for Murdoch too. The company has become rather a good neighbor—no longer on a constant acquisition spree. Murdoch himself, in the last five or six years, has become less a figure of controversy and more the ultimate elder statesman. Fox News, which rubs Chernin, a Democrat, wrong, is still an irritant, but Murdoch, with a little help from Chernin and Gary Ginsberg, has even been warming up to the Democrats.

On Wall Street, which has always been suspicious of Murdoch, investors have something like a crush on Chernin. He's restrained the beast—and by the summer of 2004, with his contract up for renewal and the Disney talk rife, he had cornered Murdoch. What Chernin wanted was straightforward. He wanted it understood that if, perchance, the company needs a new CEO during the term of his next four-year contract, it will be him.

It was galling for Chernin that Murdoch continued to single out Lachlan, even before his thirtieth birthday, even before he had any serious management experience at all, as his likely successor. Along with running the Australian newspapers (if this was the historic core of the company, it is no longer germane to the big picture), Lachlan got himself involved in a disastrous investment in a telecommunications company involving a partnership with Jamie Packer, the son of one of Murdoch's longtime rivals, Kerry Packer—together they lost a billion dollars. Not long after that, Murdoch brought Lachlan back to New York. His main responsibility is the *New York Post.* For more than thirty years the *Post* has been News Corp.'s flamboyant, money-losing (up to $50 million a year), and eccentric flagship property in the United States. It has no business reason for being other than to prosecute political and business grudges and to entertain Murdoch himself, but it remains the sentimental heart of News Corp.

Chernin, with an astute sense of his own power base, began a campaign of nearly open disparagement of Lachlan. The disparagement was Hollywood-style—that is, the veneer of smoothness, even courtliness, of deniability, of the deftest political behavior, and gracious accommodation remains the norm. But beyond that façade, the triangulation took place.

Chernin enlisted Roger Ailes, the Fox News chief and possibly the one man of whom Murdoch is afraid. Chernin and Ailes do not particularly get along, partly for political reasons, and partly for temperamental ones, because Chernin is deft and smooth and Ailes is glowering and bullish. But in this, against the prince designate, whom they both find callow, insubstantial, and, ironically, un-Murdoch-like, not to mention standing in their way, they were glad to double-team. If they both block him, then Lachlan has nothing to do besides run the *New York Post*, which neither Chernin nor Ailes care a whit about. Indeed, which because it is a newspaper—a newspaper!—neither thinks should even be part of this vast modern media enterprise.

Murdoch understands he is going to have to choose between his top executives and his son.

There are other frictions too between father and son. The family situation, which became so fraught in 1998 with the elder Murdoch's breakup and then, in 1999, with his remarriage, and which for a time was back on an even enough keel, has again hit the rocks.

When he divorced Anna in 1999, Murdoch agreed that in exchange for her giving up her community property claim to half of his assets, the trust under which his four children would inherit their father's interest in News Corp. would never be changed. Now, pressured by Wendi, he wants his older children to *voluntarily* agree to admit his two new children into the trust. Lachlan and his siblings—still bitter about the divorce—are resisting.

It's all too much for him, this emotional stuff. He always has to move the emotional to the tactical.

It's at this moment, in the spring of 2005, that an idea begins to take shape for him. As with so many of his notions, the more unexpected the thing he does, the bigger it is, the more it shakes everything up and lets him start again. It changes the conversation. It orders the mess. It's like shock therapy. This is often how he deals with his own troubles—he changes the game. He does something so epic and transformative that everybody else is stuck following his lead.

He has a habit or compulsion of upending the company every ten years or so. It's management by upheaval, or management by distraction, or management by force of will—he makes his enthusiasms everybody's enthusiasms. He changes the game so much that it stays his.

Now he's entertaining a new game changer, something that could help him take back the story.

It would help him deal with Malone—force him to solve that problem that he allowed to be created. It would help him deal with Chernin—while he had to give in to Chernin over his contract demands to get the top spot if Murdoch "departed," he'd better be damned sure Chernin doesn't wind up strong enough, nor his children weak enough, for Chernin to renew the contract on the same terms. And it would help him solve the family problem—which is, in his mind, about legacy. So he'll do what he's always been doing: creating a legacy. He'll just create a bigger one—which is, in fact, just what he's always been doing.

In the spring of 2005 Murdoch has lunch with Bruce Wasserstein, one of the most famous dealmakers of the 1980s, who more recently took over the investment bank Lazard. Wasserstein, fishing for business, mentions Dow Jones. It's impossible, but on the other hand, the business is in decline, while the Bancroft family's needs are ever-increasing . . . might be something there . . . Everybody knows Murdoch has a thing for Dow Jones, so if you want Murdoch's business, it's the obvious thing to offer him. And if you know anything at all about doing business with Murdoch, you know you have to gossip about something, have to hold out the possibility of unsettled relationships, of changing alliances, of exploiting other people's weakness, of far-flung, unthought-of opportunity. No matter that you might be exaggerating or even making the whole thing up.

Then Vernon Jordan, the Clinton confidant and corporate-board gadfly, who'd been forced by age limits to retire from the Dow Jones board, presses him: "Put the money on the table and the family will take it. They're just a bunch of coupon cutters."

Then there's James Lee Jr., vice chairman at JPMorgan Chase, almost comic in his enthusiasms and salesmanship, who's been obsessive about repeatedly urging Murdoch to look at Dow Jones. He knows Murdoch has a nagging interest in the company, and he knows Dow Jones has problems—and Lee has nothing to lose by conflating those two facts.

In May, Norm Pearlstine and John Huey, both former *WSJ* editors and now the two top editors at Time, Inc., call on Murdoch to get his support for Time's fight with the Justice Department in the Valerie Plame case over a journalist's right to keep sources confidential. They too know about Murdoch's longtime interest in Dow Jones and about offering Murdoch gossip to curry his favor, and during their conversation—which Murdoch will later claim not to remember—they point out that the Bancroft trustee at the Boston law firm Hemenway and Barnes, Roy Hammer, has once again repeated, in a current *Fortune* article, that Dow Jones is not for sale—at least not, Hammer quips to *Fortune*, for less than $60 a share.

Pearlstine, who has mentioned this as well to the Washington Post Company's CEO, Donald Graham, who dismissed the figure out of hand, will recall later, "Rupert's eyes sort of lit up, and he said, 'Huh, $60 a share.' He started trying to figure out how to get there almost as we were sitting there. Whereas Don Graham is a prudent man who would say that was an absurd price for Dow Jones, Rupert was trying to figure out how he could do it."

The *Wall Street Journal*, along with the *New York Times*, the big-three networks, and CNN, are the things he could never buy—establishment things, elite things. Indeed, at one time or another he has tried to buy every national news company in the country—

and been rebuffed. (Hence, he started his own network and his own twenty-four-hour cable news channel.) So whenever the subject comes up of actually owning what he is not supposed to ever own . . .

When Peter Chernin first gets wind in the spring of 2005 that Dow Jones is once again an idea in Murdoch's head, his reaction—beyond that Dow Jones is not available, not a chance—is Why in hell? What possible advantage would Dow Jones offer News Corp.? As Chernin sees it, everything from a corporate point of view that might be accomplished with the acquisition of Dow Jones has already been accomplished, in spades, ages ago.

This has been the premise of News Corp., which has become the premise of all other big media companies: By acquiring a famous media brand, you take over its cachet and standing—as well as its cash flow. The *New York Post, New York* magazine, the *Village Voice*, the *Times* of London, *Harper and Row, TV Guide*, Twentieth Century Fox—these are the brands that put Murdoch on the map.

Except now the Murdoch brand is bigger than all of them. Bigger, certainly, than Dow Jones and the *Wall Street Journal*. And certainly News Corp. would get no advantage from Dow Jones' pitiful cash flow.

From any prudent, standardized business-practices view—and the media business, once a business of audacious and often ridiculous moves, is becoming nothing if not standardized—trying to take over Dow Jones is illogical.

Not to mention the potential PR disaster. In the standardized playbook of modern corporations, the idea is to avoid controversy. Truly, there might not be any greater desire at the highest reaches of corporate life than to avoid bad press. Bad press kills. It hammers your share price, it rattles your board, it undermines you with your friends and family, it discourages your customers, it challenges your vanity, and eventually it gets you fired. For any executive, how the media might respond is a major strategic calculation. Beyond containable levels, if the press is going to be bad, you just don't do it.

Chernin has enough trouble dealing with Fox News. The last thing he needs is endless stories—and this is how it would play—of tawdry, dubious Fox News taking over the respected and unimpeachable *Wall Street Journal*.

Even more to the point, for Chernin the *Wall Street Journal*, however iconic, is the newspaper business—that dying animal. (Murdoch not only mocks Chernin for not reading newspapers, but points out that Chernin can't get his college-age children to read a paper: "They won't even read one. They refuse. He keeps sending out subscriptions for the *New York Times* to college and they won't even open them.") The company's newspapers in London and Australia, once great cash contributors to the company, are now, like newspapers everywhere, fading enterprises. They aren't the company's future. They aren't anybody's future. They're just Murdoch family lore.

Anyway, Murdoch is always buying Mars—at least until some other more distracting planet comes along, and then he'll be buying that. It is Chernin's job to help dissuade, distract, and keep the focus on the real business at hand, which is entertainment, not news. And while he knows that Murdoch has told his people to start a book on Dow Jones, collecting all the public data about the company's performance, Chernin isn't worried. Murdoch has been ordering up that book for the past twelve years. They call it the Olympic book because it gets forgotten about and then dusted off every few years. Dow Jones—Chernin knows, everybody knows—is not for sale, and, famously, does not want to be sold. Not now. Not ever.

It's true enough: Nobody has any reason to believe that the Bancroft family, or the people who shield the Bancrofts from people such as Murdoch, would react any differently than they have in the past. No means, as it has always meant, no.

Still, it's just a phone call. In fact, when Murdoch hears that Michael Elefante, a younger lawyer at Hemenway and Barnes, is replacing Roy Hammer, who ran the trusts for more than thirty years and is due to retire—and who has snubbed Murdoch before—he calls him up.

"I'd really like to come and see you. I've got a lot of ideas, which it'd help to share, and at least you can get to know me, or see that I'm not growing horns," Murdoch will later recall he said, trying to charm Elefante. But once again, Murdoch is rebuffed. Elefante rushes him off the phone—says he'll call him back. When he does, it's once again with a firm no: not interested, don't want to sit down with you, thank you very much, go away. (Murdoch says he hears later, through his deep network, that Elefante and Dow Jones' lawyers high-five each other that Murdoch has not offered a price—meaning, they believe, that it is not necessary for them to take a solicitation to the shareholders if it doesn't come with a firm offer. Murdoch will take heed of this lesson.)

And then something else occurs in the summer of 2005: Lachlan resigns. In 2001, Elisabeth Murdoch walked out of BSkyB for much the same reason that her brother is leaving now. Their father tempted, teased, even seemed to promise that each was the anointed, then left each looking foolish. It hurt him when Elisabeth left, and it hurts him all the more now that it is his firstborn son who is leaving—packing up and going back to Australia, which Murdoch himself has managed to get so far from (there is irony here, because Lachlan was born in London and grew up in New York and is far from Australian). When *New York* magazine runs a blind-sourced piece, clearly from Lachlan's perspective, about the Murdoch family's travails, Murdoch rails against the leaker. His closest associates don't really have the heart to tell him that Lachlan himself was obviously telling the tales.

And there is another development that summer: Murdoch has a crush. This is a theme of Murdoch's management style. He will, on occasion, become infatuated with someone and then, in not so subtle and sometimes not so logical ways—before he falls out of love—reorganize the company around that person.

It is impossible to ignore that *this* crush—or, changing the metaphor, the choice of a new son—comes as his real son is so painfully leaving him.

Robert Thomson is a Melbourne boy, thirty years younger than Murdoch—both were born on March 11, which Murdoch seems to find significant—who started at the Melbourne *Herald* as a copy-boy. He has covered Asia for the *Financial Times* (another paper that Murdoch, at various times, has desired), and helped direct the *FT*'s expansion into the United States. He lost a bake-off in 2001 to be the editor. Bitter about the slight, Thomson put out feelers about his availability—and Rupert called. They met for beers at the Dervish—a Times Square Turkish restaurant and one of the News Corp. joints (which qualifies by proximity and bad food) where Rupert and Lachlan, often with *New York Post* editor Col Allan, had their regular Friday lunch.

In one of those soul-mate flukes, Murdoch became almost immediately enthralled with Thomson for all the reasons he is so often suspicious of others. In the *FT*, Thomson has a prestige journalistic credential; he has a certain expertise in Asia (Murdoch was not someone who particularly valued independent expertise); he carries himself like an intellectual; and, unlike the garrulous reporters with whom Murdoch surrounds himself when he is in the mood for reporters, Thomson is restrained in the care with which he speaks, to the point of crypticness.

Rebekah Wade, the editor of the *Sun* in London, recalls Murdoch telling a joke after a few drinks, as they wait for Robert Thomson to arrive at a posh London restaurant. "God this is brilliant . . . what's the difference between a fridge and a poofter?" Murdoch booms to Wade. "Well, when you pull the meat out of the fridge, it doesn't fart!" But, then, seeing Thomson coming into the restaurant, Murdoch urgently whispers, "For God's sake, don't tell Robert what I said. He's a gentrified man . . . very clever."

Murdoch, in 2002, hired Thomson to take over for Peter Stothard as the editor of the *Times* of London. Their relationship deepened. Australianism is never incidental to Murdoch—he's more comfortable with Australians. What's more, Thomson's wife, Ping, like Wendi Murdoch, grew up in China. The Thomsons and the Murdochs began to spend social time together.

It is, in the summer of 2005, with his crush (or adoption) in full flower, that Murdoch begins to talk seriously to Thomson about the *Wall Street Journal*. It is as likely that Murdoch is trying to charm Thomson with this idea as it is that Thomson is trying to please Murdoch by encouraging him. They are enabling each other in what they have no logical reason to believe is anything more than a pipe dream.

It is not just that Dow Jones is not for sale, has never indicated any basis on which it might be for sale, is in fact locked up in a corporate structure that ensures against its being sold, nor that there is no possible way it can be sold without the agreement of its controlling shareholder, who has not only as emphatically as possible said no deal ever, but who is not available even for a discussion. Rather, it's that, were the stars to somehow miraculously align, the last person anybody who has anything to do with Dow Jones would sell it to would be Rupert Murdoch.

But pay that no mind. If only to distract himself from John Malone and his threatening intentions, from his issues with his son Lachlan and their mutual pain, from the demands of his wife and her own desires for legitimacy, and now the aggravations of having to renovate and decorate the most expensive apartment in New York—not to mention having to live up to it, having to be measured against both the Rockefeller history and dynasty—he is taking the next step. He and his little band are considering how exactly to buy an unbuyable company and, by so doing, change the game at News Corp. How, after fifty years of almost nonstop acquisition, to put the latest touch on his perennial unfinished enterprise—to burnish the legacy before . . .

Well, there is, suddenly, a speeded-up sense of where he wants to go, of what he wants to happen, of how he wants it to be. This most impatient of men is in a new sort of hurry.

# THREE

**The Throwback**

**FALL 2005: ANDY STEGINSKY**

He is a classical music fan and a Rupert Murdoch groupie. And oddly, those things turn out to be related. In 1997, Andy Steginsky, a money manager in Princeton, New Jersey, met Billy Cox through their mutual support of the New Jersey Symphony, just before Billy began stirring up trouble in the Bancroft family. Indeed, in a breakfast conversation with Cox—the kind of meeting any high-net-worth investment advisor might try to hustle with a high-net-worth individual—Steginsky claims to have instructed Cox on the virtues of Rupert Murdoch and News Corp. as well as corporate activism. "Life is short," said Steginsky. "Why don't you do something to make a difference?" And then, voilà, Billy Cox, joined by his cousin Lizzie Goth, started to agitate for change at Dow Jones. In Steginsky's view, perhaps not a coincidence.

As for Andy Steginsky's unusual attraction to Rupert Murdoch, that started in the early eighties. Not long after Steginsky, with a

B.S. from Ohio State, joined the Wall Street brokerage Oppenheimer and Co. in 1981, he called up the CEO of News Corp. to discuss the company's prospects. Murdoch not only took the time to sit down with the kid just out of school—it is a Murdoch strategy or character note that he is easy to get on the phone—but also charmed the pants off him. News Corp. was then an Australian company whose ADRs (American depository receipts—which is a way to buy stock in foreign companies in the United States) were only lightly traded, so Murdoch was keen on Oppenheimer's interest, even if Andy himself was nobody much.

Steginsky, besotted, came to believe in all things Murdoch with a particular zealotry, and regularly put his clients into News Corp. stock. (Years later he would acknowledge that, all in all, this had hardly been the world's savviest investment.) In 1989, when Lachlan was getting ready to go off to Princeton, Murdoch called Steginsky and asked him if he could occasionally give Lachlan a hot meal. This was both Murdoch the obsessive father as well as Murdoch the obsessive networker.

Lachlan, as it happened, also likes opera, and he and Andy became fast friends, sharing, in Steginsky's telling, a pair of headphones for hours on end.

Steginsky, a round-faced man in his late forties, has a kind of carte blanche at News Corp. He stops in when he's in town; he kibbitzes; he annoys people who are trying to get their work done. And while it is not always clear what he's doing, everybody is used to him doing it.

In September, Steginsky stops in at Murdoch's office. Murdoch, a great mentioner, happens to mention Dow Jones—and Andy Steginsky immediately recounts his possibly meaningful meeting with Billy Cox ten years ago.

"I could," he says to Murdoch, "make some calls"—which is what people say to get in on something. This gambit, combined with a giddiness to do anything that Murdoch might ask, sends Steginsky . . . well, it sends him to Rome and Prague.

Billy Cox, who was forced out not long after he started making trouble at Dow Jones, moved to Europe, settling finally with his family in Rome. Steginsky gets Billy on the phone, and Billy is . . . Billy. He's mad at Dow Jones for kicking him out; he's mad at his father, Bill junior, for not siding with him; and he's mad at everyone else in the family who has more money than he has. Billy may be on the outs with a lot of the family, but over the phone—with renewed enthusiasm for a fight with Dow Jones—he still tells Steginsky that he's sure he can get various siblings and cousins and other relatives to listen to reason now, even to meet with Murdoch. The next time he's in New York, Billy drives out to Princeton, where he and Steginsky, over a bottle of wine, sketch out the family structure and Billy gives a little brain dump about who is who, as well as who within the three branches of the family might, and might not, be approachable. Billy offers to make the introductions.

But over the next few months, Billy doesn't do much of anything except talk to Steginsky on the phone and tell him he definitely can do something. Finally, at the end of one call Billy says that if Andy were ever in Rome, that might be a good time to talk about next steps.

"And so I hung up the phone, called a limo service, and it picked me up in Princeton within an hour. I knew if I called Billy back and said, 'I'm coming to Rome,' he'd say, 'Don't come,' so I just went. I called the airline on the way and booked the ticket. I knew where he was and I booked a hotel not far from where he lives. I got there the next morning. I called him right before lunch and he said, 'It must be early in Princeton.' I said, 'Well, I'm not in Princeton, I'm in Rome.'"

Billy shows up with his French wife, Beatrice, and his son. It's the week before Thanksgiving, and the four of them have turkey in a Roman trattoria. The next day, Billy and his wife come over to Steginsky's hotel, near the Piazza del Popolo, and over more wine take a look at the Bancroft family chart that

Andy's worked up, pointing out what's wrong with it, what should be added to it, and, most importantly, giving Andy phone numbers. It's perhaps too much wine, because the next day Billy is back trying to get assurances that Andy won't be calling Bancroft family members willy-nilly—at least not on Billy's say-so. But who you *do* want to see, says Billy, is Lizzie Goth—his partner in the failed putsch of ten years before—who is now living in Prague.

"Well," says Steginsky, "let's get her on the phone."

In seconds, Lizzie agrees to see Steginsky, who immediately calls the concierge at the Hotel de Russie: "I'm the guy in room 602. Get me on the next flight to Prague."

They spend an hour together in the Prague airport. Lizzie doesn't want grief from the family again. She and Billy have been shunned enough by the family. Still, she offers her version of who's who, who might be susceptible, and who's not worth pursuing at all. Her message is clear—she understands the undeniable power of money in her family: "You can tell Rupert that, if he's interested, just put an offer on the table." And then Steginsky gets on a plane back to Rome—pausing to pick up his stuff and call Rupert, then in Sydney, with his report—and then on a flight to New York.

Steginsky's quixotic mission is to convince the Bancrofts that Rupert Murdoch is their kind of people. To the Bancrofts, however, he is their antithesis. If to the people at the *Wall Street Journal* he is bad for journalism, to the Bancrofts he is even more pernicious. If they stand for something high, Murdoch stands for something low, possibly all that is vile, louche, and corrupt about the modern world. He is the worst of the businessmen who have debased the media business.

Indeed, it is business itself, or success itself, or ambition, or striving, that the Bancroft family—once a bulwark of American capitalism and the Republican Party, but now proudly remote from commerce—has a problem with.

Murdoch, to many of them, is that most modern rough beast, an amoral technocrat, a market vulgarian, a destroyer of virtue. A man for whom everything is subservient to his business interests.

He is, and is pleased to let everybody know it, a winner-take-all businessman—the worst nightmare of sentimental, lefty intellectuals, which is exactly what so many of the Bancrofts have become.

And yet, just as obviously, this most quintessential and disturbing modern executive is, here in his eighth decade, premodern. In fact, if he had an MBA, if he was that sort of spreadsheet executive, he certainly would not want to buy Dow Jones and pay practically double its value. If there is a sense of not exactly rational entitlement on the side of reporters and editors who work at elite institutions such as the *Wall Street Journal*, they are up against Murdoch's not exactly rational entitlement too. In his years of ownership, Murdoch's *New York Post* may well have lost more money than any other media enterprise in history. (When I later offer that hypothesis to Robert Thomson, then the editor of Murdoch's *Times* of London, he will say, "I would not underestimate the *Times* in that regard.") No, it would be a mistake to see Murdoch as just another modern ill, born of the corporate state. Murdoch, who may have mastered modern business, is also a throwback, steeped in both dynastic traditions and in old-fashioned newspapering (how many are steeped in that anymore?)—a reversion to a type that is now quite unfamiliar.

**THE MURDOCHS OF AUSTRALIA**

Dame Elisabeth boasts that all of the living Murdoch family members plan to return in 2009 to Cruden Farm, the family homestead—which Sir Keith bought as a wedding gift for his nineteen-year-old bride in 1928—along with anybody who is anybody in Australia to celebrate the Murdoch matriarch's one hundredth birthday.

The gathering, the celebration, Cruden Farm, and Dame Elisabeth's longevity itself are all part of a dynastic self-consciousness that has to be understood as the anomaly that it is. Families fall apart—most in one generation, and virtually all, including the Bancrofts, within four. Only in the rarest instance does a postmodern Western family manage to maintain its structure and identity over a century or more.

The Murdochs, in their yen for centrality, their insularity, their generational codependence, and their business practices, resemble some of the world's great family dynasties—the Kennedys, the Rockefellers, the Sulzbergers.

Part of the Murdoch problem, however, is that nobody knows how significant and entitled the Murdochs are. The Murdoch story, no matter how deeply woven into the public mind in Australia, remains an Australian story. This makes Rupert Murdoch, when he finally sets himself upon the world, only slightly more familiar than, say, a Russian oligarch in London, or an African despot on the Riviera, or any old Eurotrash in New York. The Murdoch mythology, what makes Murdoch Murdoch and the Murdochs Murdochs, is only vaguely understood and not terribly cared about far from Australia.

He thinks he's something. We don't. We don't think his entitlement is worth much—we mock it, even.

But entitlement is not just about other people giving you your due. It's also a psychological condition, which can either marginalize you or make you strong. In the latter case, it can be a kind of arbitrage—you know something the market doesn't. You have all the confidence and financial resources of a disciplined and entitled family, while we, without a clue about your real lineage, have no reason at all to take you seriously. Not only do we not accord you an advantage, we believe, since we don't know you, that you ought to be at a disadvantage—meaning we're not at all attentive as you, in your entitlement, take what you want.

Such entitlement comes from a family with a set of dominant and controlling figures. (Such a heavy hand can also send family members running for so many disparate hills.)

At the center of the Murdoch family structure, dominating not just by longevity (although that surely helps) but by all manner of maternal force and wiles, is Dame Elisabeth Murdoch.

Her frequent notes to grandchildren and great-grandchildren, which now seem like the stuff of fond irascibility, must have seemed in her prime incredibly demanding, constant, and oppressive. Murdoch himself seems strikingly, and sourly, aware of this. "She was an okay mother," he told me—the first time I'd heard Dame Elisabeth described as something less than saintly. "That's a terrible thing for a son to say, in that we were a pretty close family, *but* my father came first, and, you know, the rest of us had to be sent off to boarding schools. My father was much older. He was always wanting to spend time with us and spoil us; she was always the disciplinarian."

Dame Elisabeth Murdoch is, in Australia, in the league of Rose Kennedy and the Queen Mum. What the matriarch does, the psychological operation she performs, is to infantilize everybody else in the family, keeping everybody in his or her place. Rupert Murdoch, a man of infinite wealth and power to the outside world, is, within his family, his mother's son—put in his place. Forget the empire: "I'm more interested in him being a good son."

There are in Murdoch's newspapers in Australia no Page 3 girls—they of the bare bosoms that have so successfully identified and sold the *Sun*, his London tabloid—out of deference to his mum.

When he announced his plan to marry Wendi Deng, his mother apparently told anyone who would listen that she "can't even look at the girl."

And Dame Elisabeth is not just Murdoch's mom; she is the most famous old lady in Australia, not merely a Murdoch family icon but a national one too.

Arriving in Melbourne in February 2008, I will find some 5,000 Melburnians turning out for a picnic in honor of Dame Elisabeth on her lawn. Cruden Farm, which when Keith Murdoch bought it for her in 1928 was a country estate sitting among the farms that surrounded Melbourne, is now itself surrounded by

lower-middle-class housing developments. Still, it remains a preserve of some proud, flinty Anglo character (Dame Elisabeth's
accent is more English than Australian)—something not quite of
this world. The gardens themselves, more than eighty years in the
tending, are a particularly uncommon monument. The house, a
nineteenth-century many-pillared neoclassical farmhouse, with all
of the antiques and paintings acquired by Keith Murdoch, an avid
collector, early in the century still in place, is frozen in time. It has
neither heating nor, evidently, a vacuum cleaner. Dame Elisabeth
answers her own phone—or, since it's a half-century or so old dial-
faced instrument, with the receiver alone weighing several pounds,
*hoists* it—and maneuvers around the estate in a walker, which she
lifts to and fro, or in an ancient old golf cart, which she double-
clutches, racing under the garden trellises and between the sprin-
klers. At ninety-nine, she sat for a three-hour interview and then
conducted the garden tour in her golf cart, summing up a sort of
perfect, and even attractive, noblesse oblige: "Rupert would say that
everything he gained from me was by example. I think that's probably true. One tries very hard to be an example to one's children. I
think that all of my children say that my example has been enor-
mously important to them. Rupert says it quite often, so I think he
believes it. I don't think you want to be giving too much advice. I
think you want to be leading by example. It's quite a responsibility
to be the head of such a huge family."

After three hours of Dame Elisabeth's instruction on how she
has managed to hold together a family that spans three continents,
her views on her "elderly" son's divorce ("I just bite the bullet and
get on with it . . . I remember saying to Rupert, 'Rupert you're
going to be very, very lonely, and the first desiring female comes
along will snap you up,' and he said, 'Don't be ridiculous, Mum, I'm
far too old for that'"), what makes "that wretched boy of mine"
tick ("He was very definite. I mean, he mightn't be always right,
but he was always very definite"), and his chosen profession ("I
don't care a hang about the newspapers. I don't care if I don't see a

newspaper for days. Terrible, isn't it? I'm ashamed to say."), she is off to a consolation dinner for the recently defeated prime minister, John Howard.

"She's got this almost Victorian attitude to do this," Murdoch says with some frustration. "It's her duty. I keep telling her, 'Mum, you don't have to do this, just relax. You're tiring yourself out. Go out two, three days a week, not seven days.'"

It is surely true that the ties that bind are a lot tighter where there's a lot of money—and through the early years that Murdoch built the business, Dame Elisabeth held the purse strings. (Murdoch's financial stake in News Corp. was wound up in Cruden Investments, the company Keith Murdoch left to his wife and children in 1952.)

But it's not just money—the Bancroft family will prove as much—but money combined with a daunting mythology that truly binds.

You are, in a Murdoch discussion—especially in a Murdoch discussion with Murdochs—instantly back, on a first-name basis, five generations. Not only are the names clear, but so are their characters and motivations. Their stories become an overarching historical composite, such that their descendants might easily believe they are history's living embodiment—and imperative.

William Henry Greene, Dame Elisabeth's grandfather, is an Irish railroad man. In the transition from Ireland to England to Australia he becomes the commissioner of Victoria's railway system.

He marries Fanny Govett, the Australian-born daughter of a founding citizen of Melbourne. Their son, Elisabeth's father, Rupert Greene, is born in 1870.

Rupert Greene is, in the telling, the source of the family charisma, the deadly charm that, genetically transferred to his grandson, Rupert, would seal so many deals in the latter twentieth century.

The adjectives for Rupert Greene—which we might assume are euphemistic in their ways—include *swashbuckling, popular, amusing, wild*, and *delightful*. He's a gambling man, and he challenged, in some more or less flashy and memorable ways, the upper-middle-class norms of early-twentieth-century Melbourne—an especially unflashy Protestant place. Still, he married properly: His wife, Marie Grace de Lancey Forth, Elisabeth's mother, was from a long line of British and Scottish establishment figures.

In 1927, with the Greenes firmly ensconced in Melbourne society, their eighteen-year-old daughter Elisabeth's debutante picture catches the eye of Keith Murdoch, the forty-two-year-old bachelor publisher, when it is printed in the gossip pages of his own newspaper.

Such an age difference, while mildly scandalous, creates for the Murdoch family a living historical expanse from Keith Murdoch's birth, in 1885, to the end of his wife's life—at this point, at least 123 years later. It's some perspective. (The lives of Murdoch's two youngest children, Chloe and Grace, could well bookend their grandfather's birth by more than two hundred years.)

In December 1986, Rupert Murdoch marches into the offices of the Herald and Weekly Times, the company that his father built—and which, in family lore, wronged him by frustrating his efforts to become an owner himself—and announces he's going to buy it.

This is thirty-four years after his father's death. For more than three decades, Rupert has nursed this revenge fantasy. He tried it once before, in 1979, and failed: The company's trustees enlisted Australia's oldest establishment media family, the Fairfaxes, to block him. Seven years later, he's back, and wins.

This is not just a psychological involvement with your family but an operatic involvement. It's your destiny. You literally see yourself as part of a grand plot and extraordinary story.

Indeed, Keith Murdoch isn't just the most prominent businessman and newspaper publisher in Australia: He's the hero of Gallipoli.

The battle for the Gallipoli peninsula in Turkey is the most fundamental story of Australian identity. It's the Australian version of Dunkirk or Pearl Harbor or Bunker Hill. Or greater still. It is at the center of Australia's place in the world—its relationship to the British, its ideas of mateship, egalitarianism, and anti-establishmentarianism. And, not insignificantly, it's a story later retailed by Keith's son, who helped finance the 1981 film *Gallipoli,* directed by the Australian Peter Weir and starring Mel Gibson (making Mel Gibson a star).

Gallipoli, where in 1915 the British ordered eight thousand Australian and New Zealand infantry and light horsemen to their death in a failed assault on the Turks, is not just the family's first media event; it is media as a transformative force.

Keith Murdoch is, in 1915, a young man of a good background and fine connections, whose professional potential is already abundantly clear. He's the product of two generations of Scottish-Protestant clergy, in an age when the clergy is a highest-attainment profession. The Murdochs are Free Churchers. Keith's grandfather James Murdoch, born in 1817 on the Moray Firth, of Scotland, joins upward of 470 other Presbyterian clergymen in the Disruption of 1843 to break with the Church of Scotland. The issue here—a Murdoch theme to this day—is the relationship with England. The Church of Scotland is too tight with the English establishment (an anti-English catechism became central to the Free Churchers). The schism here, however, isn't one of rebels turning their back on the establishment, but rather—and this remains another Murdoch family theme—the troublemakers arguing that *they* are the rightful establishment.

Keith's father, Patrick, is born in Scotland in 1850. Patrick, raised in anti-English Scottish Protestantism, becomes an assistant to a big-name London clergyman and then in 1878 is ordained himself and given a church in Cruden, a fishing village in Aberdeenshire.

Patrick marries Rupert's grandmother Annie Brown in 1882, and in 1884 takes a Free Church posting in Melbourne. Patrick, in relatively short order, finds himself not just a clergyman-pillar of the Melbourne community—and the immigrant waves have made Melbourne the largest city in Australia—but a leader of the Presbyterian Church of Australia.

Keith is born in 1885. He is meant to carry on the Calvinist line, but instead becomes a journalist. This is perhaps because of his terrible stutter—a grievous impediment to preaching. Still, at the turn of the century, 1885 journalism is nobody's idea of a profession. Or it is only a good idea if you own the press itself. To be a journalist from an upper-class family is to see yourself as something of a cultured industrialist. You would own the factory; the actual people who gathered up the news would be the factory workers.

Keith's father arranges a job for him on a prominent Melbourne paper.

Then, in 1908, he goes to study—unhappily, as it turns out—at the London School of Economics. He returns to Melbourne in 1910 and becomes a political writer—a parliamentary correspondent. He's a supporter of his father's friend Andrew Fisher, the Labor Party leader who is elected for three terms as Australia's prime minister. The Murdochs, in other words, are cronies and confidants of the most powerful people in the land.

Keith Murdoch, beginning his management rise, becomes the London editor of the news agency United Cable Service (the journalism business at the time is also the telegraph business). His father's chum Fisher, serving his third term as prime minister, asks the twenty-nine-year-old Keith to stop in Egypt on his way to London to look into some problems with the mail service to Australian soldiers (journalism is also closely related to mail).

Enterprisingly, Keith gets in touch with General Ian Hamilton, the commander of the Australian force in the Dardanelles, hoping to secure a firsthand look at the battlefield scene at Gallipoli.

Stringent censorship regulations are in place, not least of all because everything about the Dardanelles campaign has gone so terribly wrong. Keith agrees, in writing, "not to attempt to correspond by any other route or by any other means than that officially sanctioned."

In fact, Keith spends almost no time at all at the front. Instead, he settles into the press camp, on the island of Imbros away from the front, and falls under the spell of Ellis Ashmead-Bartlett of the *Daily Telegraph*, the dean—a drunken one—of the Dardanelles correspondents. Because of the censorship rules, most of Ashmead-Bartlett's dispatches never see print. The rules, according to Phillip Knightley (who will work for both Keith Murdoch at the *Herald* and for Rupert at the *Times* of London) in his book *The First Casualty*, about journalists in wars, allow "no criticism of the conduct of the operation, no indication of set-backs or delays, and no mention of casualty figures." Very few people in Britain or Australia, in other words, understand the enormousness of the debacle.

Ashmead-Bartlett convinces Murdoch that the deterioration of the Dardanelles campaign will only get worse. "Murdoch," according to Knightley, "must have realised that almost by accident he was in possession of information that would certainly rank as one of the great stories of the war."

Keith decides to break the censorship rules and smuggle out the British correspondent's dispatch. Their plot is discovered and the dispatch confiscated.

Acting not so much as a journalist but as a confidant of the powerful, Keith writes Fisher, the Australian prime minister, recounting everything he can remember from the Ashmead-Bartlett dispatch. It's a paean to the virtues and heroism of the Australians and an indictment of the duplicity and cowardice of the British. It is, in Knightley's description, "an amazing document, a mixture of error, fact, exaggeration, prejudice, and the most sentimental patriotism, which made highly damaging charges against the British general staff and Hamilton, many of them untrue."

Arriving in London, Keith Murdoch brags about the letter to Geoffrey Dawson, the editor of the *Times*. The *Times*—which Keith's son Rupert will own in a few generations—is then owned by Lord Northcliffe (aka Alfred Harmsworth). In the history of powerful press barons who've meddled in politics, Northcliffe ranks only behind William Randolph Hearst and Rupert himself. Northcliffe has fiercely opposed the Dardanelles campaign and, with the encouragement of future prime minister David Lloyd George—this is all at a very high level of intrigue—who also opposes the campaign, has Keith's letter sent to the prime minister, Herbert Asquith, who promptly has it printed and distributed to the cabinet.

As a nearly direct consequence of Murdoch's letter, whatever its inaccuracies, Hamilton, the British general, is removed, and the evacuation of Gallipoli begins.

Or . . . maybe it doesn't happen like that at all.

This event, so central to Australian mythology and to the rise of the Murdoch family, will be subject to natural and baroque revisionist accounts. Keith is not only *not* heroic but mendacious—a sneak, a thief, a plagiarist, and, of course, a self-promoter. Or he is the dupe of powerful men, a bit player in a larger conspiracy. Or a kind of Zelig—in the frame of history, but without real consequence.

No matter: It is a personal and media coup—Keith Murdoch becomes part of Australia's World War I mythology. On the seventy-fifth anniversary of Gallipoli, the *Times*, at that point owned by his son, will run an account of his legend under the headline "The Journalist Who Stopped a War."

The coup, in addition to making Keith famous at home, also cements his relationship with Lord Northcliffe, who becomes his mentor—his media rabbi.

Northcliffe is one of the great figures of the tale. His is the first great populist media empire. He has the touch (he helps Joseph Pulitzer create the famous one-time tabloid issue of the *World*, which appears on January 1, 1901, and a few years later begins the tabloid London *Daily Mirror*) and he has the business model: mass.

"A newspaper is to be made to pay. Let it deal with what interests the mass of people. Let it give the public what it wants," pronounces Northcliffe to the great condemnation of intellectuals far and wide.

Northcliffe's company—which will continue into the twenty-first century as Associated Newspapers, publishing the *Daily Mail,* "the voice of middle England," and arguably the most influential paper in Britain—also includes the *Daily Mirror,* the *Evening News,* and the *Observer.* (The *Mirror* and *Observer* eventually change hands; the *Evening News,* which will continue to be owned by Associated, will change its name to the *Evening Standard.*) His takeover of the money-losing *Times* in 1908 is an occasion for pretty much the same kind of censure by the upper crust and journalists that will occur when Rupert takes it over more than eighty years later.

Keith Murdoch, after Gallipoli, runs his news service out of the *Times*' office until in 1920 he is offered the editorship of the Melbourne *Herald*—the most upmarket and establishment paper in the country—which, with Northcliffe's assent, Keith accepts.

While maintaining the *Herald*'s establishment appeal, he begins to apply the basic Northcliffe formulae: contests, serials, shorter stories, beauty pageants, crime stories. More significantly, Murdoch launches a sister paper, the *Sun News Pictorial,* a morning tabloid—the first in Australia—which becomes the biggest-selling paper in the country.

In 1928, it's Northcliffe who helps convince the board of the Herald and Weekly Times company to make Keith Murdoch the managing director of the firm. Expansion is substantial and immediate. Keith adds radio stations to the group, installs up-to-date presses, and begins, through a program of acquisitions, to build the first newspaper chain in the country.

Continuing to imitate Northcliffe, Keith becomes an art collector too.

Rich, powerful, a workaholic—and not, apparently, the most likable guy in Australia—the forty-three-year old bachelor marries Rupert's mother, nineteen-year-old Elisabeth, in 1928.

Two more family themes are set in stone: Elisabeth, through her father, Rupert Greene, is the source of their son's charm and gambler's bravado; Keith, by way of two generations of clergy, is the source of Rupert's coldness, toughness, and puritanism.

Keith Rupert Murdoch is born in 1931—the boy among what will be three sisters, the heir among the girls.

Later it will be hard to get a clear picture of Murdoch's upbringing because it will come prepackaged in lots of upper-class language. That in itself will be a distinguishing fact: The Murdochs, within the context of egalitarian Australia, are living at the uppermost extreme.

His childhood alternates between idyllic and lonely, with lots of Australian country life (when Rupert is seven, his father also buys a many-thousand-acre sheep farm). It's about not being overindulged in the midst of substantial wealth—in fact, being treated with calculated cruelty to build character. Still, the mythology holds that while there is great harshness, there is great love and affection too.

And then it's off to boarding school—at age ten. Geelong Grammar on Corio Bay, fifty miles from Melbourne, is among the world's most elite boarding schools; twenty years after Murdoch's time, Prince Charles will be sent to Geelong Grammar's Timbertop program, which involves a year of living in the Australian mountains. Geelong, which into the 1990s will still be using corporal punishment, features all manner of privations. It even has a novelistic headmaster, Sir James Darling, a man whose Christian determination is to break the pride of rich kids, not least of all through the theoretically leveling virtues of sport.

Rupert, who will one day control a significant part of the world's sports programming and own stakes in a handful of professional teams, hates sports. And he hates authority. These two attributes are the classic mark of a prep school troublemaker. Nor is he popular. He is the disliked son of the disliked father—the domineering, politically meddling newspaper publisher often at odds with the other fathers of the establishment.

Rupert, it turns out, is rather unbreakable. The lesson he seems to take from Geelong Grammar is the obvious one: Fuck them all. (At his mother's eightieth-birthday party, in 1989, attended by the entire upper crust, including Sir James Darling, Rupert will even force something like an apology out of the former headmaster.)

And then in 1950 it's off to Oxford, in England, that hell/heaven for Australians.

His mother and his father take him to school—and along the way give him a bit of a world tour, including an audience for the Presbyterian Murdochs with the Pope in Rome.

The reason Keith has the time to accompany his son is that at sixty-five and in failing health (several heart attacks and prostate cancer), Keith is slowly being forced out of his job at the Herald and Weekly Times. Keith Murdoch may be among the most powerful men in Australia, but he's run up against the limitation that generations of corporate men of the future will regularly encounter: at the end of the day, even CEOs are just employees. Their power is rented—they don't own it.

Oxford is, all in all, a good time for Rupert. He cuts a figure. He's arch, he's aggressive, he's charming, he's funny, he's rich, he's rebellious (though not too rebellious), he gambles. His father is naturally worried about his left-wing airs—he sports a bust of Lenin on the mantel in his rooms—as well as his grades; he's a terrible student. But he's a focused one, too—focused on his own unique interests. William Rees-Mogg, the editor of the *Times* of London when Murdoch acquired it and who would go on to be a *Times* columnist, was an undergraduate with Murdoch and remembers Murdoch's enthusiastic interest in buying the undergraduate magazine, *Cherwell*. ("I told him," Rees-Mogg will recall almost sixty years later, "I thought *Cherwell* would never get enough advertising from the sort of ordinary university advertisers to make it profitable.")

There's a summer road trip—in a car purchased by his father—through Eastern Europe and Greece. The car is totaled in Turkey.

Then, in October 1952, Rupert's father suddenly dies.

While Keith was the chairman of the Herald and Weekly Times, in a bit of corporate shuffling that would be dubious now—and raised eyebrows then—he personally came to own both the *Adelaide News* and a significant stake in Queensland Newspapers Ltd., which owned the Brisbane *Courier-Mail*. Together with his reputation in Australia and a modest fortune, these papers are the legacy he leaves his family.

The co-executor of Keith's estate with Dame Elisabeth is Harry Giddy, Sir Keith's successor as the Herald and Weekly Times chairman, who promptly convinces her, over Rupert's protests, to sell the family's controlling interest in Queensland Newspapers to the Herald and Weekly Times. Rupert blames the owners of his father's company not just for failing to accord his father a bigger stake in the company he built for them, but also for acting in their own interests in convincing his mother to sell a key part of the Murdoch family patrimony. It's an elemental moment for him of understanding what the rich are up against: other people who are rich.

And it will remain a family sore spot. His mother, in my interview, will take careful issue with her son's resentment: "It was very hard to know what to do, because he wanted to keep certain properties and we knew that it was not possible. And that was hard, as I said, it was a very hard time because I insisted that we were not going into enormous debt and I'm sure that was the right thing. But I think he will always regret it very much that I didn't allow him to hang on to [the] Queensland interest because, you know, we just couldn't go owing a lot of money at that stage. Rupert was too young."

Meanwhile, Rupert has another year of Oxford left in which to think about the *Adelaide News*.

It's a familiar scenario: the (slightly) ne'er-do-well son who is left the father's odd media holdings at a callow age. There's Hearst, of course, who turns a failing newspaper into an empire; there's Bill Paley, whose father leaves him, in addition to a cigar company, a radio station, which eventually becomes CBS and the most powerful media company of its time; there's Bill Ziff (parts of whose business Rupert will one day buy), who inherits a few small magazines and turns them into one of the largest private media fortunes in the United States. There's Ted Turner (whose rivalry with Murdoch will be an eighties subtheme), whose father leaves him a billboard company which he turns into his billion-dollar media enterprise.

The key here is young men inheriting not just family businesses but specifically media enterprises, which by their nature seem to invite young men to think they can do it as well as anybody else. If the family business were, say, coal mining, or banking, or manufacturing, they likely would not be so confident.

So . . . a young man of particular self-confidence, entitlement, aggressiveness, with a dilettantish what-the-heckness and a deep competitive streak, prepares to take up his legacy.

But before Rupert goes home to assume his position at the *Adelaide News* he goes to work for the newspaper proprietor who, next to Northcliffe, most defines the Fleet Street style and "the black art of journalism": Beaverbrook.

William Maxwell Aitken, who will become Lord Beaverbrook, had arrived on Fleet Street by way of Canada and a profitable stake in the Rolls-Royce company, which he sold to fund his one true passion—a London newspaper company.

It's 1953. Rupert is twenty-two. Beaverbrook's *Daily Express* is at the epicenter of Fleet Street, the world's most competitive newspaper market. There are low papers (the vivid and "popular") and high papers (the stuffy and "unpopular"). Fleet Street's measures are as harsh and binary as the Nielsen ratings will be in American television a generation later.

Fleet Street is to journalism—journalism as an act of civic responsibility, that is—as military music is to music. Its essence is selling single copies: making the sale in the blink of an eye as you go past the newsdealer. Fleet Street is in the audience business rather than the news business, or it is an open rivalry between both impulses. It is also the class business. Every Fleet Streeter knows which is his class.

Rupert's brief few months on the *Daily Express* become the basis for his assumption of the chief executive role at News Ltd., owner of the 75,000-circulation *Adelaide News*.

It's really hard to say what running a newspaper in the 1950s might prepare you for. Most people who run newspapers in this era, or even work for them, will fade away, sell out, or drift into some other line of work over the next generation.

It's an archaic vocation, an experience and skill set that become progressively less relevant. It is, for one odd thing, a factory business. Everything you do is mechanically driven. If you run a newspaper, you are at least as concerned with machinery as you are with journalism. You are in the trucking, hauling, and delivery business. The noises, the smells, and the people are industrial. The sound on the newsroom floor when the presses come on is loaded, heavy, primal. While in years hence newspaper labor unions will come to seem like some odd conceit for what will have become an otherwise white-collar line of work, in the 1950s it is clear that the business operates on the backs of very big men.

The very idea of the newspaper proprietor, which Murdoch at twenty-two has become (later, he will appoint his own son Lachlan, at twenty-two, the general manager of Queensland Newspapers), is itself feudal. It is much like inheriting the estate and the big house—and all of the servants and workers and other dependents who belong to it. It comes with outsized authority. You inherit power. Arguably, the more entitled you are, the better a proprietor you are. Newspapers are about throwing your weight around. Modesty is not a newspaper virtue.

Rupert Murdoch is having, by the mid-fifties, the full flower of the experience of the family proprietor. And he is perfectly in character. He is to the manor born. He dives into the job without skipping a beat to learn it. His supreme confidence is born not just from arrogance but from incredible, relentless energy. There is in Murdoch's paper, as in so many other under-resourced papers, a sense of *Let's put on a show*. Adelaide, after all, is twelve hours by car from his home in Melbourne. He's got nothing else to do but put out a paper. To learn the business and to meddle in it.

The corollary to the idea of a newspaper as a feudal base is the idea of newspaper wars—another feudal kingdom trying to put down your feudal kingdom. In Australia's media business for most of the twentieth century there are three kingdoms that control the continent: those of the Fairfaxes, the Packers, and the Murdochs. It's like the Hatfields and McCoys in the turn-of-the-century Ozarks, or the five Mafia families in 1950s New York, or the Medici and Sforza families in fifteenth-century Italy.

The Fairfaxes are the establishment family. In their self-importance and stodginess—and ultimate collapse—they bear a distinct resemblance to the Bancrofts. The Packers are the arriviste family, vulgar, bumptious; Kerry Packer will become Australia's richest man. And then the Murdochs: in some sense the least transparent, the most disciplined and deadly, and most intelligent of the bunch.

In the 1950s, after Keith Murdoch's death, the enemy begins its advance.

The first shot is fired by Keith's former firm, the Herald and Weekly Times. Trying to get the Murdochs to sell the *Adelaide News*, the company advises the Murdochs that the HWT paper, the *Adelaide Advertiser*, plans to start a Sunday edition to go up against the Murdochs' *Sunday Mail*. Murdoch actually fights the Herald and Weekly Times to a rather modern draw—they merge their paper with his, leaving him in control, and giving HWT a 50 percent interest.

This is what newspapers do: fight great wars of attrition. If you can hold on longer than the other guy, you win. It's not so much a marketing business—headlines only get so big—as one of endurance. How much pain can you tolerate? Rupert Murdoch can always tolerate more. This becomes Murdoch's model: He forces himself and his competitors into a no-win spiral, your basic game of chicken, and they blink. It is, in so many ways—given its costs, its risks, its creation of lasting antagonisms, its psychic mayhem— the exact opposite of modern business strategy.

In the 1960s, Sir Frank Packer and the Fairfaxes, fearful of Murdoch's inroads in Sydney, put aside their differences and form Suburban Publications. The whole rationale of Suburban is to squeeze out Murdoch and his newly acquired Cumberland Newspapers Group, with its small local papers.

The battle reaches its peak on June 7, 1960, when the two sides square off over the sale of a dilapidated printing plant. Murdoch gets a bunch of thugs to head to the plant in the dead of night and push out Packer's men, who are guarding the presses in anticipation of Packer sealing the deal for the acquisition. Expecting the brawl that erupts about one o'clock in the morning, Murdoch has dispatched photographers from his newly acquired Sydney tabloid, the *Mirror*. Among the toughs captured throwing punches on the printing-room floor are Packer's sons Clyde and Kerry, whose photographs are splashed across the front page of the *Mirror* the next day, under the headline "Knight's Sons in City Brawl." Murdoch will eventually win the printing plant after a yearlong court battle.

A generation later, Murdoch's son will be in business with Kerry Packer's son.

The other point about many newspapers at midcentury is that they're a penny business. You want to make your product as cheaply as you can, and sell as much of it as possible, which you do by pricing it as cheaply as you can. It's a classic race to the bottom. There is no such thing as added value; there is no such thing as premium pricing. The business math is terrible.

Except for one thing: If you do manage to kill the other guy, it's a great cash business. The nickels and dimes pour in. Every copy you sell beyond your base amount—kept low by printing few pages and hiring fewer reporters —represents profit.

Advertising, which will later become both cash cow and, when it departs, the ultimate killer of newspapers, isn't a meaningful part of the equation—not yet. The business is selling copies at the newsstand. This is one reason why newspaper families have been so powerful—they don't just have a voice, they have a river of cash. Newspapers in their heyday are something like dealing drugs. After you kill your competitors, it's just you and your windfall profits.

Murdoch, beginning with a severely curtailed kingdom, seems to see his needs differently. While he could be the prince and the playboy of Adelaide, he understands that in order to remain a Murdoch—to compete with the Fairfaxes and the Packers—he is going to have to figure out a way to get back a kingdom. The answer—and this is not obvious or intuitive in the 1950s—is debt.

This isn't a small understanding or the beginnings of a minor play—it's the first move in a transformational strategy that will distinguish the new business world from the old.

There's another point here: He learns how to be a bank customer. And that banks, like newspapers, compete against each other. When he took over the *Adelaide News* its bank was the National Bank of Australia—also the Melbourne *Herald*'s bank. Dissatisfied with its lack of eagerness to support him in his expansion ambitions, he switches to the much smaller Commonwealth Bank in Sydney. In a short time, he's one of their biggest clients, confirming that elemental adage: If you borrow a little, the bank owns you; if you borrow a lot, you own the bank.

Within a few years of his arrival in Adelaide, he's bought, on borrowed money, a Melbourne magazine publisher, a weekly women's magazine, and the *Sunday Times* in Perth, seventeen hundred miles away from Adelaide—beginning more than fifty years of constant dislocation and travel.

Here's yet another point about debt and newspapers: The more you can sell, the more you can borrow. The louder, bloodier, and larger than life they are—the more they cater to a less rarefied audience—the more you sell. The lessons he learned at Beaverbrook's *Daily Express* help to finance a Murdoch acquisition spree across Australia, rebranding Beaverbrook journalism as Murdoch journalism wherever he goes.

It is the debt, more than the newspapers, that becomes his essential business, transforming him and allowing him to march into his father's old company thirty years later and take it over. (No matter that, within two years, he will effectively close the Melbourne *Herald*, merging it into his more profitable tabloid the *Sun*.)

Oh, yes, and while beginning his new life in Adelaide and traversing the country in old propeller DC-3s and DC-4s—a kind of role play, if you will: Rupert Murdoch, boy publisher—he gets married in 1956, in spite of his mother's and sisters' displeasure, to Patricia Booker, an airline hostess, department store saleswoman, and sometime model. With the birth of his daughter Prudence in 1958 begins the next generation and the first of his three families.

**FALL 2005**

It is in so many ways his lack of modern business manners that makes him the particular player that he is. The game, in the most primitive business terms, is about relative levels of weakness.

He is beginning to get a stream of anecdotal information from Andy Steginsky and from whomever else he might pull a tidbit from about the weaknesses of Dow Jones.

Peter Kann is clearly growing ever weaker—and it is Kann who has so systematically blocked every Dow Jones suitor.

Arthur Sulzberger Jr., for instance, who first petitioned Peter Kann for a Dow Jones–New York Times Company merger after the Telerate disaster in 1997, was back with the same message after the 2000 Time Warner merger with AOL. There was a lunch with Sulzberger and Times president Russ Lewis. Kann on the subject of the Times' interest in Dow Jones remained transcendently remote from the conversation—a seemingly disinterested observer.

"Do you understand that he wants to merge the two companies?" questioned a Dow Jones executive at the lunch.

"Of course I understand that," Kann replied.

"Well, you didn't respond."

"Of course I didn't respond."

In 2004, Ken Auletta, in a piece in *The New Yorker* about Dow Jones, hinted that the *New York Times* might have made inquiries about buying the company. This was the first time that members of the Bancroft family had heard of such possible options. There was, especially among the younger Bancrofts, an almost slack-jawed response: "How come . . . ? Why didn't . . . ? Shouldn't we have at least considered it?"

By mid-2005, when it had become clear that the fall-off in business advertising was not merely the result of a down market, that the entire newspaper industry was rapidly contracting, and that the Dow Jones share price—then at $33—seemed destined to further erode, a sense of additional anxiety had overtaken the family and its advisors. It came mostly from the younger generation, who seemed suddenly aware of their own preposterous out-of-it-ness. They simply had no mechanism, no knowledge base for asking for (not to speak of commanding) a change in the company's direction. They seemed like fools even to themselves.

A series of meetings began in the summer of 2005 and continued into the fall between members of the family trying to express their frustrations and the Dow Jones managers—which Murdoch, with his keen gossip antennae, has started to be aware of. Kann himself, sensing the drift, began to talk about moving up his retirement schedule. He will be sixty-five in 2007. Instead of leaving then, he proposes giving up the CEO role earlier, while continuing to hold the chairman's spot until his official retirement day.

There are further politics here: Kann wants to give his wife, Karen House, the paper's publisher, the top job. An indication of Kann's own confidence about how well he knows his company and how reliant the company (and the Bancroft family) is on him is his belief that he can overcome the fact that House is a figure of great contention within the company.

Earlier in the year, the Dow Jones board had appointed a committee of board members to begin to consider the succession issue—or what some were calling the House issue: Should they give her the job, or could they resist? The committee included Roy Hammer, of Hemenway and Barnes; Harvey Golub, the former CEO of American Express and executive chairman of the board of Campbell Soup; Irv Hockaday, CEO of Hallmark; and Jim Ottaway, whose family newspaper chain was sold to Dow Jones, making him, after the Bancrofts, Dow Jones' biggest shareholder. When Hammer retired in April 2005 and Michael Elefante, a Hemenway and Barnes partner, replaced him as family trustee and Dow Jones board member, Elefante also took Hammer's seat on the ad hoc committee.

Various members of the committee continued to believe that the succession ought to happen as it had always been anticipated—when Kann turned sixty-five in 2007 he'd step down as chairman and CEO before the annual meeting in April. The further logical idea was that a successor ought to be anointed and groomed under Kann but not formally given the top job until the spring of 2007. Then too, there was the also reasonable view that a search firm should be retained so that, in addition to inside candidates, people from outside the company might be considered. This was the most politic way to get around the House issue. The minority view—Elefante's view, hence the majority shareholder's view—was that there was no time to waste, that whatever was to happen, the process should be accelerated.

Nevertheless, the process goes slowly. There might be dissatisfaction with Kann, but it is dissatisfaction mixed with something
like awe—and an inability to imagine the future without him. He
remains the parent. There are 360-degree reviews of all the internal candidates, in which everybody in management reviews everybody else. Internal candidates are interviewed by the committee.
Outside search firms are identified, but as the end of the year
nears, none has yet been approved by the board.

A Dow Jones directors' meeting is convened in New York on
November 12, 2005. Present are the twelve directors representing
management, the three independent directors (Golub, Hockaday,
and former Michigan State University president Peter McPherson),
Elefante, and the three Bancroft family directors representing the
three branches of the family. The three family members are
Elizabeth (Lisa) Steele, who runs a little company that does envi-
ronmentally friendly development in Vermont, representing the
Cook branch—she's the daughter of Jane Bancroft Cook (daughter
of Jane and Hugh); Leslie Hill, an airline pilot, representing the
Cox-Hill branch—she's the daughter of Jane Cox Hill MacElree,
from Philadelphia; and Christopher Bancroft, an "investor," who
lives in Texas and represents the Bancroft branch—he's the son of
Hugh Bancroft Jr. from his marriage to Jacqueline Everts Bancroft
Spencer Morgan (Hugh junior died young and Jacqueline, with a
big inheritance, married a doctor named Spencer; she divorced him
and, three years before she died, got remarried—to her gay inte-
rior decorator. Years of litigation ensued).

There are three key presentations at the meeting, by the three
key managers below Kann—the three who have become the leading internal candidates to replace him.

One is by House herself. The next is by Gordon Crovitz, the
forty-nine-year-old Yale Law School graduate and Dow Jones lifer
who rose from the editorial page, did time with Dow Jones in
Europe and Asia, crossed over to the business side, and now super-
vises the *Journal*'s Internet strategy.

The third is by the company's COO, Richard Zannino. Zannino came to Dow Jones just five years ago, first as the chief financial officer, with a finance background at retail and fashion companies Saks and Liz Claiborne. He's held the COO spot now for three and a half years. Although he is considered as a possible successor to Kann, he was initially rated the least likely contender, for the substantially disqualifying reason that he is not a journalist. The Dow Jones CEO has *always* come out of the newsroom. This is company culture—how can you understand and value the company culture if you haven't come out of the newsroom?—and, for all intents and purposes, the company grail. Still, as the ad hoc committee explored the issue, there was increasingly a challenge to this idea. Why did it have to be a journalist? How much talent were they excluding on that basis? Wasn't it obvious that with all the issues the company is facing, it needs a broad business kind of mind in the leadership role?

Crovitz's and Zannino's presentations are uneventful. House's presentation, on the other hand, is nothing short of a disaster. She's high-handed and charmless. She's condescending. She's acting like the board doesn't count.

Well, the next item on the agenda is the CEO search. The management committee is set to recommend that a recruiter be hired—one has been selected and lined up—and that outside candidates as well as inside candidates be interviewed for the top job.

And then, following something more than a mere nod of the head, something less than a full discussion, the family members of the board—Lisa Steele, Leslie Hill, and Christopher Bancroft—together with their trustee, Michael Elefante—say no. Although these are the people who control the company, they have only ever been bystanders to its business.

But here they are saying no—*this isn't working for us.* Blindsiding everybody.

It won't be a long process, the committee tries to explain. It'll all be done in the spring.

Well, no thanks, says the family, essentially doing something they have never done before, which is to exert their control.

Indeed, one of them says, it's clear, after this morning, that it can't be *her*—that won't fly.

Somebody else then analyzes that if they pick Crovitz, Zannino will surely leave, but if they pick Zannino, Crovitz will probably stay.

So, five minutes and it's done. Zannino. Kann's exit as CEO will be announced on January 3, just after the holiday (there's actually a move to make Zannino's appointment immediate—even before he's told that he has the job); Kann begrudgingly will be allowed to hold on to the chairman's job until he reaches the Dow Jones mandatory retirement age; Zannino, before accepting the job, will get the board to agree that he can get rid of House.

The Bancrofts have raised their voice.

# FOUR

# Opposing Families

**2006**

In a certain sense, the Bancrofts are sticking it to the company with Rich Zannino.

Amidst all the class distinctions that have arisen at the company—business reporters looking down on business, managers looking down on owners, owners so long in awe of employees—Zannino's appointment is an act of something like petulance. As though the family now wants someone it too can look down on.

Rupert Murdoch has a sense he might get along with Zannino. This is partly because JPMorgan Chase's Jimmy Lee is telling him he will. Lee, who tried to get Murdoch together with Zannino in 2005 before he was even CEO (before cooler heads got Zannino to cancel that unapproved meeting), banked Zannino at Saks Fifth Avenue and then again banked him when he was a finance executive at Liz Claiborne (Lee uses the word *bank* as a verb without self-consciousness). But he is even more pleased with himself that he knows Zannino because they are neighbors in Greenwich, Connecticut, and because their sons play on the same prep school hockey team.

Lee's point about Murdoch getting along with Zannino is partly a business point but a class point as well. Murdoch, no matter his own aristocratic background, likes rough-and-ready business guys, strivers, and—possibly *because* of his aristocratic background—men who look up to him. As opposed to, say, Peter Kann, and so many others at the *Wall Street Journal*, who look down on him.

Many people at the *Wall Street Journal* look down on Zannino too—they are at the *Journal* not least of all because it gives them a pedestal on which to look down on strivers such as Richard Zannino. Partly what the people at the *Journal* look down on—and in this they are certainly joined by the Bancrofts—is business itself. Or the business of getting ahead.

Zannino got his MBA at Pace University, a New York commuter college. It's not at all clear that if Rich Zannino had gotten his MBA from Harvard or Wharton he'd be held in higher regard (he got a B.S. from Bentley College in Waltham, Massachusetts, which doesn't help matters).

Though business has become one of the dominant cultural drivers—even, arguably, where the best and the brightest gravitate—and a major journalistic story, there remains a subset of media organizations, of which the *Journal* and the *New York Times* are the leaders, in which the left intellectual brain is contemptuous of and determined to resist the right business brain. If business has conquered, leveled, or even destroyed most other journalistic organizations, then these are the last redoubts of reason, dedication, civility, grace, professionalism, fairness, and civic responsibility (all the virtues that Peter Kann embodies so earnestly).

It is this remove from the realities of business, this condescension toward people in business, and this sense of entitlement that comes from believing that you are involved in endeavors worthier than business that distinguish what Murdoch calls, with as much disdain for them as they have for him, "the elites."

Indeed, it is a rarefied position: There are few journalistic or media organizations left that are not run by the strictest return-on-investment calculation (except, contrarily, some of Murdoch's newspapers, which is quite another story).

Still, the fact that a business guy is now running Dow Jones seems more difficult for Zannino himself than for the journalists. The weight of the culture is against him. Having worked for the clothing manufacturer Liz Claiborne, Zannino is to *Wall Street Journal* staffers a "garmento." There is his "shit-eating grin"—that is, his evident insincerity and phoniness—and all-around salesman's demeanor. There are the references to his sleaziness, his oiliness, his cashmere socks, his plucked eyebrows, his expensive suits—his essential superficiality, in other words, and soullessness.

As the *Journal* moved, beginning in the 1980s, from being a strictly business-oriented publication—a trade publication of the securities industry—to being a more well-rounded, top-notch, prize-winning journalistic organization, it developed a deep suspicion about business and the interests of businessmen, in spite of the fact that business is its subject area. Of course, the resistance to the hurly-burly and undignified aspects of trade was once part of the high WASP canon of behavior, attributes that used to make you a proper Eastern establishment Republican but which now indicate that you are a proper Eastern establishment liberal—exactly like the Bancrofts, and unlike the Murdochs.

It is this inversion that now defines both families—and that will come to be at the core of the fight for both the soul and the equity of the *Wall Street Journal*.

There is almost a plaintive sense among the younger Bancrofts, the fourth generation, about their attenuation from the family business. Dow Jones has, by the modern era, floated beyond the reach, culture, and interests of the Bancrofts. Except in a ceremonial sense, it isn't even talked about in the family all that much. "It wasn't like you should work there," one family member will later reflect in an interview for this book. "We knew we owned the company but we didn't know we could work for the company. . . . Like, you are not good enough to work for the company." Somehow Dow Jones and the Bancrofts have come to inhabit entirely different worlds—a divide that Murdoch believes he is uniquely positioned to appreciate and exploit.

## THE BANCROFTS

Charles Dow and Eddie Jones, who dislike each other, start a financial news service and newspaper in 1882. They have a news-sharing arrangement with Clarence Barron, who has his own news service in Boston. Jones leaves, Dow dies, and Barron, five foot five and 330 pounds, buys their business in 1902. Okay, technically *he* doesn't buy the business; his wife, Jessie Waldron, who runs a boardinghouse, buys the business, which he will run. It is to Jane Barron—her daughter, whom Barron adopts along with her sister—that the shares are passed. Jane's sister, Martha, who has made a propitious marriage to H. Wendell Endicott, of the Massachusetts Endicotts, does not need to be left anything—hence the Barron-Endicott line is severed from the story.

Jane Barron marries Hugh Bancroft, himself quite a Boston Brahmin type (though not nearly as Brahmin as the Endicotts), who goes to work for Barron, enduring his difficult father-in-law—a bully and a screamer—until Barron dies in 1928. Hugh Bancroft runs Dow Jones for barely five years until his death by suicide at fifty-four, in 1933. Bancroft, the rival *New York Times* discovers, spent his last days reading up on poisons before stuffing the doors and windows of a blacksmith shop on his property in Cohasset, Massachusetts, and gassing himself. Suicide by coal-gas fumes.

Dow Jones' owners—Hugh's wife, now Jane W. W. Bancroft, and her children—pretty much never darken the door of the paper again. Says Jane W. W. Bancroft to Kenneth Craven Hogate, as she appoints him the company's president, in words repeated down the years at Dow Jones: "I want you to do what's best for the company. Don't you and the boys worry about dividends."

The dividends, which the company would in fact lavishly supply, support the next four generations of Bancrofts, and ancillary family lines, in aristocratic style.

It's helpful to remember that Clarence Barron is just a generation older than Keith Murdoch. In the 1920s, when Barron, who had made it squarely into the American power structure, was dining with Calvin Coolidge, Sir Keith, also having made it, was dining with Australia's prime minister.

From 1933 to the relative present, nothing much disturbs the Bancroft family—except that in 1963, Dow Jones goes public, allowing the family to take for itself a load of cash. In 1986, the company is organized into a two-tier voting and nonvoting hierarchy, so the family can get even more cash but maintain control. (Nothing changes except that they are richer.) From the time that the Bancroft family's "permanent control" plan is instituted until the present, the family will sell off more than 60 percent of their shares. That leaves them with 24.7 percent of the company's shares, but by the terms of two-tier voting structure, under which any shares that are sold immediately become non-voting shares, the family retains 64.2 percent of the voting power.

The story of the Bancroft family in 2006 when Rich Zannino becomes Dow Jones' CEO is the story of an American milieu and class that in some strange, almost macabre sense just shut down and went out of business. The WASPs—who were likely Republicans too, whose families dominated prestigious social, business, educational, and religious institutions in the northeastern United States, whose gray-flannel husbands and fathers were the *Wall Street Journal*'s archetypal readers—had given up. Capitulated. Just sat down and refused to go on.

The Bancrofts recall—in a rather jolly, pleasantly nostalgic, hard-to-suppress-a-giggle way—nothing so much as the unreconstructed New England patrician, remote and snobbish.

But even this is not exactly true. The family, or the fourth generation of the family, has mutated from its patrician roots into something much more ordinary and unremarkable and dysfunctional, and, in its way, even more remote from Dow Jones.

There's the Cook branch, representing the families of the three daughters of Jane Bancroft Cook—the Steeles, the Robes, and the Stevensons—who have become New England liberals, earnest to a fault, dependable, clichéd, crunchy granola types.

The Cox-Hill branch, the children and grandchildren of Jessie Bancroft Cox, who have lived in Philadelphia and New York, have become almost self-consciously middle-class, with many of them actually holding jobs; they are regarded as the troubled, angry, resentful people in the family.

The Bancrofts, descendants of Hugh Bancroft, live in the Southwest and southern California. They're the flashy side, the idle rich—race car drivers, equestrians, people who live in Europe, all a bit embarrassing and confounding to the others.

By the time Murdoch enters the picture, the Bancrofts have, in the geographic and emotional distance they've put between each other, largely broken the oppressive family structure. Without the money, by now they'd probably have reverted to a norm—cousins and second cousins who barely know each other. Were it not for the money, the different branches of the family would likely have no connection at all. But there is the money, binding them to this family tree and its attendant dysfunctions.

It is a family tree that from September 2005 until the summer of 2006, Andy Steginsky—both on Murdoch's behalf and to curry favor with him—painstakingly assembled.

It goes, specifically, like this.

Clarence Barron's stepdaughter, Jane W. W. Bancroft, wife of Hugh Bancroft, had three children:

**I.** Jessie Bancroft Cox, born in 1908, the dedicated horse-woman, who played mahjong with FDR, and whose Massachusetts estate, the Oaks, serves as a Bancroft family ancestral home, married William Cox, took over as family matriarch—she died after collapsing at the one hundredth anniversary party for Dow Jones in 1982—and had two children, who make up the Cox-Hill branch:

> **A.)** Jane Cox Hill MacElree, seventy-seven, who relocates to Philadelphia and marries Louis Hill, a state senator who runs for mayor against Frank Rizzo in 1975 in the Democratic primary. She has seven children—among the most vocal in the Bancroft family.

> **B.)** William Cox Jr., seventy-six, who moves to New York, and who, together with his son Billy, represents the only Bancrofts to have actually worked for Dow Jones, albeit in an undistinguished capacity. He and his wife have four children.

**II.** Jessie's twin, Hugh Bancroft Jr., who died in 1953, and had two wives and four children, who all relocated to Santa Fe, New Mexico. They make up the Bancroft branch:

> **A.)** Bettina Bancroft (died in 1996 at fifty-five), who had one child.

> **B.)** Hugh Bancroft III, fifty-eight, who has three children.

> **C.)** Christopher Bancroft, fifty-five, who has three children.

> **D.)** Kathryn Bancroft Kavadas, fifty-four, who has two children.

**III.** Jane Bancroft Cook, who was on the Dow Jones board from 1950 to 1985 and died in 2002, who had four husbands and three children, who comprise the Cook branch:

> **A.)** Martha Robes, sixty-two, who has three children.

> **B.)** Jean Stevenson, sixty-one, who has three children.

> **C.)** Elizabeth Steele, fifty-eight, who has one child.

In other words, Clarence and Jessie Barron's daughter Jane produced three children, who in turn produced nine grandchildren, twenty-seven great-grandchildren, and so many great-great-grandchildren that nobody in the Bancroft family seems to have an up-to-date count.

And while all, more or less, will weigh in on the decision to sell the company—indeed, it is likely the last event that will bring all the members of all three branches of the family together—for the purposes of this story, the focus is on the following:

Elizabeth (Lisa) Steele—she's a Dow Jones board member, holds the votes for a large stake in Dow Jones, has always been vociferous about protecting the independence of Dow Jones, and is seen as being closely aligned with both Peter Kann and Hemenway and Barnes.

Brother and sister Jane Cox Hill MacElree and William Cox Jr.—these are the oldest living members of the family and control a big Dow Jones stake.

Billy Cox III—he's the troublemaker who first breached the family's unity in 1997.

The three Hill brothers—Tom, fifty, Michael, forty-six, and Crawford, fifty-five—who've begun their own battle against the family trustees.

Leslie Hill—the fifty-three-year-old American Airlines pilot, now retired, a Dow Jones board member, and regarded by just about everybody as the most difficult, intractable, and unpleasant member of the family.

Christopher Bancroft—he's a Dow Jones board member who controls a 15 percent voting stake.

Lizzie Goth Chelberg—the forty-two-year-old equestrian, the first of her generation to control her inheritance upon the death of her mother, Bettina Bancroft, joined with second cousin Billy in the 1997 brouhaha.

It's a simple tale: While everybody lives off the proceeds of Dow Jones, they do not, by the logic of trusts and the math of reproduction, share equally. Nor is there any consistency in the way the various trusts established by Jane Barron Bancroft after her husband's suicide—most of them were set up in 1934 and 1935—are organized. So what you have is just one of fortune's inevitable messes, always ending in the acrimony and squabbling of heirs clinging to ever decreasing portions of the original estate.

By 2006, with Steginsky making his inquiries, parts of the family, spurred on by the younger members, have begun actively trying to unlock more cash from their billion dollars (give or take) that is stuck in Dow Jones and losing value. The $80 million or thereabouts in dividends that the family gets each year from Dow Jones (a significant part of the company's profits) isn't quite enough—not just because there are so many members of the Bancroft family, but because much of that money still flows to the third generation, leaving the fourth to scramble and implore. Hemenway and Barnes, which acts not only as the family's lawyer and trustee but also as their money manager, is being pressured— particularly by the Cox-Hill branch—to look for solutions. The firm brings in a few investment banks to mull over the problem.

Merrill Lynch makes a proposal that the family should radically sell down its equity. But nobody wants this—nobody wants really to change anything. They just want more money. Meanwhile, Hemenway and Barnes doesn't want to change anything either. Its business since the 1940s has largely been built on the Bancrofts and their quiescent ownership of Dow Jones—maintained, in much the same way that Peter Kann maintained his relationship with the Bancrofts, by treating them as investors who wanted to know as little as possible about their investments.

Part of the job—Kann's job with Billy Cox and Lizzie Goth in 1997, and Michael Elefante's job now at Hemenway and Barnes— is to manage the natural inclination of younger people to exert themselves.

Michael Hill has actually taken a course at Harvard specifically about what families ought to do with their businesses and fortunes. He has the idea that there are opportunities close to him that he ought to try to find something out about it. He has begun to believe that what stands between him and Dow Jones and him and his money is Hemenway and Barnes.

What Andy Steginsky has learned is that the Hills are not just unhappy with Hemenway and Barnes but are thinking about suing the firm. To Murdoch, this is, to say the least, a sign of the disarray he's been counting on. On the other hand, one solution (or effort to mollify) that Hemenway and Barnes has proposed is to create a voting trust similar to the one the Sulzberger family has at the *New York Times*—in essence, pledging the family to vote together—which would allow the Bancrofts to sell down more stock but continue, with their secure voting bloc, to maintain control. This proposal for unity would be bad for Murdoch.

But, in a sign of ultimate disarray or paralysis, neither development—neither the lawsuit nor the voting trust—seems to be proceeding, leaving the family to descend further into feuding and discord.

## THE MURDOCHS

Rupert Murdoch loves hearing the gossip about the Bancrofts. The e-mails he has been getting regularly from Andy Steginsky about the crazy Bancrofts are the high point of his day.

He is an expert on anybody who owns any media, but he has a special feeling for the history of families who own newspapers. That is his field of play. Since arriving in the United States in 1973, when he purchased the San Antonio papers, he has kept a clear schematic in his head of who is who—updated on a virtually daily basis. He admires the way the Sulzberger family has stayed unified and protects its interests. However, the present scion—Arthur Sulzberger Jr., the company's chairman—is, in Murdoch's estimation, an ineffective leader and lousy businessman (he is thin-skinned too, and more than once has tried to call Murdoch to complain about something the *New York Post* said about him—Murdoch doesn't take the calls).

The Sulzbergers are followed by the Grahams, where Katharine Graham was the first lady and matriarch of the press. Her son Donald is a low-key and methodical steward who carefully developed the company's interests in the education market; its Kaplan unit, which offers preparation for standardized tests and mail-order degrees, is now the company's main profit driver.

There are the Chandlers, with the *Los Angeles Times,* whose Times Mirror Company was the most profitable newspaper company in the United States—but the Chandler family, by the fourth generation, was attenuated and remote from the business, which was sold in 2000 to the Tribune Company (the Chandler trusts, which became significant holders of Tribune Company stock, forced the underperforming company to put itself on the block in 2007—yet another signal to Dow Jones).

There are the Binghams of Tennessee, who owned Louisville's *Courier-Journal* and the *Times* and whose family saga of good intentions coupled with incompetence and breakdown (and left-wing children) makes Murdoch cringe. There are the Ridders, who turned Knight-Ridder into the second-largest newspaper chain in the country—but earlier in 2006 Tony Ridder was forced by his disgruntled shareholders to sell. There are the families that have stayed private: the Hearsts and the Newhouses and the Coxes. The Hearsts, descendants of the greatest, or at least most iconic, newspaper proprietor of all time, William Randolph Hearst, are disengaged and passive figures, supported by a company that includes television and magazines as well as newspapers, run by professional managers. (Hearst himself made it clear in his will that he didn't want his not necessarily so bright offspring running the business.) The Newhouse brothers—S.I. and Donald, who inherited their company from their father and who are even older than Murdoch—continue to run their newspapers and magazines with great canniness. Murdoch admires them—and once tried to get them to help him buy Twentieth Century Fox—as much as they admire him. (He wonders, though, what might happen to that company going forward; there'll be a lot of Newhouse hands out.) The Coxes of Atlanta, descendants of James Middleton Cox, the Democratic candidate for president in 1920 (his daughter, Anne Cox Chambers, was Jimmy Carter's ambassador to Belgium, and is among the most powerful people in Atlanta), with their Cox Enterprises continue to own newspapers and cable stations as well as the third-largest cable provider in the United States.

The thing you have to understand—and understanding this explains so much about Murdoch's success—is that happy newspaper families are alike, and unhappy newspaper families are . . . well, they're quite alike too: In the end, they all lose their papers. As cautionary tales go, you could hardly find a more hothouse example of families gone awry, of genetic dumbing down, of the effect of idiot-son primogeniture, and of the despairing results of idle hands than newspaper families. Newspaper families provide no surer way to produce incompetence and ineffective executives, no better guarantee of shareholder antagonism.

This is his opportunity: The Bancrofts are ridiculous.

A side benefit of his close look at the Bancrofts is to make him feel so much better about the dysfunction in his own family (*dysfunction* is a modish word that irritates him—he uses it only because his children say it so often). The Murdochs, who have had their problems, are not, he is confident, heading in the Bancrofts' direction—not yet. The situation with his children was bad after the divorce, and it got much worse after the introduction of Wendi, followed by the birth of his young children—there were several anni horribili—but they have all managed to persevere. Lachlan's break from the company, painful as it was, actually helped things.

Anyway, whatever he did, and whatever Anna might say about his absenteeism—and Homeric it could be—he has done something right. Or Anna has done something right. Or good genes are just good genes.

## PRUE

Prue, Murdoch's daughter with his first wife, Patricia Booker, is the only one of his children not directly competing for his business affections. But her husband, Alasdair MacLeod, after a News Corp. stint in London, took a high-ranking spot in Australia in 2004, so Prue is hardly neutral in the News Corp. sweepstakes. What's more, her children, James, born in 1991, Angus, born in 1993, and Clementine, born in 1996, are the oldest grandchildren, which strategically positions them in the dynastic stream.

Then again, Prue has morphed into the official family wing nut. She gets away with saying what the others won't, even things that the others won't *think*, and she takes the various family members much less seriously than they do themselves. This involves, not least of all, seeing her three oldest half siblings as, each in their way, master-race prototypes. Where Prue is short, plump, unfashionable, and rather disheveled, her half siblings are each striking, precise, intense—almost too good to be true, at least at first glance. Indeed, both her brothers married models, each of whom bears an uncomfortable resemblance to their husbands' mother, Anna— striking, precise, intense—and hence to their husbands' sister Elisabeth, who is her mother's clone.

Prue's mother, Patricia, whom Murdoch met and married in Adelaide, was always regarded by Murdoch's mother as less than she should have been. When he divorced her, in 1966, she married a bad-news Swiss jet-setter by the name of Freddie Maeder, with whom she began a partying life (funded with her former husband's money), often leaving Prue behind.

When Rupert and Anna Torv marry in 1967 (she is not on the face of it a much better match—an Estonian Catholic is not exactly a catch in Anglo-Protestant-centric Melbourne), nine-year-old Prue begs to live with them. They move together to London in 1968. Prue is the difficult stepchild to a pregnant stepmother—and it's all pretty much downhill from there. Her schooling is a disaster (Murdoch, trying to be an Australian egalitarian, first sends Prue to a London state school—she doesn't last a term), her behavior often incorrigible, and her relationship with her stepmother at the very least strained and often much worse. Then there's the move to New York—she's fifteen and suddenly plunged into the Manhattan private school world at Dalton. She's way out of her element among the New York rich kids. She's one of the few Dalton students who don't go on to college. Murdoch, at this point, still doesn't see girls as having much of anything to do with what he does, certainly not as part of the future of News Corp. In fact, the only job Prue gets at News Corp. is a girl's job—when she returns to London, she's briefly a researcher at *News of the World*'s Sunday magazine.

At twenty-six, she makes what seems to be a favorable marriage to Crispin Odey, who will go on to be the highest-earning hedge fund manager in London. But a year later, they separate. Prue goes back to Australia—partly because her mother is in bad shape, in the midst of the depressions she will go in and out of after Freddie squanders the fortune Murdoch gave her on a failed orange juice company in Spain. At one point, Rupert and Prudence actually go to Spain together to retrieve Booker after she suffers a breakdown there. (Murdoch paid for her medical care and to set her up again in Adelaide before she died in 1998.)

In 1989, Prue, back in London, meets and marries Alasdair MacLeod, a Scotsman who shortly goes to work for Murdoch. Prue is strongly against Alasdair going into the family business—but Murdoch offers him a job behind Prue's back.

Her resentments and general feeling of exclusion from the family continue and come to a head in 1999 when she is plastered on the front page of the *Sydney Morning Herald* under the headline "Forgotten Daughter." Still furious about remarks her father made at a press conference in 1997 in which he'd referred to "my three children," Prue agreed to sit for the only interview she'd ever given up to that point. In the interview she recounted how, after her father's public slight, she had had "the biggest row I've ever had with my father. I rang up, I screamed at him, I hung up. He was very upset. He then sent the biggest bunch of flowers—it was bigger than a sofa—and two clementine trees."

The interview appears the day of Lachlan's wedding to Australian supermodel Sarah O'Hare. But Prue, who hasn't seen the interview, arrives at Cavan—the 40,000-acre sheep station outside of Canberra Murdoch bought in the 1960s—for the wedding and can't understand why everyone is so tense.

It must be "your fault," she says to her father, telling him it has to do with the separation.

"It has nothing to do with me," Murdoch says. "It's your fault."

"You've got Wendi holed up in a hotel in Sydney, and you've got Anna here hating you. Why is it my fault?"

"Did you not see the front page? You've upset them all."

And yet she is in some ways the child Murdoch is most comfortable with—or at least the child who is least afraid of him. Within News Ltd., in Australia, people remark that she treats her father more like a husband—an irritating husband she has to beat some sense into.

For her part, she finds it just slightly unsettling that he regularly mistakes her for one of his sisters.

Prue is the only ally he has when Wendi comes into the picture (still, she tells an Australian documentary filmmaker, he was a "dirty old man"). And indeed, during the divorce negotiations with Anna, who is trying to guarantee that neither his new wife nor possible new children would gain an interest in News Corp., Anna tries to assign Prue a lesser position in the family trust.

## ELISABETH

Murdoch's ideas about girls seem to change substantially with Elisabeth, born ten years after Prue. This is partly about the broad cultural change that's happening as Elisabeth is growing up. But it's also that Elisabeth is growing up in New York—a particular age in New York when so much of the focus, especially in the circles she and her family move in, is on the success, achievement, advantages, and connections of the children as well as the parent.

Elisabeth goes to The Brearley School, where Murdoch is hardly the only billionaire father and where Elisabeth is not even the most notable heiress.

It's a hothouse of competition—academic and social and, not least of all, for ultimate worldly position.

He begins raising her with an idea of how he was raised. When Elisabeth is in the ninth grade, he sends her to Geelong Grammar, the same school his parents sent him to that he hated. It isn't any better an experience for Elisabeth. She's back within a year.

She is often uncontrollable—including a suspension from school for drinking. She fights more with her strict, formal mother than with him. Away so often, he's the good guy.

He doesn't actually want to know what she's up to. He's careful not to know.

Petronella Wyatt, the daughter of his friend Woodrow Wyatt, has Liz, in her memory of a teenage summer trip, climbing on the back of a Vespa and roaring off with an Italian man who chatted them up in a Roman bar.

She goes to Vassar College from Brearley. In her senior year, she falls in love with Elkin Kwesi Pianim, the son of a Ghanaian political prisoner. Murdoch sends Elisabeth to work for News in Australia after she graduates—not without thinking the distance might end her relationship with Elkin. But she wants to come back. In September 1993 she marries Elkin in a huge Catholic wedding in Los Angeles. Elkin, of course, goes to work for Fox.

But Elisabeth remains restless. She convinces her father to help her do something on her own. He suggests that television stations are a good bet. The following February, weeks away from having her first baby, Cornelia, with a loan from Australia's Commonwealth Bank facilitated by her father, she and Elkin buy two small

NBC affiliates in California for $35 million. She's a harridan of a manager—ripping through the staff, sacking many old stalwarts, and slashing operating costs. Eighteen months later, she and Elkin sell the stations for a $12 million profit.

She gets into Stanford Business School, but her father says he can teach her much more than she could learn in any old MBA program. "I called my dad and said, 'I've gotten into Stanford and I'm going.' He said, 'Are you fucking crazy? No, you are not. I can give you a much better MBA of life than anybody at Stanford can give you, you know. Come work for me.'" She joins BSkyB, based in London, in 1996, reporting directly to the CEO, Sam Chisholm, then promptly becomes pregnant with her second child. She also becomes a high-profile figure in the London media social scene. Meanwhile, Elkin, who is running the couple's small venture capital company, Idaho Partners, along with his brother Nicholas Pianim, launches an upmarket Afro-Caribbean weekly and buys the sponsorship rights for London's annual Afro-Caribbean Hair and Beauty Exhibition. He also tries to launch a television station specifically for black audiences.

At Sky, she clashes publicly with Chisholm, who refers to her openly as a "management trainee." Murdoch, in this instance, chooses his child over his manager, and in 1997 Chisholm resigns. But Murdoch, annoyed by Elisabeth's failure to get along with Chisholm, her latest pregnancy, with her second daughter, Anna, and the increasingly critical reports of her London life, doesn't give her the top job. Elisabeth "has some things to work out," he tells Mathew Horsman, a reporter from the *Guardian*. "She has to decide how many kids she is going to have, where she wants to live." He adds of his children, "Currently it is their consensus that Lachlan will take over. He will be the first among equals, but they will all have to prove themselves first."

Elisabeth starts working with Matthew Freud, great-grandson of Sigmund and the most notorious PR man in London, on a rebranding campaign for Sky—and, not incidentally, on an effort to improve her profile in the press. Their affair shortly becomes public.

Disappointed by Lachlan's ascendancy within the company, and taking her mother's side in the marital battle with her father, *and* once again pregnant—by Freud—Elisabeth resigns from Sky in May 2000, saying that she plans to start an independent production company.

The tabloids revel in details about her on-again off-again relationship with Freud and her breakup with Elkin. Freud even briefly walks out on her when their daughter Charlotte, born in November 2000, is three months old. Over both of her parents' objections, she marries Freud in the British wedding of the year at his family's country home in August 2001.

Although she has publicly said that she will be primarily a passive investor in Shine, the independent production company she is backing, and that she intends to spend more time with her children, by the time her father is thinking about buying the *Wall Street Journal* she's running the biggest independent television production company in the United Kingdom.

Two months before he bids for the *Journal*, she will finally give birth to a boy, Samson Murdoch Freud.

## LACHLAN

He's the first son, which has a profound pull on Murdoch. It also may be that frictionless, affable, constant Lachlan is easy to get along with. Uncomplicated. This is what makes him, in the eyes of the many Murdoch-philes, not Murdoch enough. Curiously, though, it makes him more Australian, which has become his adopted, or in a sense reclaimed, home.

Within a few months of his abrupt and emotional leave-taking from News in 2005, he and his wife, Sarah, have not just settled into Sydney but have become pop culture figures—he as famous in Australia as Prince William in England, and she the head of the major Murdoch charity, and in 2007, the fetching hostess of a popular morning show. They're the king and queen of Bronte Beach. Australia is his place.

He was born in London in 1971 but grew up in New York. It was a wholly upper-class, establishment—*liberal* Eastern establishment, to be sure—American upbringing. Dalton and Trinity in Manhattan. Then Phillips Academy in Andover, Massachusetts. Then Princeton.

After Princeton, Lachlan spends a couple of months at News Corp.'s Sydney headquarters as a management trainee before it's announced in August 1994 that he will become the general manager of Queensland Newspapers, the Brisbane-based publisher of the *Courier Mail*. This is, remember, the newspaper that the Herald and Weekly Times trustees convinced Dame Elisabeth to sell to the company after Keith Murdoch's death. So at twenty-two—the same age at which his father took over the *Adelaide News*—Lachlan takes his management role. (Not incidentally, in the rival Packer dynasty, Jamie Packer, who is four years older than Lachlan, has begun to take over duties from his father.) Three years later—Lachlan's preternatural good looks, signature tattoos, motorcycle, and famous name having made him an iconic Aussie—he's promoted to running all of News Corp. in Australia.

That year, 1997, the Murdoch children are summoned to New York, where Rupert tells them that he's settled the issue of succession and that Lachlan will end up running the company.

In 1999, Lachlan marries Sarah O'Hare—all of the Murdoch children get married young—who is the face (or bottom, actually) of Bonds, the most famous Australian underwear brand. The wedding at Cavan, at which Prue blows up at her father, is front-page news in Australia—the romance of the year, an Australian fairy tale. At Anna's request, Wendi Deng isn't invited and waits in a hotel room in Sydney.

Lachlan is a constant newsroom presence in Australia, carefully modeling himself, just as his father had done decades before, as the boy publisher. Among his closest friends in the company is Col Allan, the boozing, bad-tempered editor of Sydney's *Daily Telegraph*, whom Lachlan later appoints as editor of the *New York Post*.

In 1999, his father brings him back to New York as the head of U.S. publishing and then eighteen months later gives him the title of deputy chief operating officer—officially the number three guy at News Corp.

But, other than the *Post*, he has no real job—he's resisted everywhere else at News Corp. in the United States. It's a lesson that his brother and sister both take keen note of: Being too close to their father, and the people who want to be close to him, isn't a propitious move. Quite the opposite: To be at a distance, at a far remove from the old man, makes them the Murdochs everybody who is also distant from the old man wants to get close to.

Officially, Lachlan will say he's moving to Australia to give his sons, Kalan, born in 2004, and Aidan, born in 2006, a better life.


## JAMES

Unlike Lachlan, James *is* like his father, News Corp. people believe. Or at least he tries to be. But it may not be so much his father that he's emulating as some generic idea of the advanced business figure. In open-necked white dress shirt and steel-rimmed glasses, he's aggressive, implacable, focused, remote, fit, precise. His father is obviously proud, even perhaps slightly afraid of him, but, one might suspect, a little confused by him too.

His father, being a more clearly primitive business creature, is perhaps most mystified by James' self-conscious MBAisms—even more mystified because James does not have an MBA. He is so effortlessly programmatic, reductive, and process-oriented. And he's a marketer—the one thing his father has never been.

Counterintuitively, James' diffidence or contrariness, his relative shunning of the family business, is what seems to have paid off. At fifteen, while working for the *Daily Mirror* in Sydney, he was famously snapped sleeping during a press conference, and the photo appeared in the rival *Sydney Morning Herald* the next day. A bleached-blond hipster, with various piercings, he drops out of Harvard in his junior year, after spending time in Rome, vaguely thinking about a career as an archaeologist. Instead he decides to make the hip-hop label he's started in college, Rawkus Records, his full-time career. He swaps out the bleached-blond hair and earrings for a rugged beard and eyebrow stud.

Rawkus is a critical if not quite financial success, with Mos Def and, early in his career, Eminem on the label. His father agrees to buy Rawkus in 1996, and James goes to work in News Corp.'s music and tech division.

In 1997, he's made the head of News America Digital Publishing, a job he will later describe as "doing triage" as he attempts to fix the old empire's missteps into digital media (though he does not particularly fix anything). His wardrobe changes to sharp suits and thick black glasses in his new persona as the young entrepreneur.

When the Internet bubble bursts, James is shipped out to Hong Kong to run the ailing Star TV business, where he becomes, echoing his father, an apologist for the Chinese government. Among the Murdochs, not a famously verbal bunch, he develops a reputation as the family polemicist. In 2000, he delivers the Alternative MacTaggart, the formal contrarian address, at the Edinburgh Television Festival, and excoriates both English-language centricity and Hong Kong's democracy movement. The next year, with his father sitting in the audience, he delivers a speech at the Milken Institute in Los Angeles accusing Western media of being unfair to the Chinese government and describing Falun Gong as a "dangerous" and "apocalyptic cult." (Tunku Varadarajan, in the *Wall Street Journal*, characterizes James as a college dropout involved in the "craft of craven submission to the communist regime in China.") Sky Asia turns its first profit in his third year of running it. His father promptly moves him to Britain to run BSkyB.

Around this time, inside News Corp., James becomes "the real thing." Among the reasons James has come to be described in this language (usually when phrases are repeated at News Corp. it means that Rupert has said them first) is that he is not his brother. The consensus that has formed around James as the better successor comes, at least in part, from the fact that he was farther from the company and from the top job. So the more James was praised, the more that took from Lachlan's inevitability. The more James was praised, the more his father had an alternative. This reinforces the idea that staying away from the epicenter of News Corp. is the better strategy—one now being followed by Lachlan.

James gets up early, works out at the gym, arrives in the office before anyone else, and leaves in time to put his kids to bed. He has a black belt in karate. Unlike his brother and sister, he stays out of the gossip columns. He tells his PR advisor, "You will be a success in this job when the press starts referring to me as the reclusive James Murdoch." Unlike his father, he has refused to comment on his political views (with the exception of his China coddling) and doesn't court politicians.

He's introduced to his wife, Kathryn Hufschmid, an Oregon-born model, by Lachlan's future wife, Sarah O'Hare, at a yacht party in Sydney in 1997. The couple get married just outside Old Saybrook in Connecticut in 2000, not long before James is shipped out to Asia to head up Star.

The private wedding, a year after Lachlan's Australian royal-styled affair, was something of a reunion for the family. Wendi and Rupert attended, as did Anna and her new husband, William Mann. Dame Elisabeth made the trip from Australia. James read a poem by Pablo Neruda to his bride, and Kathryn responded by quoting James Joyce.

While in Hong Kong, both Kathryn and James sat for a handful of magazine profiles and made occasional statements to the press, but as soon as they arrive in London, she disappears from the media spotlight, her name only briefly appearing in reports as James' wife.

The couple have two children, Anneka, born in 2003, and Walter, born in 2006.

## GRACE

Grace, born in New York in 2001, is fluent in Mandarin. As Rupert Murdoch begins to plot to get the *Wall Street Journal,* he's also worrying about getting Grace into private school in New York. He wants her to go to Brearley, where Elisabeth went. He recruits Gary Ginsberg, who knows the Kennedys, to help him get Caroline Kennedy, a Brearley alumna and board member, to write a letter on Grace's behalf.

## CHLOE

Chloe, born in 2003, is fluent in Mandarin too.

Murdoch talks about his children, and their relative potential, with the same openness and tactical nuance that he talks about anything else that might affect the company. He seems to assume that everybody else has a stake in his kids—that they are figures in the body politic, corporate assets, historic personages.

Murdoch's projection about his children manages to be both compellingly normal and obviously creepy at the same time. This normalcy and creepiness are reflected in the way the company treats them. Except at the highest possible levels of the company, the Murdoch children are accorded not just deference or standing but a kind of love. They represent something—him. Even at the highest levels, the price for pushing Lachlan out was to then declare an alternative Murdoch child, James, "the real thing," the real Murdoch.

There are now few families living this blood story, this blood imperative. Generally, any effort at this kind of dynastic construct is met with easy ridicule. It's an extremely difficult modern conceit. It may be an impossible one. The press scrutiny alone for young people upon whom has been bestowed too much money and too many expectations is deadly. But in this, obviously, the Murdoch children are spared considerable pain—a significant part of the media protects them. And so they have been able to coalesce into dynastic shape.

They're certainly like the Bushes in their level of advantage, connections, resources, and focus on family entitlement. But they may be more Kennedy-like. The insularity is powerful; there is a sense, especially among Anna's children—Elisabeth, Lachlan, and James—of being part of a rarefied order, of being judged against it, of there being no escape from it. They are trapped in the Murdoch bubble, in its exceptionalness.

The insularity can seem to take the form of an almost puppy-love closeness. It's one of Wendi's first impressions of the family, that they're always kissing each other and saying "I love you." They can't have a telephone conversation—and they're always on the phone with each other—without many protestations of love. Wendi, from a carefully unemotional Chinese family, is a bit weirded out.

And yet there's an ordinariness to it. Rupert Murdoch is a man obviously burdened by family issues; equally, his children are burdened by a complicated and demanding father. The Murdochs are as fraught as any family, and as connected as the closest of families—there are seldom days he doesn't speak to each of his children. He's not just weighing their futures but plotting their futures with them. He's not just the patriarch but the mentor and strategist. And if he's often been the remote father—full of murmured regrets—he is also the long-suffering one, stoically standing by as his children fail to heed him.

So it's a sort of yuppie professional family, everybody in love with everybody else's success—and everybody just a little too competitive about it and oppressed by the demands.

In the spring of 2006, as he's getting Andy Steginsky's reports about the dysfunctional Bancrofts, he decides to finally resolve his family's filial and financial dilemma. But he does it on television.

This is both because he does see it as historic and, in its way, necessarily public, but also because it's easier than doing it in person. Also, it makes it a fait accompli. Decision made. Done. Dealt with.

He's been standing between Wendi and their two children, on one hand, and his adult children, on the other—he has to cast the deciding vote. Which he does on *Charlie Rose*.

With the birth of Grace and Chloe, the family's financial situation becomes untenable, as his and Wendi's children, by the terms of his divorce agreement with Anna, are barred from the Murdoch trust and fortune. Wendi's position is clear: *Rupert, fix it.*

In this issue of great moment, nearly a matter of state, over the trust, a complex, almost historic agreement—proscribing control over the News empire—Wendi is, to say the least, a discordant note. First of all, she talks constantly, without guile or niceties, boiling it down, reducing, stripping away all conceits, formality, pretense. Indeed, if that has been the essence of Murdoch-style journalism, he must have been shocked to be so outdone.

His older children resist. They're furious. In projecting their royalness, it seems to them a terrible breach of etiquette for Wendi—Wendi of all people—to want to interfere with their historic birthright. It is, however, not just Wendi. If she's prodding—really prodding—Rupert is himself not about to forgo this further shot at immortality, given two more children, and half-Chinese children, no less.

It's a long negotiation that begins before Lachlan's departure from the company and that takes place primarily on the phone with children and their advisors mostly in different countries.

And then, Charlie Rose. His show is a forum that business leaders, especially those in the media, often use to stroke their reputations, or to make valedictory pronouncements, or to smooth over

PR problems. Rose is a deferential and often treacly host (many of the media figures he hosts in turn help underwrite his show). His hourlong conversation with Murdoch, which airs on July 20, 2006, is a meandering hodgepodge that seems to mostly focus on Britain in the 1980s. But then it turns to the message it seems he's there to impart—it's a muddled, almost coded message, which makes sense to only his family and to those people advising the family on the sticky trust issue. And virtually all of those people are caught off guard. He has either told Charlie Rose more than he intended to or, keeping his own counsel, gone off script to make the private public and therefore definitive.

> Rose: While you have said that you would like to have a
> member of the family succeed you—
> Murdoch: Yes, I think that's a natural desire.
> Rose: You've said. Either sons or daughters, you'd like to
> have—
> Murdoch: They've got to prove themselves too.
> Rose: Where does that stand today? Succession. Lachlan—
> Murdoch: It's really up to them.
> Rose: But, to great pain, when Lachlan left it was painful
> for you.
> Murdoch: If I go under a bus tomorrow, um, it'll be the
> four of them will have to decide which of the ones
> should lead them.
> Rose: Your four children?
> Murdoch: Yeah, well, and my, uhh, the two little girls are
> too young to consider this at the moment.
> Rose: Now do you consider them? You've said they are all
> my children.
> Murdoch: They'll all be treated equally—financially,
> absolutely.
> Rose: You ran into some buzzsaw within the family because
> of that decision?

Murdoch: No, just on a question of power. Would their
       trustees have votes and these things at the moment,
       you know? We've resolved everything very happily.
Rose: It's your personal business. So, if something happens
       to you, if you get run over by a bus when you leave
       this studio, the four kids have to decide who among
       them ought to be the heir apparent.
Murdoch: In terms of power, yes, in terms of leadership.
       They'll all get treated equally financially.

What this means—and the various advisors all note that they would not have liked to be Rupert Murdoch watching *Charlie Rose* with Wendi Murdoch when it aired that evening—is that he has acceded to his older children's settlement proposal to admit their young half siblings into the trust economically but to exclude them politically. They will benefit from the company but have no say in how it is run.

Among other elements, this guarantees that Wendi will not be able to act as the regent (with two votes) for her minor children.

Rupert Murdoch's ambitious, largely functional family is, in a certain sense, what he believes he's offering the *Wall Street Journal.* The Bancrofts, he further believes, given their lack of ambition, deserve to lose their business. Similarly—and this is another aspect of the class subtext—he doesn't believe that management of the company should have the right to control because, well, it isn't their money.

Which is, in a way, the point of his intersection with Richard Zannino.

Zannino, as a conventional manager—even if his MBA is from a night school—understands that capital controls. That it's only in a strangely anomalous and inverted world that it does not. That, actually, at Dow Jones, it's crippling that capital doesn't control—

the cost of keeping capital out of the hair of the business managers is that they have to turn over all the money the company makes. Capital, if it were running the company, would understand that the company needs to reinvest profits to thrive and grow. Indeed, given the weakness in the newspaper business, there is periodic talk about selling the Ottaway chain of newspapers, which Dow Jones acquired in 1970. But the company knows that if it does sell Ottaway, the money will likely be immediately distributed to the Bancrofts.

Shortly after Zannino is made CEO, he gives his presentation on the state of the company and his plans for renewal to the Dow Jones board. Even in his optimistic scenario, he only feels comfortable projecting, in five years' time, a rise in the share price from mid-thirties to $45. He understands, even with his night-school MBA, that this means that he, like Peter Kann, will have to placate the Bancrofts. That he will have to, in some sense, fool the owners of the company—providing them with the money the company needs in order for them to remain quiescent enough not to sell the company or, worse yet, think they could run the company themselves. (His own appointment is evidence that this could happen—that these know-nothings could assume greater control.)

He understands that he has risen to a CEO job that really can't be done. He can only fail at it.

Hence, when Jimmy Lee, his neighbor from Greenwich, Connecticut, and fellow hockey dad, calls him about scheduling a get-together with Murdoch—now that Rich is actually the CEO—he goes for it, without any hesitation. Indeed, he neglects to tell anybody at Dow Jones—not chairman Peter Kann, not anybody else on the board, not the company's lawyer, nor any representatives for the Bancrofts—that he is meeting with Murdoch and an investment banker.

Lee is a semi-legend on Wall Street. "Semi" because he is partly a punch line too. He's a caricature of an investment banker, eighties-style—white collar on his striped shirt, slicked-back hair, Martha

Stewart-worthy wife and children, and a regular table at the Four Seasons. In April 2000, he was famously plastered on the cover of *Forbes* in floral suspenders and touted as the greatest financier since Mike Milken (earning him the nickname "Suspenders"). But a bona fide legend, too, because he has been in the game, at the top of the game, for as long as anyone, a player in a long list of famous deals. Jimmy has banked Rupert since the late nineties.

Lee first gets a taste of Murdoch business at the Sun Valley conference for media moguls hosted by Allen and Company each year. At a conference in the late nineties, Lee runs into "the boys"—Lachlan and James—who are talking workouts. And so, at five o'clock the next morning, Jimmy is up and chasing the three Murdoch men to the gym. (Murdoch himself, in his oversize sneakers, has long been a stoic exerciser—not so much a fitness buff, but a man determined to keep going.) This convivial conversation in the Sun Valley gym leads to another, more businesslike one, which leads to JPMorgan Chase getting a role in News Corp.'s efforts in 2000 to go after DirecTV.

After that, now in the constellation of News Corp.'s bankers, Lee keeps trying to move a deal—any deal—to the front burner. Because everybody knows the *Wall Street Journal* gets Murdoch's attention, Lee keeps bringing it up—telling Murdoch about how tight he is with Rich Zannino because of the hockey-dad thing, how key Rich is to what's going on at Dow Jones, and what a mess it is down there and how something's got to give.

Actually, it's by no means clear who, in the end, will pay Jimmy's fee. JPMorgan Chase has had a relationship with Dow Jones—if there is a deal, Jimmy would definitely be interested in banking Dow Jones. But Murdoch would be the better play—except if Dow Jones gives Murdoch the cold shoulder and gets interested in somebody else. But first things first.

Jimmy tells Rupert—who's partly inclined to believe the company will give a new CEO at least a few years to see if he can work a turnaround—that Rich is hot to trot. To Rich, Jimmy renews his offer of an important rite of passage for any media business honcho: an introduction to Murdoch. And now, because Rich is the CEO, he doesn't have to clear the meeting with anyone.

Of course, Zannino knows that Lee is shopping him. At the same time, he regards his de facto openness to being shopped—why else go out to dinner with an investment banker and someone who has made no secret of wanting to buy your company?—as a white-lie pretext to meet Murdoch. Who in his position wouldn't want to meet Murdoch? The truer point, though, is that Zannino wouldn't necessarily know which is the real pretext for what—is he pretending to be a seller in order to meet Murdoch, or pretending he wants to meet Murdoch in the hopes of selling to him?

The get-together happens at the Links Club on 62nd Street on the Upper East Side of Manhattan. It's a place at which neither Zannino nor Murdoch is particularly comfortable. It's Jimmy Lee's place. He's putting his imprimatur on the meeting. It's a WASPy, stuffy, rather ridiculous old-fart place. (The Wall Street guys have taken over all the venerable establishments.)

A banker, at this point in a deal (substantially before there is a deal), is kind of a professional annoyance. His job is to be the unsubtle one, even the clown. Let the principals blame the gaucherie of bringing up business on him. But Murdoch is an exceptional client. Whereas, to most bankers, the principals so often get off track and need to be prodded back into line, with Murdoch there is the sense that, even as he dangerously digresses, he knows where he is going. As it happens, this is not necessarily because he knows where he is going, but because he is Murdoch. Everybody knows what Murdoch means. If you're sitting with Murdoch, it's, well, big. You end up assuming a lot about Murdoch—most of all that he must know what he is doing.

In fact, on the most obvious level, Murdoch can seem rather out of it. That's partly the hearing issue, which no one acknowledges. On the other hand, this sense of him not listening to you, of him just taking the conversation anywhere he wants, makes him more

Murdoch too. He's on a higher plane. You're just pleased to see what Murdoch is really like—and not sure what to make of it, but nevertheless fascinated, captivated. It's not something you've seen before: this old man, among the world's most powerful men, musing, mumbling, forgetting, recovering with a sharp remark.

Zannino is nervous and eager to please. He wants to be liked, respected.

Lee knows that Murdoch, if just automatically, is making an estimation about Zannino's type. Is he one of *them* or not? This is the way Murdoch assesses everyone. Are you pretentious or are you not? Do you want to make money or are you interested in other sappy stuff (like what the hoity-toity people think of you)? Are you wet or are you made of sterner stuff? Do you hate him or not?

Now, Murdoch has made many deals with *them* types. It's a simple technique to make a deal with one of them—Murdoch just denies that he is Murdoch. As it happens, people are often so relieved to find out that he is actually soft-spoken, reasonable, intelligent, and witty that they relax. They're so relieved they lose their critical faculties. They all of a sudden believe, for some reason, what they want to believe about him. (It's this relaxation on their part that has often gotten him accused of being a liar—and while in truth he does lie or misrepresent, isn't it their fault for believing him? Is he expected not to take advantage of their lapse in judgment?)

By the drift of the conversation into the larger media world—they talk a lot about *American Idol*, Fox's blockbuster show (a show that Murdoch's daughter Elisabeth first mentioned to him when it ran on British television as *Pop Idol*)—it's immediately clear to Murdoch that Zannino is not one of *them*, he's not Peter Kann. Zannino is not interested in newspapers for themselves. He's obviously interested in business as a larger construct. He's more interested in deals—the higher business currency—than the product per se.

They're over the sensibility hurdle.

Now, what Murdoch has to do is weigh Zannino's level of resistance without confronting it. Were he asked outright, Zannino at this point would be forced to commit himself to not being a seller. Murdoch wouldn't do that—wouldn't put him in a corner. What Murdoch is trying to figure out (his drifting almost visibly moves to acuteness) is if it's worth the time and energy to create a situation in which Zannino might come to him.

How do you turn a nonseller—a man who has far more to lose by selling than he has to gain—into a seller? Into your partner in a deal? How do you make him your ally? How do you loosen him up? How do you subvert? How do you make an intractable situation fluid?

Of course, there is no reason, this evening at the Links Club, to believe that Murdoch is thinking about any of this, that he's thinking about anything other than the opportunities of reality television. Murdoch's lack of introspection, his disinclination to talk in large, abstract, or theoretical ways, is his form of poker. He's listening to you (though, you suspect, not really listening) or he's rambling about something not too relevant.

Zannino leaves dinner not quite sure what *that* was about, feeling, somehow, that he has not interested Murdoch quite enough—feeling just a little bad about himself.

# FIVE

# The Outsider

People are against him. They are against him because . . . well, he is who he is and they are who they are. He stands here; they stand there. His world is his world—it is not necessarily a part of other worlds. He exists in opposition. You are with him, you are against him, or you are irrelevant to him. Arguably, he has overcome most obstacles by that simple analysis. If you are against him, then you are his enemy and he fights you—it becomes binary. Sometimes it seems that he creates enemies just because it simplifies the world.

This makes him somewhat less than rational as a businessman —noneconomic, even. Wanting to buy the *Wall Street Journal* is not simply about one company that has analyzed that it might gain an advantage from acquiring the assets of another company. It is more about one man who believes he can profoundly adjust the balance of power between those who are for him and those who are against him.

And he's right about this. The *Wall Street Journal* sees itself as opposed to *him*. It represents something he cannot have, *should* not have. He wants it because they don't want him—it's fairly primitive.

On the other hand, part of his method is to place the most economically irrational of motivations into a straightforward marketplace context.

It's almost a sleight-of-hand play on his own character. He's not outsized, dramatic, mercurial. He's methodical, thoughtful, and, seemingly, extraordinarily reasonable. Everybody around him acts as though they are involved in considered economic pursuits, rather than substantially primitive ones; they have convinced each other of this, and often have convinced the world. For almost a year now, John Nallen, the number two accountant at News Corp. and part of Murdoch's inner circle on the eighth floor of News headquarters at 1211 Sixth Avenue in Manhattan, has been quietly updating the book on Dow Jones as new pieces of information emerge about the company. The level of Murdoch's interest in Dow Jones can be measured by how frequently the book is updated. How much is he talking about Dow Jones? Nallen is tracking and anticipating, trying to make everything logical about this wildly imprudent pursuit.

Richard Zannino, too, has been able to pretend that he is engaged in a perfectly straightforward, even workaday discussion of mutual business interests—instead of what it obviously is: Murdoch, in his us-against-them mode—almost Cold War–like in its notions of loyalty and betrayal—is evaluating him, judging him. Will Zannino turn? Will he come over? Will he be the mole?

After their dinner at the Links Club, Murdoch has been pacing his moves as he takes in more information, as Andy Steginsky continues his intelligence gathering. Learning that the Bancroft family's solidarity is much less than it seems and that its moral high ground is pretty shaky to boot, he has Jimmy Lee take the next step with Rich Zannino as soon as summer is over and everyone is back at work.

In October, Lee invites Zannino to lunch with Murdoch in a private dining room at JPMorgan Chase at Park Avenue and 47th Street. Once again Zannino does not tell his board or his shareholders that he's meeting with the company's most eager suitor and his investment banker. The meeting is self-consciously secret. By plan, Murdoch and Zannino arrive at JPMorgan Chase thirty minutes apart.

The stakes are high for Zannino. If he allows this to proceed, it results either in a sale of the company or, quite likely, in his own dismissal. He could be an amply rewarded hero who will go on to run another substantial company—or a business disgrace whose career will stall out. The threshold issue for Zannino is whether Murdoch will go the distance. That, if the game begins, will Murdoch see it through—can he carry a deal across the finish line?

What Murdoch has to estimate is if Zannino will play the Judas role. Not just selling the company but selling it to the very person it derives part of its identity from, by virtue of his not owning it.

And Murdoch has to figure out his price. At what level will Zannino go for broke?

This is not all about Zannino as a turncoat; in part it's also about him as a rationalist. Can Zannino find a way to believe that what he is doing, or what he is allowing to happen, is the best thing for the company? Later Zannino will insist on his literal responsibility: to increase shareholder value. In order to take that position, he must be the ultimate rationalist. He's decided that he can't increase shareholder value. He's given up that point of pride.

It is partly too about Zannino's sense of his own role. The people around him—the family, the board, fellow executives—are saying one thing: The company is not for sale. But they may not mean that. They may just mean they personally don't want to sell the company; they don't want that burden, that scarlet letter. But—and Zannino is acutely aware of this point—the board, with family members leading the charge, threw out Kann, the guy who expressly did not sell the company (or increase shareholder value) in favor of Zannino.

At the *Journal* there will be the lurking suspicion that Zannino might have engineered the whole thing. The theory here is that even for Murdoch—coming up with the right price, then having to depend on Zannino's acquiescence, then getting the family to fall into place—it's just too much good fortune and coincidence and amazing chess playing and successful manipulation. The true conspiracists will put it all on Zannino.

The problem with the conspiracists' theory is that it turns Rich Zannino from a fledgling CEO—a longtime climb-the-ladder company man, a man very pleased with his own chance elevation to the top spot, a quiet, eager-to-be-liked, eager-to-be-respected, eager-to-live-in-Greenwich man—into an extraordinary rebel.

Still, if not a rebel's nature, Murdoch sees something in him—plasticity, ambition, openness, reverse snobbery (he's more in awe of Murdoch than he is of the *Wall Street Journal*).

Of course, nobody has to believe they are thinking about this or, in fact, about anything—except having lunch in the JPMorgan Chase private dining room. Even if, as it happens, Jamie Dimon, the new CEO of JPMorgan Chase, stops in for a little chat—adding to the sense of moment.

It's obvious, though—the predator, his bankers, and the air of attention can only mean something large is expected, that Rich Zannino is being asked to choose.

In fact, nothing happens. It's all, pretty much, a replay of the spring dinner. Which is exactly the point. Zannino becomes the rebel and turncoat just by going along, by not changing tone, by not seeming skittish, uncomfortable, resistant.

Zannino is falling for Murdoch's trick. Murdoch has a way of seeming like the most rational player. Even if everybody knows—and they do; how can they not?—that Murdoch has it in for established norms and polite society and customs of the nation, that, at root, he is always making some primitive, emotional, I-can-live-only-if-you-die assault, still, he always somehow makes it look as if the numbers add up.

The outsider is surrounding the insiders.

But first there's another piece of business to take care of. It's the kind of move that marks him as different not just from you and me, but from other businessmen too. He's so outside, so from his own world, that he can't be trusted to behave with the same logic or emotion as the rest of us.

The past six years of his career have been largely spent pursuing DirecTV, the satellite television network owned by General Motors. He has staked his reputation and much of News Corp.'s reason for being on his satellite vision. He has pursued DirecTV so assiduously, so single-mindedly, that, at one point, he even considered buying General Motors to get it. He has invented some of the media businesses' most baroque and far-fetched financing strategies to do the deal. When he fails in his quest, because EchoStar, the other major satellite competitor to DirecTV, makes a last minute bid, which GM, in 2001, partly out of antipathy to Murdoch, accepts, he still keeps going. He finally succeeds after waging a fifteen-month antitrust battle. It's the pinnacle of all his aspirations. It's the top of the top. It's his most megalomedia dream come true. It is, he says, the absolute necessary synthesis of all that he's worked for—and it has finally all come together.

And then, in late 2006, he shrugs it off—as though it hardly ever existed. Puff! Not important. That he might have told the world DirecTV was the most vital component of News Corp.'s business is something that he can, apparently, readjust—ignore. If he has to change reality, flip it, reinvent it, he can. It may be a sort of narcissism—nobody exists but him, therefore he can do what he wants. Or like a certain authoritarian, even Orwellian, regime—he can merely change the facts, rewrite history. Anyway, he long ago gave up trying to justify himself.

In order to make his bid for Dow Jones, he's got to get rid of John Malone, his largest shareholder since Malone's midnight raid on News' Australian shares in 2004, when Murdoch was preoccupied with election-night anxieties and festivities. Malone, he knows, will go ape shit about a Dow Jones bid. Malone won't sit still for Murdoch buying . . . a newspaper. Murdoch would have to fight two battles at once: against Malone and for Dow Jones.

Malone's threatening presence within News Corp. had bedeviled Murdoch for two years now—it was a cold war. Neither man would blink. But now his desire for Dow Jones clarifies Murdoch's thinking about how to deal with Malone. Simple: He'll pay the cost and fuck it. That is, New Corp.'s shareholders will pay the cost.

What Malone wants is a steal. Malone doesn't want Murdoch to pay him money to go away—Malone would have to pay taxes on that and he has a great tax aversion—he wants Murdoch to sell him something for cheap. So if that's what Murdoch has to do to get the *Wall Street Journal*, get screwed by Malone, that's what he will do.

In this marvelous, bravura way, Murdoch declares DirecTV to be irrelevant to his interests and goals and gives Malone a good deal on it. And that is it. No looking back.

You don't really have to offer many excuses or justification when you've come to believe you live outside and above everybody else's fairly contemptible world.

## HIM VERSUS THEM—BRITAIN FROM 1968

Why should Rupert Murdoch be so difficult? So stubbornly the "other"? So impatient in his position? So ambivalent about his own desire for acceptance that he believes his own mythology about his determined outsiderism?

It could be an Australian consciousness. He's the product of a nation whose artifice is lack of artifice, which inevitably comes into conflict with everybody else's rituals and proprieties.

Or it could come from what happened to him at Oxford, or, for that matter, at Geelong Grammar. In these two experiences of being thrust out into the world, he found himself marked, cut off, not accepted. This caused him not so much to figure out a way to fit in, to submit, as to lead a parallel existence.

Or it's his appetite for risk. The prudent world seems weaker, lesser, more fearful to the gambler.

Or it's his actual displacement. He literally isn't at home. He's not so much an immigrant, eager or forced to fit in, as a colonist, living in his own preserve, certain of his own superiority.

Or it's the nature of his business. He's in the tabloid business. He's the whoremaster. The ruder you are, the more papers you sell. You can sugarcoat this, or not. In some perversely honorable sense, he chooses not to do so.

Then, having taken this on—having become the outsider, the person apart—he has to push back ever more forcefully against the pushback. Sensing his own ostracism, he sits it out even more defiantly.

He began as an insider; became an outsider because people didn't understand he was an insider; became such a successful outsider that he becomes, once again, necessarily an insider.

But by that point, having only contempt for insiders, he has to find ways to be an outsider again. Offending polite sensibilities becomes his hobby and calling card.

Such outsider-insiderism, such shifting sense of place, of the barometric pressure of social judgment, becomes even more complex when you make Britain such a great part of it.

It would be curious to rewrite the Murdoch history with him skipping England and coming directly to New York. It'd all be less kill-or-be-killed. Less about the premium on disruptiveness. Less about him against the rest.

Murdoch in England is a never-ending fight with the establishment. He uses the word *establishment* partly as the Brits do, to suggest toffs and Eton and plummy accents, but expands it to include any other power center that he's against—for instance, and not incidentally, the BBC. So there is the left establishment, and the journalistic establishment, and the banking establishment, and the royal establishment, and of course the trade union establishment. He wins; they lose.

Curiously, the establishment shortly found itself rather in awe of him. He was a new sort of spectacle, in part even a comic figure (the villain you hissed at—enjoyed hissing at). The journalist Chapman Pincher describes his and everyone's great amusement at seeing Murdoch, in the early seventies, arrive at a manor house for a hunting weekend "in a brand-new shooting suit, with knickerbockers—you could see it was absolutely brand-new—and what looked to me, as an old hand, like an absolutely brand-new twelve-bore, side-by-side gun"—and then, never having fired at a pheasant before in his life, to have bagged a ton of birds.

The credit for his victories belongs, however, as much to his timing as to his natural talents.

During his career, England is substantially reinvented—with Murdoch at the center of it. He might be one of the prime change agents, but the superstructure really puts up a pretty meager resistance. Britain's labor-socialist establishment is so sclerotic that it's an easy target for any entrepreneur with a little management and organizational acumen.

It's actually handily preyed upon by all sorts of outsiders. After Murdoch, there's his nemesis, Robert Maxwell, the Czech; there's Conrad Black, that other would-be Murdoch, a Canadian; Tiny Rowland, of a German father interned during World War II; Mohamed Al Fayed, an Egyptian; and then, later, the Russian billionaires. Compared to this bunch, you can begin to make the case that, relatively, Murdoch's a proper gentleman. And yet, he similarly offends upper-middle-class sensibilities. All of these guys are opportunistically feeding on the passive, depressed British body. And while they are allowed to feed—pretty much gorge—they are still regarded with contempt, mockery, and condescension. They can have money, but they can't have standing (until they ultimately take that too).

In London, as an Australian, Murdoch is marked as particularly uppity, unsuitable, and not serious. He makes bumptious and arrogant noises about buying the *Mirror*, Britain's greatest tabloid. When he's rebuffed by its owner, IPC, he starts buying shares in the parent company—although nobody seems to take this as much of a threat. He's merely obnoxiously calling attention to himself.

And yet, the obnoxiousness has a certain value. He so insistently and loudly expresses his interest in buying into Fleet Street that one of his bankers puts him on to the *News of the World*, which, right away, Murdoch becomes desperate to buy.

His immediate interest in the *News of the World*—a ridiculous, almost campy British Sunday paper whose specialty was sexual perversity of a particularly English kind (spanking), crime, and scandal—suggests two things: that newspapers did not necessarily mean news to him but rather theater and spectacle, and that the rather priggish Murdoch would fit his tastes to what was for sale (and what he could buy).

The *News of the World* has been run for nearly a hundred years by the Carr family. At its height, in 1950, as a pre-television diversion in a postwar Britain dying for diversion, *NoW* had a circulation of 8.5 million; by 1968, when it comes to Murdoch's attention, it is down to 6 million. For sixteen years, the paper has been run by Sir William Carr, who, at the earliest possible hour for lunch, walks the few blocks from the *NoW* headquarters on Bouverie Street, just off Fleet Street, to the Savoy Grill, where he stays late. Even with circulation dropping, the share price falling, and Sir William in his cups, the family thinks its position is unassailable. Sir William's family owns 27 percent of the voting shares, and Sir William's cousin, Professor Derek Jackson, owns another 25 percent.

The professor, however, tired of his relatives, decides to sell.

Enter Robert Maxwell. The Jewish, Czechoslovakian-born Maxwell (who will become known as, among other things, the "bouncing Czech") is almost twenty years into the forty-year fraud he is perpetrating—engendering only mild suspicion—on the British media industry. He uses his company, Pergamon Press, a publisher of, among other things, specialized scientific literature (so his interest in the *News of the World* is even quirkier than Murdoch's), whose value he has inflated by various financial subterfuges, to make a stock offer of £26 million for *News of the World*. The professor puts Maxwell into the catbird's seat by agreeing to sell him his 25 percent.

Several things are about to happen:

Murdoch, through his courtship of Sir William Carr, and through a series of promises that he will not keep, is about to pull a jujitsu move, which, along with the broken promises, will stick to him as a kind of signature (indeed, this hoary old deal will one day be dredged up and endlessly cited by Dow Jones partisans).

He is also, to his great annoyance, for the next twenty years, about to become associated, indeed hopelessly identified, with the crooked Robert Maxwell—they are both the two interloping R.M.s of the British media business.

And he is about to become branded, through to his core, as among the most exploitive and most vulgar publishers working in the English language.

Anyway, it's really nifty jujitsu. Murdoch, even though he's been posturing about buying up IPC shares, doesn't have the money to counter Maxwell's offer. On the other hand, Sir William appears to welcome death more than he'd welcome Robert Maxwell—likely not so much because Maxwell is a crook as because he is Jewish.

Murdoch is the Protestant antidote, albeit without the necessary cash.

Murdoch, having won over the Carrs (Sir William admires Murdoch's mother), gets them—after he threatens to walk away from the deal and leave them helplessly saddled with Maxwell—to make him, along with Sir William's nephew Clive, co-CEO of the company. Sir William will become chairman, with a seven-year contract. The *News of the World* will then acquire certain assets Murdoch owns in Australia. In this semi-flimflam exchange, Murdoch's Australian company will get 40 percent of the *NoW* company. His 40 percent, and Sir William's 27 percent, means they can block a sale to Maxwell. Sensing that he holds the upper hand, before the deal closes Murdoch seriously backpedals on the agreement to be co-CEO and insists he get the role alone—and without too many options, save Maxwell, the Carrs agree.

Meanwhile, Murdoch and Maxwell are trying to gouge each other's eyes out. Maxwell even tries to buy News Ltd. It all ends in a huge dustup at the shareholders' meeting on January 2, 1969, with Murdoch, the presumptive heir, and Maxwell, the losing pretender, fighting bitterly to the end.

Not long after, Murdoch, who agreed not to buy any more shares in *News of the World*, turns around and buys part of the professor's stake. The justification for this is—well, there is no justification. You take what you can get.

In short order, he forces Sir William to resign, and then gets rid of all the other Carrs, who, too late, understand that they were lambs led to slaughter.

Murdoch seems remarkably dense about how he's regarded. He doesn't pick up the signals. His press image is seldom a topic of interest for him, or even of conversation (as it is, quite often obsessively, with so many other public men). It may be that he is so temperamentally opaque that nothing gets through. Or it may be that high regard is, quite uniquely, not what he's about. To be held in the esteem of the British public and press is the least of his ambitions. He may not even be aware of this as a measure of anything important or telling or valuable. He occupies a different world.

For an international businessman and would-be tycoon, he's incredibly parochial. He's just an Australian come to London to do some business. That's how he sees himself—proudly, as an opportunist. Britain is something to take advantage of, not to be part of. In outsider fashion, he creates a little circle of cronies around him. That becomes his finite world.

Bert Hardy is one of his first retainers. Hardy has been an advertising salesman for the *Mirror*, the leading British tabloid. In Hardy's view, there isn't a sense of great strategy and big picture, and certainly not destiny, about Murdoch. At the outset, at least, he sees Murdoch as the leader of a little group of small-timers trying to keep their businesses—lame, faltering businesses at that—on their feet. It's a patchwork; it's ad hoc; it's seat-of-the-pants; it's all-consuming. It's a condition in which no other reality can quite exist—you're just too busy.

Murdoch, arriving in England, hasn't bought himself marvelous cash-flow-producing prestigious brands with his new businesses, as he will in the future. This isn't the world of private equity, of financial logic (an amount invested produces a predictable amount returned), of cutting costs to produce more free cash. It's sweat equity. The harder you work, the quicker you respond, the cheaper you do it, the greater chance you have of making your business work. The difference here is that Murdoch, acting like the narrow-focused, tight-fisted, do-what's-necessary manager of a gasket-making company in, say, Manchester, is acting like this in the newspaper business in London. He doesn't get that all eyes are on him.

One of Murdoch's early "scoops" at the *News of the World* is to serialize the memoirs of Christine Keeler, the call girl who six years earlier was at the center of Britain's biggest postwar sex scandal, the Profumo Affair. The thing is, John Profumo, the disgraced defense secretary, has devoted his postscandal life to charitable works and is now seen as something of a paragon of British social virtue. Thus Murdoch becomes the rude so-and-so for dredging up the whole sordid mess. The Press Council, an industry self-monitoring group, issues a public condemnation of the Keeler series. In a huff, Cardinal Heenan, Britain's ranking Roman Catholic, pulls an article he had agreed to write for the *News of the World*. The Profumo Affair becomes the Murdoch Affair.

Murdoch himself—pleased to have sold more copies with the Keeler story than the *News of the World* usually sold—seems strangely casual and unconcerned about the backlash. Demonstrating that he's not averse to a public role but that he has little comprehension of its nature, he uses the controversy to get himself on television.

On the air he's artless: "I don't agree it's sleazy for a minute," he says to the interviewer, David Dimbleby, in I-am-not-a-crook fashion. "Nor do I agree that it's unfair to the man. I have the greatest sympathy with him, but it doesn't alter the fact that everybody knows what happened. Certainly it's going to sell newspapers."

It is, however, his interview with David Frost, in the autumn of 1969, after publication of the Keeler article, that puts Murdoch—as well as Frost—on the map. Frost's show has been running on London Weekend Television for three weeks when, as Frost will later say in his memoir, "it caught fire" with "an interview with a new arrival on the London scene."

The interview is notable, on Frost's part, for its heavy shocked-*shocked* tone—as though Murdoch's even bringing up the Profumo Affair, one of the most well-covered scandals in British history, was simply outrageous behavior. It's notable for the ferocity of Frost's attack—sarcastic, prosecutorial, and sanctimonious. And notable for Murdoch's implacableness: His instinct is to resist and inflame, rather than smooth and mollify. And notable because Murdoch completely bombs.

Frost himself assumes that Murdoch will sidestep the issue with some sort of mild mea culpa so that the show, which Murdoch has been convinced by Frost will be "friendly," will focus largely on an Australian entrepreneur's success in London.

But Murdoch, accompanied by Anna, Bert Hardy, and his PR man, John Addey, runs right into it. His own conception of himself as a hands-on, man-in-a-hurry, commercially astute guy—characteristics that in another decade or so would become de rigueur for every entrepreneur—morphs publicly into the figure of the dark, morally suspect, sadistic villain. It's a relentless forty minutes in which Murdoch, with evident pride, takes practically full responsibility for the Keeler book excerpt.

"I certainly subedited a tremendous amount out of the book," he proclaims.

"You have done that yourself?" confirms Frost, before holding him to account: "Since we talked on the phone this afternoon, I spent four dismal hours reading through the [Keeler] manuscript. What did you think of it when you read it?"

Thus begins perhaps the only public inquiry into Murdoch's tabloid philosophy.

"What is your argument of positive merit?" demands Frost. And this becomes his leitmotif: making Murdoch define the good he does.

"Arguments of positive merit in this is that for the first time the whole story is being told," Murdoch tries.

"But it's not," says Frost. "All these books have come out. . . ."

Murdoch retreats. There is nothing wrong, he says, "in telling a story twice."

"If you admit that the story has been told twice, then we are making progress," says Frost, treating Murdoch like an errant schoolboy. "But, I mean, you started off by saying there were new things. I went through this. I combed this through very carefully and I could not find any new facts in it at all except a couple of minor personalities."

Then, midway in the show, a taped interview with Cardinal Heenan is introduced, which Murdoch says he wasn't told about. The prelate excoriates Murdoch on air and defends the worthiness of John Profumo's current philanthropy.

Frost then singles out John Addey, sitting in the audience, for clapping loudly when Murdoch defends himself. "Your PR man's going mad again. Your PR man is the only person who's applauded —you must give him a raise."

And then there is a point where, with narrowed eyes, Murdoch seems to focus on his position. The entire controversy has been whipped up, he says, "by members of the sort of establishment" who, he analyzes, would not otherwise "want to be seen with Mr. Profumo anywhere."

Frost cements Murdoch's position: "That's an Australian view of England—it really is, you know. I mean, it doesn't work that way anymore there, you know. It really doesn't. I mean, of course there a lot of daft old-school ties in this country and so on, but it doesn't work like that—the Establishment are not as well organized as that."

"You reckon?" says Murdoch sourly.

The interview, a smash success for Frost (Frost and Murdoch actually occupy similar media places—the first of the independent media entrepreneurs), confirms everybody's position. Murdoch, to Frost's audience, is a disreputable, un-British interloper. Britain, to Murdoch, is ruled by a hypocritical, self-sustaining establishment— which, he clearly understands, doesn't want him. (After the show, Anna says to Frost, who has invited the Murdochs back to the hospitality suite for a drink, "We've had enough of your hospitality.") Everybody's position, in fact, is enhanced. The establishment rises in condemnation of Murdoch, as Murdoch becomes determined to have his revenge.

Murdoch doesn't seek to recast himself as a more sympathetic character, more appreciative of British opportunity, more observant of British protocol, more obviously a supplicant to British approval—what any PR specialist or marketing consultant might have suggested. He goes in a radical and opposite direction. He rejects cultural Britishness. His rejection reflects his ever-hardening binary philosophical position: You're either successful, and hence significant, or you're not successful, and hence insignificant. And at this point in time, nearly every British institution, commercial strategy, and fundamental method of economic or social problem solving is failing.

It's a key differentiator. Most, perhaps all, of the entrepreneurs attracted to Britain and rising in it are looking for a broader kind of approval—they have major social aspirations—whereas Murdoch is only market-driven. Earlier than most, he understands what will become the central trend of the last quarter of the century: Success trumps.

What's more, he seems, in contravention of his conservative personality, to understand that the deftest commercial strategy in Britain is the affront. From the Rolling Stones to the *Sun*'s bare-breasted Page 3 girls, any slap at convention in this passive if disapproving society promotes you.

And yet, he is no rebel. He certainly never sees himself as louche, rude, or disreputable, nor, as moguls are apt to, larger than life. That is part of his constant irritation with Robert Maxwell, his confounding doppelgänger, who *is* louche, rude, disreputable, and large (He's "mad," Murdoch will often say). In some sense, Murdoch is a perfect antiestablishment storm—precisely because he believes he *is* the establishment in his very core. He is a perfectly presentable, perfectly well-bred, exceedingly mannerly, highly competent business executive, without personal eccentricities or evident grandiosity, who owns ever more politically conservative newspapers. He isn't trying to upset the establishment or take from it. Rather, he is its legitimate defender (to the extent that the establishment is one in his image). As his Free Church Scottish ancestors believed they were the true Church and the established church the pretenders, so for Rupert.

Storming out of the Frost show, he says to Bert Hardy about London Weekend Television, the producers of the show: "I will buy this company." And he does.

He will note to me almost forty years later that he hasn't spoken to Frost since.

"I feel like saying, 'I'll get the bastard one day,' " Murdoch will say to me, adding ruefully, "but he'll die before I get him."

The *News of the World* establishes Murdoch as a new and unnatural character in British public life. He becomes—and will continue to be for over four decades—the "Dirty Digger," in the characterization and nomenclature of *Private Eye,* the satirical weekly. To be called a digger—first used to refer to the Aussie soldiers sent to their deaths by British officers at Gallipoli—is something of a compliment among Australians. In *Private Eye*'s usage, it becomes both a reference to *News of the World*'s reporting on dirty laundry and an ethnic slur.

But it is the *Sun* that makes Murdoch a player in Britain, and whose success makes it possible for him to show little or no interest in submitting to, as it were, British rule.

After building up, over almost twenty years, his Australian chain of more or less tabloidy newspapers (most of them more middle-market than downmarket), one of his central business perceptions is that Britain, that storied destination of ambitious Australian hacks, has only one significant daily tabloid—the *Mirror*—and it is putting on untabloid-like airs.

The *Mirror* is owned by IPC and run by the most famous publisher of the day, Hugh Cudlipp. In Murdoch's view, as he will recall forty years later, Cudlipp has allowed himself to become corrupted; instead of focusing on being a great editor, he is more concerned about hanging out with the "champagne people." In Murdoch's telling, Cudlipp has committed the worst sin of newspaper proprietors: He's turned his back on the working stiffs by trying to take the paper upmarket—and is failing dismally. The *Mirror* was made the biggest-selling paper in postwar Britain by Harry Guy Bartholomew, who, in Murdoch's encomium, is "a great journalist," meaning not a great finder of facts but a great packager, showman, and drinker (it makes you a greater packager and showman if you can do this and drink prodigiously at the same time). "He'd be standing in God knows whose bar from about three in the afternoon and have proofs sent to him," Murdoch will gleefully recall to me. "They had to go to press at four in the afternoon to get the papers to Scotland and everywhere. But he was a great journalist. He was out at the bar, reading these pages and he'd throw them back and say, 'Put the fucking picture spread back in.' "

According to Murdoch, the *Mirror* "had a lot of spirit in it and it was absolutely anti-establishment and the soldiers' paper in the war. They loved it. It gravitated across, over a period of twenty years I guess at best, to this paper striving to be something it wasn't in its past." The tabloid has, in Murdoch's view, become preachy and teachy, demonstrating the kind of liberal earnestness and clunkiness that will become one of Murdoch's favorite targets.

For Murdoch, the competitor—in this instance a self-satisfied and not very spirited one, but one nevertheless with a five million circulation—defines the market. He not only covets this market but, owning the weekly *News of the World*, needs a daily paper to keep the presses busy the rest of the week.

He makes a short, unsuccessful effort to buy the *Daily Sketch*, a fading tabloid owned by Northcliffe's heirs, Associated Newspapers (the *Daily Sketch* was ultimately folded into the *Daily Mail*), and then begins thinking about starting a tabloid of his own.

Then, in 1969, Robert Maxwell puts the *Sun* into play.

The *Sun* began life as the *Daily Herald*, a left-wing broadsheet owned by the Trade Union Congress, and was the largest-circulation paper in the United Kingdom in the 1930s. After the war, the *Daily Herald*'s circulation went into free fall. IPC, the *Mirror*'s owner, bought the paper in 1961, repositioning it a few years later as a paper for the new youth market and renaming it the *Sun*. With the paper's circulation continuing on a downward spiral—circulation had fallen by almost half, to 850,000—IPC begins to consider closing it in 1969. With the unions threatening to make trouble for other IPC papers if the *Sun*'s jobs are lost, Maxwell offers to take the paper off IPC's hands. The understanding is that he'll cut jobs and run a limited-circulation paper that will not compete with the *Mirror*.

Getting wind of the deal, Murdoch, knowing that the unions would resist the Maxwell plan, writes a "confidential" letter to the "relevant parties," which include the unions, saying he'd be interested if Maxwell can't come to an understanding with the unions. Murdoch knows the unions will never let IPC sell to Maxwell if there is an alternative. With Murdoch having gained the support of the unions (whose power he will later destroy), IPC is forced to sell its paper, for a discount price similar to that offered by Maxwell, to the man who would become IPC's most tenacious competitor.

The almost instantaneous success of Murdoch's *Sun*, which will become one of the two most profitable and most powerful media outlets in Britain, is due to Murdoch's big investment in television advertising ("Pussy Week in the Sun"—a whole week of coverage about British cats—was one of its especially successful promotions) and his positioning of the *Sun* as a working-class antidote to the fusty *Mirror*.

It is an entirely new sort of package, a kind of inky precursor to *Married with Children*, the lower-middle-class gross-out comedy that will launch the Fox Network in the United States. The *Sun*, celebrating downmarketness—it's fun to be *us* rather than *them*—directly makes the British connection between the working class and sex (Page 3 girls) and, indeed, between alcohol and sex. It also makes a bolder grab at popular (i.e., media and celebrity) culture than any British paper before it—and it takes a combative, bold, political line.

In addition to suddenly giving Murdoch a power base, the *Sun*'s startling success turns Murdoch, in the establishment view, into England's most disreputable and dangerous media figure. He's some commercial genius at a time when it's just beginning to become clear, in an unsettling sort of way, that this is a powerful thing. That others sense this power makes him all the more disturbing and noxious.

It's almost impossible to exaggerate how quickly Murdoch becomes the bogeyman in Britain. He is at this point practically the antithesis of British manners and virtue. The reaction to Murdoch, at first from the most conservative parts of British society but then more and more from the left too, is a mixture of apoplexy and British resignation. He is the rough beast.

There is nobody who better embodies that mood than the queen's husband, Prince Philip, who for the next forty years will use Murdoch as his personal bête noire. Indeed, at a moment when the British royal family is at nearly the zenith of its popularity, Murdoch is always full of casual disparagements and nasty gossip about it.

To the left, Murdoch represents rampant commercialization—he becomes *Private Eye*'s archetype for vulgarity ("Thanks for the Mammaries" is the *Private Eye* headline inspired by the *Sun*'s chesty Page 3 girls)—and this is even before he becomes stridently right-wing.

It bothers him hardly at all. As for *Private Eye,* of course it would be after him. "They were almost a sort of Establishment in a strange English way" is his almost fond dismissal when he recalled *Private Eye*'s campaign against him for me almost forty years later. There are even elements of being the "Dirty Digger" that he clearly takes as a compliment. Prince Philip's ill regard is to him an accomplishment.

He's not conflicted. The disapproval directed his way is, in a sense, negative reinforcement of epochal proportions. The more everybody disapproves, the more he succeeds.

What's more, he's working all the time. Or he's in transit, that other leitmotif of his career, shuttling between continents. He often doesn't get what people are saying because he's not around to hear it. The excitement and motion of his life dwarf the heckling. He's running back and forth to Australia, a regular diet of twenty-five-hour flights. Also, he's beginning to go to America. For an adrenaline junky, for a success junky, for a newspaper junky, he's living the life. This is the more-more-more moment: *This is the feeling I want to sustain and keep re-creating.* He had a similar feeling back when he was traversing Australia. Decisions, action, money.

Still, while such a feeling can, perhaps, handily sustain you, the pointed snubs and low-level contempt are likely more difficult for the people closest to you.

It is, after all, a dramatic relocation for his family. When they uproot from Melbourne and land in London in 1968, Rupert and Anna have been married for little over a year. He is thirty-seven. She is twenty-four. Like his first wife, Anna is undereducated, provincial, not yet ready to be a would-be international press lord's wife. Her calm forbearance is a kind of stoicism. She's the interloper's wife.

Later it will be hard to conjure the closed-down, hidebound, judgmental, highly nuanced sense of manners in almost any particular stratum of late-sixties British daily life, high or low. If it is changing, if Murdoch himself is a symptom of that change, actual daily life has yet to be fully informed.

The Murdochs are simply not invited anywhere. They have no friends (except Rupert's employees). They have money but no entrée.

Anna is the pornographer's wife.

Then, in the last week of 1969, something happens that will further stain the Murdochs' life in London: There's an attempt to kidnap Anna. The Murdochs, returning to Australia for the Christmas holidays, lend their car, a Rolls-Royce, to Alick McKay, one of Murdoch's executives. McKay's wife, Muriel, takes the car one day on a shopping trip and is never seen again. The kidnappers, issuing million-pound ransom demands, have mistaken Muriel McKay for Anna.

Oddly, this is the incident that makes Murdoch internationally famous. What's more, the kidnapping and the bizarreness of the mistake become tied to the Murdoch brand. There's a massive publicity moment, provoking a torrent of conspiracies and invective against Murdoch. One letter: "I will let Mrs. McKay go if the *News of the World* and the *Sun* publicly announce that they will not corrupt our kids any more by printing all that filth."

Murdoch is not just the Dirty Digger: To him dark, threatening things attach. Indeed, Mrs. McKay is murdered and fed, possibly, to pigs.

And then another incident. In 1972, at their country place in Ealing, Anna Murdoch, on a rainy night, accidentally runs over an elderly woman in her BMW and kills her. (The Murdochs end up giving the car to Bert Hardy.) It's a story that's almost wholly covered up—but it leaves Anna feeling all the more isolated.

Murdoch, single-minded, without self-doubt or equivocation, is nevertheless at this moment in an unnerving position. He has a business that every day is more successful. It's a success that, in itself, is making his life, and his family's life, more difficult. In order to manage his life, he will have to negotiate the terms of his success. There is such a thing as being *too* successful.

It will be difficult to continue to be the Dirty Digger. He's pushed the envelope too far. England is too small.

His solution to the problem of his outsiderness is to make himself, in a sense, the ultimate outsider—a kind of exile.

The literary exile leaves his geographic home to be free to write. There is a similarity to the way Murdoch leaves first Australia and then England to create this separate sphere in which he operates as the man apart.

You can never really catch him.


**MARCH 29, 2007**

It's the provocation. He gets people to react to him. And he doesn't fear or even, apparently, worry about the reaction.

The *Wall Street Journal,* along with the *New York Times,* has stayed safe, in part, because people fear having their good names compromised if they go after it. This touches the media's sense of propriety. And you offend the media's sense of propriety, particularly its sense of propriety about itself, at your own great risk. Among the most galling and confounding aspects of the Dow Jones bid is that Murdoch is so blithely willing to violate the norms. He has no institutional respect. He has no fear of offending the community. How do you deal with someone who doesn't care what you think of him, who is somehow beyond public sanction?

During most of the winter, his people on the eighth floor continued to analyze the Dow Jones business. The company is trading no higher than the mid-thirties; Murdoch has heard about Rich Zannino's estimate of getting the share price to, tops, $45; Merrill Lynch, in its presentations to the Bancrofts about selling down their holdings, advises that $45 seems optimistic (Murdoch has heard this too). On News Corp.'s eighth floor, even understanding that Murdoch wants to be able to make the most attractive offer possible for Dow Jones—if he decides to go ahead with an offer—they put an uppermost value on the company of $50 a share.

But Murdoch insists they should offer $60. It is a decision to violate the norm—to be the unreasonable, disruptive, fuck-you outsider. Dow Jones management and the Bancroft family might act sanctimonious and high and mighty. But he is calling their bluff.

He leaves word with Rich Zannino's secretary in New York that he'd like to speak as soon as possible. He's apologetic when Zannino, on vacation at the Ocean Club in the Bahamas, calls him back, but says he's eager to see Zannino. How about March 29 at News Corp.?

Zannino's reaction: "Uh-oh! Why is he calling me directly and why now? Does he want to offer me a job, does he want to have another benign meeting, or is he getting ready to strike?"

Suspecting something large, Zannino might here too have consulted with others at the company. If the goal is not to sell the company—and there is no reason, at this point, to assume that this mandate has changed or will change—Zannino might have headed this off.

If he has any doubts, as he pulls up outside the News Corp. building that morning he gets a call from Jimmy Lee, saying, "Have a good breakfast."

It is, again, for Zannino an "Uh-oh!" moment.

They have breakfast in one of the nondescript dining rooms on News Corp.'s third floor. Murdoch, for a provocateur, actually tends to beat around the bush. They spend the first forty-five minutes again discussing *American Idol*, Murdoch's plans for the Fox Business Network, and declining advertising revenues at newspapers.

But finally, he turns to it: "Well, I'm thinking about making an offer to buy Dow Jones."

Zannino demurs a bit: "You know, Rupert, you know as well as anybody, this isn't my call, it's the family's call. And the family has consistently—and Rupert, even as recently as our last board meeting—said that they're committed to the independence of Dow Jones and they have no interest in selling the company."

Murdoch says, "I know that. I was thinking I'd take the offer directly to the board. I know the family feels that way. I've called Elefante in the past. He won't even take a number. The number I'm thinking of is . . . sixty."

Zannino: (internally) *Holy shit!* (externally) Silence.

Murdoch goes on, "So I'm thinking I'll just take that directly to the board to try and get that through the board. Should I call Hockaday, should I call McPherson, should I call Harvey Golub? I think I'll call Harvey Golub."

Zannino responds, "Well, you know Harvey's chairman of the governance committee. He's one of the most savvy board members we have, so you know. So that's who you would call."

Zannino: (internally) *I've got to get the hell out of here.*

Murdoch: "So that's what I'm going to do—I'm going to make an offer to the board. Did I just make an offer to you?"

Zannino: "No, you didn't. You mused about wanting to buy Dow Jones. I told you the family has the call and it's not for sale, and you told me you were going to contact the board."

Zannino is trying to find his balance—he's walked out to the farthest point, and now, teetering on the precipice, he's trying to come back. Zannino tells Murdoch he isn't going to tell his board about the offer, because it's really not an official offer, suggesting to Murdoch that if anybody asks him about it, he should say he was just joking about the $60.

But, in the car, Zannino understands that the breach has just occurred—that he's let Murdoch in. He breathlessly calls Joe Stern, the Dow Jones general counsel, and tells him: "He gave me a number." And, mindful of his driver: "I'll tell you what it is when I get to the office. It's nuclear."

Back at the Dow Jones office, each successive person let in on the news understands that the breach is real—and that they can't close it. More to the point, no one is strong enough to close it.

Murdoch has correctly analyzed that Zannino, who might have blocked his access to the board, has not. And that Michael Elefante won't block his access to the Bancroft family. Zannino and Stern first call the Dow Jones outside lawyer, Art Fleischer. Then they call Elefante. Both Zannino and Stern note to each other that Elefante doesn't say "Hell, no," on the phone, which Roy Hammer would have said. Hammer, Zannino adds, would certainly have said, "Fuck him and the horse he rode in on!" Elefante, instead, says: "I have to consult with family members, my fellow family directors and other family members, before I can give you a reaction on this." And to himself (after *Oh, shit!*): *Great price, but it's from the master of evil incarnate.*

When Kann arrives at work that afternoon, Zannino and Stern tell him about the $60 offer.

"Boy, that's a big number," Kann says. "What did Mike say?"

Zannino tells him, "Mike didn't shut it down."

Kann's real question, however, is: "Why the fuck was Rich going for breakfast with Murdoch?"

The outsider is practically in.

# SIX

**His Art**

**APRIL 17, 2007**

Two dinners are taking place in Manhattan, blocks from each other. The first involves Murdoch and two Melbourne colleagues. The second, members of the Bancroft family.

That afternoon the News Corp. board met and approved Murdoch's outsized bid for Dow Jones. The board—all men, partly because Murdoch believes that women talk too much—may not be the most docile in corporate America, but it is certainly among the most reverential. Outside directors are supposed to be of a stature to judge and monitor and take to task a company's senior management. The News Corp. board, a collection of successful but hardly exceptional businessmen, has the added hurdle of having to assume equipoise with Rupert Murdoch. They do not pretend to try. In the instance of Dow Jones, an acquisition that might reasonably have raised many doubts, if not objections, was greeted with a rather giddy sense of adventure. The question was not should they but could they—it was not the logic of it but the challenge that was compelling. Having unanimously approved the deal, a letter was forthwith delivered to Peter McPherson, who will the next day, April 18, assume the chairmanship of the board of Dow Jones.

That evening, in celebration, Murdoch goes to dinner with Melburnian Sir Rod Eddington, a genial and avuncular former airline executive who ran both British Airways and Ansett, an Australian airline that News Corp. acquired a controlling stake in; Murdoch put Sir Rod on the News board in 1999. The other Melbourne bloke joining them is Robert Thomson, who has been in constant contact with Murdoch about the deal, virtually commuting back and forth between the London *Times* newsroom in Wapping and News Corp. HQ on Sixth Avenue in New York. They go to Milos, a Greek restaurant on 55th Street near Sixth—where Murdoch can get a plain grilled piece of fish.

They are all pleased with themselves, on tenterhooks about what's to come, and almost stagily careful about what they are saying, or how they are saying it, out in public. This is easy for Thomson, who is almost pathologically cryptic, and next to impossible for Eddington, who never seems to stop talking.

Eddington, who has known Murdoch now for more than twenty years, is actually worried about what Murdoch might be facing. Rupert has been amusing them with the latest details he's learned from Steginsky about the Bancrofts. Many members of the family, even those not particularly inclined to side with Murdoch, are turning out to be their own best and meanest chroniclers, telling Steginsky on a blow-by-blow basis who's firm and who's crumbling, who's on the wagon or off, who's taking their meds and who isn't.

It sounds to Eddington as if this might quickly get pretty messy and bogged down.

"You need to show two things in this deal—a lot of charm and a lot of patience," says Eddington. "And you only have one. I'm not saying you're not charming."

Impatience is one of Murdoch's key character notes—an attribute that appears in countless situations, one responsible for so many abrupt turns of conversation or of the state of play, the characteristic that may have resulted in his reputation in some quarters for being antisocial. He fidgets, his eyes wander, his fingers tap, and then he forces the issue—peremptorily, often rudely, sometimes brutally.

And yet here they are in such a delicate deal.

Family deals are the dogged low end of the mergers and acquisitions business. The high end of M&A is when great public companies agree to be combined or to be acquired, or reverse-merged, or restructured, or to have significant divisions rolled out or rolled up. This is finance, with intricate and original logic and symmetries—the business of bankers, lawyers, and principals. It is what is called in the M&A trade "a process," that is, something orderly, routinized, fungible, knowable, predictable. This represents the great sense and sensibility of capitalism—the great accomplishment. The administration and accumulation of wealth, so the thinking goes, has largely left the hands of parochial, narrowly focused entrepreneurs and uninformed, emotionally addled families and has been placed in the hands of professionals—masters of business administration.

Nobody wants to be a hand-holder, a cajoler—nobody wants to do the widows-and-orphans thing. Nobody wants to get down in the primal muck of a family and its inheritance.

Except, actually, Rupert.

A secret (one of them) of Murdoch's success, the grease of his career, is his ability to deal with, and prevail in, highly personal, profoundly emotional transactions in which the stakes are not just financial but deeply related to ego, turf, and family. This impatient man has an extraordinary tolerance for the ambivalence of nonrational players—and a keen eye for their weaknesses.

While the Melbourne boys are on West 55th Street, various members of the Bancroft family are sitting down to dinner around the corner on West 52nd Street at the "21" Club. For years, members of the Bancroft family have gathered for dinner on the night before the Dow Jones annual meeting.

Now they are faced with an offer to buy the company at almost twice its current value. But in the nineteen days since Murdoch told Rich Zannino over breakfast that he wants to buy the company, and Rich Zannino and general counsel Joe Stern called Michael Elefante to see how the family would react to such an offer—understanding that the family's ability to react was highly time-sensitive—no one has told the family.

The family board members—Chris Bancroft, Leslie Hill, and Lisa Steele—have been told, but they have been rather threatened with all manner of insider-trading violations should they tell their relatives.

Rich Zannino joins the Bancrofts for dinner at the "21" Club and gives a little talk. On the eve of Dow Jones' most momentous annual meeting, the CEO talks to the company's principal owners about . . . the Red Sox. Recall that in 1982, the Bancroft family's seventy-three-year-old matriarch, Jessie Bancroft Cox, at a one-hundredth-anniversary party for Dow Jones—also held at the "21" Club—said, "What the hell's the matter with my Red Sox?" and keeled over dead. Ever after this—and Zannino has been so informed—the Boston Red Sox have been the subject of choice when management speaks to the Bancrofts (disregarding the fact that few of them live in Boston anymore).

After Zannino gives his little talk about the Red Sox, it is Peter McPherson's turn. McPherson is about to become the chairman of the board of Dow Jones, and this is one of his first introductions to the family as a whole. It is good—and calculated—Murdoch timing: Put the offer in the hands of a brand-new chairman. McPherson, sixty-six, is a blustery, portly, academic administrator. He got the chairmanship because the logical candidates, Irv Hockaday and Harvey Golub, were either too old or unwilling.

Hence, the mustachioed McPherson, fond of chewing on an unlit cigar, is greeted with a skeptical "Who's he?" by the Bancrofts.

McPherson, faced with having to deal immediately with the most significant event in the history of this century-old company on the first day of his chairmanship, speaks to the controlling shareholders about . . . binge drinking on college campuses.

## 1977: HIS DEALS

Among the reasons Murdoch will achieve a business status at times rather close to that of, say, Jay Gould or Michael Milken or the chiefs of Enron, is that his deals so often seem so unfair. It defies logic how he gets what he's gotten, so therefore he must have tricked people into giving him what he has. His dealcraft isn't blue-chip dealcraft.

Most major corporations hire big investment banks and brand-name law firms and top management consulting firms in order to create a great, diffuse decision-making consensus. What's done is done with someone else's approval. Everybody gets ample ass coverage. That's the point: Whatever decision is made, whatever transaction occurs, whatever destabilization of a company, an industry, and/or the entire economy results, it's the product of a consensus of the most respected business mandarins in the land. Everybody has done what they've done acting on the advice of someone else. There are rules and conventions that are followed. Ritual and propriety are obsessively observed.

Over the years, News Corp. will largely, if begrudgingly, come to follow these rules and conventions. Peter Chernin will prove to be as process-oriented an executive as you're likely to find in the media business. Murdoch mostly goes along with this, albeit grumpily. But even thirty years later, he will still see himself as the alien, which in the beginning he is, the man without roots in the community, which in the beginning he doesn't have, the usurper, who has not paid his dues.

When Murdoch moved his family to New York in 1974—when business protocols were still largely straitlaced and blue-suit—his intention was to make acquisitions in the United States. The first step in that process would be to buy yourself business legitimacy by hiring the biggest law firm and the most prestigious investment bank that would have you.

The fact that Murdoch doesn't go this route means:

He's simply too small-time to be of any interest to the big boys.

He doesn't even aspire to the big leagues—he's looking at two-bit deals that wouldn't be of any interest to powerful businessmen. He has, in other words, no illusions about his status.

He doesn't care; in fact, he has an entirely different, whether instinctive or strategic, conception of how he means to work, and who can work with him.

He has problems with authority.

The media business in the early seventies isn't considered to be particularly respectable on military-industrial-complex-biased Wall Street, so Wall Street wouldn't want him anyway.

Likely it is all of these things.

Commencing his American initiative, Murdoch hires himself a twelve-man local New York law firm with virtually no experience in the field of mergers and acquisitions. The firm is called Squadron, Ellenoff, Plesent, and Lehrer. Like a thousand other little firms in the city, it handles minor litigation, trust and estate matters, and other small-time commercial transactions. It's as different from the major business firms—Paul, Weiss, Rifkind, Wharton, and Garrison, the firm of the Kennedys; Milbank, Tweed, Hadley and McCloy, the firm of the Rockefellers; Cravath, Swaine, and Moore, the firm of IBM; Lord, Day, and Lord, the firm of the *New York Times;* Weil, Gotschal, and Manges, the firm of General Motors—as Australia is from the United States.

Howard Squadron, the senior partner, is a minor politico in the city. He has no stature in the business world, has done no deals of the kind that Murdoch will shortly be doing. Murdoch met him in conjunction with a book publisher he owns in Australia and some matter involving the distribution in the United States of a line of astrology titles. Years later, when biographers look at Murdoch's beginnings in New York, they will cast Squadron as a legal power broker. But his eminence will derive entirely from Murdoch. Murdoch, as he did with Commonwealth Bank in Australia, will quickly come to dominate the firm. It will have no other real allegiances. (In 1990, when News Corp. will merge its Sky satellite network in the United Kingdom with British Satellite Broadcasting, Goldman Sachs, its banker on the deal, will be required by News Corp. to use the Squadron firm to do significant aspects of the legal work. Goldman will decide the firm is not up to the job and assemble a "shadow" legal team to redo the work of the Squadron attorneys.)

And then Murdoch hires Allen and Company. Hiring Allen and Company as your investment bank not only does not give you blue-chip status, it says you are the opposite. It sends up a red flag. Started in the 1930s, it's a firm that, up until the media becomes a blue-chip industry, is entirely outside of the business establishment.

When Murdoch comes along in 1976 and hires Allen and Company's Stan Shuman, he is hardly hiring a firm—he's just hiring a guy with a briefcase.

Murdoch isn't going to be dominated by mandarins and experts, nor by standard practices—he isn't going to be high-handed by somebody more authoritative and more respectable than he. Murdoch does not like people with big egos, as Arthur Siskind—the corporate partner at Squadron, Ellenoff who handles much of the day-to-day News Corp. work and who, in 1991, will join News Corp. as its general counsel—comes to appreciate. He isn't about to give up any aspect of control.

Murdoch's first two deals in New York, with Dorothy (Dolly) Schiff of the *New York Post* and Clay Felker of *New York* magazine—both of which shock the city, both of which seem to occur in the dead of night—are about his charms and skillful manipulations.

One secret of Murdoch's seemingly underhanded deals, and his sudden materialization as a player and contender, is the courtship. Where other businessmen run the numbers, Murdoch deals with personalities. Against the best advice on the game, he plays the man, not the ball.

The man he courts and plays most adroitly, and who becomes the agent (willing and unwilling) for his first dramatic acquisition in New York, is *New York* magazine editor and publisher Clay Felker. In the anti-Murdoch mythology, the two men now represent the extremes of the media business—one the honest creator, the other the cynical acquirer. In fact, Murdoch's advantage is to realize how much they are alike.

The age of the media operator has begun—media guys who leverage the profiles and reputations they gain from buying media properties to buy other media properties.

Murdoch immediately sees Felker as a contrast to the other key player he's met and courted in New York: Edward Downe Jr., the owner of Downe Communications. In the early 1970s, Downe, a society figure who will later marry the socialite Charlotte Ford and be convicted of insider trading and tax evasion, owns the largest magazine publisher in the U.S. Its flagship title is the *Ladies' Home Journal*. He owns, too, cable TV systems, radio stations, direct mail, and magazine subscription fulfillment companies. It's an odd sort of precursor to the future Murdoch empire—except that Downe, unlike Murdoch and Felker, does not see himself as the brand. He's just a guy who's invested in a bunch of stuff.

Downe, who, like Felker, sees Murdoch as an easy mark, is trying to lure Murdoch to become an investor in his business. But Murdoch doesn't especially like Downe—he finds him a disengaged, lazy, snobbish figure. What's more, he can't afford a meaningful stake in Downe's company—and he isn't, if he can help it, a noncontrolling investor. And he really wants a newspaper.

In 1973, not long after he buys the San Antonio papers (there are afternoon and morning papers, which he merges into one), Murdoch meets Felker at a dinner party Kay Graham of the *Washington Post* throws for him. Graham is Murdoch's one substantial contact in the newspaper business in the United States. Graham's father, Eugene Meyer, knew his father. When Rupert was younger, they socialized in each other's countries as visiting newspaper royalty. Murdoch, not long after he settled in the United States, began to fantasize about buying the *Washington Post*. Or, with only slightly less grandiosity, he considered competing with the *Post*, eyeing the *Washington Star*. Washington would be a suitable base for him. That would give him liftoff. But he hesitated. It was an unusual moment of sentiment, his decision not to compete with Graham, or an unusual moment of caution and fear. He judged her a scary competitor. What's more, he couldn't remotely afford the *Star*—although he never strictly aligned his plans with his bank account.

Sentiment will not save Clay Felker (though thirty years after he buys Felker's company and cuts short Felker's meteoric rise in the media business, Murdoch will voice brief regret about losing the friendship).

Like Murdoch, Felker is an outsider in New York. He's a midwesterner, from Missouri. His relationship to the New York establishment is to hustle it and to thrive in spite of it—or on a parallel track to it. In *New York* magazine, he perceives that the city's establishment is on the verge of transition and that his magazine could become the old establishment's rival.

Felker, the city's most successful media upstart, is a sort of New York Svengali—in the pages of the magazine and in the emerging new social scene in New York, he's creating a set of personalities and defining new centers of power to compete with the old.

He is, in this, a perfect if unwitting tutor for Murdoch.

At Felker's suggestion, in the summer of 1974, Murdoch takes a house in East Hampton, just through the hedges from Felker's own house.

Felker spends a good part of the summer monologizing Murdoch about the New York media scene—who's up, who's down, who's going after whom. It is partly through Felker's example that Murdoch figures out the dangers of a summer house in East Hampton, Manhattan's media enclave by the beach—it's too exposed, the conversation too uncontrolled, the gossip too unguarded. Wounding Felker, Murdoch buys a house in upstate New York, a farm in Old Chatham. But Felker is working Murdoch (at least he believes he is the one doing the working, rather than the reverse). Felker sees Murdoch as his discovery. Many of Murdoch's initial acquaintances and introductions in New York are through Felker.

Felker suggests what schools the Murdoch children should attend. Murdoch's daughter Elisabeth, age six, enrolls at the Nightingale-Bamford School on the Upper East Side, then a year later switches, trading up to The Brearley School on East 83rd Street. His daughter Prudence and son Lachlan enter Dalton, on East 91st Street.

There isn't any more distilled collection of the ambitious, the determined, the wealthy in Manhattan than at a handful of schools mostly on the Upper East Side. The parent body is some ideal combination of the hereditary social set, the most economically powerful at a given moment, the lawyers and bankers who work for them, and a dollop of celebrities, together with all of their spouses. Clubbiness and ensuing relationships and connections is one of the reasons you go (or have your children go) to these schools. Oddly, it's a world that rather appeals to Murdoch. It isn't Geelong Grammar. It's much more fluid, commercial. It's where the elite meet—but to do some business. There isn't much more pretense here than the pretense of moving up. Such schools are not just where smart children make lifelong connections but, also, where smart parents hook up. In the history of New York schools and the connections they facilitated, none may be so profitable as the introduction of Stan Shuman of Allen and Company to Rupert Murdoch at a parent function at the Dalton School, where Shuman's son Michael, and Murdoch's son Lachlan, both five, are in kindergarten together.

Murdoch takes naturally to the New York form of hustle—to its efficiency, its lack of pretense, its dollar domination. In London it is tricky to just call somebody up—that would be a downright suspicious move. In New York, you can connect seamlessly with anyone. Murdoch, a reluctant socializer, is a brilliant networker. He's one of the early geniuses of the form. It's a form that lacks prescribed social niceties and inefficiencies and thrives on direct value-added chat: just who you know. The Murdoch progress in New York is all about efficiently extracting information.

In the beginning, it is not clear who's hustling whom. Felker, along with most everyone else in New York, assumes that Murdoch is the rich foreigner, hence easy pickings. The rush to offer him things is not to benefit him but to take advantage of his optimistic newcomer's buying mood. One would be foolish not to seize the opportunity that a rich foreigner presented.

When Felker introduces Murdoch to Dolly Schiff, the owner of the *New York Post* (seventy-three-year-old Schiff has a crush on fifty-one-year-old Felker), he knows he is introducing a potential seller to a wannabe player in a manic buying mood. Both Felker and Schiff think they've lucked into something a little too easy. Murdoch, with his I'll-buy-anything purchase of the San Antonio papers and his hapless launch of the embarrassing *National Star*— his low-end tabloid meant to compete with the *National Enquirer*—seems like pretty classic dumb money.

When Murdoch goes down to the Allen and Company offices and engages Shuman to represent him in the matter of Dolly Schiff's *New York Post* (Shuman's first assignment is to sit next to Schiff at a dinner party Murdoch will shortly throw), Shuman too is rightly skeptical. But a fee is a fee.

Nobody quite knows that the deal-making style Murdoch is developing is that of the available outsider. To be underestimated is a cultivated part of his affect. The advantage of always moving on—a key advantage of the con man—is that it takes a while for your reputation to catch up with you.

What he's already done in London, now he'll do in New York.

The fading newspaper business—in the first of its many fade-outs, television and growing labor problems having depressed the value of papers in the sixties and seventies—gives Murdoch certain advantages. He can afford to buy himself both exposure (owning a paper makes you a public figure) and, because he has an appetite for vividness, cash flow (the more blood, the more sales).

Of the three daily New York papers in 1976, the *Post*, which, for two generations has been the sentimental favorite of working-class Jews, is the marginal one, not least of all because there aren't any working-class Jews anymore. The first death-of-the-newspaper moment is just about coming to an end (it got into full swing with the great New York newspaper strikes of 1962–63 and 1966, which resulted in the closing of four of the city's seven dailies). Across the country, afternoon papers—the *Post* in the seventies is an afternoon paper—have closed or merged with morning papers. Most urban markets are moving toward the consolidation into single-owner markets.

The *New York Times* has the quality, Manhattan-centric market; the *Daily News* has the working-class outer-borough market. Unless one of those two wants to acquire the *Post*, there is not going to be any other logical buyer. Murdoch, in some sense, is an old-fashioned newspaper buyer: a man who believes that showmanship—being a better carnival barker—can save the day. He is, furthermore, another classic sort of newspaper buyer: a rich man who wants a platform (forgetting the fact that he isn't all that rich at the moment). In 1974, those two characteristics make him a market of one.

While Dolly Schiff probably has the wherewithal to maintain the *Post*'s cash needs, she is deeply relieved—and somewhat incredulous—to find an interested, charming (she is famously susceptible to charming men), promising buyer. Actually, many other people in New York, in its journalism and media community, in its political circles, are relieved too—the anemic *Post* is about to be rejuvenated.

Overnight, Murdoch is a pet of the city. There's little goodwill he isn't accorded. On the night he makes the deal for the *Post*, he and his small team, along with the lawyers from Squadron, Ellenoff and Stan Shuman and his people at Allen and Company, take a limo from the "21" Club, where the deal is signed, and go on to further celebrations at Elaine's, the restaurant-bar at the center of the journalist-media-political chattering class that is entirely ready to embrace Murdoch. "You did it! You fucking did it!" Elaine's proprietor, Elaine Kaufman, shouts at Murdoch as he comes through the door.

Murdoch, in one move, has achieved insider status in the city. This is what people like Murdoch—if not Murdoch himself— aspire to. It's power, affirmation, and a great social life. You become part of a rarefied and constantly self-congratulating class. This is irresistible for most every ambitious person—perhaps even more so for a foreigner, an outsider.

One night at Elaine's is apparently enough.

He proceeds to chuck it all with his hostile pursuit of *New York* magazine.

He does this even before he's the formal owner of the *Post*. The *Post* is his on December 30, 1976. One day later, news of his attempt to take over *New York* magazine hits the *New York Times*. As he's being congratulated for his takeover of the *Post*, he's effectively waging a stealth campaign—quite like the stealth campaign he'll be waging in thirty years for the *Journal*—against the people who are congratulating him.

As much as the *Journal* represents, second only to the *New York Times*, the official establishment voice, *New York* magazine in 1976 represents the official voice of, well, an evening at Elaine's.

Born in 1968 out of the *Herald Tribune* (it began as the paper's rotogravure magazine supplement), it is, in a sense, the inheritor of the city's great newspapers—the *Journal American*, the *World-Telegram*, and the *Sun*, which all closed during the strikes of the 1960s. *New York* magazine, which in the 1980s will come to articulate and be the poster child for the new money culture in New York, began as a reinvention, or last gasp, of New York's newspaper culture. Which was precisely what has caught Murdoch's eye: its tough-guy flamboyance, its newsprint bona fides and romance. (The facts that the tough-guy newsmen will turn against Murdoch and that under Murdoch *New York* will become the great yuppie magazine are another story—a further irony of time and circumstance.)

Murdoch's takeover of *New York*—his sense of the opportunity, his stalking of the magazine, his flipping of its investors—is among those events that make Murdoch Murdoch. Or it's the story out of which other people make Murdoch Murdoch.

The facts, the actual chain of events, of who said what to whom, become part of an imbroglio nearly ideological in its density, conspiratorial in its motivations. It's a Rashomon moment that will recur with so many of the Murdoch deals—everybody has his own version of how Murdoch manages to do what he shouldn't, logically, be able to do.

The writer Susan Braudy will later recount in meticulous detail her weekend in East Hampton at the Felker house with her then-boyfriend, *New York* magazine writer Aaron Latham, and their trip through the hedges to have dinner at Rupert and Anna's, served, charmingly, by Elisabeth and Lachlan, at which Felker reveals his frustrations with his board—and Murdoch discusses only the price of paper. This same conversation, or at least one similar enough, is said to take place with different secondary participants in a taxicab or at a Yankees game or at Murdoch's house in upstate New York.

What is clear is that on one side there is Felker and his writers and, on the other, a set of board members who have grown weary of Felker for the most predictable reasons: He spends too much money and gets all the attention.

It's a difficult bunch. Each board member is, in his fashion, a serious prima donna. Among them are the chairman, Alan Patricof, a small-time investor who, with his flip of the company, will turn himself into one of the city's best-known media financiers; Carter Burden, the heir to Cornelius W. Vanderbilt and one of the most significant social figures in the city (he and his wife, Amanda Burden, the stepdaughter of CBS founder Bill Paley, were a New York "it" couple of the 1960s—Amanda Burden went on to marry Warner Communications chief, and Murdoch nemesis, Steve Ross); Bartle Bull, another WASP society figure; and the board's counsel, Ted Kheel, the most prominent labor negotiator in the city.

The striking thing is not the disputatiousness, irascibility, and egocentricity of the *New York* magazine board—although, even for a media company board, it is rather extreme—but that Murdoch is able to corral and manage them. One of the reasons Murdoch's ultimate acquisition of the company comes as such a shock to Felker is Felker's perfectly reasonable judgment that nobody could deal with this colossally dysfunctional group. There is nothing in Murdoch's background to explain why he should have the political and social skills to deal with some of the most serious egomaniacs in New York. Indeed, *New York* magazine is, in so many ways, a New York thing, as distinguished from a business thing. He would seem to have as reasonable a chance of prevailing in this world as an automaker from, say, Seoul would have arriving in Detroit.

And it is not just the run-amok personalities for which he has to muster some canny appreciation; not at all intuitively, he has to appreciate the magazine itself. To understand what this particular property can buy him.

Because *New York* magazine, for all the attention it gets, is still just a bit of local color. It has a relatively small circulation. The company is losing money. Oh, yes, and with *New York* comes the *Village Voice*, that left-wing insane asylum Felker acquired two years before and which, perhaps among all the publications in the world, is the least congenial to Murdoch.

So what does he see?

He sees a deal. If the idea is merely to buy things that you can afford, the turmoil at the company gives him that opportunity and a discount.

But after that comes the more complicated and astute perception. Whereas more cautious businessmen would reason that it's not a great idea to enter a business by engendering profound ill will in the industry in which you hope to succeed—that, in fact, goodwill is a primary currency—Murdoch has the fairly new sense that making a splash is the all-important thing.

Just getting the deal done makes you something. It comes down to, as it so often has for Murdoch, a strong-arm percentage play.

Felker's deal with Carter Burden, a significant shareholder in the *Village Voice*, provided that after the acquisition of the *Voice*, Burden got 24 percent of the *New York* magazine company—but if he wanted to sell, he was obliged to offer it first to Felker. He could not just put it on the open market. This meant that Felker, with his 10 percent—together with the 24 percent that Burden couldn't sell to anyone before offering it to Felker, along with his other allies—was pretty much guaranteed continuing control. There was one loophole (at least in Murdoch's telling and as his justification): If the company lost money for four consecutive quarters, Burden would be free to offer his shares on the open market.

Murdoch represents something of a pure experiment. How do people react when an outsider arrives? Felker himself, when he took over the *Village Voice* two years ago, did it with some of the same tactics as Murdoch will use at *New York* (the owners of the *Voice* sued Felker for the same reasons that Felker will eventually sue Murdoch), but, of course, Felker was less an outsider than Murdoch.

"We are faced with a sudden transfer of control . . . to a foreign publishing conglomerate controlled by a man whose journalistic approach appears alien to us and whose commitment to our city is untested," declare "the editors, writers, artists, and photographers" of *New York* magazine in a letter to the board of directors.

What kind of person is willing to be such an outsider, to tolerate being so reviled? What kind of temperament and constitution are required? This is not obvious or intuitive.

The pathology can be missed only by those who are simply too stunned by the accomplishment. In weeks, he's achieved a level of business recognition that would ordinarily take years—note that, in the editors and writers' statement, he is now a "foreign publishing conglomerate"—at the expense of his own reputation.

Felker's fatal mistake is thinking that Murdoch might be his saving grace. He proposes that Murdoch take a stake in *New York*. Murdoch, despite his friendship, sees the opportunity. He fairly judges that if Felker is offering him a piece of the company, he would offer it to others too, meaning a transaction will likely occur and that the company is in play.

The only real issue, from this view, is 51 percent. Carter Burden and his ally, Bartle Bull, together own 34 percent. Alan Patricof owns 10 percent. The investment banker A. Robert Towbin has about 10 percent. Felker has 10 percent, and so does Milton Glaser, a Felker pal and the magazine's art director. The rest is held by small, public shareholders.

Murdoch's approach is around the back. He's talking to anybody he can talk to—sucking up information, counting votes. It's politics. It's junior high, and you're trying to figure out, through the friends of the girl you have a crush on, what's her level of interest in you.

This may not be anything more than an incredible appetite for gossip. This is what gets him going. He's a kibbitzer. The right shading of who wants what, the sense of dispute, of grievance, the opening—having that information moves him. (Murdoch sometimes seems startled by his own success, even embarrassed slightly by, in the recounting, the way the pieces have fallen together.

"Luck. There's just been a lot of luck," he'll say. All these side conversations, these countless emissaries, this nonstop phoning, this incredible focus on the game mean he has the wherewithal to create more lucky opportunities than most.)

Patricof becomes the key ally. Patricof himself has used *New York* magazine as a way to trade up, or bootstrap himself, into a position of some significance. Beginning with a minor financial interest, he's managed to get his 10 percent of the company. He's been vying with Felker for dominance too. Indeed, Felker has been trying to push him out of the chairman's slot on the board. Felker wants that job for himself. What's more, the stock, which has traded as high as $10 a share, is down to $3.25. Patricof is looking to get rid of Felker or get out himself—at a big number.

Burden, however, holds the power. And he has a short attention span as well as a dilettante's sense of direction. He won a seat on the city council, but this is starting to bore him. His investment in the *Village Voice* was about wanting to be a crusading publisher. He sold out to Felker and *New York* magazine because being a crusading publisher turned out to involve much too much aggravation. Now here he is, the largest shareholder in *New York* magazine, a position that should be pleasantly diverting but instead is aggravating him. If he could wash his hands of all this, he would. True, he could just sell out to Felker. But, honestly, he has come to loathe the man.

On the other hand, he doesn't like Murdoch either. Or doesn't think he likes him. Who is he? An Australian. Everything about him is dubious. But Burden's lawyer, Peter Tufo, has been talking to Murdoch. Tufo seems to think he'll pay as much as $8 a share. Get them out of this whole thing. Solve the whole Felker problem.

For Burden, the key point is not to have to think too much about it. So, sure, he'll sell to Murdoch. Fuck Felker. Theoretically, he has to offer his shares to Felker first, but now he's being told, on some finer reading of their agreement, he doesn't have to. *So, fine. But don't bother me anymore.*

This is the state of play when Murdoch shows his hand to Felker: He's picked up the votes.

Felker mounts a brief rally—in the press as much as in the boardroom. He gets his friend Kay Graham to say she'll rescue him. This is a little bit of a guilt thing, because, after all, she introduced Murdoch to Felker. She let Murdoch in. This will all come round— so many of the players are fixed. Murdoch, understanding the Fairfaxes and Packers, knows this. Thirty years later, Dow Jones will petition the *Washington Post* to rescue it. (Graham's lawyer, Martin Lipton, who dives into the *New York* magazine mess with the *Washington Post*'s late bid, will over the years come to know Murdoch well and do work for him, and, as it happens, be retained by the Bancroft family in the face of Murdoch's bid.)

Carter Burden is in Sun Valley skiing and in no mood to take Graham's or Felker's calls. But, just to make sure, Murdoch charters a plane on New Year's Eve 1976, flies to Sun Valley, and puts a check for $2 million into Burden's hand. It's done, except for the shouting.

The next two weeks will begin to define Murdoch in New York and in the media world. He's the outsider. He's the big guy picking on the little guy. He's the thief. He's the guy who forecloses on widows and orphans.

The backlash is fierce. But there is a level of the din that he just doesn't hear. Partly, it's that he's used to it (and he will become ever more used to it). These kind of ad hominem attacks are what naturally accompany anybody who's in the press. Your competitors, in the business of creating controversy, attack you. Also, he doesn't really have to be concerned with what people think of him. If it works, it works; if it doesn't, it doesn't, and he can just pick up and leave. He understands that he doesn't really belong here. Any move he makes is bound to disturb. So what the hell.

The Murdoch takeover of *New York* magazine is the big first event in one of New York's pivotal and fateful years: 1977 (Son of Sam, the blackout and subsequent riots, and the city's brush with bankruptcy). *Time* magazine puts him on the cover as King Kong striding over the rooftops of Manhattan. *Newsweek* declares, "Press Lord on the Attack." Simply, Murdoch is made—in those several weeks of heated and rancorous attention, he is *created in America*.

As a parting shot, Jann Wenner's *Rolling Stone* magazine—a key competitor of the *Village Voice*—runs an account of the *New York* magazine takeover by *New York* magazine writer Gail Sheehy. Sheehy, who will later marry Felker, sets in stone the version of Murdoch as the enemy of decent journalists everywhere, the practitioner of businesses practices so underhand and vile that no decent people could ever have a chance against him.

# SEVEN

# The Eighties—
# Business Guys

MAY 1, 2007

The cultivated courtliness, or lack of coolness, at Dow Jones that has kept it outside the media gossip world is about to be seriously upset by the e-mail Gary Ginsberg receives at 10:46 A.M.

"I know," reads the message from David Faber at CNBC.

Ginsberg is still recovering from the winter publicity firestorm when—not entirely unrelated to the bid for the *Wall Street Journal*—News Corp. turned against one of its stars, the publisher and Murdoch confidant Judith Regan, who was preparing to publish a theoretical "confession" by O. J. Simpson, and then to follow up with a Fox television interview. This was an entirely Murdochian event, but, faced with a sudden media backlash over the tasteful-ness of paying Simpson for his confession—and with a bid for the respectable *Wall Street Journal* on his mind—Murdoch uncharac-teristically punted on the Regan project. Equally uncharacteristi-cally, when Regan—the type of tabloid character whom Murdoch has always indulged—acted out in response, he fired her. Ginsberg's immediate thought when he gets the e-mail from Faber is that for the second time in six months, he'll be managing the biggest media story going.

A baby-faced forty-four-year-old with a perpetually rumpled open-neck dress shirt, Ginsberg hotly disputes his frequent designation as "Murdoch's PR guy." That implies he's a functionary who, after the company acts, processes the information about its actions—sending out the press release. Ginsberg is sensitive on this point, not least of all because whatever he does he gets paid a healthy seven-figure salary to do it, so it'd better be more than handing out press releases. And you certainly don't want to be perceived as the PR guy to somebody who's perceived to be the Devil (you might be on the side of the Devil—but not as his PR guy).

Before coming to work for Murdoch, Ginsberg was planning a historic and public career as an intimate of his schoolmate at Brown University, John F. Kennedy Jr. In addition to starting a magazine, *George*, which wishfully conflated politics and entertainment, the friends were planning their political future. Ginsberg, a lawyer, worked in the Clinton White House for a stint. He was also briefly an on-air personality at MSNBC. It was idle fantasy—and something more—imagining himself with JFK Jr. in the White House.

Since joining News Corp. in 1999, six months before JFK Jr.'s death, he has had a new sort of corporate communications job. It isn't *just* corporate communications. It's something closer to what the communications director does in the White House. Or, considering that Murdoch is one of the most politically influential men in the world, Ginsberg's job is a greater one. He is the point man for all of the information going out of the company, as well as all of the information coming into the company. Ginsberg has gone, in eight years at News Corp., from an unlikely figure—a liberal Ivy League yuppie and Kennedy-phile in a company that has contempt for Ivy League liberal yuppies and for the Kennedys—to a central one. His job is (although no one at News Corp. will ever say it like this) to protect Murdoch from himself. Or to protect News Corp. from its worst and basest impulses. When Ginsberg was first interviewed for the job, in the aftermath of the shit storm following Murdoch's abrupt cancellation of Hong Kong's last British governor Chris Patten's book—because of negative comments Patten had made about various Chinese government officials with whom Murdoch was then trying to curry favor—the main question for Ginsberg was how they should have done it differently. Ginsberg said the obvious: They shouldn't have canceled the book, since that just called attention to it.

Ginsberg is everybody's point man. Peter Chernin, the president and COO of News Corp., calls Ginsberg. Murdoch's children call Ginsberg. Wendi Murdoch calls him. He is the Murdoch interpreter.

Everybody confers with Ginsberg about what the old man is thinking—not least of all because the old man doesn't necessarily ever say what he's thinking, or say what he's thinking to any one person in any consistent way—and if he does, he mumbles so much, and his accent is so thick, that you might not understand him anyway. Everybody tends to have just their piece of the story—Ginsberg pieces together the pieces.

Dave Faber's scoop about Murdoch's offer of $60 a share for Dow Jones, Ginsberg understands, will change the story.

Ginsberg's preparedness—or rough-and-readiness, or media savviness, or sense of reality and its plasticity—is at dramatic odds with what anybody at Dow Jones can offer. Nobody there seems to quite get their heads around the situation they'll face if Murdoch's offer goes public before they decide what to do about it.

The Dow Jones board has, in essence, handed over the next step—and the leadership of the process—not to mergers and acquisitions specialists (ideally ones with a good media sense) but to a sleepy Boston law firm. To, specifically, Michael Elefante of

Hemenway and Barnes, where they are more used to the vagaries of doddering families than to the sharks of finance and media. Trying to wash their hands of the matter, the board said to Elefante—who represents the controlling shareholders and who, as the trustee, holds the controlling vote, practically speaking—*You have to tell us what the family wants to do.* Elefante was asked to begin canvassing the family shortly after Rich Zannino's breakfast with Murdoch on March 29, and while he began consulting with advisors and the family board members, he didn't tell the entire family for three weeks.

Instead of telling the family there had been a $60 offer, they were asked to consider what they might do in the event of a hypothetical offer with an unspecific price.

Finally, on April 20, Elefante and the rest of the family trustees at Hemenway and Barnes commenced a series of exasperating phone calls with each of the family members. Elefante was unable to communicate adequately to the family—perhaps because he didn't quite understand—that there were two issues, each as relevant as the other. Whether they wanted to sell (and for how much) was one issue. The other was that if they didn't make their feelings known before the offer became public, then they'd have to share the whole tedious decision-making process with the marketplace.

Elefante finally convened a family-wide meeting on April 24 at the Hemenway and Barnes offices on State Street in Boston. Almost all the adult Bancrofts, plus banking advisors from Merrill Lynch and lawyers from Wachtell, Lipton, were either in the room or waiting to be connected by conference call. Except the phones didn't work. And then a fight broke out between an ailing seventy-six-year-old Bill Cox Jr., whose son led the 1997 rebellion, and who would only see the *Journal* sold over his dead body—he repeatedly banged his cane on the floor for emphasis—and his nephew, the obstreperous Crawford Hill, who very much wanted the money. Still, mostly the family was at least against being forced to make up its mind, and certainly against Murdoch, though not necessarily against $60.

The family's race against the clock—to declare its desire before the bid was leaked and the market is able to declare *its* desire—was hampered by their inability to appreciate several overriding business factors:

While the family controls the voting shares, in a public company such control is not absolute. As soon as the bid goes public, other constituencies will have a powerful say, potentially in the form of shareholder suits.

The family believes that if it *does* want to sell, it can pick the buyer—who would never, ever be Murdoch—which necessitates there being other bidders.

Murdoch's $60 bid is preemptive; he is offering a substantial premium for the privilege of trumping everybody. If the offer goes public and no bidders emerge, the family will lose the leverage to negotiate a higher price with Murdoch.

Not understanding these factors, the Bancrofts also did not appreciate that the circumstance is a perfect bit of business triangulation. Either (a) they turned down Murdoch flat—and had better do it quickly—or (b) they negotiated with him, which, since Murdoch didn't yet know there won't be other bidders, might mean the family could get more than $60 a share.

What they chose—angst and ambivalence—isn't a tenable option. The public outing was imminent and inevitable.

In the days since the offer letter was received from Murdoch, the company's executives, board, and family of controlling shareholders had begun, after a period of deer-in-the-headlights paralysis, to do what was necessary—necessary, at least, to avoid shareholder lawsuits: assemble the apparatus of bankers and lawyers.

Zannino pushed aside longtime Dow Jones advisor Roger Altman, the former deputy treasury secretary in the Clinton administration, who now runs the investment firm Evercore Partners. Altman is close to Peter Kann and well grounded in the company's historic bias against selling. Zannino instead had hired

Goldman Sachs, which usually represents Murdoch. The family itself hired Merrill Lynch. Dick Beattie, one of the most iconic takeover lawyers of the age of takeovers—and, as it happened, one of Gary Ginsberg's mentors when Ginsberg was an associate at Beattie's firm, Simpson, Thacher—was retained by the special committee of the board. Marty Lipton, *the* most iconic takeover lawyer of the age of takeovers, was hired by the Bancroft family (Lipton was already advising Elefante about how the family could sell down its holdings but still retain control). Art Fleischer, of Fried, Frank, Harris, Shriver, and Jacobson, is also involved as Dow Jones' outside counsel.

On the News Corp. side, assembling quickly, you have News Corp.'s longtime bankers at Allen and Company (who are in the mix partly for sentimental reasons and partly because Nancy Peretsman, an Allen partner, counseled the two dissident Bancroft family members in 1997); a buddy of Ginsberg's, Blair Effron at Centerview Partners; Andrew Steginsky; and Jimmy Lee, along with his people at JPMorgan Chase, who will become everyone's favorite as the leaker.

At any rate, one of the more than one hundred people who knew about Murdoch's $60 offer alerted Faber (he says it was a source at an investment bank) to "not the biggest deal, but a jaw-dropping one."

But since the leak has become the *deus ex machina* of the deal, it is likely that it was less than random—part of the movement of forces against what will turn out to be the Maginot Line protecting one of America's most prestigious and historic franchises.

Along with Murdoch's superhuman sense of the long term, there is his indifference to the weight of the obvious: There isn't anyone who believed that Dow Jones was vulnerable, except Murdoch—which is where the leak comes in.

Serious businessmen don't brag about the deals they've lost; serious businessmen don't pursue deals that can't be done. And they don't go up against the implacable resistance of the voting tier of a two-tier stock company (Murdoch's own company was organized this way). Except if they can show that the resistance is not implacable.

CNBC's Faber is an ideal target for the leak. He works for a 24/7 business news channel and can go on the air immediately. Faber's audience is every trader on Wall Street. From his mouth to their next trade. On his report, the stock, trading at $36, can rise close to Murdoch's offer of $60.

The more the traders bet on Murdoch—the closer the share price gets to $60—the harder it will be for the company not to do the deal. It's like a run on the bank, but in reverse. Every share-holder and option holder in the company is being promised a wind-fall. Would the Bancroft family and Dow Jones management have the mettle and the meanness and the confidence to take it away from them—and themselves?

An ironic element here—an aspect of the strange and incestu-ous relationship of the press, which Murdoch intimately under-stands and which often underlines his PR game—is that, after Dow Jones itself, this news could be most detrimental to CNBC.

For more than three years now, Murdoch—who twenty years ago launched a fourth television network, and eleven years ago launched a 24/7 cable news network—has been planning to launch a business news network whose goal would be to devastate CNBC. Competing with Murdoch is difficult enough, but it could be a whole breathtakingly new level of competition if Murdoch owns the *Wall Street Journal*.

Murdoch seems to understand perhaps better than anyone else that the established media can often be counted on *not* to work in its best interests. (If it were his network, Fox News, that obtained information that put its business interests at issue, you can bet it would act quite differently.)

This will become a major charge against Murdoch during the takeover battle, that he uses his media outlets for his own interests.

Meanwhile, CNBC and its parent NBC have not used the information they possess—have not leaked the leak, which would give Dow Jones the opportunity to shoot down the offer—to undermine the deal that could lead to its own undermining.

This is not the only point of media irony. The *Wall Street Journal*, that great organ of business media, and the one with the most at stake, has the story too. They have been sitting on it for two weeks. Murdoch himself, in mid-April, had communicated with the *Journal*'s editor, Paul Steiger, about the offer. Steiger, the world's most important business editor, had the world's most important business story, and decided—thereby keeping the $60 offer in play—not to use it. Had the *Journal* revealed the offer and the company's rejection of it—even just its usual pro forma rejection—the deal might have been quashed.

When Ginsberg reads the e-mail from Faber, he feels a certain dizziness. And he has the sense that the other side must have its head up its ass—that they have lost control of the process.

## THE EIGHTIES

The modern, million-plus-circulation *Wall Street Journal* was created by Barney Kilgore, the most famous newspaper editor nobody has ever heard of. (What's called Dow Jones' Princeton campus—but which is really in South Brunswick, New Jersey, and whose usefulness Murdoch will regularly question during the takeover battle in 2007—is named the Bernard Kilgore Center, and features a statue of Kilgore with his sleeves rolled up.) Despite his success, Kilgore is unheralded for three reasons: He edited a specialized business paper, he was a conservative in the liberal age, and he was a modest guy—indeed, that modesty, or reticence, or ambivalence toward whatever is popular still informs the *Journal*.

He's been dead and all but forgotten for forty years by the time Murdoch is trying to buy the paper. (His contemporaries in stature,

Henry Luce at *Time* and Harold Ross at the *New Yorker*, have yet to fade into comparable obscurity.) But Murdoch knows Kilgore. Because of his conservatism or because of his success—or both— he's Murdoch's idea of a great editor and great man. To Murdoch, the *Journal* has mostly gone downhill since Kilgore. Richard Tofel, an executive at the *Wall Street Journal* from 1989 to 2004, will begin his book about Kilgore with Murdoch's views, taking his title—*Restless Genius: Barney Kilgore and the Invention of Modern Journalism*—from Murdoch's estimation that Kilgore founded journalism as we know it.

Some of Kilgore's innovations surely suit Murdoch. In Tofel's description of Kilgore's editorial strategies, "stories needed to be shorter; fewer needed to 'jump' from one page to another." Kilgore, in the *Journal*'s "What's News" column—still the most widely read part of the paper—invented news summarization. Kilgore's no-nonsense packaging of news and facts is Murdoch's idea of a quality paper. It's a Murdoch fixation: Almost all newspaper stories are too long, including the *Wall Street Journal*'s. (Some of Kilgore's other innovations, however, notably the "A-Hed," the *Journal*'s signature quirky front-page story, puzzle and irritate Murdoch. The idea of the anecdotal lead, which defined Kilgore's idea of "sprightly" writing, is a dubious indulgence in Murdoch's eyes.)

But what Murdoch will eventually buy is not Kilgore's *Journal*. Kilgore is as relevant to that modern *Journal* as Murdoch himself is relevant to, say, the anonymous titans of industrial production. Murdoch and the *Wall Street Journal* are, ultimately, creatures of the 1980s. Each is transformed by the decade; each helps create the decade. As money achieves a different value, a different meaning, during this period, so did Murdoch and so did the *Journal*.

The *Wall Street Journal* that existed before the 1980s existed as business did: as a discrete entity, as a specific and relegated function. The pre-1980s *Wall Street Journal* covered a set of industrial-related functions. It was a business paper speaking to exceedingly narrow-bore businesspeople. Its readership consisted of investors, executives, and retired investors and executives. Its readership reached 1.775 million in 1979, making it the largest paper in the United States and reflecting the creeping expansion of business that will shortly change modern life. But that change had yet to happen. "To the people who edit the nation's daily newspapers, the *Wall Street Journal* has always been a kind of stepbrother. A member of the family, yes, but without much family resemblance , . . and is certainly not a paper of general appeal," noted the *New York Times* when the *Journal* surpassed the *Daily News* to become the nation's largest-circulation daily paper. This had as much to do with the nature of business as with the emphasis on earnings reports in the paper: Business had yet to spill over into everyday life. Business hadn't yet become a key part of the culture. Business hadn't yet become a dramatic event—a *news* event. Business didn't yet involve so much money.

The *Wall Street Journal*, before the eighties, was a one-section paper, no bigger than forty-eight pages, with three usually well-reported and carefully written front-page features, a column of short items, and two columns of summary. Inside you had a rather mindless collection of earnings-related stories with a heavy focus on large-cap stocks, commodities, and credit markets (in the mid-forties the *WSJ* merged with the *Chicago Journal of Commerce*, pioneering the then-fanciful notion that readers who cared about equities and readers who cared about commodities might find a common interest in a newspaper). It was all a calculated business gray inside: just two types of headline, the single-column head and on occasion a two-column head. (When the stock market crashed in October 1987, editors felt it was inappropriate to use a two-column headline because the paper had used only a one-column head for the 1929 market crash that began the Great Depression.)

Its growth happened partly because it was so limited. As a thin, one-section paper it could more easily be printed at disparate locations around the country. The paper was able to grab a national audience of business readers because local papers had such weak business coverage. During the fifties and sixties, an overwhelming number of readers of the *Journal*—nearly all of them, in fact—read another newspaper as well. The *Journal* became the business addendum.

In 1982, Gannett launches *USA Today*, a national newspaper with ambitious circulation plans, promising an abundance of stock-and-option quotes and general-interest business coverage—for twenty-five cents where the *Journal* charges fifty cents. At the same time, focusing on the specialized business audience, *Investor's Business Daily* launches. What's more, the *New York Times* begins to roll out its national edition—and launches its own freestanding business section.

And a trend that began in the seventies—the migration of individual investors into mutual funds—is becoming the norm. If you own eight or ten different stocks, you might want to check them every day. If you give your money to an anonymous management fund, you tend to lose some of your interest in the market's day-to-day ups and downs.

At the same time, one of the greatest advertising bull markets is under way—newspaper advertising will more than double between 1980 and 1989, from $14.8 billion to $32.4 billion—from which the *Journal*, with its paltry number of pages, is unable to benefit.

The transformation of the *Journal*—which includes going from one section to two in 1980, and then, in 1988, to three—is masterminded by the bright-young-men triumvirate of Warren Phillips, a foreign correspondent who became the chief executive in 1975 and chairman in 1978; his protégé, Peter Kann, the Pulitzer Prize–winning reporter who in his career at the *Journal* will never file a business story; and Kann's protégé, Norm Pearlstine.

The premise is an expansion of business news beyond companies and markets: To see business as a major narrative event with dramatic characters and constant plot developments, to see business as a national pastime.

Pearlstine will later say, "I thought, we'll have a law page every day, because sometimes it feels like there are more lawyers than people. I thought we ought to cover accounting on a regular basis, not just because of tax but because there were a lot of accountants who saw themselves as a service industry for business. The paper had terrible technology coverage. [Technology] was covered by one reporter who covered everything from Xerox to IBM to AT&T, and then they had a reporter in San Francisco who divided her time between health care and semiconductors."

The very idea of a *Wall Street Journal* reporter changes—culture and lifestyle reporters come to business. Business, after all, is becoming the single greatest story of the decade: the deregulation and ensuing free-for-all of the Reagan years; the sea of liquidity created by a booming stock market; the rise of financial titanism; the birth and meteoric growth of the personal computer industry and the effect of personal computers on business culture (spreadsheet software arguably creates the finance culture); the ascendancy of the charismatic CEO and businessman superstar (Lee Iacocca, Donald Trump, Steve Jobs, Bill Gates, Andy Grove); the rise of Michael Milken and the pursuit of Michael Milken; and, not least of all, the development of a literature and media to celebrate business. Indeed, in many ways, the *Journal* is the preeminent source of this literature: *Barbarians at the Gate*, by Bryan Burrough, about the takeover of RJR Nabisco; *Den of Thieves*, by James B. Stewart, about the rise of Michael Milken; and *Oil and Honor*, by Thomas Petzinger, about the takeover of Penzoil, were all written by *Journal* writers, and each book began as a *Journal* story.

Murdoch enters the decade as a minor, if voluble, figure in the publishing world and will leave it as one of the era's business superstars. He will become one of the characters the *Journal* is writing about, which, in turn, helps create this business culture he is a beneficiary of. The eighties message is that playing the game means you're worthy of the game.

Arriving in the eighties, Murdoch is actually in a place disconcertingly similar to that of Donald Trump: He's got ambition much larger than his asset base. And he's faced with a similar conundrum: How do you jump-start your own standing? How do you get taken seriously?

In London's *Sun*, he's got a good cash-flow engine, which (again like Trump) means that he can borrow money. This is another eighties point. If you're underleveraged in the eighties, you're going to recede; if you're overleveraged, you'll advance. Overleveraging yourself, at a time before the geometric value of debt is understood (if you buy a $10 million enterprise with only $1 million cash down and it doubles in value—and the eighties are the decade of spiraling values—then you've just made a 1,000 percent return on your money), requires a particular eighties kind of temperament—which Murdoch, like Trump, has. It's a high tolerance for uncertainty, the ability to keep numerous balls in the air, and a lack of any evident ambivalence.

You're an action figure. No nuance here.

The internal financing of Murdoch's restless efforts to enter and stay in the deal flow comes from a fundamental contradiction in his ideological position—and another alignment of the eighties stars. He's an anti-monarchist. Almost everything about the British royal family annoys or repels him; everything about the people who surround the royal family nauseates him. The *Sun* is as dismissive of the royal family as any mass-market British publication could ever be. And yet the internal cash flow of News Corp. becomes highly dependent on the *Sun*'s obsession with Diana, Princess of Wales. The more Diana is in the news, the more papers are sold—particularly copies of the *Sun*. If the eighties represent a convergence of publicity seekers and publicity givers, each rewarded by the market for their efforts and their symbiosis, then the relationship of Murdoch and Diana is an apogee of the era. The great, roaring bull market for newspapers in the United Kingdom during the eighties and nineties is fueled by Diana—and when she dies in 1997, the newspaper business will also start to die.

It's cash flow combined with restlessness—a businessman's ADD—that defines an eighties temperament. Murdoch is pulled by his sense (not so much strategic as nervous; it's his impatience) that something is going on somewhere else. In the early eighties, he cannot yet articulate the global media vision—it doesn't mean anything yet. What he's pursuing is the wherewithal of money itself. If the banks will lend money, it's a lost opportunity not to take it. It's exactly the instrument that his father lacked—you get to take control with someone else's money. He knows too—and it's like a monkey on his back—that other people are also seizing this new opportunity.

The temperamental restlessness is important. He literally can't stop moving. This too becomes an advantageous eighties trait. He's got an iron will coupled with an iron bottom. With the move to the United Kingdom, he was merely extending his range (and jet transportation was getting better). With the move to the United States, he's at a level of dislocation and constant global movement that may not be matched by anyone in the world. It's so extreme that it must be having an impact not just on his metabolism (the *Chicago Tribune* and the *Independent* in Britain have both reported that he "reportedly" takes enemas before long flights) but also on his sense of both place and possibilities. Not to mention how it's exacerbating what we might already infer about his intimacy issues. What's more, right up until the late eighties, he's traveling on commercial flights, not private jets.

His first eighties deal, the financially dubious acquisition of the *Times* of London and the *Sunday Times* in 1981, makes him one of the world's most famous newspaper proprietors—arguably the most important private citizen (or, actually, noncitizen) in the United Kingdom. Presto! It's another eighties point: The deal reinvents you.

What Murdoch gets is a business that over the next twenty-five years or so will never make him any money—and which may cost him as much as a billion dollars. While the *Sunday Times* is Britain's leading *Sunday* "quality" paper, at about 1.5 million circulation, and returns a robust profit, the paper's problem is that, having been acquired in 1959 by Canadian Roy Thomson, who founded the Thomson Corporation, it got itself linked to a tar baby when Thomson acquired the daily *Times* in 1967.

But the money-losing daily paper is among the world's most famous journalistic enterprises. Over two centuries, it has been the consummate example of a paper coming to reflect the dominant values of the dominant class. Indeed, the *Times* helped to define the British idea of class. It exists for that reason more than for an economic one.

By the eighties, it has become not just a poor economic proposition but an untenable one. This is partly because of its relatively small circulation—about 200,000 in the seventies—but mostly because the print unions have largely achieved economic control of the newspaper business and are bleeding it.

Roy Thomson died in 1976 and his much less sentimental, less starstruck son, Kenneth, took over. In 1978, he announced that unless the company could get concessions from the typesetters' union it would close the papers down. The unions went on strike anyway. The strike (or lockout) lasted a year, costing Thomson, who continued to pay the salaries of the other unions, £40 million, and in the end Thomson capitulated, rehiring the printers and getting no concessions or savings in return.

Then, in August 1980, the journalists went on strike, which was the last straw and, as Thomson saw it, the final betrayal: He put the group up for sale in October. Eager to avoid severance costs of more than £35 million associated with closing the paper, which he announced he'd do if he couldn't find a buyer, this was officially a distress sale.

Among the potential buyers were Associated Newspapers, owners of the *Mail;* the ever-dubious Robert Maxwell; Atlantic Richfield, the American oil company, which, in a fit of odd diversification (characteristic of that corporate era), had bought the *Observer;* and separate groups led by the *Times'* editor, William Rees-Mogg, and the *Sunday Times* editor, Harry Evans. And Murdoch.

Nobody else except Murdoch would agree *not* to close the daily *Times*.

Murdoch is beginning to practice eighties finance. The deal itself gives him access to greater deals, which, if need be, would cover the cost of this one.

There is, too, the other element, not at all eighties: his newspaper fetish. He is, in some sense, helpless not to try to buy any newspaper that might be for sale. His advance here is to couple his newspaper fetish with a greater eighties avariciousness. Every purchase, every deal, is in service to the next deal. His compulsion to buy newspapers is becoming a compulsion to buy just about anything.

And he's started to conflate the idea of all media. Entering the eighties, separate media disciplines—newspapers, television, books, movies, music—had separate owners. Leaving the eighties, one owner will own all. This happens in part because of Murdoch's cash-flow needs.

His thinking is less visionary or abstract than it is practical. His television station in Australia has a significantly greater profit margin than his newspapers—allowing him to buy more newspapers (in other words, owning newspapers remains the point). In the United States, newspapers not only have unimpressive cash flows (at least second-tier newspapers, which is all he owns) but also don't reach a national audience. He needs national impact. He's really not interested in Chicago or Boston or San Antonio (this is one reason why he'll continue to own the *Post*—it's in New York). He needs to hear the sound he makes.

Still, because he can, he buys the *Herald* in Boston and the *Sun-Times* in Chicago. News Corp. is suddenly, with his Australian, British, and American holdings, one of the largest publishers in the world. He's got the two ingredients that make the business world take you seriously: the ability to get financing and the ability to command the attention of the media (not least of all because he is a buyer of the media).

It's a story—the Murdoch progression from wannabe to serious player—told most particularly by the *Wall Street Journal.*

After Murdoch's takeover of the *New York Post* and *New York* magazine, the *Journal,* itself in the earliest stage of trying to find a way to write about business as more than just share price or quarterly results, sent a young David McClintick to profile Murdoch. McClintick will later write one of the seminal eighties books, *Indecent Exposure*, about the greed, foolishness, and naked power struggle that nearly destroyed Columbia Pictures. But in 1977, McClintick and the *Journal* were still groping toward a style. The profile highlighted not just Murdoch's newcomer status but the newcomer status of this form of writing in the *Journal* itself. The front-page piece opened with a description of a painting of two dead sheep being shorn in a drought, by Australian artist Clifton Pugh, which was propped against a wall in Murdoch's new office at the *Post.* "Few if any *New York Post* editors or writers have seen the painting. Nor has anyone from *New York* and *New West* magazines and the *Village Voice* . . . But the starkly elemental yet ambiguous work serves as a rough symbol of the hopes, doubts and fears of the publications' employees as they contemplate the prospect of working for Rupert Murdoch. Is he, as well as the field hand in the picture, interested in essentially making something good out of a bad situation? Or are they cynical opportunists, bent only on stripping a carcass of its profitable remains?" (This is the kind of narrative prose that will make Murdoch scowl the most when he later sees it in the *Journal.*)

Although Murdoch is frustrated by the U.S. newspaper market, he continues to pursue it obsessively. He considers buying the afternoon Hearst paper in Baltimore, the *News American*, with the idea of making it a Washington, D.C., paper too. The *Los Angeles Herald Examiner* is also on his list. Neither purchase happens. He focuses, briefly, on making a bid for *Newsweek*, the newsmagazine owned by the *Washington Post*, but is talked out of it by Ed Kosner, his *New York* magazine editor, who spent much of his career at *Newsweek*. He's envious of Gannett's launch in 1982 of *USA Today*—and will offer to buy it.

He's entering what, in business terms, can only be seen as a manic phase.

News Corp. has a surge in growth not only because of acquisitions but because of the dramatic upswing in advertising. (In 1984 the company's revenues will top $2 billion; Time, Inc.'s revenues in 1984 will be $2.8 billion.) The *Sun* alone, fueled by the Princess of Wales, is throwing off $50 million a year in free cash flow—meaning it can finance upward of $500 million in new acquisitions.

At the same time, he's pushing the limit. The company's debt at times exceeds its assets. One way to lower this ratio, counterintuitively, is to buy more: Get more cash flow by assuming more debt.

The problem is that there just aren't that many newspapers to buy.

The idea of cross-platform ownership, although it is not yet called this, of a horizontally integrated media company is about to be born. It is born not out of a farsighted, sophisticated, abstract business construct, but out of the need to spend money, to do deals.

Equally, Murdoch, whose real and in some ways singular intention is to buy newspapers, has come to understand that other kinds of cash flow might help him in this regard. He is, in effect, trying to rationally finance the sometimes irrational.

Then there's another element fueling the mania. Here too he's demonstrating an eighties sensibility: He sees business as a competition among individuals. For him this goes back to the Fairfaxes and Packers, and, more recently, in London, to Robert Maxwell. In the United States, players are beginning to emerge. "The *Wall Street Journal* library," the *Journal* says, "maintains books of clippings of stories about 'personalities,' the people who dominate the pages of this and other newspapers. In the past few years few individuals have accounted for more clips than Carl Icahn, Irwin Jacobs, Carl Lindner, David Murdock, Victor Posner and the late Charles Bluhdorn." The *Journal*'s profiles of such individuals will come to define the era; a piece the *Journal* runs on Carl Icahn highlights the paper's soon-to-be-classic use of anecdote, recounting the New York financier's shouting match with C. E. Meyer Jr., the president of TWA, in a "half deserted bar at the Waldorf-Astoria hotel."

By the mid-eighties the cast of characters is set, with the *Journal* providing something like fanzine coverage: Drexel Burnham's enigmatic financier, Michael Milken; the arbitrager Ivan Boesky; the British corporate raider Sir James Goldsmith; the Texas oilman-turned-raider T. Boone Pickens; Murdoch's Australian nemesis (and sometime partner) Robert Holmes à Court; the upstart Ronald Perelman (with his surprise bid for Pantry Pride, the supermarket chain), and, of course, their bankers (e.g., Bruce Wasserstein) and lawyers (e.g., Marty Lipton).

Murdoch is taken with the outsiderness of these guys—they all come as if from nowhere and are making king-size trouble. They're playing his game, taking his role.

There isn't such a state of play in the newspaper business in the United States—it's hard to make a splash. Murdoch is surprised to find the U.S. newspaper market a fairly tame and boring place. There are no personalities. There is little competition.

Even in the greater media business—dominated by aging, entrenched players—he arguably has only one peer. Steve Ross built Warner Communications into a mini media and entertainment conglomerate. He started with funeral homes (owned by his father-in-law) and traded up to parking lots. Then, starstruck, he bought a talent agency and acquired the name and remnants of Warner Brothers to reconstitute the movie studio. From there he went into music and, presciently and disastrously, into video games.

Murdoch's view of Ross in a sense presages his view of the other media barons who will shortly begin to populate the territory. Assessing his competitors is the one place where Murdoch is systematically analytical rather than reflexive and instinctive. He loves to analyze other people's weaknesses. He collects information about them—as they do about him.

Ross's Warner was until 1983 the country's most high-flying media company. Then, with a radical drop in revenues at Atari, the video game company it acquired in 1976 (this might be the first instance of a traditional media company acquiring a new media company with catastrophic consequences), its shares collapse. Murdoch begins borrowing money to buy Warner's shares.

By the end of 1983, he has spent nearly $100 million to acquire 6.7 percent of the company. Not only is he now Warner's largest shareholder, but since he's exceeded 5 percent, he's obliged to disclose his position—which, with its clearly threatening implications, makes him a presumed takeover player. With companies and industries becoming, in the eighties, like sets of dominos (once one goes . . .), Murdoch's move can be seen as putting the whole media business in play.

As it happens, Murdoch is not that good at the game (yet)—he doesn't end up taking over Warner. Still, because the Warner guys are themselves thought of as such tough players (thugs, relatively speaking), the fact that Murdoch has gone head to head with them—and, at that, forced Warner into serious lockdown mode—means that Murdoch emerges from this as a man who's made his takeover bones.

Indeed, the Warner guys react to Murdoch in such a way as to suggest that he is more capable than he really is. After all, it is far from certain that he could have put together the financing to take over Warner. But Ross, vulnerable in the wake of the Atari fiasco, freaks. He dives into a deal that will bedevil Warner for years to come, and of which, sixteen years later, Murdoch will be the ultimate beneficiary. Chris-Craft Industries, another mini-conglomerate with media-related assets, agrees to take a 19 percent stake in Warner in exchange for a 42.5 percent stake in a Chris-Craft subsidiary that owns independent (non-network-affiliated) television stations around the country—a company Murdoch will acquire in 2000.

Because foreign nationals are not allowed to own more than 20 percent of any U.S. television station, the Chris-Craft deal makes it impossible for Murdoch to take control of Warner.

Murdoch sues, not least of all because if he gives up the fight for Warner, its shares, including the ones Murdoch owns, will take a precipitous drop. Although News Corp. accuses Warner of "a pattern of racketeering"—echoing fraud charges then pending against Warner executives in connection with a shady investment in a theater in Westchester County, New York—Warner neverthe-less manages to effectively paint Murdoch as the predator, the unsavory element. For Steve Ross, the former parking lot and funeral home king, long rumored to have mob ties, to successfully portray Murdoch as the unscrupulous one is a good indication of both Murdoch's sudden credibility as a wheeler-dealer and of the fast-growing Murdoch backlash. Indeed, Harry Evans, the London *Times* editor whom Murdoch pushed out of his job, publishes his memoir, *Good Times, Bad Times* in 1983, with its devastating por-trait of an amoral, duplicitous, and ruthless Murdoch—and is then promptly recruited by Steve Ross to help in the Warner anti-Murdoch campaign.

For his part, Murdoch has reporters from the *New York Post*—including his favorite, Steve Dunleavy—investigate Ross and Warner. Dunleavy goes as far as to call Ross's old headmaster at Columbia Grammar and Preparatory School to ask about his grades.

Finally, in 1984, Warner pays Murdoch to go away, buying his stock back for significantly more than it is worth and giving him a quick profit of $40 million—effectively making him a green-mailer, that species of financial bottom feeder already becoming part of eighties mythology.

Murdoch, not surprisingly, likes the game. Both the conflict and the profits suit him, not to mention the publicity. He's elevated himself from mere publisher to international financier—a player, a man to fear. And, perhaps most important, a man whom capital seeks out.

So he does it again two months later. Backed by a consortium of banks, he goes after the St. Regis Corporation, a paper company. A decade before, Time, Inc., in what turned out to be a disastrous combination, acquired a forest and paper company. But Murdoch, quite likely, does not really want St. Regis. He's suddenly in a fur-ther business—beyond publishing, paper, or even media. It's the barracuda business. And, with the quick $37 million he makes on his St. Regis stock when the company sells itself to Champion International Corporation to avoid Murdoch, he's now making a lot more money in the barracuda business than he is in the actual media business.

He's getting good at it. The takeover business—the financial bully business—requires somebody with the balls for conflict, the appetite for risk, and the ability to make quick decisions. And you can't bother about being hated. Indeed, in that department, his two greenmail episodes in the mid-eighties further color his character: Long after the greenmail has been forgotten, the scent of bully-boy financial skulduggery will cling to him. But, unlike the other financial bully boys the *Journal* is covering during this time with great devotion—Icahn, Pickens, Goldsmith, Perelman, Asher Edelman, and others even less scrupulous—Murdoch feels guilty.

For Murdoch, it's about owning stuff. As much as the quick cash and the heat of battle appeal to him, he's a proprietor. His father did not own, and he wants to own. He's old-fashioned. He's a man not of capital but of assets. He wants to be able to walk through what he owns. Jet in and be part of it, however briefly. He wants to be able to explain it to his mother, who demands explanations. It is hard to explain greenmailing. What's more, honestly, he's not all that interested in just having more money. Between money used for personal cosseting and pleasure and status symbols and money used to buy another newspaper, there's no contest.

Yet he is like those people—Icahn, Pickens, Edelman, Goldsmith, et alia—too. He understands, just as they understand, that the moment to act is *now* ("We don't have a grand 10-year strategy," he tells the *Journal* after the Warner battle. "We've gone where opportunity has led us.") and that the action itself is self-sustaining. Plus he seems, as they seem, to have a temperamental advantage over other businessmen. It's a lack of worry about the future. And, too, the willingness to do things alone.

At the end of 1984, thirty-one years since he took over the *Adelaide News,* ten since he moved to New York, he does the biggest deal of his career. He spends $350 million for a group of . . . hmmm . . . trade magazines. The tabloid publisher is now the world's leading publisher of magazines for people in the aviation industry and for travel agents. If you want to price a six-year-old Boeing 767 coming off its first lease or get a discount on a block of rooms in Atlantic City in midsummer, go ask Rupert, proprietor of, among other titles, *Aviation Daily* and *Hotel and Travel Index.*

This unlikely acquisition actually has several vision points. This seemingly boring trade magazine deal has unexpectedly attracted a lot of attention. It's one of the biggest sales ever of publishing properties. Bill Ziff, who, like Murdoch, took over some fledgling titles from his father thirty years before, has built a significant magazine empire, which has helped redefine the nature of advertising. His titles are all niche, special-interest, targeted publications. Along with his trade journals, there are his consumer titles: *Modern Bride, Popular Photography, Yachting, Car & Driver.* His decision to sell almost everything he owns is so unusual in the media business that he has to come up with an excuse: He's dying.

The deal is so big that Murdoch can't hope to afford it all (another indication that he never could have completed the Warner deal). So he bids for the trade publications, and CBS (with a hapless vision to diversify into print) bids for the consumer titles, ultimately paying $362.5 million.

The size of the deal and the active bidding for it suddenly open the door to other big media sales—indeed, within the next five years every significant media company will change hands. It will no longer be necessary to pretend you're dying in order to sell a company—everybody's doing it. (A few months after the Ziff deal is completed, Murdoch observes a comely young woman on the same flight he's on to Palm Beach. As she disembarks, she runs into the arms of a tanned and fit Bill Ziff, who will live another twenty-one years.)

Murdoch, having played his part in opening up the media deal flow, is now at the heart of it. (Any property that comes up for sale he'll be called about—he's a buyer of first choice, first approach; he's atop every investment banker's call list.) The fact that he is stuck with $350 million worth of trade magazines, which could not interest him less, is not so much an inconvenience as part of the compounding effect of the deal flow that he's helped begin. The market is further heated up by everybody's efforts not just to sell or to buy but to sell one thing in favor of buying another. The media is now a trader's business. Indeed, Murdoch will very profitably rid himself of these trade magazines—as will CBS rid itself, also profitably, of its part of the Ziff deal—as a way to move into the movie business.

At this moment, in 1985, Murdoch is still a dedicated newspaper proprietor—fully two-thirds of his time is devoted to his papers, half of his time to literal newsroom matters: stories, headlines, coverage, politics, editors. But, again, there just aren't enough newspapers to buy with all the capital available.

Hence, television.

Television stations are one of his fixations—in part because, given his immigrant status, his inability to buy television stations rankles him. He has no particular feel for network programming, but he likes station cash flow—Channel 10 in Australia is one of his big earners. As early as 1977, after the acquisition of the *Post* and *New York*, he had the Squadron, Ellenoff lawyers research just what it would take for a foreign national to buy stations in the United States. Alas, there's no way around this; it would take U.S. citizenship, which even in the seventies he started to consider—he was willing, but his mother was the immediate impediment.

Another fixation is HBO, the leading pay-television channel in the country. Murdoch has a great respect, or in some sense child-like awe, for technology, but he's pretty clueless himself. He's got no practical grasp and very little intellectual grasp of technological transformation. But certain things strike him—it's almost the shiny-object syndrome. Still, while HBO catches his eye, cable, which is the actual technological revolution of the moment—the one that HBO depends on—doesn't.

HBO speaks to his precise self-interest: It's a form of U.S. television that, because it doesn't involve television stations, he could own as a foreigner. What's more, HBO, which Time, Inc. started in 1972, is distributed by satellite. Satellites tickle him. He likes their stateless sense—that they might be beyond ordinary controls, outside of political interference and regulation.

Also HBO is then just recycling Hollywood movies. He does the calculation in his head: Buy the movies for X, resell them for X+. It's dealmaking, not programming.

His fixation logically becomes about the idea of the film library. If he can *own* the titles, he's in the loop. Again, in order to understand this, it's necessary to understand not the vision but the lack of vision. Two-thirds of his mind is still concentrated on newspapers, some more than nine thousand miles away from Hollywood. What he's doing with the balance of his attention is thinking about what he can do to ensure that he can buy more newspapers when he needs to.

Indeed, when he buys Twentieth Century Fox, there are few people who have ever come to Hollywood less enamored with the place, less temperamentally suited to it, than Rupert Murdoch. It rubs against his every grain: its excesses, its sexuality, its anti-work ethic, its lax dress code.

The fact that he will play the Hollywood game as well as anyone is quite possibly due to his antipathy for the place. He's here not for glamour but for cash flow.

He buys 50 percent of Twentieth Century Fox from the real estate magnate Marvin Davis, who, with commodities trader and financial schemer Marc Rich—who shortly flees to Switzerland to avoid fifty-one counts of fraud and tax evasion (to be pardoned eighteen years later by Bill Clinton)—purchased the studio in 1981. Davis, who bought out Rich's interest for $116 million, sells it to Murdoch for $250 million in March 1984.

Murdoch may be the first person to come to Hollywood who has no interest in the movies or stars or show business itself. Davis, Murdoch's new partner, is an especially vivid example of a Hollywood grotesque—obese and starstruck—who appalled and annoyed Murdoch.

Now, the Murdoch without particular social aspirations has nevertheless always made a point of knowing other dealmakers. He has gradually pushed, in his ten years in the United States, to know everyone at the dealmaking level of American media. This, in itself, is a kind of new perception about the nature of business. He's an early, consummate networker. He dispenses with the country clubs or the golf course and the artifice that he has any other interest but business. He's not interested in social contrivance and ritual and propriety, which have imposed a formality and courtliness and exclusivity on the business world (and have had the effect of keeping interlopers out).

He's interested in efficiently knowing who he needs to know.

This includes John Kluge, who has assembled the largest collection of independent television stations in the United States. In a sense, because Murdoch has no friends and therefore does not judge people on the basis of compatibility, he can get along with Kluge, a man with whom few people get along. Kluge is a media mogul prototype. A bully and vulgarian of limited interests, he takes his public company, Metromedia, private in a legendary screwing of his shareholders, which makes him the first media billionaire. (When Kluge, at sixty-seven, married his third wife—a thirty-two-year-old—Anna Murdoch was the matron of honor.)

In March 1985 Murdoch agrees to pay a huge premium for Kluge's six stations—almost double what stations are selling for at the time. It's a transformation premium: He goes, in little more than a year, with the Twentieth Century Fox deal and the television stations deal, from a print publisher to the first truly all-media media company.

The television deal sets in motion the kind of radical changes and conflicts of interest that few companies can endure. Which is a key difference between News Corp. and other companies: Murdoch reduces the corporate issues to personal issues—it's about what changes and contradictions *he* can endure.

Buying Kluge's stations is the quintessential too-much-risk, too-many-moving-pieces virtuoso deal that helps turn business into such a satisfying spectator sport in the eighties. You cannot miss its existential proportions. If he pulls it off, he'll be among the most powerful men in the world; if he falters, he'll be roadkill.

Initially Davis is in the deal as well—which means that the stations will cost News Corp. an out-of-pocket $832.5 million, significantly increasing its already serious debt load. But Davis backs out of the deal in the middle of the financing, and the burden on News Corp. doubles. Murdoch also determines to get rid of Davis altogether, buying him out of the studio, which will call for another

$325 million—and put Murdoch just behind the biggest entities in the media industry, the networks and Time, Inc.

In part, this is just a sign of the times: the sudden tolerance for heretofore undreamed-of levels of debt. After all, this is the most fundamental eighties alchemy: producing cash when you don't have any. But on Murdoch's part, it is also a simple financial trick. It's the strange and wondrous advantage of dealing through so many different countries and financial and legal systems. In the United States, preferred shares, the type Murdoch is granting to the television station bondholders, are considered debt—you *have* to pay their holders what you said you would pay them before you pay anyone else; these preferred shareholders are not, like common shareholders, owners who are part of the fate of the enterprise. In Australia, however, preferred shareholders *are* considered own-ers—hence the value of their interest is not a balance-sheet minus but a balance-sheet plus. In the United States the television deal makes News Corp. worth $1.6 billion less; in Australia this makes it worth $1.6 billion more, which Murdoch can borrow against. (The *WSJ* will further point out in 1988: "Under Australian accounting principles, TV licenses, titles and other intangible assets aren't deemed to have any finite life and thus don't have to be counted as good will and gradually written off against earnings. Another quirk of Australian rules: News Corp. can eventually write up the value of . . . assets on its balance sheet if it thinks the prop-erties are worth more than it paid. Such a write-up would raise shareholders' equity and increase News Corp.'s borrowing ability.")

What's more, while heretofore determined not to sell assets, he immediately resolves to sell assets. "I need to sell you to buy tele-vision stations," he says to David Schneiderman, the publisher of the *Village Voice*. Likewise, he sells the *Chicago Sun-Times*. As it happens, each sale helps confirm the higher value of his assets, which helps him borrow even more money: The *Village Voice*, whose $7.5 million purchase in 1978 included *New York* and *New*

*West* magazines, now fetches, on its own, $55 million. The *Sun-Times,* bought two years before for $90 million, commands $145 million.

Among the series of fraught and radical decisions involved with his acquisition of the stations, none is as emotional as the one to take up U.S. citizenship—except not to Murdoch. It is everybody else who has a how-could-you? reaction. The message is clear—or it is received in this clear form: He will do anything to get what he wants, even abandon his own country. Forgetting the fact that he has lived in the United States for eleven years, and will go on to live in the United States for, at the very least, the next twenty-three years, adopting U.S. citizenship seems to be proof of his extreme cynicism.

Emotionally, the most troubling aspect of his great transition from print to multimedia magnate turns out to be the prospective loss of the *New York Post.* He believes, in fact, he can stare down the rule against owning a television station and a newspaper in the same market. He's succeeded in getting waivers from the FCC through 1987, and, as he prepares for Christmas with his family that year, he has every reason to believe that the waiver will be extended. After all, the money-losing *Post* has little chance of being bought by another "philanthropic" newspaperman. But in a move that has all the hallmarks of typical Murdoch stealth, his old rival Teddy Kennedy, whom Murdoch has so frequently maligned in the *Boston Herald,* manages to sneak a piece of legislation through Congress as an attachment to a catchall appropriations bill that prevents the FCC from extending any waivers to the cross-media ownership laws or granting any new ones. The Supreme Court will eventually strike down that provision because it is directly aimed at Murdoch, but not before he is forced to sell the *Post* to real estate developer Peter Kalikow, who shortly afterward goes bankrupt.

But most tellingly, he does the one thing he's sworn never to do, risk his control of the company—if the stations don't perform, the bondholders will take over News Corp. He's betting it all.

In the eighties there are many figures playing as aggressively as Murdoch—and lovingly covered by the *Wall Street Journal*—who will be only ever so vaguely remembered two decades later. And then there are others, including Murdoch, who are not necessarily that different in intelligence or nerve or cash position, but who will become, by the financial plays they execute in the eighties, among the wealthiest people who have ever lived.

So what is the difference between the former and the latter? Luck? Audacity? Crookedness? Or some kind of true belief, some special trust, in the nature of market forces and how the system is being transformed that lends you some further ability to hold it together?

It is hard to see Murdoch, so consummate a figure of cynicism and opportunism, as a true believer. And yet, as the eighties progress, as he goes from, relatively speaking, your most basic baling-wire-and-duct-tape business guy to a new sort of figure in the world—a man who on the basis of his own reputation has seemingly unlimited access to capital—Murdoch becomes one of the most righteous advocates of the changes that helped make him. He is, and sees himself as, the ultimate product of the liberated market—that is, when he does not see himself as the liberator of markets.

This is the point in his career when he is perhaps most in danger of the overreach, of the hubris, that ruins so many other figures of the time.

Indeed, in him the triumph of the markets is, as it will be in others, suddenly infused with Hollywood style. Murdoch—who, over the millions of air miles he's traveled, has up until now insistently flown commercial—learns that his subordinate, Barry Diller at Fox, has his own plane. Murdoch decides he ought to get one too. The mogul ethic is born.

And now his climactic eighties moments are at hand.

Except, not yet—first there's some personal business. This occurs out of view of most of the world. Indeed, he is using his eighties might to do something very un-eighties. He buys his father's old company, the Herald and Weekly Times, which, with his own holdings, gives him almost 60 percent of the newspaper market in Australia.

The deal is significant not just because of its impact on Australia (and its price: $1.6 billion) but because it makes no sense from the point of view of the new global media company he's created in the United States. Or it only makes sense if one is to conceive of the company not at all as a coherent vision, a calculated strategy, but as a hodgepodge of Murdoch's own interests, hankerings, experiments, bets—and personal, idiosyncratic acts of dominance. It makes no more sense, at this point in its development, for News Corp. to monopolize the newspaper business in Australia than it would for Time, Inc., to monopolize it.

From the strict eighties point of view of brutal corporate rationalization—wherein a company should be a cold and efficient instrument for maximizing value—the renewed interest in Australia seems preposterous. But from that other eighties construct, the charismatic CEO—wherein certain rare executives are believed to be so prescient and all-knowing that they can, like a big star who can carry a dog of a movie, defy logic—is what you're betting on.

The second climactic moment of the Murdoch eighties is Wapping—the newly built headquarters and printing facility for his U.K. newspaper operation in east London. Grasping historical imperative and the zeitgeist, he makes common cause with Reagan and Thatcher (Murdoch might arguably join them as part of the eighties values triumvirate) and in 1987 breaks the British print unions after a strike that lasts more than a year.

The success of his move is not just in the breaking but in the historical revisionism. At the time, having erected a prison-like, totalitarian-seeming printing complex on the bank of the Thames and then secretly moving his strikebreakers in and keeping his unionized workers out, he creates one of the ugliest, potentially most explosive standoffs between labor and management in industrial history. Murdoch is anathema to all right-thinking liberal people. He is the thug, the brute, the boot.

At twenty years' remove, however, there will be only one story line: The union printers are thieves and nihilists who hold newspapers hostage and have brought the business to the point of bankruptcy (they are also censors who will regularly stop the presses over articles they don't like), and Murdoch is the bloke who finally says, *Enough!* What's more, he is the clever bloke, creating at Wapping one of the most brilliant subterfuges, one of the grandest deceptions—he manages to convince the unions that he is starting an entirely new paper there—since D-Day. He's even credited with some altruism: It is his move against the unions that empowers his competitors too, indeed even provides the wherewithal for the *Independent* to launch and compete directly against Murdoch's *Times*.

It doesn't stop. He owns a minority position in William Collins & Sons, a leading British book publisher, and so acquires the U.S. publisher Harper & Row ($300 million), and shortly thereafter turns around and scarfs up the rest of Collins, which he has previously promised not to touch. And suddenly News Corp. owns one of the world's biggest book publishers—a business or pastime (reading books) he has almost no interest in at all.

He grabs 20 percent of Pearson PLC, which owns the *Financial Times*. His notion is either to buy Pearson outright or, failing that, get it to give him the concession to publish the *Financial Times* in the United States. (This doesn't happen.)

He hits number eight in 1987 on *Forbes* magazine's list of the four hundred richest Americans, with an estimated net worth of $2.1 billion.

Oh, and there is the *South China Morning Post*. For $300 million he converts a minority stake into a controlling interest because

Dow Jones, with 19 percent, decides it doesn't want to be in business with Murdoch and agrees to sell him its shares. (Doing this deal is the first time Peter Kann meets Rupert Murdoch.)

And there's the greatest cash suck News Corp. has ever faced: the launch of the four-channel Sky satellite service in Britain. While he wins his battle to launch before his better-funded competitor BSB, the problem is that it's a business without customers—and, practically speaking, without a business plan. Indeed, he's launched into the void before anybody has satellite dishes to support his programming.

Then, straining all credulity, he makes his costliest purchase so far. For $3 billion, he buys Triangle Publishing, which owns *TV Guide*.

And he is thereby, at the close of the 1980s, $7.6 billion in debt—and shortly to be on the brink of ruin.

But pay no attention to that.


Dow Jones in the late eighties, with its three-section *Wall Street Journal*, the world's dominant business information brand, misses the main point of its own success: The *Wall Street Journal*, for better or worse, construes its role as that of observer, its job as journalism, rather than seeing its business as business. That, because business has become so complex, so competitive, so fetishized, really—and because the amounts of money in business have become so much greater—information about business has become so much more sought-after and valuable. While the *Wall Street Journal* understands that the business world has undergone a profound change in character and function, it doesn't understand that it should, accordingly, undergo such a change too. Its resistance may well be honorable—if you change your function, you change your meaning. It wants to stay a newspaper, that leisurely, narrative, fussy, everyman thing.

Meanwhile, other, lesser providers of business information—not least of all Michael Bloomberg's new company and Reuters—

are servicing the business information customer with much more specific, efficient, accessible data for which they can charge a hell of a lot more.

Murdoch, who, like the people at Dow Jones, enters the eighties as principally a publisher, a man who understands the publishing business, exits it as a practitioner, a connoisseur, a lover of business itself—committed to going wherever the transforming nature of business per se, and the media business in particular, takes him.

The people at Dow Jones enter and exit the eighties as newspaper people.

**MAY 2007**

Late in the day on May 1, after CNBC's disclosure of Rupert Murdoch's bid for the *Wall Street Journal*, Michael Elefante publicly releases the results of the poll he's been trying to conduct since the April 24 family meeting. By his tally—and he's careful to describe the equivocal nature of the count—family members representing slightly more than 50 percent of the vote seem to be opposed to Murdoch's offer. The message here, of course, is not about the majority being against the deal, but rather that the historic, vaunted, implacable opposition of the family is so weak. It is a sign of such clear uncertainty, ambivalence, and, apparently, consideration of the offer that by the end of the market day, Dow Jones, which has been trading in the thirties for the past three years, closes at $58.

At their hastily convened board meeting the next day, the new financial reality is explained in terms that nobody on the board had quite ever appreciated or considered. The nature of trading practices that began in the 1980s, which the *Wall Street Journal* wrote so vividly about, has now consumed the company. That is, between

David Faber's first report of the offer at noon and the close of the market, Dow Jones has had a profound turnover in its shareholder base. Its long-term, stalwart, and, to a degree, understanding holders of its common stock have been replaced by arbitrageurs— including Warren Buffett—who have bought the stock at well north of its natural price and who will only be satisfied if there's a deal (Murdoch's or anyone else's) struck for $60 or higher. In other words, Dow Jones is now formally in business with partners who will do everything possible to make it sell—and who will be impossible to live with if it doesn't sell.

And then, on May 5, another 1980s-style shoe drops.

Four days after news of the Murdoch offer for Dow Jones goes public—and likely spurred on by this announcement—Canada's Thomson Corporation, one of the world's largest publishers of business information, and Reuters, the news service and business data supplier, announce their plan to merge, presaging all sorts of vast dislocations in the market.

This could seem just like Murdochian dumb luck. Here he is trying to buy a company and, voilà, its two most logical saviors— his most logical competitors for Dow Jones—decide to merge, meaning they won't be able to bid for Dow Jones. What's more, Dow Jones, already dwarfed as a supplier of financial information, is suddenly even more circumscribed, reduced, limited.

Even Murdoch thinks he's been strangely and inexplicably smiled on by this development. But other than that, the announcement is so fortuitously timed for him, it seems rather predestined—just one more piece of historical inevitability that Dow Jones has been in denial about for years.

*Oh, shit,* is what Michael Elefante thought when he got the call on March 29 about Murdoch's expected $60 bid for Dow Jones.

*Oh, shit,* is what he thinks again when, five weeks later, he hears about Thomson and Reuters.

# EIGHT

**It's a Tabloid World**

Murdoch is restless—annoyed by the Bancrofts' lack of response to his offer.

While he knows what they must think of him, he still can't believe that they really think this—they must just be listening to other people who don't know him.

He decides to write directly to the family. He means his letter to be from one newspaper family to another. He talks about his father being a wonderful guy and mentions Gallipoli (which may be puzzling to members of the Bancroft family not up on their World War I secondary-battle history). He talks about his own children and how News Corp. is a family company. And that he thinks that interfering with the *Journal* and its long history of editorial independence would be bad for business. He mentions that he'd be amenable to an editorial board structure similar to what was put in place at the *Times* of London and *Sunday Times* newspapers when he bought them in 1981.

The Bancrofts receive his letter as though it's a communication from a far-off planet: While it is perhaps meaningful, there's no sense that a timely response might be in order.

It's confounding for him being out here in what feels like limbo. He isn't often ignored.

**MAY 18, 2007**

By all rights, the bottom should have fallen out of the deal. Or, if the issue actually was the standards and practices of journalism and the Bancroft family's commitment to protecting the same—and if a bald demonstration of Murdoch's idea of standards and practices was needed to remind everybody about what exactly was at stake—the deal should have died on the spot.

That morning, "Page Six," the *New York Post*'s gossip franchise run by Richard Johnson, publishes an item about itself. Scooping everybody else, "Page Six" confesses to a long list of extraordinary ethical derelictions and abuses of power of which it will shortly be accused in a lawsuit by a disgruntled former employee.

One disgruntled former employee is piggybacking on the charges of another disgruntled former employee, and both stories provide a window into the Murdochian tabloid world. In 2004, Ian Spiegelman, a "Page Six" legman of long standing, used the page to wage a vendetta (his e-mail threatened violence as well as bad press) against a demimonde flack over a woman. In 2006, Jared Paul Stern, another legman on the page—both Spiegelman and Stern had rather styled themselves in the tradition of the most cynical and noir gossip columnists of the forties—was accused by supermarket billionaire and Bill Clinton friend and partner Ron Burkle of conducting a shakedown. Burkle, who was secretly video-taping the meeting, had Stern name him a price for arranging favorable coverage and for smoothing the unfavorable.

Stern, who was fired shortly after Burkle made the claims, is now threatening to sue News Corp., in the process revealing that Johnson himself took at least one bribe, which "Page Six" now admits to (terming it a "Christmas gift"). In addition, Stern is set to claim in his suit that the editor of the *Post*, Col Allan—the thirty-four-year News Corp. veteran and Murdoch family favorite—was regularly provided with liquor and sex at a New York strip club. While "Page Six" does not deny that he frequented the club, it advises nevertheless that Allan's behavior was "above reproach." The litany of other claims that have been acknowledged with great umbrage and fulmination but not explicitly denied (save for boilerplate protestations about "smears and lies") include all manner of other extortions, pay-for-coverage schemes, and, in one instance, the allegation that the price of Lachlan Murdoch's house in Australia, when purchased by the actor Russell Crowe, included a guarantee protecting Crowe from bad press in the *Post*.

Prepublication, these revelations caused vast panic on the eighth floor at News Corp. Genie Gavenchak, the company's compliance lawyer, found that Allan did in fact, despite denials, use his credit card at the strip club in question—so they knew the jig was up, and the story would surely come out. It was Gary Ginsberg's idea that "Page Six" ought to gossip about itself, and, in fact, Ginsberg negotiated the "confession" with Allan.

Allan believes he's about to be fired and, certainly, Murdoch is furious with him and deeply worried about how the Bancrofts will react. Murdoch, nevertheless, used to suffering the bad behavior of hacks, lets it ride.

## HIS NEWSROOMS

The newsroom at the *Wall Street Journal*, in the World Financial Center—put up on the landfill from the excavation when the

World Trade Center was built in the 1970s—has seemed to Murdoch, on the few times he's visited, rather more like the back-room of an insurance company than a news operation. It's quiet, orderly, businesslike—or, you might say, strangled, repressed, dead. Murdoch didn't think the place, so "depressing and without energy," could be the newsroom. They obviously need, he will tell me later, "a change of culture, a change of scenery."

Newsrooms in Murdoch's world are id places, where reporters express instinctive impulses that, ideally, mirror the unexpressed impulses of their readers. Murdoch's favorite reporter, his totemic reporter, over the fifty years of his newspaper career is Steve Dunleavy, who worked at News Corp.'s Sydney paper, the *Daily Mirror*. In the 1960s, he preceded Murdoch in heading to New York. Now, at sixty-nine, he can be found on many afternoons—and mornings—drunk at Langan's, among the least appealing bars in Manhattan (think tourists in funny T-shirts), but where anybody who is anybody at the *New York Post* stubbornly congregates. Similarly, in Sydney, on any given evening you'll find the cream of News Ltd.'s reporting staff at the Aurora, a twenty-four-hour last-stop bar filled with slot machines, fluorescent lighting, and the occasional white Aussie male salsa dancer. It's the only remaining nongentrified spot in revivified Surry Hills, where Lachlan Murdoch has his chic offices.

Newspapers, to Murdoch, are an ungentrified idea. They are an immediate, often crude act. The energy you feel in a good news-room comes from speed, good reflexes, and that highest Murdoch standard, a lack of pretense.

The *Journal* newsroom in New York and its annex in South Brunswick, New Jersey, are foreign and desultory places to Murdoch—unlike the truly horrifying places where his reporters have in years past worked (and found secretly exhilarating).

From Peter Chippindale and Chris Horrie's classic account of Murdoch's *Sun, Stick It Up Your Punter!*:

The horrible conditions in the rackety old Bouverie Street building only added to the air of adventure about the enterprise. . . . Inside, the building was cramped, dingy and smelly. The corridors and stairway were cluttered with leaky vats of acid and various other chemicals used in the process department to make plates for the presses. The ceilings were a tangle of ducting carrying electrical and drainage systems which had haphazardly evolved over the decades, defying any logical system of safety or planning. On one occasion an acid drain split overnight and the *News of the World* hacks arrived in the morning to find the typewriters on their desks reduced to smoldering and partly dissolved lumps of metal. Facilities were rudimentary. The toilets were foul and swarmed with bluebottles in the summer. The canteen was filthy and infested with rats, giving the hacks another excuse to get out of the office into the Fleet Street pubs, where they could tap into the grapevine of what was happening at the other papers. . . .

But the squalor did make Bouverie Street an exciting and unpretentious place to work, with the day always dominated by the subconscious anticipation of press time, when there would be a deep rumble from the basement as the presses began to roll.

Such traditions and theatricality are not so much the point for Murdoch (he's hardly a sentimentalist—he ultimately moved the *Sun* and *News of the World* to antiseptic conditions in Wapping, and the *New York Post* from rat-infested digs above the trucking bays on South Street to News Corp.'s headquarters on Sixth Avenue) as the basics. Murdoch has a fixed notion of journalism—tinkering with it or dressing it up doesn't, to him, make it significantly more than it is. He has, in fact, a visceral revulsion, or contempt, for the dresser-uppers. It's artifice. It's fake. It's disreputable. And it always results in copy so much longer than it needs to be.

"There's levels and levels of editing," he will tell me incredulously after an early tour of the *Wall Street Journal*'s newsroom. "Every story gets edited about five times. Then it goes down to Princeton, where they put the paper to bed, there's 150 people there and they say, 'We do everything in a final edit to make sure everything is absolutely right and we check the sources and stuff.' And I thought, 'Oh my God, it's a wonder anything ever gets in the paper or on time.' " (He will often tell this story with the number of edits varying from 5 to 8 to 8.7.)

This has been a consistent disconnect—what American journalists think of when they think of news and what Murdoch thinks about news. To Murdoch, even the word *tabloid* is misunderstood. "Tabloid" in the Murdoch context is an idea of immediacy, sharpness, efficiency, and emotion—it's news at its most visceral and powerful and entertaining. The craft, and it is a high craft, is compression. Necessary and vital compression: The tabloid tradition in Britain and Australia derives in part from newsprint rationing after the First and Second World Wars. When Murdoch took over at the *Adelaide News*, newsprint was still controlled. Hence, during the Falklands War in 1982, when the Royal Navy sank Argentina's warship ARA *General Belgrano*, Murdoch's *Sun* famously reached the pinnacle of the form by delivering the news in a word: GOTCHA.

"Tabloid," in the modern U.S. context—to most people at the *Journal*, certainly—is about celebrities and gossip. It's faux news. Tabloidism is a modern journalistic illness, a virus—spread most of all by Murdoch himself.

But Murdoch is, more accurately, not a modern journalist but the last representative from an era when a newspaper was its own advertisement, when it had to sell itself.

Newspapers as sellers of news—as loud, unsubtle, rude instruments, as midway-type entertainment (games of chance, horoscopes, funny pages)—were, of course, the American form too. The

Hearst and Pulitzer empires were built on such papers. Any city with two or more papers fighting it out was certain to have a version of carnival news: cheaper (cheaper to produce, cheaper to buy), blunter, louder.

Then American papers—American news—turned orderly and genteel. This happened as newspapers, feeling television's competition, figured out a new business model: monopoly (largely by absorbing secondary papers). And then the big chains—Gannett, Knight Ridder, Tribune Company, Advance—replaced local owners. What's more, the American city as a working-class redoubt was transmuted into ghettos and suburban flight. The newsstand, and with it the battling urban evening newspaper, died. But a newspaper controlling its geographic position—not so much the city as its piece of the great expanding suburbs—had a monopoly on local ads. In a single-newspaper market, local advertisers often had no alternative but to advertise in the single paper. So a newspaper's best strategy was to be sedate, mannerly, uncontroversial—to offend no one, and not to call attention to the fact that it has monopolized the market, which it would certainly do if it screamed and bullied.

The dominant news voice in the United States has become a network television voice. News was now a serious, weighty, basso profundo affair, delivered by men of unimpeachable integrity and, relatively speaking, zero personality. News, bland news, self-important news, suddenly defined a kind of respectability and upward mobility. For the middle class, Walter Cronkite rather than William Randolph Hearst or a chain-smoking city editor came to represent the news.

The business itself was transformed from a workingman's profession—reporting had been a semi-white-collar job that didn't require a college education—to an Ivy League one. This is sometimes called the Watergate effect—the press's own good press during the investigation and pursuit of Richard Nixon, together with its evident power, made it a profession of choice. Also, during this time, the newsgathering function was being overtaken by the information-processing one—more specialized skill sets were required. Then too, there were fewer and fewer newspaper jobs; employers got to be choosier.

Arriving in New York in the early seventies, Murdoch—whose papers are in markets where television news is hardly a factor, and are still staffed by working-class reporters—is struck by one overpowering sense of the market: American news is lazy, stultifying, pickle-up-its-ass, boring. This suggests, to a man who has spent twenty years selling news in some of the most competitive news markets in the world, great opportunity.

In this regard, he is both right and wrong. In retrospect, it will be possible to see his years in America as a process of wrestling with what he does not understand about the American news market—a losing fight that, oddly, will make him a winner. It's partly out of frustration with American newspapers that he will come to build an entertainment empire. It's partly because he doesn't doubt himself that he will continue to try to succeed at news, and build Fox News, and bid $60 a share for Dow Jones. The $60 offer will indicate to many observers, however, that he still does not understand the American news market.

By the time Murdoch arrives in the United States he's mastered one business model: single-copy sales. Advertising is a modest adjunct to this greater business strategy. Indeed, at the beginning of his career, Murdoch is kept out of the "quality" media and the "rivers of gold" classified advertising revenue by the dominant Fairfax family. His son Lachlan, in a discussion about his father, will later point out that if Dame Elisabeth had not sold the Queensland newspapers, which were the upmarket part of the Keith Murdoch legacy, as opposed to the downmarket *Adelaide News*, then her son would have begun his career with a quality broadsheet (in Brisbane), rich in classified advertising—and Lachlan's father might not have ever become a tabloid king.

Murdoch's only real deviation in Australia from the single-copy tabloid strategy is the *Australian*, the first national newspaper in Australia, a quality broadsheet that he launched in 1964—the only newspaper he'll ever create, as well as the proof positive of his journalistic bona fides that he'll cite over and over again in the battle for the *Journal*. The *Australian*, whose respectability keeps his mother happy, will lose money for nearly thirty years.

It's the *News of the World* and the *Sun* that are his principal models. They are downmarket as an identity, with a precise and calculated form—constantly refined (even if refinement means vulgarization) and sharpened. And they sell like crazy.

It's media magic, his reconstruction of what he thinks of as the perfect tabloid form. Murdoch himself may be sour about and disaffected with Britain, but Britain embraces his *Sun*. Its tone is pitch-perfect. It is so spot-on that it effectively revolutionizes the form itself—in modern Britain, the tabloids become the most powerful media, breaking stories, setting the agenda, electing politicians, changing the culture. To question the form means you're standing on the sidelines. Questioning it, turning up your nose at its cultivated noxiousness, its calculated downmarketness, would make you something like an intellectual arguing against television, or a sixties parent decrying rock and roll. Successful media is its own justification (a key Murdoch precept). It is not possible to overestimate how much the *Sun*'s success has transformed even Murdoch's idea of the tabloid. He feels he has found the secret. What's more, the *Sun*, with profit margins as high as 60 or 70 percent, has become the most significant part of his business and will remain so for nearly twenty years. It not only becomes the primary revenue source, supplying the cash flow for his other efforts, but it also gives him his extraordinary power base in the United Kingdom. The *Sun* becomes one of the key levers to push the transformation of Britain itself. It changes Murdoch too, giving him a sense of just how large his ambitions could be.

The *Sun* and the *News of the World* are what he somehow hopes to bring to the United States. The size of this dream is disconcertingly huge—to be able to create a national tabloid with the success and impact of the *Sun* on a U.S. scale would be massive.

And yet, judging by the incredibly boring newspapers in the United States, it seems almost like a no-brainer.

Such sales as the *Sun* and the *News of the World* are having in the United Kingdom are dependent, however, on working-class men (ideally with the same interests, i.e., soccer) who buy papers, and newsstands where they can buy them.

The absence of those key factors in the U.S. market is an indication of how little Murdoch knows—and how hard it is to dissuade him from going forward when he wants something. Part of the reason he sends his early U.K. coterie in America packing back to London is that each of them perceives, in the face of his stubborn enthusiasm, that the U.S. market is inhospitable to the British tabloid model.

In a car culture, in the great rolling suburbs, the only place the middle class gets to truly eyeball the cover of a periodical is in the supermarket. And all the middle-class people doing this eyeballing are women.

The Murdoch formula—his tabloid magic, his working-class insouciance, his badgering and bullying—is for men. The aggressiveness, the girls, the sports, the jokiness, the news—all for men.

Supermarkets in America do not really sell newspapers. Supermarkets sell magazines. And tabloids, aka "the tabs." In the seventies, an American tab is a magazine/newspaper hybrid—it fits into a supermarket checkout rack—that merges two publishing genres: the fanzine (with slavish attention to celebrities) and the fantastical (accounts of aliens and grotesques and deviants with only the barest pretense of being factual). The *National Enquirer* — MOM BOILED HER BABY AND ATE HER!—which sells four million copies a week and is published by the Pope family, with its supposed organized-crime connections (Mafia boss Frank Costello is rumored to have put up the money for it), is the height of the form.

Murdoch's idea of a tabloid as a media property that could become a powerful working-class institution comes face-to-face with the American reality that a tabloid is a product that defines not only its readers' lack of standing but that of its owners. This is confounding and frustrating to him—and, significantly, an entirely different business and cultural climate from any he's ever been in. He has no background in soft celebrity gossip targeted at women.

It's important to keep in mind how premodern Murdoch is. He's a fifties guy. A guy's guy. From an era when guys talked about guy stuff.

But now comes the stubbornness and the relentlessness and the conviction that he can do whatever it takes. That, going forward, is the important thing. You set something in motion and then you try to control it. Doing it is what defines you.

In 1974, he launches the *National Star*. This is his American tabloid—not at all what he had in mind, but, nevertheless, he is playing it as it lays. Because although this is not the kind of paper he wants to be publishing, it does have another virtue that moves him: single-copy sales.

In this instance, the money overrides his ego. It doesn't really bother him that the *Star* is further poisoning his already problematic reputation. He's not only a British tabloid publisher, which is one thing, but he's now the proprietor of the lowest form of media in America. You can't go further down than this. The publisher of a supermarket tabloid doesn't get to eat out in Manhattan with the other parents at Brearley and Dalton.

Still, say what you want, one fine morning in August 1977 Elvis Presley dies. Steve Dunleavy had just published a book about Elvis—it's the King as a drug-taking debaucher well on his way to death. Murdoch scoops up the U.S. rights, and after the first install-ment of the serialization of the book, the *Star*'s circulation jumps from two to three million. The *Star* will serialize the rest of Dunleavy's Elvis book twenty more times, and at four million copies reach an equal footing with the *Enquirer*. (Murdoch will sell the *Star* for $400 million in 1990 to the *Enquirer*'s parent com-pany.)

But never mind the *Star*. It will be the *New York Post*—acquired almost three years after he launches the *Star* —that will truly demonstrate his belief in the potential of the tabloid in America.

The oldest paper in the city is, virtually overnight, transformed into a British tabloid—a species of newspaper that New York has not seen in two generations and which, over the next thirty years, will only ever lose money.

It is almost impossible to exaggerate how determined and how wrongheaded Murdoch is with the *New York Post*. It is another one of those things that shadow his reputation: No matter how wrong he is, he won't give up. That's scary. In this regard, he's beyond all reason. It is a grand and stubborn obsession.

In fact, after he is forced to sell the paper in 1988 to comply with rules that prohibit a proprietor from owning a newspaper and television station in the same market, he will move political mountains to get the *Post* back when its new owners bring it to the brink of insolvency in 1993. He can't entirely breathe with-out it.

The *Post* exists, in some sense, like a perfect fantasy world. A tabloid newsroom in a world where there are no such things any-more. They pretend, at the *Post*, that this is real work, legitimate work, sustaining work—when, in some sense, it is more? like a theme park. (For that reason, I will tell my own daughter, casting about for her first journalism job, that there is no newspaper as wonderful to work at as the *New York Post*.)

Nor can you argue that it hasn't, on its own terms, been wildly successful. It is just, oddly, that this most commercial of papers is not, well, commercial. Upscale-centric New York advertisers treat the *Post* and its three-ring-circus sensibility with contempt.

Still, Murdoch's New York British tabloid arguably becomes the second most influential paper in America—the paper that everybody in the media business reads first. The *Post*—the only real daily tabloid in America—embodies and influences the circus of pop and media culture that has migrated to so many other media outlets and which has left so many newspapers behind.

Meanwhile, the reason cited by Murdoch's detractors for his keeping the *Post* alive—that it wields disproportionate political influence—seems a strained one, considering that by 1996 he will have Fox News. And by 2007, he'll be losing $50 million a year on the *Post*—which could buy a lot of lobbyists and political leverage (which, at any rate, he already has bought).

The *Post*'s early losses don't in the least dissuade him from his plan to build an American tabloid newspaper empire. Wherever there's a second paper—an imperiled second paper—he's buying or trying to buy it. He considers launching a morning competitor against the *New York Daily News* which he'd call the *Daily Sun*. He tries, in 1982, for the *Courier Express* in Buffalo, but the unions rebuff him (and the paper closes—"We voted to die with dignity," says one reporter). At the end of 1982, he buys the *Boston Herald American*, the also-ran against the dominant, establishment *Boston Globe*. In 1983, in Chicago, historically one of the greatest newspaper cities in the world—the setting of Ben Hecht and Charles MacArthur's classic newspaper farce *The Front Page*—he buys the *Sun-Times*.

His is a classic and anachronistic newspaper business plan: With boldness, sassiness, sexiness, and wild promotions, he'll make big gains against the dominant paper. Because the tabloid style of journalism requires a much smaller investment than the starchy, information-heavy papers, it ought to be a no-lose formula.

Except he loses. Each of his American tabloids, save the *Post*, is a kind of listless version of a true Murdoch paper. Stories are short; there are more pictures, there is more crime coverage (murder and rape), but there isn't the tabloid joie de vivre. He is betwixt and between—and disengaged. American newspapers aren't any fun. Also, they don't make money.

At least he understands the basic issue: Advertisers want to reach an aspirational middle class, and such a middle class reads a paper above its station. "Everybody in this country wants to get ahead, get a piece of the action," he will tell biographer William Shawcross. "That's the fundamental difference between the Old World and the New World. There's not the self-improvement ethic in England that there is in this country."

And yet, even with this unprepossessing American experience, he remains committed to the tabloid model, unable really to see beyond it, believing that the visceral impact of tabloidism has to prevail—and, indeed, it finally will, on the Fox network and on Fox News.

Murdoch's tabloid stars are, in some striking co-dependency, extraordinarily loyal to him—and he to them. This may be because there is really nowhere else to do what they do than to do it for Rupert—no other well-paid corporate outlet for their kind of behavior—and because he relies on them to do what he personally, and temperamentally, can't do. They're his weapon, his amusement, his idea of romance. His personal *fuck you*.

In the media business, which more and more strives for respectability, many of his favorites border on the unemployable. They exist only because he lets them exist. They get to be employed by a public company only because his control of the public company is so sui generis. These are Rupert's reprobates.

As Murdoch first starts to think about pursuing the *Wall Street Journal* in late 2005, Rebekah Wade, the thirty-seven-year-old editor of the *Sun*—still Murdoch's largest and most profitable publication—is sitting in a jail cell in South London. She was out the night before with Murdoch at a birthday party for his son-in-law, Matthew Freud, who is one of Wade's close friends. After leaving Freud and Elisabeth Murdoch's home in Notting Hill, Wade—who's been running a campaign in the *Sun* against domestic violence—got into a drunken brawl with her husband, Ross Kemp, an actor who plays a tough guy on Britain's most popular soap, *EastEnders*. At 4:00 A.M., the terrified husband—more than twice the size of his wife—calls the cops, who arrive at their Battersea home to find him with a busted lip. Wade is arrested and fingerprinted and gives a DNA sample before being thrown in a cell for eight hours to sleep it off, even as Murdoch sits waiting for her at News International's Wapping headquarters for their 8:00 A.M. breakfast meeting. It's the biggest story in the other British tabloids for more than a week. Wade continues to be one of Murdoch's favorite editors and he frequently discusses moving her into the executive ranks of the company.

And Richard Johnson. Not only does he not lose his job because of the "Page Six" bribery scandal, but in some sense the bribery business actually seems to confirm Johnson's status for Murdoch as an old-time, walk-on-the-wild-side, dangerous, rule-bucking, proudly cynical newspaperman.

At Fox News, Bill O'Reilly, flouting News Corp.'s own rules on sexual harassment, is caught up in a lawsuit that—complete with phone transcripts—accuses him of brutal sexual stalking and bullying. It's handled as an internal matter.

And then there is, in some long-running act of newspaper sentimentality, Steve Dunleavy at the *Post*. There is almost no contemporary explanation for him. He exists so much outside of the norm that no one tries explaining him. He's just part of the News Corp. background—that's in some sense his real function: to demonstrate that News Corp. is unique, proudly unreconstructed, can't be brought to heel. Besides his pompadour, which even after weeklong binges still manages to be upstanding, Dunleavy is most famous for drinking like . . . well, Dunleavy.

Dunleavy stories, whether true or not, are part of News Corp.'s identity. Such as: He was once having sex with an (insert Norwegian heiress, "*Post* cub reporter," "redheaded temptress," "political source" here) in a back alley on a cold winter's night when a snowplow ran over his foot and Dunleavy didn't notice. (When Pete Hamill, an old-school New York journalist, was told about the supposed accident, he responded: "Was it his writing foot?") And another: A fresh-faced copy kid shows up for work early at the *Post*'s offices on Sixth Avenue and finds Dunleavy in his usual position, passed out under his desk. The problem is, nobody's told the copy kid that this is just the way it is. So the copy kid rings 911 for an ambulance. The paramedics say, "Don't worry about it. It's just Dunleavy."

Dunleavy may be the oldest journalist on any payroll in the city who still turns out for the big crime—and no matter how many drinks he's consumed that day, whether a sip of orange juice or twenty vodka tonics, his stories never really make any sense.

Alcohol and tabloids go together. (Murdoch once banned alcohol from the premises in London, but he nevertheless can sometimes seem in awe of great drunks.) In a city where overdrinking has become a grievous gaucherie, it's possible to find *New York Post* editor Col Allan swishing tomato juice at Langan's in the afternoon before he commences an evening of drinking. When Allan first came to New York in 2001—brought to the *Post* by Lachlan—he was preceded by stories of pissing in the sink at the *Daily Telegraph*. (These stories seemed partly designed to horrify New Yorkers.) The alcohol is accompanied by temper tantrums and strip joints.

Lack of restraint and decorum is also Allan's newsroom management style. Not only is he a legendary screamer—the morning news meeting is a daily and by now ritualistic drama of reporters and editors having the shit screamed out of them—he's a deeply disorganized one. This disorganization, however, facilitates a tabloid effect because there is no reasonable and procedural process for gathering the news. Hence, Allan is the one who is left to dictate what the news is going to be that day. Which sometimes backfires. For instance, blotto during the 2004 Super Bowl, Allan failed to appreciate the importance (even the tabloid importance) of Janet Jackson's notorious public breast baring—and the next day's headline was about Super Bowl advertisements.

Still, it is exactly this lack of process, or lack of traditional news sense, that has made Allan in News Corp. parlance and context a "genius." Having no news, he can take a press release or AP wire story of no consequence and package it with a great headline and terrific picture into a perfect tabloid crisis. In Australia, a minor upturn in the census figures for unwed mothers became NATION OF BASTARDS. For a pro forma report about lower test scores in schools, Allan singled out a local high school class and, over its picture, slapped the headline THE CLASS THAT FAILED US. At the *Post*, France, Germany, Russia, and Belgium voting against the UN Iraq War resolution became THE AXIS OF WEASELS. James Baker and Lee Hamilton, who chaired the Iraq Study Group, became SURRENDER MONKEYS.

The other part of his genius, of course, is his devotion to Murdoch. (One day, according to News Corp. legend, Allan and Roy "Rocky" Miller—who will retire in 2008 after forty-seven years at News Corp.—were sailing with Murdoch, and Murdoch took a sensitive phone call. Murdoch cupped the phone and said to his boys, "Would you mind . . . ?" Naturally, they both jumped into the water, then swam in circles until Murdoch invited them back on board.)

The point, distinct in corporate America, is about the kind of flamboyance that makes for shameless and sensational journalism, or about having people who know they exist only at the boss's sufferance (he'll tolerate them and nobody else will)—or, perhaps most of all, about his own personal amusement.

A News Corp. executive in London sits next to Murdoch at a dinner and, boldly, brings up the subject of Rebekah Wade, whose continuing rise in the company is confounding to other more disciplined players. He explains fondly, "She's a larrikin," the Australianism for a much-loved rogue.

Perhaps most vividly, in the larrikin regard, there's Judith Regan—the ultimate News Corp. product who, in fact, is sacrificed in part for the *Wall Street Journal.*

She may be the only American Murdoch has ever met who instinctively got the Australian and English tabloid thing—that mix of combativeness, extremism, sexuality (or not sexuality so much as dirty talk), and sanctimony. If there were a Pulitzer Prize for tabloidism, Judith Regan would have certainly gotten it.

Her abrupt end at News Corp. comes in December 2006, not long after Murdoch's second meeting with Richard Zannino. The scandal that is blowing up around her—the kind of scandal that Murdoch almost never runs from—is something that everybody else in the company (just as anybody in any company would) wants to rid themselves of as quickly as possible. Only Murdoch himself might be able to save her—and in the past, he would have. He's saved her many times.

He hesitates here, and then folds. He is choosing the *Wall Street Journal* over the ultimate tabloid confection—the staged confession of O. J. Simpson in book and television form.

There was a concerted and telling effort at News Corp. to disappear Judith, or at least the Judith of Murdoch's affections. To distance Rupert from her. In the telling, she was just an HR problem. The greater truth was that she was not just a News Corp. employee but its creation. Not just unemployable anywhere else, but Rupert's pet. Not just his pet, but an example to him of what a journalist should be—the last of the tabloid originals, a throwback, full of piss and vinegar, larger than life.

Book people, no matter that he owns one of the world's largest book publishers, put Murdoch into a sour and impatient mood. Their sensibility is not just different from his but the sensibility he is most against—snobbish, literal, phlegmatic, establishment.

Judith Regan, however, is a working-class Irish-Italian from Long Island, who acquired poise at Vassar and then, in some downwardly mobile twist, went to work for the *National Enquirer*. She had a child without getting married (well before this was respectable) by a man who'd shortly end up in prison for dealing drugs. Needing a more stable life than following tabloid stories, she got a part-time job at Pocket Books, one of the Simon and Schuster paperback imprints, where, spectacularly, and almost immediately, she started to produce bestsellers, and where she became in no time at all a fabulous irritant to the book publishing business. Hers was a level of vulgarity and fury perhaps never before seen in the book world. Murdoch, who met her in early 1993, took to her right away—and hired her, not least of all, to annoy the people at HarperCollins. With Murdoch's protection, she not only got away with her obscene, grotesque, often funny, not just politically incorrect but reprehensible, not necessarily truthful monologues (definitely monologues—she doesn't really engage in conventional conversation) but expanded their range and frequency.

What she communicates most forcefully, and what Murdoch has always found so appealing, is that she both hates authority and loves power.

The proximate cause of why she is fired in late 2006 involves charges that she made anti-Semitic comments to a News Corp. lawyer, but the truth is, she regularly squared off against myriad ethnicities, sexual orientations, genders (she actually manages to be both anti-women and anti-men). Murdoch either loved her bilious, vitriolic, manic, gynecological, anti-everybody-and-every-propriety conversation or loved the effect it had on everybody else at News Corp. who had to put up with it. Her inappropriateness was, in a sense, a demonstration of his power.

Indeed, she was the perfect demonstration that inside News Corp., if you have Murdoch's nod, you have vast powers of your own. It's quite impossible to imagine her fantastic and improbable career being possible without someone exactly like Murdoch in her corner.

A year before her final tumble out of favor, in a state of pique and hubris notable even for her, she made the unilateral decision to up and relocate her publishing company, Regan Books—a division of Regan Media, itself a division of HarperCollins, a division of News Corp.—to Los Angeles from New York, a move the *New York Times* found significant enough for a front-page story. In the *Times'* view, Judith's moving her boutique publishing imprint to Los Angeles was possibly a harbinger of a major shift in the media landscape (the view inside HarperCollins and News Corp. was, as always, substantial marveling and vexation at her uncanny publicity talents).

But more to the point, one the *Times* entirely missed: She had become anathema at HarperCollins headquarters in New York— not just a reviled figure but a mocked one—and had to get out.

In the tumble of ethics charges surrounding Bernard Kerik, former New York City police commissioner and business partner of former mayor Rudy Giuliani, when he was nominated by President Bush to be homeland security chief in December 2004, it emerged that Judith was one of his two mistresses (he was cheating on his wife with Judith, but on Judith with another mistress), trysting with him in a special Ground Zero apartment and working out at the gym together. It was part of her tough-guy thing: Men are brutes, so go with the most brutish of them. She herself had a thing for cops and underworld types—as tabloid people usually do—talking often, and not necessarily in an amusing way, about having her former husband bumped off. When Judith lost a cell phone at the office, she had Kerik send out New York City police to the homes of Regan Books employees whom she suspected of snatching the phone.

The Kerik debacle officially made Judith a tabloid figure herself. There was the paranoid part: She'd threatened the unfaithful Kerik with what she had on him, then began accusing people, including News Corp. people, of threatening her because of the way she might hurt Giuliani's presidential chances. (After she is fired, this becomes the central charge she levels against News Corp. in a $100 million lawsuit—it canned her to protect Rudy.)

"Judith" became, as much to News Corp. insiders as to anyone else, a punch line.

And yet her corporate bad behavior (or otherwise self-destructive behavior) continued to hold the interest of the boss.

Part of the tortured explanation at News Corp. about how the O. J. affair happened involves separating Rupert—who is now said to have soured on her earlier, during the Kerik affair—from Judith. Rupert, News Corp. people say, started to regard her as a "really embarrassing aunt you keep at a distance."

"He did not seek out or relish her company," is the official, dyspeptic status report on their relationship. Indeed, Murdoch will later maintain he spoke to her only "once every couple of years."

And yet Rupert personally approved the O. J. deal.

Indeed, he would: O. J. Simpson confessing, or even seeming to confess, to two of the world's most famous murders would be one of the greatest tabloid stories ever told.

The Fox network took on the O. J. project with Judith as its central figure—if she wasn't exactly a television celebrity, she was, after all, a News Corp. celebrity—without dissent from anyone at the network or at News Corp., and, in fact, with apparent approval from News Corp. COO Peter Chernin. The appetite for both O. J. and television confessions being constant, Fox had every right to expect that an O. J. confession might do some of the biggest numbers of the year.

The furor over the book and show erupted in the week before Thanksgiving. Murdoch was at his ranch in Australia when the announcement of the book and the interview was made on November 14, 2006. Gary Ginsberg was on his way back from Australia. By the time Ginsberg landed, his BlackBerry was going crazy.

Arguably, the tabloid landscape in America had suddenly shifted.

O. J., who had begun the present tabloid epoch, was in a sense ending it, causing a sudden, mass reversion to a shocked-and-appalled bourgeoisie sensibility. Judith's market value took a direct hit.

While this was evident to Ginsberg, it was not yet evident to Judith—or, for that matter, yet to Murdoch. She continued to work the publicity levers. This was going to be the biggest on-air interview since Michael Jackson confessed to sleeping with little boys. Potentially way bigger. Meanwhile, O.J.'s victims' families—the Browns and the Goldmans, astute media practitioners—went into full attack mode.

Fox affiliates began to react, expressing distaste and reluctance to air the two-part interview.

What's more, Fox News, in an almost insurmountable internal political complication for Judith, turned its vaunted media venom on the project. The possible reasons for this slap were varied: tensions between Fox News chief Roger Ailes and News Corp. COO Peter Chernin; an effort to distance Fox News, with its version of heartland moralism, from the Fox network (always a dicey branding issue), with its outréness; or Ailes' antipathy to Regan—he'd moved her short-lived talk show off the air. It's also worth noting that Ailes, among the most formidable people in modern media, had, after his marriage ended in the nineties, once gone on a date with Judith, describing it ever after as "the scariest three hours of my life."

In some sense, News Corp. had joined the rest of the American media in being against Judith. Murdoch was her only holdout. And it is not at all unlikely that he might have continued to protect her were it not for knowing that soon the battle for Dow Jones would begin and the last thing he needed was to be harboring the woman who was trying to give O. J. Simpson blood money.

And then there occurred the raging, loaded, fraught, contemptuous, abusive, allegedly anti-Semitic conversation—this one with Mark Jackson, the HarperCollins lawyer. They must have been waiting for it, could have counted on it like the sun rising—Judith going bananas.

When she did, the cooler corporate heads at News Corp. went to Murdoch—one can only imagine with what satisfaction—and, finally, he ended it.

After she's fired, Judith begins telling friends that something has changed at News Corp. That it isn't the same company anymore. Rupert himself has changed. The treatment he received for his prostate cancer several years ago has made him soft. And Wendi Murdoch is part of the problem. It's Wendi's craving for respectability that has made Rupert weak. She's . . . liberal! Peter Chernin is a Democrat! Gary Ginsberg worked for Clinton! Rupert is forsaking his tabloid heart in the quest for mainstream, yuppie respectability. The greatest media company of the age has become like any other—pathetically concerned about what people think.

Of course, there might be something to this.

Still, in the aftermath of all this, it is Judith who is left representing the psychopathology of the media—its shameless self-promoters, so without a moral center, so motivated by their own grandiosity and need for attention that they have bankrupted the culture—not Murdoch.

There is one other not insignificant point in the tension between Murdoch's tabloidism and other more elite, if you will, kinds of journalism: How much does he realize, or accept, the difference?

The *Australian*, his respectable, mostly money-losing 1964 start-up—it would eventually make a slight profit—is thought by many to be the best paper in Australia. But in lots of ways it has been a dogged act of good behavior, churchgoing rectitude—a kind of philanthropy. His stated mission, from the beginning, was to create a paper that his father would have been proud of. Then, along the way, it turned into something to deflect his mother's disapproval. Along the way too, it has clearly become a personal point of pride—and part of the proof offered to the Dow Jones share-holders that he can, indeed, do "serious" journalism. But it is a calculated anomaly—and not a model that he has chosen to repeat.

The *Times* of London is the other example of Murdoch on a higher plane. The *Times* is usually crisp and straightforward—without affect, and without much personality. It's utilitarian. What he seems to have no feeling for, or a resistance to, is a high-end sensibility—the conceits, the snobberies, the look and feel, and the attention to detail that help create a more articulated, nuanced, and exclusive voice.

But perhaps the best example of his stubborn resistance to a select sensibility, to the upper middle brow, was his plan, in 1994, to have his Fox network create a show that would compete with *60 Minutes,* CBS's enduring, hoary, high-end Sunday news show. The idea here was not just to try to steal a piece of a lucrative market—*60 Minutes* had one of the highest advertising rates in television—but to help raise the cachet of the Fox Network. For this exercise in high-end programming, he personally chose as the co-anchors former *Sunday Times* editor Andrew Neil and . . . Judith Regan.

This colossal or farcical disconnect—the angry and foul-mouthed diva moderating a new show for the high-minded—might suggest that he really doesn't get the aesthetic fine points. Or, even more tellingly, that he suspected that the high-end audience really wants, given its druthers, an in-your-face option.

The show died, after nearly a year of preparation, under the weight of the genre mix-up—which had the additional virtue of helping him see that he ought not to try to play on the high end but to continue to pit himself directly against it.

**MAY 23, 2007**

Murdoch ultimately sees the distinction between what he does and what the elites of journalism do as not so much about journalism as about turf. The elites, so-called, have a good thing going, a monopoly of their own, and they don't want to let him in. So the way to keep him out is to say he doesn't have the stuff, doesn't know how to do the job, will ruin the neighborhood.

He isn't admitting to anybody that the whole mess with Richard Johnson and "Page Six" is just adding fuel to the fire—he is made of sterner stuff than that; he doesn't cut and run—but the truth is, he's pretty sick about it. The Bancrofts know nothing about him; he suspects that none of them has even ever read the *Post*. But he is sure they all know now about whatever it is that Jared Paul Stern and Ian Spiegelman are saying. And, indeed, if any of the Bancrofts have any contact with people at Dow Jones—and anyone at the *Journal* who has the wherewithal to reach out to the Bancrofts is doing so—they are now getting the "Page Six" story (and all the other stories about the "Page Six" story) e-mailed to them.

Before this, the Bancrofts may only have assumed Murdoch is some helluva piece of work, but now they have proof. You can't get slimier than "Page Six"; you can't find someone who runs a slimier organization than Rupert Murdoch.

Indeed, family members will report that Pulitzer Prize–winning reporter James Bandler turned up at their house to lobby them to say no to Murdoch. Bandler accidentally left a "pitch book"—outlining Murdoch's sliminess and all the reasons why the Bancrofts shouldn't sell—on the lawn of one of the family members' homes.

Murdoch begins to feel the momentum recede—he really might not get Dow Jones.

What he does not know is that Lisa Steele has been moving away from her emphasis on liberal morality and focusing on, well, business.

Steele, fifty-eight, a liberal New England aristocrat (in 1996, *Forbes* named her mother, Jane Bancroft Cook, as the wealthiest woman in Massachusetts) living outside of Burlington, Vermont (an alternative-lifestyle capital), and running a "sustainable and socially conscious redevelopment company," is the Bancroft family member who, by nature, is most repelled by the very idea of Murdoch.

It is her family—the Cook branch—that has been most unwavering in its belief in Dow Jones. While others sold down as much of their shares as possible, she and her sisters held.

On May 14, there was a conference call that Mike Elefante had set up involving him, the three family board members, and Michael Costa from Merrill. It was to be a run-through on Costa's part for the presentation he was going to give to the whole family on the twenty-third. The mood before the call was of a relative level of superiority. If they were in a certain maelstrom, they were getting used to it—whatever the pressures, the decision was theirs, the family's, to make when they made it, after the facts were in. Even Michael Elefante—more impatient than he knew he should be with the more difficult family members—still felt this would be a long process of weighing many factors before arriving at a considered decision.

But it was Mike Costa—affable, reassuring, without airs, not someone you'd expect to say anything profound—who changed the mood. Costa's main point was that the combination of Thomson and Reuters removed the two bidders who might—just might—have reached Murdoch's $60 range. And, in Costa's estimation, that left nobody else.

What's more, Costa felt—and Merrill was working the numbers—that Thomson-Reuters materially changed the business environment for an independent Dow Jones. There followed, then, a bit of discussion about Murdoch's letter—these so-called editorial protections he was bringing up.

Two days later, Steele, along with Chris Bancroft, Leslie Hill, and Elefante teleconferenced into the Dow Jones board meeting where Clare Hart, who ran the newswires and digital business, spoke. Hart's presentation too was unexpectedly grim. Thomson-

Reuters had turned everything upside down. The entire basis of Dow Jones' profitability was, in essence, compromised. Its business would be under relentless competitive pressures.

Throughout the next week, Elefante and Steele end up speaking frequently with each other. Elefante knew where Steele (and, in turn, her sisters Martha Robes and Jean Stevenson) was going.

At the same time, Steele was having mournful conversations with Peter Kann. He was certainly against selling, but he understood, or said he did. They go back too long for him not to. The sense of a shift in Steele's views make them all talk about the editorial-protections stuff—it was something for Steele to hold on to. Kann demurred about what he thought Murdoch's word might be worth.

Everybody's at the Bostonian Hotel for the family meeting on the twenty-third (except for Chris Bancroft and Bill Cox Jr., who says he's fed up with these people). The atmosphere is tense— although the overriding sense is that the family still remains opposed to Murdoch, there's a feeling of deeply divided agendas, of loyalists and of potential betrayers of the family trust. They're all asked to sign confidentiality agreements. (Indeed, Leslie Hill accuses Billy Cox of being the source of leaks from their meetings—most of all to the *Journal* itself.) Mike Costa is there. So is Josh Cammaker from Wachtell, Lipton.

Elefante opens the meeting with a five-minute talk in which he says he's changed his position: Even if he doesn't personally want the company to lose its independence, it's time to explore a sale, if not to Murdoch, then to somebody. With the Reuters-Thomson deal, that's the only reasonable fiduciary view. Lisa Steele also reverses her position: Her branch of the family simply lacks the "appetite for risk" that an independent Dow Jones would require. And, especially, if it is possible to sell the company but ensure some measure of protection for the editorial integrity, well, then that's what they ought to be thinking about.

Cammaker is delegated to draft a statement about the family's current wishes. Still, nobody calls or writes Murdoch—who is nearly beside himself with worry and a sense of lost opportunity, and even belated fury at "Page Six" and Richard Johnson and Col Allan.

The next day, the *Journal* goes with this: "An influential member of the family that controls Dow Jones & Co. said he opposes selling the company to Rupert Murdoch's News Corp. for fear such a step would endanger the *Wall Street Journal*'s independence. 'Why would I risk that?' said Christopher Bancroft, who also is a Dow Jones director, in his first public comments about News Corp.'s $5 billion bid. 'I'm open to any situation that benefits the *Wall Street Journal* and Dow Jones and its shareholders. At the moment, I don't see anything that would do that.'"

Murdoch's worry about the deal and his irritation with his tabloid reporters' inability to keep their noses clean will result, for the first time in News Corp.'s history, in the implementation of an ethics test for his reporters (granted, if you don't pass it, you just keep taking it until you do), and the very counterintuitive practice of gossip reporters signing confidentiality agreements about their work as gossip reporters.

# NINE

# Who's the Boss?

A key reason the *Wall Street Journal* has achieved such lofty standing is that it has not really had any active input, much less interference, from its proprietors for seventy-five years. Independence, along with a good budget, tends to make for quality journalism. The reason Murdoch's papers don't get awards or respect (at least from journalists who don't work for him) is that he's as involved a proprietor as any.

The hatred of Murdoch by the great population of journalists who don't work for him is stoked by many things, but underlying all these things—and forming the real, gut-level antipathy for him in the newsroom at the *Wall Street Journal,* a sense of the end of the world—is the structural difference that he actually runs his newsrooms. If you work for Rupert, you do his bidding. You submit to Rupert. He gets his newspapers wherever he is in the world, gets out his red pen—just like his father before him—and puts a cross through stories that shouldn't have run, circles a photo and draws an arrow to show where it should have been placed, notes a head-line that should have been two lines rather than one, and so on.

He denies that he interferes—sort of (he doesn't actually want people to think he's not involved). The people around him, his executives and his editors, defending their own bona fides, deny this categorically. This—such denials about interference—is the artifice that Murdoch and his people believe everybody is practic-ing. They actually don't accept that a hands-off structure truly exists anywhere. And if it does exist, then something has gone rad-ically amiss—and you've a fool for an owner.

From his view—and understand that, except for his brief internship with Beaverbrook, he has only ever worked for himself; he has no idea, really, how other journalistic organizations func-tion—it would be absurd and irresponsible for him *not* to run his papers.


**MAY 31, 2007**

As the *Wall Street Journal* deal progresses in slow motion, all the ritualistic behavior—the wooing, the assurances regarding edito-rial independence—on Rupert Murdoch's part ought to be under-stood not necessarily as farce, but certainly as Kabuki. And yet the earnest Bancrofts respond earnestly.

This is partly a sense of the turn in mood—if Lisa Steele and her sisters are going for the deal, and carrying Michael Elefante with them, that's a major shift—but there is an additional purpose-ful feeling. A kind of *Let's hear what the man has to say.*

While Murdoch would gladly lead the Bancrofts into exactly the kind of trap they are walking into—showing their hand before the other guy shows his, revealing their intentions well before it is necessary to reveal them—the Bancrofts are really going out of their way to be naifs and victims. Selling a company, or not selling a company, is a highly codified drama in which a buyer or seller ultimately bests the other by their knowledge of the nuance of the process. It's balletic. And the Bancrofts are now on the verge of committing some ghastly, and mortal, ritual missteps.

How is this happening? True, Michael Elefante has little idea what he's doing when it comes to mergers and acquisitions, but that's why he's hired Wachtell, Lipton, the most hallowed M&A firm in the country. The family's advisors, Merrill Lynch along with Wachtell, should have told the family that the moment they start negotiating on editorial agreements they won't get a price higher than $60—because they are effectively telling Murdoch they're willing to do this deal for the editorial protections.

But the problem is . . . well, the Wachtell and Merrill people won't say it's the most frustrating deal they've *ever* done, but it's close. So frustrating that they just want to get the deal done—get their fee and get out. If the client won't acknowledge the rituals in a highly ritualized situation . . . if people don't listen, if they can't listen no matter how you explain . . . well, fuck it.

It's Josh Cammaker who has to put this ungodly mishmash of wishfulness and good intentions into some sort of statement.

Meanwhile, the *Journal* itself isn't helping. A good part of the family's information is coming from the paper itself. It's coming from reporters who are calling up whatever individual members of the family they can get on the phone and sharing with them the latest gossip they've heard—and, in return, hoping for family gossip—which is then passed from one family member to another. Or they're reading it in the paper itself—the *Journal* is churning out all manner of wacky stuff coming from inside the family (the wackier the family member, the more likely it is he or she is talking to reporters, most likely reporters from the *Journal*).

Indeed, from reading the *Journal* the Bancroft family comes to believe that, in fact, it is more than likely *not* selling the company—at least not to Murdoch. On May 31, the paper, reflecting the anybody-but-Murdoch view sweeping the newsroom, reports the possibility that Dow Jones will be sold at a lower price to an alternative buyer because the family hates him so much. (That same day, Billy Cox sends an e-mail, which he leaks to the *Journal*, accusing family members of leaving him out of the process, and saying they don't have "the foggiest idea what is going on." Murdoch, he adds, is the best person to sell to.)

The three family members along with Michael Elefante go into the May 31 Dow Jones board meeting believing that the Bancrofts are in control of the process. They'll meet with Murdoch and solicit his views on editorial protections, and to boot they'll begin discussions with other possible buyers. Then they'll weigh their options. What could be more reasonable?

The board, waiting now for nearly a month to hear from the family, has remained in its disinterested pose—that is, *It's the controlling shareholder's duty to advise us of its desires.* But as the meeting begins—most participants are connected by telephone, which compounds the sense of confusion—the mood gradually shifts from disinterest to concern to incomprehension.

Elefante begins by reading the Josh Cammaker–drafted statement that the family wishes to release. It says that the Bancrofts want to explore alternatives with regard to the future of Dow Jones and, at the same time, meet with Murdoch to discuss his ideas about protecting the editorial freedom of the paper.

There is a painful irony here, because reporters from the *Journal* are at that moment, in an exercise of editorial freedom or subversion, receiving what seem to be virtually real-time reports from the board meeting. Elefante, who has begun to regard the *Journal* staff as yet another pressure group lobbying his clients against a sale, will wonder later if a *Journal* reporter isn't surreptitiously listening in on the call. Indeed, the Dow Jones board will later consider whether to discuss an investigation into the leak, but it decides in light of the Hewlett-Packard scandal—wherein members of the HP board authorized phone taps—to grin and bear their own leaker.

Various members of the board now try to clarify what they've heard. The Bancroft statement, they begin to realize, goes too far.

It opens the door to *all* discussions. It's saying, *Yeah, we're for sale to the highest bidder*—when, in all likelihood, the highest bidder has already bid. The only leverage they have with the highest bidder is him thinking there might be another bid. If you make it clear that there isn't, and they've already been advised that without Reuters or Thomson there probably isn't . . . *Shit.*

There's a sudden moment of disarray—which is duly reported in the *Journal*—in which the board does not know what to do or what's about to happen (or what has *just* happened). Peter McPherson asks the Bancroft representatives to drop off the call while the rest of the board discusses the implications of the Bancroft family statement. Michael Elefante objects, arguing that there is no reason for the family not to participate. Dick Beattie, representing the board, argues that the board, in this instance, may have different fiduciary duties than the family does. The family representatives begrudgingly agree and accept their time-out.

The board conversation is basically, *How can these people not know what they're doing? Are they so hopeless? What are Wachtell and Merrill doing? How can they be so hopeless?* The board consensus is that the family should be asked to withdraw this statement.

When the family comes back on the speakerphone, Chris Bancroft says, in effect, wait a minute, the family didn't mean to say that the company was for sale.

Dick Beattie says . . . *Ahhh . . . Um.* He's just at that moment looking at the *Journal* Web site and . . . *Ahem* . . . the family's statement has already been posted by the *Journal* reporters who are eavesdropping on the call. (The *Journal* reporters who have posted the story will subsequently report the fact of the post.)

Murdoch is thus alerted to the sea change in the family's views—and to the potential success of his editorial integrity gambit—by the very publication he intends to buy. Indeed, the family has opened the door to eliminating any other potential bidders—Murdoch, who has been working the phones and feeling out all the other potential bidders, is sure there won't be any—and to certifying him as a reasonable editorial steward.

That's the beauty of an editorial-protections plan—it commits them so much more than it commits him.

How can they not know this?

## IT'S HIS NEWS

It was Murdoch's takeover of the *Times* of London—for which he made similar promises of editorial protections—that turned him from a vulgarian operating at the margins of the business into, well, a threat to truth.

The transformation of the paper is an event that is still bitterly contested, in which who did what to whom, who was righteous and who not, and what has been lost and what saved are still, more than twenty-five years later, touchy matters.

The anti-Murdoch argument is that he took an upmarket paper famous for its probity, detail, and specialized focus on matters of policy and government, with long-practiced standards and traditions of fairness, restraint, expertise, and impartiality, and transformed it into a middle-market paper expedient about its coverage and its quality controls, casual about its areas of expertise, and willing to sacrifice the attention to detail sought by a limited group for the general-interest superficiality sought by a larger audience. All true enough.

Murdoch himself argues that between 1981, when he bought the money-losing paper of record for the establishment, and now, the transformation that has occurred at the *Times* simply mirrors what's happened in the news business overall. General-interest news outlets that once maintained a strict, hierarchical sense of news have—in the face of competition from specialty outlets and in an effort to attract a wider, often younger or more female demographic—embraced a softer, more feature-oriented idea of what's important. And sure enough, that broadening and softening could just as easily define the transformation of, for starters, *Time* magazine and the *New York Times*.

Not to mention that Murdoch has turned a twenty-four-page broadsheet selling not much more than 200,000 copies a day into a 120-page tabloid selling 700,000 copies a day.

But it is not just that such a transformation occurred, and it is not just the nature of the transformation, but that he bullied it into being. In fact, he carried it out as something of a jihad against *Times* people themselves—anyone who represented the older order was part of the problem. The transformation was a statement about who he was and who they were. Of what he wanted and what they'd have to become—or get out.

He blames the journalists who worked at the paper for not knowing that they had to change—for resisting his program of change. The way he sees it, he is strong, direct, practical, and strategically deploying his own money; journalists, given their natural inclinations, are weak, self-indulgent, and, given the opportunity, absolutely sanguine about wasting his money.

The proof of their fundamental weakness and incompetence is that if they had been doing their job right, he wouldn't own them—and be doing their job for them. Murdoch sees journalists mostly as necessary functionaries who don't get the big picture.

In his view, there are two kinds of reporters: the ones who acknowledge their limited range and repertoire—few, after all, know all that much about the complicated businesses that employ them—and accede to his direction, and the ones who *think* they know, and who believe in their own importance and righteousness. The former are skilled craftsmen—Murdoch accepts what they do as a useful trade; the latter, in the Murdoch view, see themselves, delusionally, as intellectuals, as arbiters of right and worth. The former are beholden; the latter believe—again, delusionally—that they are independent from their proprietor. The former have no pretense—they know they're hacks; the latter crave respectability (that respectability is, in part, earned by hating him).

This is, for him, the fatal weakness of papers such as the *Journal* and the *New York Times*—that they are fundamentally about respectability rather than about the needs of their readers and their proprietors.

And so, Harry Evans. Evans, who was promoted by Murdoch from the editorship of the more successful *Sunday Times* to the editorship of the more prestigious daily *Times,* may have done more damage to Murdoch's reputation than anybody else. First, he's an elegant and trenchant writer, and in 1983 when his book *Good Times, Bad Times,* with its portrait of Murdoch as a modern monster, was published, Evans was the most famous journalist in Britain. It was the most respected newspaperman of the age against the most loathed proprietor of the age (or if he wasn't quite yet the most loathed, Evans would help make him so).

Murdoch may have started with a misguided smidgen of PR thinking along the lines of, *Get Harry Evans to run the* Times *and the furor over my having bought the* Times *will be somewhat allayed.* Just as likely, though, it was a calculation that by moving Evans out of the *Sunday Times* editor's slot, he was putting all his editors' chairs in motion, giving him a fluid situation to mess with.

The structure for editorial protections that Murdoch accepted when he bought the Times Newspapers, and which he almost immediately, publicly, and shamelessly subverted and ignored, is the precise structure that he offers the Bancrofts. And the one that they accept pathetically, stupidly, guilelessly, desperately, moronically.

The Evans book could not have been more stark. Beyond who is the bigger prima donna, Harry or Rupert, the book's message was clear: Murdoch will *always* have his way. It is, to him, physically painful not to have his way. Maintaining neutrality would be torture. The paper would not be a reflection of Harry Evans, it would be a reflection of Rupert Murdoch. Simple.

Murdoch partisans and Evans detractors (of which it turns out there are a lot—especially combined with the detractors of Evans' wife, Tina Brown) describe a scenario in which Evans was the spurned lover. He was infatuated with Murdoch, wanted to be in Murdoch's circle, wanted to be the favored son (even though Evans is three years older than Murdoch). He was envisioning his own ascension to entrepreneurial, managerial, and financial heaven. Having not gotten there, having not impressed Murdoch enough, Evans, in his memoir, was just expressing his great disappointment with himself. He was a wounded bird.

For Murdoch detractors and Evans partisans, Murdoch is just an out-and-out liar. A fraud. What he says he'll do, he doesn't. What he agrees to, he reneges on. He makes everybody his pawn. And he's a frightening bully, so the people who might stand up to him don't.

Certainly it's true that Murdoch manipulated his way out of the editorial agreements he made to take over the *Times*. Indeed, he obviously made the agreements with the *Times* and with the British government (as a way to avoid having to come before the Monopolies Commission) as he is making them with the Bancrofts, knowing that they are weak and unenforceable and more about other people's need for a fig leaf than about any reasonable idea of governance.

And, likely, it's also true that Evans did have grand, mogul-ish aspirations for himself. Judging from his own later transformation into an American of high social standing, and, with his wife, a consort of the rich and celebrated, Evans was, like Clay Felker, a would-be Murdoch. In fact, Evans has since rather developed a specialty as a courtier to capricious billionaires, having gone to work for Si Newhouse, who owns Condé Nast, who eventually pushed him out, and for Mort Zuckerman, the real estate magnate who owns the New York *Daily News*, who pushed him too. Similarly, his wife went to work for the movie producer Harvey Weinstein, and he pushed her. (Indeed, Tina Brown, encouraged by Harry Evans, became, in her moment astride the publishing business, almost as controversial a figure as Murdoch himself, and for many of the same reasons—she's become the product of the journalism she publishes; it's all about her.)

In hindsight, it is hard to see Evans' brush with Murdoch as much more than two alpha media figures wrestling for control. Murdoch merely had the advantage of a better business sense.

Ultimately, they both seem to have helped create each other's character: Murdoch is a brilliant and manipulative bastard; Evans is a brilliant and easily manipulated man of taste and honor.

Exercising a heavy hand as a newspaper proprietor is actually much harder than it looks. Newspeople have something like a structural talent for ignoring their owners. Newsrooms, evolving over more than 150 years of difficult and entitled proprietors, have developed an organizational model designed, in part, to maintain a distance from the actual guy in charge. In a typical structure, only the editor communicates to the owner (or, even more remotely, the editor communicates to an executive who in turn communicates to the owner). It's the editor's job to be the buffer—not so much to carry out the owner's mandates and desires, but to carry out the minimal level of the owner's mandates and desires and still keep his job.

From a newspaperman's perspective, the owner is almost invariably a lesser sort, a weak heir, a self-dramatizing buffoon, or a corporate know-nothing. Newspapermen have, classically, measured their careers not so much in terms of the news outlets they've worked for but in terms of the owners they've had: bumptious owners, crazy owners, meddlesome owners, weak owners, bureaucratic corporate owners—and, only in rare Camelot moments, fair, reasonable, responsible, appreciative, hands-off owners.

It's instructive to consider the legacies of Murdoch's three most direct owner-operator peers (each of whom he helped destroy):

Robert Maxwell, whose likely suicide by drowning in 1991, off the back of his yacht *Lady Ghislaine* as it cruised around the Canary Islands, happened just as his empire was about to implode; Conrad Black, whose trial for looting his own company was in progress during the Dow Jones battle; and Ted Turner, who made a fortune almost as great as Murdoch's but lost his company.

Maxwell owned the Mirror Group in London, which he overpaid for, and then, obsessed with doing what Murdoch did, overpaid as well for the *Daily News* in New York. Maxwell wanted to own newspapers and media outlets for many of the same reasons Murdoch wanted them—for influence, for cash flow, and because, like Murdoch, he had a chip on his shoulder and owning media was a best-revenge scenario: You had the last word. But Maxwell was an exaggerated and comic figure. A tyrant—an obese tyrant. And a needy one. All his appetites were out of control. He was, in fact, a type of proprietor that newspapermen have a secret fondness for: an aberrant being, a ridiculous figure whose excesses provide a dramatic and amusing narrative—and whom you don't have to take seriously. Maxwell confirmed what everybody knows about proprietors: They want to own, but they don't really want to pay attention.

Conrad Black, like Murdoch, emerged from a small market—provincial Canadian newspapers—looking for a larger stage in London, where he acquired the Telegraph Group. Like Murdoch, he was an inveterate right-winger, intent on retailing his conservative views—and on gaining political influence for himself. He was, in this case like Maxwell, the proprietor as comic fool: grand, dismissive, self-important, striving, humorless, full of social and political zeal ("bullying, bombastic, verbose and vain," the *Guardian* called him). And yet he would come to be, as proprietors go, an idealized, even cherished one, because he could be handled, appeased —"a benign, applauded beast," according to one British press commentator. (His idea of interference was to write famously turgid and pompous letters to the editors of his publications—for publication.) To own a newspaper, a fancy newspaper, was for him about being elevated by it, to be seen in its reflection, to have a lifestyle appropriate to it. The newspaper, and the people who worked at the paper, indulged him. Indeed, when the *Daily Telegraph* found itself going head to head with Murdoch's *Times*—with Murdoch cutting the newsstand price by half and costing the *Telegraph* 500,000 readers—Black was unable to stop being indulged (or even able to cut back on his indulgences) and began to loot the company to support his various homes and high social standing. Black, who took particular pleasure in appearing in ermine robes after being appointed to the House of Lords, had, leading to his downfall, perfectly normal human needs and weaknesses—to be liked, respected, praised. It is not clear that Murdoch—who could not be less interested in the House of Lords—does.

With CNN, Ted Turner outflanked Murdoch—he created the first truly electronic counterpart to a newspaper. Murdoch would assiduously try to buy CNN and then would eventually start Fox News to compete with it. Turner became as associated with his news operation as Murdoch is with his. A television guy, he reinvented himself as a newsman. This had never quite been done before—wherein a fundamental entertainment/distribution guy takes command of a news operation. This worried Murdoch. In the contest of media alpha proprietors—men who were directly shaping the news they owned—Murdoch finally had a doppelgänger. On the other hand, Turner was roguish, larger than life, liberal, more often than not operating at the edge of self-control. In a way, Murdoch seemed to envy Turner's charisma—particularly since even Turner's newsroom appeared enthralled by Turner. But Turner, Murdoch could also see, wanted to be liked. He was a press hound. A mascot—like Maxwell and Black, a comic figure. In some strange sense, CNN had become so strong and so successful and so branded that it was larger than Ted, so he could not interfere with it. And then, like Maxwell and Black but minus the criminal complications, he lost financial control of his company and, ultimately, of his newsroom.

Victory has allowed Murdoch to be somewhat generous in his assessments of his former enemies. When asked which newspapermen he admires, Murdoch thinks for a good thirty seconds before answering: "He's gone now, but in London I've got to say Conrad Black. He backed his editors, backed his writers, they loved him, and he pushed the paper very hard."

About Ted Turner he says: "Mike Milken said to me, 'You don't know the advantage you've got in this country. Nobody can guess what you're going to do next and that you're nuts. And there used to be two of you. That one's finished. Ted Turner.'" Murdoch bursts into laughter.

About Maxwell: He rolls his eyes.

However much each of these proprietors was personally difficult, there was a set of formalized routines that developed around them. The *Mirror* newsroom in London could deal with the corrupt, irascible, and none-too-stable Maxwell in relatively practiced fashion. It was easy to make Black happy—with praise or social cachet. It was always easy to distract Turner— most of all with more press.

But Murdoch's management style is oddly unpredictable, partly because of his spectral quality. He's almost never there—except when he is, overwhelmingly, there. Hence, when he's *not* there, he's there as a palpable absence. Given the hundreds of separate news organizations he's running (together with the hundreds of other non-news organizations) at any given time, you never know when you're on his mind; you never know when he's going to walk through your door.

What's more, he appears so often without announcement—a controlled, quiet, mostly polite (alarmingly polite) presence, suddenly involved in the details of your work. "Murdoch drifted in like a ghost," says Piers Morgan, who edited the *News of the World* for Murdoch. "Literally creeping up on us without any fanfare at all. I'd heard this was his deadliest weapon, his ability to just appear and scare the daylights out of you."

Here is a real-time report on Murdoch in the *New York Post* news-room, detailed as it occurred, sent to me minutes after it happened:

*He slips into the newsroom just after 3:00. Rupert looks exactly like any other guy in the newsroom—rolled-up blue shirtsleeves, not too fancy, slacks. And he walks top-heavy too—that way news editors have of leaning forward into their stride, on a mission. But unlike newsmen who stomp around, gesticulating loudly, abrasively, draw-ing attention to themselves—Murdoch is silent. Even his steps—not a sound. Really, nobody is noticing him.*

*He's standing behind a new reporter. Four seconds pass before the reporter feels eyes on him and turns around. I'm not sure he even knows it's Murdoch.*

*Murdoch (quietly, matter-of-factly): "Where does Richard sit?"*

*The reporter gets that it's Murdoch, stiffens, responds with some panic and confusion: "Richard who?"*

*Murdoch looks around and spots Richard—Richard Johnson, of course; there's only one "Richard" at the* Post—*at the end of the floor and walks off.*

*Murdoch quietly stops behind Johnson—and waits. Ten seconds. Richard turns from his computer and looks surprised—and Richard never looks surprised.*

*Politely, matter-of-factly, Rupert says: "Could you do me this favor?"*

*Murdoch hands Johnson something—it's an invitation to Ivanka Trump's jewelry collection launch (I check it out as soon as he leaves).*

*"I see her in the gym every day and she looks nothing like that photo you ran of her the other day."*

*Mr. M turns and walks back the way he came, down the news-room corridor, past the managing editor offices, looking at no one. And no one looking at him.*

Such appearances are reported throughout the empire. He's not there, and then he is there. He's not engaged, and then he's caught

up in the most basic details, overly focused, abrupt, nagging. Or gossiping—his habit is particularly to hang around the business section reporters looking for a tidbit, or looking to drop one. It may be
that his shyness makes it a problem for him to integrate into a situation—so he doesn't arrive and acclimatize, doesn't get the lay of
the land, the sense of the situation, but rather just begins, awk-
wardly, from his own point of reference. Not being socialized, he
just starts off on what he's thinking about. The effect of this is that
somehow everybody feels *they* have been adrift and *he* is the solid
mass.

His moods, or his mood swings, are frightening. This is not
because, like Maxwell, he can veer easily into grandiosity or petulance, but because his moods occur in a finer range—so that you
don't quite know *what* his mood is, other than to sense that his
attention and humor and purpose have rather shifted. The moods
may be subtle, but they're also intense—the moods of a relatively
inexpressive person.

Constant jet lag doesn't help. This cordial, even courtly man
can, at times, suddenly seem dangerous. Out of nowhere he can be
cranky, impatient, short. "Old Grumpy," they called him, only half
affectionately, in the office of Star TV, his Asian satellite operation.
(He's at his most jet-lagged in Asia.) He cuts you off. You know—
or suspect you know—when he's lost interest in what you're saying
(because he's a polite man, he keeps listening even through his evident distraction—causing panic in whoever is speaking to him).
What's more, he's on uppers and downers to deal with the jet lag,
which makes his glass of wine quite lethal. "He gets completely
legless, he's a real bloody two-pot screamer because he's always taking sleeping pills," says a former Australian executive who has
drunk with Murdoch at bars and in his homes around the world.

One effect of all his travel is to reduce almost everything to its
immediate moment in time. It's in front of him now and he deals
with it—giving him extraordinary decision-making reflexes. But
it also means that everything is a surface, just one dimension. He

walks into a situation and plays it as it lays. It is not really that he has a system of thinking—like a Jack Welch–style methodology or formula to impose—but rather a set of reactions.

Depending on his mood and his level of sleep deprivation, his reactions often come with prickliness, a hectoring or carping quality, a rat-a-tat-tat of complaints and put-downs and contempt. A certain piercing sense of dismissal and disappointment. You have not approximated or anticipated what is in his head at that moment, so you've failed him.

And then he is gone.

Interestingly, the result among the News Corp. faithful is often not ill will toward Murdoch, but self-doubt.

After he moved Harry Evans, in 1981, from the *Sunday Times* to the *Times,* he appointed Evans' deputy Frank Giles to the *Sunday Times* editor slot. It was obviously a matter of expediency. Giles was sixty-two—a caretaker. He was there to hold the fort and maintain some consistency while Murdoch figured out what to do in this most substantial and complicated takeover of his career.

But it was a terrible mistake. Giles' memoir, *Sundry Times,* is a horrifying portrait of upper-management cruelties, of a pervasive atmosphere of mockery and contempt, of the collapse of all newsroom ritual and propriety. You read it with a constant cringe, awash in Giles' hurt and desperation. The point, most of all, seems to be about the cost of standing your ground. Giles, an upper-class sort, was the ultimate anti-Murdoch figure—as in antimatter. The two simply couldn't exist together in the same universe. He was at Times Newspapers for more than thirty years; he came out of a tradition of watchfulness, objectivity, quiet judgment. He was, in his laconic way, as contemptuous of Murdoch as Murdoch was of him.

Here was the editor who had been promised, by force of law, his independence and who was trying to claim it.

Here was Murdoch, "intemperate and disagreeable," with his "bitter animus, stridently voiced," "deliberately seeking, through extravagance of language and extremity of views, to get a reaction or a rise," when not otherwise "non-communicative," appointing lieutenants who egged him on "in his impulsiveness and ape him in intolerance and rudeness," who were constantly engaged with him "in muttered conversation," with Murdoch's face "framed in a scowl which seemed to stop not far short of malevolence." Every memo from Murdoch, every conversation with him, was meant to disturb, undermine, unman, threaten, criticize, and harass. The portrait is all the more grim for Giles' obsessive understatement:

> It is important here, for the sake of accuracy, not to exaggerate by suggesting a perpetual state of guerrilla, or sometimes open, warfare between me in my office, on one side of the street, and Murdoch and Gerald Long [his lieutenant] in their offices on the other side, each visible to the other. Evans tells the story of how Murdoch would amuse visitors to his office by firing imaginary pistol shots at my back, clearly discernible through the big plate-glass windows across the street.

But finally, what Giles is describing is not a new plan or forceful business strategy being implemented by Murdoch and company, but instead a world without any plan at all, without any particular endgame other than the constant expression of Murdoch's "restless temperament" and the implementation of his "authoritarian management" style. Which is, in part, what led to Murdoch's biggest editorial debacle, *The Hitler Diaries,* which is among journalism's all-time greatest hoaxes. Indeed, here is an important nexus: For serious journalists, Murdoch's 1983 publication of *The Hitler Diaries* is a mortifying, inexplicable, credibility-destroying event; for Murdoch, it's just one of the cons and flimflams that happen in the ad hoc, impromptu, on-the-fly news business, so why beat yourself up about it?

The diaries were concocted in Germany by a Hitler memorabilia fetishist with the tacit participation of a journalist at Gruner

+ Jahr, one of the biggest publishers of magazines and newspapers in Germany. The diaries were offered for sale for international publication and vetted and authenticated in a slapdash process of journalistic wishfulness and giddiness. Nobody's journalistic wishfulness and giddiness was greater than Murdoch's, because he'd lucked into a great journalistic theatrical event (in Britain, Hitler sells as well as sex).

As it happens, one of Britain's greatest Hitler scholars and most respected academics, Hugh Trevor-Roper—Lord Dacre—sat on the *Times*' editorial board. Murdoch dispatched him to Hamburg to pass judgment on the diaries. Although he didn't even touch them, he gave them his imprimatur. They were duly scheduled for publication, though in a typical Murdochian this-hand-that-hand failure to communicate, the first publication was shifted from the *Times* to the *Sunday Times*. Enter Phillip Knightley, the *Sunday Times*' legendary investigative reporter—the Aussie who also worked for Rupert's father—who smelled a rat. Knightley badgered Lord Dacre, who in short order got cold feet. His hesitation, however, was communicated to the *Times* and not the *Sunday Times*—which didn't hear that its expert no longer believed the diaries were authentic until the presses were ready to roll.

This is the point at which Murdoch struck a blow against effete and wishy-washy academics and championed journalistic immediacy and swashbuckling. Or he struck a blow against truth and focused solely on profit. Anyway, he delivered the now immortal journalistic injunction: "Fuck Dacre, publish!"

And for better or worse, he didn't look back.

It is this strange combination of lack of doubt, impulsiveness, high-risk behavior, a striking capacity to ignore everyone else, and a disinclination to seek cover that makes him the central, even heroic, presence in his newsrooms. It is his great certitude that makes him, in the words of former *Sunday Times* editor Andrew

Neil, the Sun God. He's got dark, magical powers—insidious powers that border on mind control.

He's the disappointed, disapproving, impatient, but constant father. A News Corp. editorship under Murdoch is a position in which your authority, your professional grade, is always temporary—you hold it only so long as he is not in the room (or the country). As soon as he arrives, you surrender it. As soon as he arrives, everything you are doing is up for immediate review. You're reduced to a factotum. Again, not because he is so much a demanding son of a bitch, but because his is a parallel universe, which you can't intersect with, but which, through some sort of magnetic force, controls your universe.

Neil, who has had a substantial career since leaving Murdoch —and who was among Murdoch's most successful editors—has also made a secondary career of critiquing and analyzing Murdoch. He can't seem to let Murdoch go. In his book *Full Disclosure* (and in every morsel of publicity that has linked him with Murdoch since), he essentially defines himself against Murdoch—having survived Murdoch, having been in the ring with Murdoch, having on occasion stood up to Murdoch, and finally, of course, having been spit out by Murdoch makes Neil worthy. Murdoch is his whale.

From the outside looking in, the fear, or horror, of working for Rupert Murdoch is not just of dealing with a man who will, with few exceptions, always have his way, but of being part of an organization that invariably, and necessarily, acts in his interests. In other words, the very act of professional journalism is subverted by working for him. To work for him is to do his bidding, to follow his line, to execute his desires, to support his needs, to grind his axes, to act on behalf of his empire, to carry out his policies, to be a citizen of his nation-state with all its demanding nationalism.

Of course, virtually everyone within News Corp. emphatically denies that this is so.

How can this be? How can they insist upon this unreality—it's precisely this insistence that bedevils other journalists—while so blithely, so unrepentantly, so obviously propping up Rupert's version of reality?

The truth is, in many ways coming to work for Murdoch as a newsperson is not entirely a bad situation to find yourself in. First of all, it's the most successful, most thriving, and largest news organization in the world. And while it has never been the most commodious operation—it takes pride in its lack of comforts—it nevertheless allows for a pretty good standard of living. There is certainly no feeling of existential dread—*Could all this go away tomorrow?*—which is the feeling at so many other news organizations in the markets dominated by Murdoch. It is pretty easy, in the 60 percent of the market he controls in Australia, at his dominant papers and broadcast outlets in the United Kingdom, at the *Post* and at Fox News in the United States, to feel a sense of relief that you've made it to a safe harbor.

Granted, in many instances you would not actually have arrived at this safe harbor but grown up within it. Relatively speaking, News Corp. is a closed organization. It promotes from within. It's suspicious of outsiders. You're set apart at News.

You are also kept apart. Literally, in London, out at Wapping, you are sequestered. But the larger psychological apartness results from being treated with suspicion or contempt by non–News Corp. journalists. The more you commit yourself to Murdoch and News Corp., the more you are not one with the greater journalism fraternity.

Robert Thomson, the *Financial Times* editor whom Murdoch hired to run the *Times* of London, went from full-fledged member of the quality press in the highest standing to Murdoch henchman. "He is," confided a former editor of the *Times* to me, "the *Times* editor most under Murdoch's thumb, most willing to bend, to accommodate, to positively respond."

But Thomson, because he came from outside, is somewhat of an exception. News Corp. originals, because they've never much interacted with the greater journalistic fraternity, therefore never have to think of themselves as judged by it or traitors to it. It is partly this lack of interaction that creates the sense that News Corp.

people, Murdoch people, are less than top of the class, that they have fewer options—which is why they're at News Corp. and *grateful* to be there.

Jesse Angelo, the managing editor of the *New York Post,* is one of the rising stars in the News Corp. journalism firmament. He is a pridefully regarded figure at the *New York Post* in part because he went to Harvard. (Pedigree does not ordinarily exist in a Murdoch newsroom, because nobody much has one.) But, in fact, he has succeeded because he's shed Harvard—to the point where it seems incongruous that he ever went. Angelo was James Murdoch's best friend at the Trinity School in New York, with their friendship continuing at Harvard (James dropped out; Jesse tried to drop out, but his mother sent him back). Sponsored by the Murdochs, he went to the *Sun* in London as a junior reporter, then to Australia to do a stint as a reporter under Col Allan, and then to New York and "Page Six" at the *Post* before he was picked up on the *Post*'s most vaunted of sections, Business. The *Post* is a studied—and successful—working-class exercise for him. He's become of the *Post* rather than of journalism.

When I asked him, one evening after the paper had gone to bed, who his friends were among other journalists in the city (an arguable flaw among most journalists is that they tend to associate mostly with other journalists), he at first didn't seem to know what I was trying to ask. I was wondering, I said, if his Harvard association gave him access to the Harvard journalism mafia in New York (the very group that Murdoch hates most—and that hates Murdoch most). Answer: No. The elite at News Corp. must prove that they've shed any hint of elitism or, even, desire for respectability.

It is part of the character of working for Murdoch—at least if you want to be in character (and success at News Corp. demands being in character).

It's deeply tribal. (In the early years in New York, Murdoch actually tried to slightly lessen the tribalism by suggesting that News Corp. Australians might think about living somewhere other than in the apartment complexes of Roosevelt Island, in the middle of the East River.) Loyalty has to be proved over and over again. That's the job: to prove your loyalty. When Col Allan came from Australia to take over at the *New York Post*, he spent his first three months merely observing—then purged the newsroom of the people he felt were less than loyal, less than 100 percent Newsites. The company is largely run—this is most pronounced on the newspaper side of the company—by lifers, men who have no significant professional experience other than working for Murdoch.

At the CNN greenroom in New York, it is always a cocktail-party-ish affair of the city's top-tier journalists and commentators and other chattering-class grandees. There's always a current of people who know each other—who have worked together and socialized together for years. At the Fox News greenroom, a famously gritty place, the crowd tends to be made up of unknown experts, homegrown oddities (e.g., a former local judge who has become their legal expert), and eerily photogenic women wearing, even for TV, a vast amount of makeup. This is not just about sophistication versus populism, upscale versus downscale, but a fundamental aversion to the journalistic inner circle.

Roger Ailes, the Fox News chief, tells prospective talent coming from other networks that they ought to think twice about working at Fox, because they won't ever be able to go back again. (In the case of the newscaster Paula Zahn, when she left Fox for CNN, Ailes made it seem like she'd been cast out—that CNN was settling for sloppy seconds.)

And yet this is not at all to say that anybody in the news business at News Corp. regards their status as second-class. Just the opposite: It's there but for the grace of God when it comes to everybody else at other places. It's about a noncom class and an officer class, with the noncom class being the heart and soul and purpose of this man's army and the officers being parodies of themselves, sacrificing adventure for some attenuated, oppressive idea of respectability.

Journalism, when you work for Murdoch, is good sport. It takes *only* the combat seriously.

The idea of higher calling, of blah-blah responsibility, of reverential bullshit, is some class thing about trying to make the job more important than it is, and has nothing to do with making the news direct, powerful, and fun.

The effect of this, of the creation of this very clear and insular culture, is that the process itself is not open to question. The idea that someone would not understand that the organization has its interests would define someone who was not going to be part of News Corp. for very long. This is Rupert Murdoch's newsroom—wherever it is (and wherever he is). Being Rupert Murdoch's newsroom, pursuing Rupert Murdoch's interests, hitting Rupert Murdoch's enemies over the head, gives the whole place personality. Other journalists might take exception to Murdoch's heavy hand, to Murdoch using *journalism* to fight his battles, but, elementally, readers don't—in a sense, they like it; it's a clarity that they *get*.

Part of the sport, for readers and for Murdoch journalists, is understanding, accepting, and getting a kick out of the fact that the news media can still crack the whip, and that making trouble is what gives it snap—readers like to know that their paper can stick it. And that when the paper uses its power, you're part of that power—you can feel pride in that, and strength. Going after people is part of the fun—having power is fun.

When MSNBC's Keith Olbermann attacked Fox News chief Roger Ailes on the air in 2007, Ailes informed NBC CEO Jeff Zucker that he would have both the *New York Post* and Fox's Bill O'Reilly attack Jeffrey Immelt, CEO of NBC's parent, GE. O'Reilly told viewers, "If my child were killed in Iraq, I would blame the likes of Jeffrey Immelt," because GE has business in Iran, a country that the United States accuses of supporting Shiite militias in Iraq.

Murdoch, during the investigation of Conrad Black, promised to go easy on the story (killing at least one aggressive story in the

*New York Post*) if, in return, Black's *Telegraph* airbrushed criticism of Murdoch's decision to appoint his thirty-year-old son CEO of BSkyB.

From News Corp.'s point of view, this is just about the day-to-day management of its news assets. If someone strikes you, you strike them back *hard*—it's effective and it's fun. If they cry uncle in the face of your demonstration of power, well, you've proved your point—you've confirmed your power. So you lock in your advantage, protecting your own position and putting something in the favor bank too.

What's more, you have to know how to extend and leverage your power. This is about power that is best understood in a semi-feudal sense. It's about a fiefdom that not only has its own central-ized power but confers power on other people, who then return some tribute—in the form of information (hence all this actually *does* serve a journalistic function) or in the form of more power and the furtherance of the company's interests.

Howard Rubenstein, for instance, has built a massive New York PR practice, one of whose chief assets is its ability to wield influ-ence at the *Post*. In a perfect information loop, he represents Murdoch's PR interests and as well represents other people who have PR interests involved with Murdoch's *Post*. This is, within the *Post*, regarded as one of those elements that is not so much annoy-ing as characteristic—"that's a Rubenstein client" is a particular News Corp. status (extended to everything from major companies to local restaurants).

One of Rubenstein's methods is to arrive in the *Post*'s news-room and to cross it slowly, in public view—sometimes with a client in tow—making his way directly to the editor's desk. The message to *Post* reporters is clear: Howard has grease.

If you're embroiled in scandal, that scandal might well be mit-igated at the *Post* if you hire Rubenstein. In 2006, for instance, the *Post* got wind that a student at the prestigious Collegiate School had threatened "to go Columbine"; with *Post* reporters at its door, the school was savvy enough to hire Rubenstein and have the story downplayed.

There are greater and lesser agents of *Post* power. When in 2003 I wrote a book that had some less than kind things to say about the movie producer Harvey Weinstein, I was the butt of a ferocious attack on the *Post*'s "Page Six." "What gives?" I asked, calling up the page's editor, Richard Johnson, with whom I'd been on affable terms. "Never underestimate the power of Harvey Weinstein on this page," said Richard, more matter-of-factly than threateningly. (Weinstein, actually, had hired Johnson as a screenwriter.)

So, if designees and hustlers and bullies can come to have extrajournalistic influence and power in Murdoch newsrooms, imagine the power Murdoch himself has. It is direct from Murdoch's lips to the page. There's an excitement, an electrifying sense of accomplishment, when you give Murdoch what he wants, when you know that it comes directly from the boss. (It doesn't really matter that Murdoch is often full of inaccuracies and self-serving rumors; he's full of juicy gossip and good stories too.)

Simon Jenkins, in his book *The Market for Glory*, about the great newspaper proprietors, makes a point that would never be made by an American press critic—that dubious motives and good journalism might coexist. Beaverbrook, for instance, whose *Daily Express* displayed calculated "malice towards often innocent 'enemies,'" as well as not necessarily warranted "generosity to friends," was nevertheless "a master journalist," in Jenkins' view. "He had an instinct for news and a belief in the authority of a good reporter to command the reader's attention."

That's the Murdoch position: News Corp. has to represent its proprietor's (and, by extension, its shareholders') interests while at the same time giving consumers what they want.

It's a position at diametric odds with that of what Murdoch would call—using his catchall term for the sanctimonious—the "Bishops" of journalism, who, you cannot convince him otherwise, merely hide their interests while continuing to flog them, and, quite possibly because they've so internalized their own phoniness, more often than not fail to hold their readers' or viewers' attention.

The entire rationale of modern, objective, arm's-length, editor-driven journalism—the quasi-religious nature of which had blossomed in no small way as a response to him—he regarded as artifice if not an outright sham.

Even as the discussion proceeded about the protections for the *Wall Street Journal*'s editorial independence, Murdoch would go through the paper every morning slashing and stabbing its pages, full of annoyance, contempt, and incredulity.

Is there a way for a Murdoch editor not to submit and be trammeled—not to be wholly Murdochified?

Actually, it's become something of a subgenre of literature—editors who have worked for Murdoch and gotten out alive (often just barely) and then written a book about it.

There are so many of these accounts that it can start to seem as if the point of journalism, or the central experience, is to have dealt with Murdoch. The details of your dealings with the other powerful men of the age pall in comparison—Murdoch is the ultimate test.

Former *News of the World* editor Piers Morgan, who clearly anticipates someday going back to work for Murdoch and who remains on good social standing with Elisabeth Murdoch and her husband, Matthew Freud, has written what is meant to be a fond memoir. "He truly is Citizen Kane, though from my experience so far nowhere near as malevolent. It makes me laugh when I read what a vile monster he is," he writes, while at the same time helplessly making a pretty good case for Murdoch's malevolence. There is Murdochian vindictiveness, implacableness, and a corrosive disposition (however masked by courtliness) that Morgan is, during his editorship, constantly trying to weigh and anticipate and dodge. When he leaves News Corp. to edit the *Sun*'s main competitor, the *Mirror*—ostensibly because he wants to run a daily paper—what it feels like in his account is that he's fleeing Murdoch. Not out of any specific antipathy—he's clearly fascinated by him and has no issue about journalistic scruples—but because he can't relax with Murdoch as his boss. Every second working for Murdoch is a second spent thinking about what Murdoch wants. He inhabits you.

## JUNE 4, 2007

Editorial integrity suddenly somehow becomes for the Bancrofts the paramount issue. It's beyond price, beyond the issue of continued independence, beyond the fraying family relationships, beyond a developing antipathy for the family advisors (there is the not incorrect feeling that the advisors are steering them to sell). This has become the pride issue—the face-saving issue. The moral stand: editorial freedom.

Murdoch, of course, had seen this countless times: an impossible, or, even pathetic, effort by the *ancien régime* to try to ensure the good behavior of the new regime. If you really want any of this, you keep control. If not, you don't. The rest, Murdoch understands, is just guilt (or feckless superiority).

The meeting on June 4—it's the first face-to-face between Murdoch and the Bancrofts—takes place in the big conference room at Wachtell, Lipton on West 52nd Street. Wachtell may be the most profitable law firm in the country, but its real estate is entirely humdrum. It's faceless, unprepossessing, discouraging. Soaring ambitions are tempered here.

For Dow Jones and the Bancrofts, it's Michael Elefante, Lisa Steele, Leslie Hill, Chris Bancroft, Peter McPherson, Marty Lipton, and Josh Cammaker. For News, it's Murdoch, Dave DeVoe, Lon Jacobs, and, yet to arrive—flying in from Europe—James Murdoch.

Marty Lipton is shepherding the meeting. This is good for Murdoch, whom Lipton is clearly not immune to. Indeed, Lipton and Murdoch are fellow veterans of the great corporate realignments of the 1980s and '90s—they've been made by the same forces. They are the substantial historical personages in the room; everybody else is . . . well, everybody else.

The News Corp. people, who will leave the meeting some five hours later in a celebratory mood, believe from the start they've got a lovefest going. The first two hours are spent in getting-to-know-you chitchat. Mostly, they're waiting for James to arrive—Murdoch feels James will really carry the day. "I brought in James," Murdoch recalled to me later, "so they could see that we're a family company and they might say, 'Look, you're an old man, you could drop dead tomorrow and what are we doing,' and so on. Okay? So I thought I'd have James there." (In somewhat typical News Corp. fashion, although James is the secret weapon, he's a last-minute one. In fact, Jimmy Lee says he was the one who asked that James be there: "That was actually my idea. I called Rupert the day before the meeting and said is there some way to get James there. It was tough but he did it.")

But meanwhile, he thinks he's putting on his best charm offensive. Leslie Hill is asking—grilling—him about China. Has he bent over backward to accommodate the Chinese government? What about booting the BBC off Star TV? What about the HarperCollins China book he canceled, the one by Chris Patten, the last British governor of Hong Kong? Murdoch feels he's on, he's handling this all very deftly. But Hill, who has actually gone into the meeting with a pretty open mind, decides Murdoch is ducking the issues.

They're at a huge table—they're all sitting miles from each other. Murdoch isn't really listening to them and they can't really understand him. He's monologizing, slipping in and out of his heavy mumble and unfinished sentences. Elefante finds himself thinking, *The guy is really old.* He was anticipating being impressed—it's Rupert Murdoch, after all. Instead he's impressed by how unimpressive Murdoch is.

Then lunch, catered in the conference room. And then—finally—James arrives. James takes the floor. Elefante understands that James is there to snow them. Elefante isn't unimpressed. If James doesn't end up adding much, he's at least got presence—youth, good looks, confidence. But glib. Scarily glib. He can say anything well (unlike his father, who appears to them to say nothing well). Murdoch, for his part, proudly believes James has really impressed Lisa Steele with, particularly, a bit of "tree-hugging" talk.

After almost three hours, they finally get to the editorial-protections discussion. It's James who lays out how the *Times* of London agreement works. Now, Murdoch's letter about editorial protections was sent almost three weeks ago. But nobody seems to have done any research about what the agreement entails. Nobody has even looked up the details of the *Times* agreement. They're hearing about it here, really seeing it, for the first time. They even say, dumbly, *Well, it looks good on paper.* They ask how it will work, even having read in the *Journal* that in key instances at the *Times* papers it hasn't worked at all.

Lipton asks the News Corp. guys to leave the room while they confer.

It's a basic negotiating trick—let the other guys cool their heels. But, in fact, the News guys are so pleased with how things are going—reassured by the Bancrofts' lack of focus and general cluelessness about the most basic notions of editorial process—that they don't mind at all that they've been sent out. Indeed, they sit happily in another Wachtell conference room for nearly two hours before they're asked back in. They feel this meeting is the great leap forward; they've connected.

It's during this time, with the News guys out of the room, that Marty Lipton tries to give the family members, along with Elefante and McPherson, a context for thinking about editorial protections—trying to tell them what's realistic from a legal point of view and what's in essence ritualistic. What he does not tell them is that it's baloney—that any such agreement is and will be only what Murdoch wants it to be. In some sense, by maintaining the artifice that this is a discussion among equals, among like-minded men of goodwill, Lipton is selling the idea of the agreement. (He certainly isn't saying, *Listen to me, you fools, this is all chump stuff!*)

In fact, when the News guys return, Lipton says of the editorial protections, "Are you prepared to give it the force of law?"

"Sure," says Murdoch, ready to hug them all. He'll say whatever they want him to say if they'll sell him the paper.

Murdoch is amazed these people are actually taking this seriously. Really, given everything—not least of all his own well-known history—it is preposterous that they would.

And yet, "It ended up," Murdoch will later recall, "with Elefante and Lipton seeming to be helpful and all the others very happy. We thought that it was a great afternoon. We never expected it to turn out like this."

Chris Bancroft asks, in a more gentlemanly than antagonistic sense, if he can trust Murdoch. Murdoch, somewhat hilariously, says that he should just ask around to see if he's a trustworthy person or not.

The Bancrofts promise to respond in writing with regard to the editorial protections. And the meeting is adjourned.

The News guys repair, in a self-satisfied mood, to the Grand Havana Room, a cigar bar atop 666 Fifth Avenue, around the corner from the Wachtell, Lipton offices—though only Lon Jacobs actually has a cigar.

# TEN

# Rupertism

In the *Wall Street Journal*'s narrative of events, significant potential bidders are circling the company. There's a conversation between Microsoft and GE about a partnership to buy Dow Jones. Then there's talk of a GE-Pearson hookup. GE, the parent of NBC, also owns CNBC, which Murdoch's new cable business channel will compete with. What's more, CNBC has a long-term content relationship with the *Journal* that a Murdoch takeover will imperil. Pearson, for its part, owns the *Financial Times*, which will face a new competitive threat from a Murdoch-owned *Journal*. Another rumor has Pearson merging its *Financial Times* with the *Journal* to create a new, separate company.

Then there's Warren Buffett, the storied investor who is on the board of the Washington Post Company, and is thus perceived to have an interest in newspapers. Buffett is suddenly—apparently through no fault of his own—considered to be one of the *Journal*'s possible saviors. (The irony here is that Buffett has invested heavily in Dow Jones after the announcement of Murdoch's proposed deal and is actively calling directors and urging them to sell.)

The source for most of the optimism about Murdoch alternatives is Leslie Hill, the Dow Jones board member and former airline pilot, who has developed a single-minded belief that she can save Dow Jones from Murdoch and that she herself might be a reasonable choice to head the company. The reporters with whom she's speaking encourage her in this—"I Fly with Leslie" signs appear in the newsroom.

She pressures Michael Elefante into attending a meeting with her and Brian Tierney, the marketing executive who put together an investor group that, in 2006, bought the *Philadelphia Inquirer*—which since then has fallen further and further into extremis. Hill also gets a meeting at Dow Jones for MySpace founder Brad Greenspan, who bears a grudge against Murdoch and News Corp. over News' acquisition of MySpace. Greenspan proposes that he'll raise the money to buy 25 percent of Dow Jones and thereby protect it from Murdoch.

Chris Bancroft, meanwhile, is also using the *Journal*'s reporters to help him make a market. His antipathy is not toward Murdoch per se—but if a deal is to be done, he wants more money. He's on the road, looking for private equity firms or hedge funds that might be willing to put up the cash so he can buy a controlling share of Dow Jones and block the deal—thinking he too might not be such a bad CEO.

Ron Burkle, who has emerged as a suitor in many bidding wars for media companies, now emerges, at least in the pages of the *WSJ*, and partnered with the *WSJ* union, as a potential savior for Dow Jones.

As it happens, the alternatives to Murdoch are much more real in the minds of these suddenly attentive Bancroft second cousins and in the *Journal*'s own reporting of the alternatives to Murdoch than in actuality. But the effect of the *Journal*'s reporting and its aggrandizement of unlikely saviors, along with the evident futility of the Bancroft family's heroic or mock-heroic efforts to find another buyer, serves most of all to make Murdoch look better and better—or at least singular.

The initial optimism about a blue-chip suitor that would value and support the editorial independence of the *Wall Street Journal* shortly fades into a more clear-eyed view. A company such as GE, for instance, which early on was the board's favorite alternative to Murdoch, exists for no other reason than to impose rational, regulated behavior on its various businesses. That would surely mean, it soon becomes clear to *WSJ* reporters, that the newsroom head count could be at risk if the business were run by GE on the strictest economic terms.

After all, the *Wall Street Journal* is not—at least nowadays—a terribly rational construct. Murdoch, say what you want about him, is one of the few Fortune 100 CEOs empowered to not act rationally—for instance, pouring a lot of money into newspapers simply because he likes newspapers. What, after all, does GE or private equity or Ron Burkle, for God's sake, care about newspapers?

And then there is the sotto voce point, cherished by only a handful of *WSJ* true believers—but they are and always have been the important handful. An odd and fundamental truth about the *WSJ* is that it is a profoundly conservative newspaper—irascibly and militantly conservative. It is part of the anomalousness of the *Wall Street Journal*. Most of the paper makes every effort to exist as an entity without a political agenda; if there is such an agenda, it is unassumingly liberal. But the two editorial pages, the penultimate pages of the first section, speak in the most determined conservative voice of any newspaper in the nation. Arguably, they are the country's most influential newspaper pages—regularly supplying more support and valuable ideas to the conservative establishment than any other paper or magazine. Indeed, it is not entirely far-fetched to argue that this—these pages, this mission—is the *real* reason the *WSJ* exists, and why the paper's independence has been protected so tenaciously for so long. Peter Kann and Warren Phillips, key members of the Dow Jones board, along with the determined, scary, radical figures on the editorial page, not to mention the deeply Republican older members of the Bancroft family (no matter that the offspring have become liberals), have in the past been united—in some sense have even conspired—to protect the *Journal*'s wherewithal to argue its pure conservative view. Kann's deft avoidance of all takeover approaches is, not inconsiderably, because there really is nobody out there who might be a reliable steward of these views.

The *Journal* has managed to protect its editorial voice, and actually give it great respectability, by sequestering it inside a relatively liberal newspaper. It's a neat trick—and a fragile construct. One that Ron Burkle or PR-minded GE likely would not understand. Indeed, few at the *Journal,* save its innermost circle, understood this. The younger Bancrofts surely don't. In fact, one of the things that troubles the younger Bancrofts most is the paper's political stance—which is yet another reason the Bancrofts have been so adroitly kept at a distance. The inner circle of the paper has been protecting not just a quality paper, but this other mission.

In this regard, Murdoch understands he has a singular advantage. In 1997, when he went down to the Dow Jones offices to see Kann—free-market, small government, anti-regulation, America-first believer, no matter how mild-mannered he might appear—this was an aspect of what he was saying: *We're on the same page, you and I—and about how many buyers can that be said?*

If this inner circle has to choose between the anodyne sensibilities of most major corporations—GE most of all—and such insubstantial, blowing-in-the-political-breeze figures as Ron Burkle, or Rupert Murdoch, well, there is really no contest.

The newsroom may want Donald Graham at the *Washington Post* or even the Sulzbergers at the *Times,* but as Karen Elliott House, Peter Kann's wife and the paper's former publisher, will acknowledge to me in the aftermath of the deal, among the most senior editorial managers, Murdoch is much preferred to the assorted liberals.

If he is a bad choice, he's still the better one.

## THE POLITICAL MAN

If you're not with Murdoch, even on a modest point, you're a *liberal*, or—though this appellation has dwindled in the past decade or so—a *commie*. It's important to get the tone right here. It's not necessarily even all that disdainful. Said with exaggerated resignation or incomprehension, it is often semi-affectionate. Murdoch's sisters, for instance, are "the socialists." Gary Ginsberg is often waved away with "Well, you're a liberal." Murdoch is almost not making a point about ideology. It's more a point about temperament—his versus yours. The way he sees it, he's the last reasonable man standing.

Are you sentimental or are you realistic? Are you a basic sort or are you fancy? Do you know the value of a dollar? (Particularly *his* dollars.)

What he is is a fifties sort of dad. In fact, he *is* a fifties dad. (His daughter, Prudence, was born in 1958.) In the international media circles that he's moved in for the last generation, this fifties dad thing has become a particularly rare sort of sensibility. So when he sees it, he embraces it. While this sensibility is, most prevalently, found among right-wingers, specific policies aren't only what he's looking for or what attracts him. It's rather the articulation that moves him: a lack of equivocation, a firm declaration, a clear identity, a fundamental compression, a lack of evident complication or obvious neurosis—along with, of course, the various tax, regulatory, and fiscal policies that will benefit him personally.

How he would like the talk to be, how he would like the world to be—suffused with patriarchal definitiveness—finds one of its highest reflections on the *WSJ* editorial pages. This is his true temperamental home. These pages hew more closely to Murdoch's views than, perhaps, even those of any of his own publications (including the conservative political magazine the *Weekly Standard*, which was launched with Murdoch funding in 1995, but is often more wonky than declarative). They lack equivocation, they revel in their own certainty, they *sell* it. "You can't write a fifty-fifty editorial," one of the pages' first editors, William Peter Hamilton, a Scotsman like Murdoch, once wrote. "Don't believe the man who tells you there are two sides to every question. There is only one side to the truth."

They are, quite likely, the only editorial pages in the country that are actually avidly read. They may even have their own dedicated readership—a hundred thousand or two hundred thousand hard-core conservatives who buy the paper *for* the editorials. They're informed by them, galvanized by them, in love with them.

On our editorial page we make no pretense of walking down the middle of the road. Our comments and interpretations are made from a definite point of view. We believe in the individual, in his wisdom and his decency. We oppose all infringements on individual rights whether they stem from attempts at private monopoly, labor union monopoly or from an overgrowing government. People will say we are conservative or even reactionary. We are not much interested in labels but if we were to choose one, we would say we are radical. Just as radical as the Christian doctrine.
—William Henry Grimes, 1951

The editorial pages, ruled by the editorial page editor, exist so apart from the rest of the paper that they function almost like a separate business. Until the *Journal* headquarters were remodeled after 9/11, the editorial pages even had a separate lobby entrance, where you walked past the photograph of Ronald Reagan, one of the pages' mainstay heroes.

It's a different kind of calling on the editorial pages—a kind of faith. This is about orthodoxy. Free trade, low taxes, anti-regulation, anti-collectivist—and later, anti-communist and pro-Israel. They're proud and determined ideologues—ideologues (at least on their best days), not partisans (the *Journal* editorial pages eviscerated George H. W. Bush when he abandoned his no-new-taxes pledge—arguably costing him a vital part of his base, and hence his presidency). The pages' editor—now Paul Gigot—is invariably the linear descendant of William Peter Hamilton, that steadfast, aggressive, absolute believer in market virtue. (The Dow Theory is his: "Beneath the fluctuations in individual stocks there was present at all times a trend of the market as a whole." And too: "The market represents everything everybody knows, hopes, believes, anticipates.") From Hamilton to Thomas Woodlock to William Henry Grimes to Vermont Royster to Joseph Evans to Robert Bartley to Paul Gigot, for over a hundred years, the position, values, and affect of the page remain largely fixed. There is no effort at consideration, balance, or even analysis.

This is one facet of the deal in which Murdoch has been able to avoid scrutiny: There aren't liberal views for him to subvert at the *Journal*—at least not on the editorial page.

And yet, for the pages' editors, there is grave concern: Can anyone, in the end, be sure what Murdoch actually believes in? Or if he believes in anything? Or if what he believes in necessarily has much bearing on what is expedient for him to *say* he believes in?

That suggests that his principles are fungible—that he's ultimately a pragmatist. If he's not faulted for being a right-wing reactionary, then he's faulted for having fair-weather ideas. But that too may be wrong—this focus on his ideas. It may just be that what ideas he has are thin. It's not ideas he's pursuing but sensibility. He's looking for other people who, along with whatever else they might believe, believe in the credo of winning—that winning is the point; that, policywise, giving wherewithal to likely winners is the point. The free market ought to rule, in other words. But, too, the free market should rule in favor of the strongest people in the free market. Likewise, all winners have virtue.

That's his ideological framework. That and what the last person he's talked to—and whom he's moved by—has said to him.

At the same time, these views he leans toward, or these people with views he leans toward, ought to be able to sell papers—which is the point about winners.

In his own mind he has only ever been entirely consistent: He has never wandered in the wilderness or confronted ambivalence. Being warlike is his point. He likes to be the cause of the conflict. He likes to set the house on fire and watch all the fire engines drive maniacally down the road. With a little critical interpretation, there is a certain autistic quality to his attention—a certain detachment, an overemphasis on his own needs and desires. He is, relatively speaking, incapable of seeing that his views have changed— that they ever have changed.

There is, politically, Red Rupert, Reagan-Thatcher Rupert, Roger Ailes Rupert, and Slightly Readjusted Rupert. And What's-Good-for-Rupert Rupert.

In all of these views or stages, there's the same basic philosophical operation: fundamental contrariness. The point about being a contrarian—especially one with decisive views—is that you stand to gain a lot more leverage than just being one among many. Murdoch wants to be out in front of a position. After all, he's in the tabloid business. It is important not to underestimate how much he actually sees his political position as an editorial act—his politics, he believes, enliven his papers. He's not only using his papers to sell his views. He's using his views to sell his papers—choosing views that will sell not because they're consistent or popular but because they're dramatic.

(Not that he doesn't fixate: In late 2007, the *Sun*, in London, will frequently devote its front page to the anti–European Constitution campaign, an issue so boring, even Murdoch admits, that the paper is losing a hundred thousand readers a day.)

There's also the sense that his politics are more about whom he is aligned against—which person annoys him most—than of what policies he is for. In politics, as in business, he needs an enemy, or at least a clear opposition that he can demonize. Conveniently, his political enemies, so often representing the establishment (or, anyway, his construct of the establishment), are often his business enemies (i.e., the *New York Times*). Red Rupert—who would become, as the ultimate fifties dad, the very opposite of Red—was the son of a thirties dad. Rupert's politics were one of the most basic and divisive issues between him and his father. His father was an Edwardian sort of conservative, very much part of the royalist, upper-class Australian tradition—a tradition in which Rupert's mother grandly continues. Keith Murdoch found his son, with all the accoutrements of anti-establishment radicalism, to be distasteful and alarming. Rupert's politics, to his father, were part of the boy's entire pattern of lack of discipline, focus, purpose.

Undoubtedly all this was true—he certainly wasn't much of a student—but he was reacting then, as he would for the rest of his career, to entrenchment. It is hard to stand out by behaving yourself—by following everybody else. That's not an efficient avenue for ambitiousness. To be his father's son, to adapt to upper-class Melbourne society, would require a controlled and docile and patient temperament. This is true too of Oxford, heavy as it is with ritual and propriety. As an Australian, he didn't fit in anyway. *So*, he reasoned, *I might as well hang my hat on not fitting in*. Hence, at university in postwar England, he became a radical—a theatrical radical, an obnoxious radical (with a really fancy car). The point, or among the points, was to be noticed—and, as well, to piss off his father. The only way you really got Sir Keith's attention was to annoy him. As a media lesson, this would be invaluable: If you annoy the establishment, it listens to you.

But a key point about Rupert's anti-establishmentarianism is that he's never removed from the establishment—or, that is, never removed from power. His views certainly aren't shaped by powerlessness. His acquaintanceship with the levers of power, even as a young man, is deep and practiced. Australia is a small country where power and politics, *success* and politics, are, for all practical purposes, one and the same. That's an argument about the quid pro quos and incestuousness and mutual back-scratching and conspiracies often made about the power elite in the United States. But it wouldn't be an argument you'd have to make in a small country. It's obvious and understood that all the powerful and successful people know each other and are involved with each other. It's a fully networked society. Rupert, as the son of one of Australia's most important businessmen and one of its undisputed press lords, has had, from an early age, access to everybody who counts in the country. What's more, he understands, because he's witnessed it, that nothing happens without a systematic program of influence among the people with influence.

Murdoch doesn't have a conception of reality, of performance, of achievement, that doesn't involve a layered involvement with politics. His business discussion is always shifting into a political discussion—not just because he enjoys political gaming, but because this is business reality. Your political connections are as germane as your balance sheet. This really has nothing to do with ideology at all. The measure of his business success, of his rise, is his ability to influence politics.

But, first, there is his early lack of ability to have meaningful clout and influence.

The 1950s conservative Australian government of Robert Menzies, largely in the pocket of established media companies—the Fairfaxes, the Packers, and the Herald and Weekly Times, Murdoch's father's old company—has little interest in helping Murdoch. As the *Adelaide News* becomes more determinedly left-wing, Menzies becomes more determined to hinder Keith

Murdoch's son—including forcing Murdoch into a major fight to win the single television license available in Adelaide. (Fifty years later, Murdoch, who has little interest in the past, can remember every detail about Menzies' efforts to thwart him.)

At the same time, the *Adelaide News* enters its first serious journalistic campaign: a defense of Rupert Max Stuart, an Aboriginal man sentenced to death in the murder of a nine-year-old girl. It's a campaign begun by Murdoch's editor Rohan Rivett—his father's handpicked editor, who was given the job not least of all because, while living in England, he befriended and looked after the young Murdoch at Oxford at Sir Keith's behest. Murdoch, in an early instance of editorial interference (and enthusiasm), takes direct control of the Stuart campaign. He coordinates the *Adelaide News'* ferocious attack on Sir Thomas Playford, the longest-serving premier of South Australia.

Playford has Murdoch and Rivett brought up on charges of seditious libel. While they are ultimately acquitted, the boy publisher is held up to calculated ridicule. It's an ordeal meant to remind him how much he's overstepped his place. (Murdoch's frustration and helplessness result in, among other things, his firing Rivett, the person most responsible for the early success of the *Adelaide News*.) Murdoch, the simple machine, learns such lessons well: You'll always be vulnerable to people who are more powerful than you—hence, you yourself must become ever more powerful.

Then, in a more worldly lesson about power and about the nature of the big time and the small time, Murdoch goes to the Kennedy White House.

Murdoch stops in Washington after a trip to Cuba in 1961 with a Sydney *Daily Mirror* correspondent because Kennedy's press secretary, Pierre Salinger, has promised the young publisher an audience with the president. In the Oval Office, Kennedy—"very, very charming, he showed us around his office, quite an experience, I was only thirty years old"—starts talking expansively about West Papua, a big story at the time in Australia. Indonesia wants to get control from the Dutch, who have held control since 1895. Kennedy says he's sending his brother Bobby out there and he's going to tell Indonesian president Sukarno that the United States is going to change its position.

Murdoch intends to write the story himself, but the *Mirror*'s local stringer, a reporter at the *Washington Post*, realizing its import, alerts Salinger, who blows his top, insisting what Kennedy spoke of was off the record. Murdoch holds his ground until, flying to New York's Idlewild Airport, his plane is met on the tarmac by Secret Service agents who hold everyone on board as Murdoch is directed to call the Australian ambassador. Murdoch will recall that the ambassador is "pissing his pants" about the story—and he tells Murdoch that Salinger has pledged that if Murdoch runs the story, he'll never get another visa again.

Murdoch, in the retelling, will break into hysterical laughter at this point, remembering his own sense of his place in the world, his sense of how far he had yet to travel, and his certain sense of when to fold. Hence he does come to *understand* that Kennedy's talk *was* off the record, later allowing as how—more laughter—"this was one of my weaker efforts in journalism." There will be no bitterness or resentment in the retelling, just enjoyment at the adventure and even gratitude for the lesson: The big time is different from the small time.

Then there's his first clear act of using his papers to gain influence—to project and to seize power. This is the story of Gough Whitlam, the left-wing Australian prime minister, who is elected in 1972 with Murdoch's support. But it is also, in its way, the story of Watergate. The backdrop to one of the greatest demonstrations of press power in Australia—Murdoch's deposing of a prime minister—is the greatest assertion of press power in the United States.

Murdoch is aghast at the press's politicking in the campaign against Richard Nixon. (Murdoch is back and forth to the United States during the Watergate investigation, and moves here with his family in 1974, just as Nixon resigns from office.) But as likely,

Murdoch's ire here is competitive too. What he's witnessing is the paramount example of press influence. And he's nowhere near it; he's not a player on this level. But we know he wants in. Indeed, *Rolling Stone* founder and editor Jann Wenner meets Murdoch in 1974 and compliments him on the newly launched *National Star*, telling him he's especially impressed by the *Star*'s political column and is curious about its writer. Murdoch tells Wenner, proudly and sheepishly, that he's been writing the column himself under a pseudonym. (Then Murdoch inquires about buying *Rolling Stone*.)

In the aftermath of Watergate, Murdoch, harrumphy about the U.S. press and the Woodward and Bernstein putsch ("The American press might get their pleasure in successfully crucifying Nixon, but the last laugh could be on them. See how they like it when the Commies take over the West," he will tell friends), finally steps up to being a true political player. "The Dismissal," which is what this historic moment in Australian politics is called, is the Australian Watergate.

Edward Gough Whitlam is, in the late 1960s and early '70s, the model of Murdoch's sort of politician. Ideology aside—Whitlam is the leader of the Australian Labor Party—he listens to Murdoch, confers with him, huddles with him at the Murdoch sheep farm outside Canberra. Whitlam becomes the darling of Murdoch's *Australian*, Murdoch's left-leaning quality paper.

But having gotten elected, Whitlam promptly stops speaking to Murdoch. Having, in Murdoch's view, "single-handedly put the present government in office," he is now snubbed.

When Australia's maritime union, in protest against the resumption of American bombing in North Vietnam in 1973, organizes a boycott against U.S. ships coming into Australian ports, the Whitlam government, crossing both Murdoch and Nixon, sides with the union. The Nixon government tries to enlist Murdoch's help—but the Whitlam government resists its most important supporter.

Murdoch, still in the Labor camp, begrudgingly supports Whitlam once more in 1974, when he is reelected. But they continue on a fast slide into acrimony. There's Murdoch's odd venture, in 1974, into bauxite mining with Reynolds Aluminum, which needs licenses that the Whitlam government resists granting. And then, later that year, there's the Whitlam devaluation of the Australian dollar, which costs Murdoch in his foreign exchange dealings.

And then there is the theory that Murdoch is in cahoots with the CIA. That when, in 1975, Whitlam begins to use Australia's deep anti-Vietnam sentiment to agitate against a major U.S. spy station located in the Australian outback, the CIA enlists Murdoch in a regime-change strategy.

Murdoch's *Australian*, once firmly liberal, moves, in the campaign against Whitlam, dramatically to the right (where it will mostly remain). The foremost example of Murdoch's capacity to be a principled publisher becomes the primary weapon in the battle to get rid of Whitlam. With intimations of sexual and financial scandal (the sexual part turns out not to be true, the financial part equivocally true), the *Australian*, in a campaign led personally by Murdoch—who himself takes to writing articles—breaks the government, which has been paralyzed by a budget crisis. Sir John Kerr, the governor-general of Australia, the figurehead appointee of the British Crown over the Commonwealth, does what has never been done before—he fires the elected government in 1975, precipitating a constitutional crisis.

Seventy-five members of the *Australian*'s newsroom write a letter protesting the anti-Whitlam campaign, which is followed by a demonstration and a one-day walkout by all the journalists at Murdoch's Sydney-based papers.

Murdoch, dismissing the protests, prevails.

In 1975, shortly after he moves from his summer house in East Hampton to the more isolated property in Columbia County in upstate New York, Murdoch gets a recommendation to call a young woman, with a house nearby, who works in state government.

"State government" must have been what made the tumblers click here—in Australia, regional governments are significant power centers—because he's not somebody who's just looking to be sociable with the neighbors. Her name is Marian Faris Stuntz, otherwise known as Cita—she's a Democrat, working for then New York governor Hugh Carey—and she begins to give him a tutorial on New York state government. (This is even before he's bought the *Post*.) "He would ring me up three or four times a day," Stuntz will later recall, "and would say, 'Who is this guy Mario Cuomo? What is this? I heard something about this, I heard something about that.' He was sucking up information about state government like a sponge."

Within his first year of owning the *Post*, he entirely alters the political landscape in New York. In a precise calculation, he decides to use the *Post* as an instrument to elect somebody—he understands that it doesn't really matter whom, just that the *Post* be responsible. After interviewing each of the prospective candidates for New York City mayor, he settles on the perhaps least likely guy—that is, the one who needs him the most. It's Ed Koch, a congressman from Greenwich Village, single, rumored to be gay (Murdoch has a typical old-school Australian man's antipathy to "poofters"), funny-looking, with a counterintuitive campaign style: He whines, complains, cavils. The entire paper is put in service to the Koch election. The *Post* is transformed into an ebullient narrative of Koch's presence, charm, and inevitability. The least charismatic man in the city becomes the most charismatic. Thirty years later, Joyce Purnick, the *Post*'s political reporter during the Koch campaign, will still be shaking her head: "Murdoch didn't change a word of my copy. But my copy was irrelevant—it was dwarfed by, hidden beneath, this package of huge pictures of Koch and great personal stories about him. And relentless day-by-day celebration."

Koch is elected mayor in 1977, making Murdoch, only a few years after his arrival in New York, suddenly one of the most influential men in the city. Koch is not just his political coup but a business and personal one as well. The *New York Post*, which has begun its course of losing News Corp. tens of millions of dollars a year, has started to earn its keep.

It's so very basic (as with all things Murdoch):

1. You can't succeed unless you have political influence.

2. It's more efficient to get political influence by starting with a new group than with the entrenched group—established power doesn't give people outside the establishment very many opportunities.

3. Likewise, the new people vying for power need you more than the entrenched people with the power.

4. Your power and influence put in service to the upstarts will be magnified if the upstarts win.

5. The upstarts always eventually win.

6. In general, while conservatives are better for business, any political faction that owes you something is better than one that doesn't.

Ideology is only one aspect of Murdoch's political instinct. In general, he wants characters who provide the best story—that is, the most conflict. In that he is like any journalist. This is his sport. He's in awe of public power and how it unfolds. But unlike other journalists, there's no pretense about him being on the sidelines. He's not just telling the story, he's actively involved in *creating* the story. What's more, he's a character in the story too, even in some sense—at least as he understands the story—the hero.

More than any other journalist, Murdoch reflects, epitomizes, and benefits from the great conservative tide. He's on the zeitgeist. This, in part, results from a temperamental distinction. In the middle of the 1970s, he's building, plotting, pushing back when everybody else is settling in, resigning themselves, acquiescing to the long decline. It's the decade of stagflation and the City of New York going bankrupt. It's the great funk.

Murdoch is the countertemperament. If everyone else appears to have given up on the idea of gaining a personal and business advantage, Murdoch hasn't gotten the message. As an outsider, he's just not quite aware that the party's over.

What he's compulsively drawn to is action, opportunity, the center of attention. A vital element in understanding his political consciousness is understanding its shallowness. For an ideologue, he's done little of the reading. Ideas are of marginal interest to him; he's a poor debater (although he can raise his voice and pound the table).

And then there is the fact that at all times he's being fed what he wants to hear. In a way, he himself is like a politician. He has people supporting and reinforcing his positions. He lives in a vacuum of, as it were, relative quackery (not unlike many politicians). Of course, even the dubious information he receives is compromised by the fact that he doesn't really listen. What he's looking for is just the top line—the executive summary, not the nuance. So, at any given time, he has this amalgamation of half facts, quasiprejudices, shorthand analysis, and cockeyed assumptions, with a smattering of gossip. All combined with his massive certainty and determined nature. That's the basis of his and his newsrooms' political agenda.

(One afternoon at lunch, during an interview with Murdoch, he will suddenly have the urge to point out to me his new understanding of the Muslim situation—that Muslims have an inordinate incidence of birth defects because they so often marry their cousins. Gary Ginsberg, mortified, pauses, his fork in midair, and says, "Ahhh . . . really? Wow. Hmmm . . . That does explain a lot.")

Such views as he adopts and promulgates derive in part from his collection of columnists, who in turn are often trying to write what they think he wants to hear, and who are, too, his social life. Or, if not his actual social set, his social buffers or social amusements, as well as his fundamental gossip sources and intellectual advisors (gossip and intellect go hand in hand for Murdoch).

It's useful to look at the brain trust that's supplying him with much of his political intelligence during the vital Reagan-Thatcher years: Woodrow Wyatt and Irwin Stelzer, both Murdoch foot soldiers competing for his attention.

Wyatt, thirteen years older than Murdoch, was a Labour MP until he lost his seat in 1970. He was made head of the Tote—the office that governs horse racing—in the United Kingdom, where-upon he began his precipitous slide to the right. Wyatt became a tel-evision talking head, with his signature floppy bow tie, for the anti-labor side of the Labour Party, until the Labour Party asked him to shut up and declared him just this side of persona non grata.

Murdoch meets Wyatt in London after the acquisition of *News of the World*, when the Murdochs are making the effort to climb, or at least find, the social ladder in Britain. Wyatt, a veteran social climber, had become a nexus for bankers and aristocrats and titans of industry. He is also a man with the kind of authoritative-sounding, if not necessarily informed, unified-field-theory opinions that Murdoch likes. Murdoch is suitably impressed by Wyatt's no-nonsense views about labor nonsense. What's more, Wyatt, like Murdoch, has a young wife, Verushka, who is Hungarian; Anna, Rupert's wife, is Estonian—and, like Murdoch, a young daughter (Petronella Wyatt would, like Murdoch's daughter Elisabeth, become, in a generation's time, the talk of London).

Wyatt is the kind of Brit who would seem to confirm all Murdoch's Brit prejudices—a snobbish, eccentric anti-Semite with many former wives and indiscreet affairs, obsessed with, more than anything, the state of his wine cellar. "He was a figure," the *Independent* will write on his death, "albeit a slightly ludicrous one, in the land." But given Wyatt's immediate and fulsome apprecia-tion of the new publisher in town, Murdoch finds him talented and amusing, even prescient and sage.

Within a few years, Murdoch will, under Wyatt's tutelage, come to see the real nature of rot and decay in British life (per Wyatt: unions) and, within a few more years, the real hope for the future (per Wyatt: Thatcher). Wyatt is instrumental in arranging the early contacts between Margaret Thatcher—still a dark horse among the Tories in socialist Britain—and Murdoch. The Thatcher victory in 1979 is a serious elevation for Wyatt, not least in terms of his usefulness to Murdoch.

Shortly after Murdoch buys the *Times* in 1981, he gives Wyatt columns in the *Times* and, as well, the *News of the World*. Amidst the randy vicars and spanked schoolgirls, there's Woodrow Wyatt articulating the virtues of the free market in a column called "The Voice of Reason." The columns, surely more valuable to Murdoch than to readers, are drippy encomiums to all things Thatcher. (They are, reportedly, always her first read of the day—some say her *only* news read of the day.)

Wyatt is a terrier at Thatcher's skirt. Her press secretary, Bernard Ingham, who spends much time trying to fend him off, will recall for me how obsessive Wyatt is in hounding Mrs. Thatcher: "A bloody menace. He thought he was running the country by ringing her up at eight in the morning. Poisonous little twerp, he was."

Almost no one in the Murdoch organization has any use at all for him—his columns relentlessly promote not only Thatcher but himself—except Murdoch. The various memoirs by Murdoch hands invariably characterize Wyatt as a great annoyance or comic relief. (In turn, Wyatt, who becomes a memoirist and prodigious diarist, will take his revenge—when his diaries are published posthumously—on those who slight him, or edit him, or deprive him of opportunities for income enhancement, or serve him poor wine.) But Wyatt understands—and frequently points out without restraint—that he is under Murdoch's personal protection.

Wyatt may actually be Murdoch's closest friend during the 1980s. Their families vacation together and socialize together.

Wyatt also becomes not just somebody who is influencing Murdoch on his anti-union position but a significant player in the battle for Wapping. It's Wyatt who brings Murdoch moderate union leaders who will supplant the radical leaders. It's through Wyatt that Murdoch is introduced to Frank Chapple, head of the electricians' union, who agrees to have his membership undermine the printers and typesetters.

Wyatt is the model of a Murdoch columnist and ideologue: The significance that the column gives him is, in turn, used in the service of News Corp. He is, too—and this mightily helps his standing—a courtier. Mr. M. is his singular client.

When Wyatt dies in 1997, having sacrificed his News Corp. pension for more cash up front, it is Murdoch who has to step in and bail out Wyatt's widow, Verushka, and his daughter, Petronella, who herself becomes a columnist for the *Spectator* and *Sunday Telegraph*. (Petronella, not incidentally, later becomes a protagonist in a sex scandal that makes it big in the *News of the World*—she's the lover of Boris Johnson, the married Tory MP and future mayor of London, and a prominent figure in a roundelay of sexual intrigue involving the *Spectator* magazine and the highest reaches of government in 2004.)

It is the other vital member of Murdoch's 1980s brain trust, Irwin Stelzer—who will later feel the sting of Wyatt's diaries (Stelzer apparently stores his expensive wines improperly)—who negotiates the payout to the widow Wyatt.

Stelzer is an American. He's an economist who—and this is attractive to Murdoch—has actually made money: He's started and sold a forecasting company. Murdoch meets him because his attractive neighbor in upstate New York, Cita Stuntz, who's explained the inner workings of New York State government to him, is dating Stelzer. (Stelzer is trying to take her out for her thirty-fifth birthday, but Cita tells him that Murdoch has already made the invitation, so Stelzer calls Murdoch and asks if he can split the check, and hence gets invited along—which is how he and Murdoch meet.) Stelzer's economics specialty involves regulatory matters, and on this issue—Stelzer, as a business advisor, is of course anti-regulation—he and Murdoch agree and bond.

Stelzer is furthermore a gossip, a man about town, a raconteur. Having just bought the *Post* and *New York* magazine, and not having found any sort of like-minded brotherhood in New York, Murdoch now has Irwin. It's a kind of meeting of the minds that you wouldn't necessarily, or easily, find in Manhattan in the late seventies: two free-market, anti-regulatory, self-styled libertarians. Murdoch likes expressive people whose opinions he shares—who offer him opinions that he can adopt for himself.

Irwin is also a kind of Anglophile. Actually, he's Murdoch's kind of Anglophile: He likes everything about England but the English. Murdoch enjoys Stelzer's British-type pomposity even more for Stelzer's being an American. When Stelzer and Cita are married, Murdoch gives them a dinner party in London, where he introduces Irwin to Woodrow Wyatt, who Murdoch thinks will share Irwin's views.

In fact, Irwin finds Wyatt to be a rather ridiculous British eccentric, not to mention an anti-Semite and, he'll eventually conclude, "a lying son of a bitch," and he considers Wyatt's wife, Verushka, to be "stark raving mad." Wyatt, in turn, hits on Stelzer's new wife.

Now Stelzer and Wyatt are competitive courtiers. Murdoch is on the phone with each of them every day. They're functioning not just as columnists—Stelzer also gets column space in the *Sunday Times*—but as his eyes and ears.

Cita and Irwin have a house in Aspen (it's at the Stelzer home that Claudine Longet, the former Mrs. Andy Williams, renting the place for a few weeks one winter, kills her lover, "Spider" Sabich), and Anna and Rupert follow them there. Rupert comes over one day, in Irwin's telling, and says, "It's not fair for me to keep taking your ideas," and offers to begin paying him a consultant's fee. Irwin says, "I don't think my wife would approve—you're one of her friends," but then Anna calls Cita and says, "We'll never be allowed to have dinner with you again unless Irwin takes the money." Voilà. Irwin is now business advisor, researcher, and speechwriter as well as columnist.

Stelzerism and Murdochism are all about the defense of the free market, of Israel, of American clout. Stelzer, through Murdoch, arguably helps make this heretofore complicated, even tortured combination of positions quite a mantra. It's early neoconism.

Stelzer ultimately takes on the role of a kind of Murdoch intellectual spokesperson. That is, when Stelzer talks, people come to believe it's Murdoch talking. Likewise, Stelzer, in addition to his personal work for Murdoch and his columns for Murdoch publications, becomes a Murdoch representative and diplomat to the Reagan administration and almost any other place Murdoch needs a voice, an argument, or some intelligence. At the same time, not always to Murdoch's liking or to the liking of other people in News Corp., Stelzer becomes a kind of freelance Murdoch exponent. Stelzer runs his own Murdoch portfolio. That portfolio will eventually come to include British prime minister Tony Blair and his people, who will regularly make pilgrimages to Stelzer to find out what Murdoch might be thinking.

Murdoch's politics, opinion, and general discourse, along with whom he favors and whom he's against, are less the product of his developing and increasingly conservative worldview than of the odd troop of conservative-minded irregulars who find their way onto his relatively impatient wavelength.

Along with Wyatt and Stelzer, there are, at other times, other oddities. There's Maxwell Newton, once the darling of the Aussie left, whom Murdoch appoints as the first editor of the *Australian* and then fires. He arrives in New York to, of all things un-Australian, quit drinking, and his redemption comes in the form of a business column in the *New York Post*, which basically echoes Murdoch's own growing romance with Reaganomics. There's John Podhoretz, a strange, abrasive, Asperger's type, whose father, Norman, is a guiding eminence of neocon conservatism, who becomes a *New York Post* columnist too and helps convince Murdoch to put up the money to start the *Weekly Standard*—which will become the leading journal of neocon opinion. And there is Eric

Breindel, the former socialist and junkie (his incipient career in liberal politics was ended by a heroin bust) and social figure (Harvard, friend of the Kennedys, friend of Henry Kissinger, lover of *Washington Post* heiress Lally Weymouth), who, as a *Post* columnist, becomes a virulent anti-Arab, anti-welfare, anti-communist voice. He brokers the relationship between Murdoch and Rudy Giuliani (Murdoch didn't like Giuliani, not least of all because he prosecuted his friend and financier Michael Milken), which results in the *Post*'s endorsement of Giuliani in the New York mayor's race. (Breindel will die of AIDS in 1998.)

If Murdoch likes talking to you, if you can hold his attention, and if you're the last one to have talked to him, then often your opinions can be his, no matter that you might be odd, pompous, ludicrous, or flat-out nuts—especially if, additionally, you have a simple argument to make and are also a suck-up.

The liberal people who are now closest to him have come up with a construct for his politics, which are so often just this side of offensive or even intolerable to them: He's a libertarian. Fundamentally, they'll point out, he's not really even political because he hates politicians (or if he doesn't hate them, he at least generally regards them as weak-willed tools). He's on his own tangent, so pay no attention.

And yet, with his politics, he keeps the people around him in some state of fright and discomfort. Which is also part of the point of his politics: He likes the people around him to submit.

Here's something else that's key: It's painful for him to speak personally. He grips and clutches and descends into muttering and murmuring when forced to talk about himself. Politics is his substitute for speaking personally. Politics, in his testing and teasing, is his way of connecting to somebody. At the family dinner table, it's his way of engaging with his children. It is not so much indoctrination—his children have all become relative liberals, after all—but, arguably, a way to express concern, disapproval, curiosity, and affection, and to get attention. It's like how other men use sports as their replacement for not talking personally.

And then there is Anna Murdoch and her politics, as there will be Wendi Murdoch and her views.

Anna Murdoch is a Catholic conservative. In his role of dutiful husband, as it was as dutiful son, he's a practiced mollifier of determined and irritated women (he's away so much that Anna is pretty much always irritated). He's striving to make peace. He gets along better with Anna when his conservative positions are in order. He spends not a small amount of time discussing with Anna and various retainers whether or not he should become a Catholic (he does not). His conservatism helps offset the irreverence, even calculated sacrilege, of his tabloids, which offend Anna (as they do his mother). When the *Sunday Herald Sun* runs a cartoon that makes fun of Pope John Paul II for his encyclical restating the Church's prohibition on birth control, the paper's editor, Alan Howe—the longest-serving Murdoch editor—receives a handwritten fax from Murdoch telling him how appalled he is by the criticism of the Vatican and how disappointed he is in Howe's decision to run the cartoon.

And then there's conservatism as it reflects on his feeling that he's a big swinging dick. It's alpha, macho, aggressive. He's at his most conservative in the mid-to-late eighties—just when he's become the world's biggest, baddest businessman. He's playing to his brand. He's a straight-down-the-line social conservative— against abortion, gay rights, immigration, you name it. A fiscal conservative—the smaller the government, the better the government. A warrior conservative—in the eighties he's all for Thatcher threatening to nuke Beijing as a tenable position during the negotiations over the future of Hong Kong (this, of course, before he tries to win the favor of the Chinese for strategic business reasons in the 1990s). He even supports Pat Robertson—the wing-nut television evangelist and Christian-right politician—for the Republican nomination in 1988.

If there is a moment of dangerous grandiosity in his career, it's in the late eighties. His dealmaking frenzy represents the triumph of Reaganism and Thatcherism and the free markets and the collapse of so many regulatory impediments—and it represents his own triumph. Indeed, his conservative politics track the manicness of his dealmaking. The more deals he makes, the more conservative—the more strident, pugnacious, out there—he becomes. It's his free market and he'll make the rules for it.

But News Corp.'s banking crisis in 1990, his being-and-nothingness moment, changes him. It's a personal ending of the eighties for him. He's forced into a vastly more conciliatory and accommodating mood. Humility in all walks is part of the price of his bailout. The crisis brings new discipline not just to his business but to his political views. He isn't an independent state after all—he learns that he can't function like one. In a way, he's getting a grip.

Also, he sees the fate of Reaganism (it turns into George Bush–ism) and particularly of Thatcherism (an ignominious end for her, and then the shift to John Major–ism)—not to mention the fate of so many of his eighties cohorts, including Michael Milken, who's off to federal prison. He's running scared. He has to not just escape his own financial predicament but survive a zeitgeist shift.

Not only does he not like George H. W. Bush or John Major very much, they don't like him. What's more, they owe him little. If they've been made by the forces he's helped create, he hasn't helped them directly. He's distant from them.

And so he turns—if not on a dime, in a wide swing.

He may be losing his ideological fire, but he's still left with one of the best political organizations outside of politics. All CEOs tend to have a lower-level function that they're most comfortable with and which becomes their point of management style and emphasis—so your CEO might be the real CFO, or real marketing chief, or real operations guy, or real M&A person. Murdoch, at News Corp., is the government affairs specialist. (It's one reason he's become so close to Gary Ginsberg—because that *is* what Ginsberg does.)

Murdoch's good at government relations—a rare talent. There is just something about the process here being so character-focused, and about the system being so basic and mechanical—you apply pressure here and yield a result there; weakness responds to power; you scratch my back and I'll scratch yours—that fascinates him. "He spends a few days in Washington and he gets full of energy," says the Republican pollster and consultant Frank Luntz, who has advised News Corp. and accompanied Murdoch on Washington visits (and gone on to be an on-air commentator at Fox News). "He's in his element. He knows who everybody is and everybody wants to meet him."

Again, it's not ideology. It's all function—it's all craft. It's the investment that he's made over so many years in politics and in politicians paying off.

Indeed, in the nineties, post-Reagan-Thatcher, he begins to play a profoundly nuanced and plastic game: He figures out that a right-wing guy with even the mildest possible suggestion of moderation can have incredible clout with the liberal guys.

He really can't stand the Clintons. This is partly because they can't stand him and partly because they seem so sloppy, so unfocused, so undisciplined. On the other hand, he gets results from them; they jump. He gets the federal waiver he needs to get the *New York Post* back. He manages to have the Clinton FCC close its eyes to the fact that Fox television stations are actually, and contrary to the law, owned by a foreign company. (He has also assiduously courted the Republican Speaker of the House Newt Gingrich, including arranging for HarperCollins, the News Corp. book publisher, to give him a rich book advance.)

But it's in Britain that this ironical fluke of ideology—that the left can be more responsive to him than the right—really pays off. His working of Tony Blair is quite a thing to behold (as is, conversely, the Blair working of Murdoch).

The diaries of Alastair Campbell, Blair's communications chief, present an almost step-by-step primer on the art of submission to Murdoch—how much you need to give up, how much you can hope to retain. It's a hard, humiliating business that shapes the Blair candidacy and defines New Labour. The Murdoch in the diaries is an implacable presence: You come to him, and only when you've given enough does he give. It begins with Blair coming to address a News Corp. conference in 1995 at a gathering on Hayman Island in Australia. The event is distinguished not just by Blair's Murdoch-placating talk but by everybody in Australian politics warning him about the difficulties of dealing with Murdoch. "Murdoch," says Paul Keating, the Australian prime minister, whom Murdoch has supported, "is a hard bastard and you need a strategy for dealing with him." There are the difficulties of dealing one-on-one with Murdoch: "I tried to prise him open a bit about what he was thinking," says Campbell, "but despite the twinkle in his eyes, and the general warmth, he was very guarded. Any attempt at big talk was reduced to small talk pretty quickly." And on Murdoch's address to his own editors: "Chilling, to watch all these grown men, and some women, hanging on every word, and know that an inflection here or there would influence them one way or the other."

It's a leitmotif of dealing with the Murdoch media: "In the end, they [Murdoch editors] would do what they were told." Recounting a meeting at the *Sun*: "Afterward [Blair] said that was not a good meeting and they are not very nice people . . . I said did you notice the portrait of Murdoch in the room where we had lunch? It was one of those in which the eyes followed you round the room. Hilarious. But they were all a bit Moonie-fied."

It's a further irony, which Murdoch enjoys, that his most powerful political statement in the United States, when he becomes most publicly and vividly identified with the right wing and the "vast right-wing conspiracy"—which the Clintons will see themselves as martyrs of—comes just at the point where he is the least committed to the fervent right: Fox News.

Just as Fox News is taking the mantle of Clinton-Lewinsky and crafting its rambunctious, propagandized, intolerant, bar-stool conservatism, Murdoch has become involved with a junior staffer. Not only is his lover vastly younger and more liberal than he, but she will shortly cancel out Anna's influence. He actually has to mollify now in the opposite direction—he's got to be more liberal to foster peace at home. What's more, Peter Chernin, the News Corp. house liberal, continues to gain importance in the company—and importance to Murdoch.

But Fox News is a perfect reflection of Murdochian what-the-market-will-bear politics. It reflects, too, Murdoch's very odd combination of mischief and sanctimony—that perfect tabloid formula.

Fox is, in so many ways, the ultimate Murdoch product—all the lessons are combined and they all work. He produces, finally and successfully, his American tabloid. Up against CNN, a much larger, much more established, much more respectable competitor, he counterprograms. Fox is self-consciously downmarket, rude, loud, opinionated. This not only defines a lower-end, secondary news market, but does it in a way that's much cheaper than how the other guy does it. Lack of respectability is cheaper than respectability. That's tabloid.

It's all about torturing the other guys too. Your marketing premise is that you'll push it until you get a rise out of them. The establishment makes the anti-establishment possible. This is simple. CNN is Keith Murdoch and Fox is Rupert Murdoch. This is what he's learned.

On the other hand, he could not have done this alone, because he's too respectable; he might even be too liberal by this point.

Hence, his alter ego: Roger Ailes.

In a sense the success of Fox is random, or kismet: almost entirely dependent on the fact that Murdoch lucks into a television guy whose affect—bumptiousness, irascibility, succinctness, obvious outsiderness—entertains him. What happens to Murdoch is that he gets a crush on Ailes. For a very long time, having dinner with Ailes is the most galvanizing thing in Murdoch's life—it makes him feel in the game, it's pure pleasure. Indeed, he gives Ailes what he has never given any of his editors—never given the *Times* of London, even though his pledge has the force of law, and likely never will give the *Wall Street Journal*, although he'll swear he will: fundamental editorial independence. It is understood that Murdoch can't go behind Ailes' back and talk to the talent and executives at Fox News without him first talking to Ailes, and that Ailes himself can't be overruled about what goes on the air.

There is, of course, an exceptional reason for this: It's television, not a newspaper, and Murdoch doesn't know from nothing when it comes to television news. At a newspaper, he's confident about his ability to meddle; with television, he's, with good reason, not at all confident (he doesn't even like television all that much). And it's also a calculated business decision: He needs Fox to be pushed further than even he might naturally go.

Indeed, the apoplexy that Fox News regularly arouses in liberals is aroused too within News Corp. It may be one of Murdoch's measures of how successful Fox and Ailes are—how much they're getting to the News Corp. liberals, not least of all Chernin and Ginsberg.

(Ginsberg is Murdoch's ever-present example of what fun it is to mess with liberals. Ginsberg, practiced in his acquiescence and tolerance, could also be Murdoch's best indication of going too far. One Christmas, Murdoch, to bedevil the Jewish liberals at News, not least of all Ginsberg, pays for crèches to be placed on every reception desk throughout News Corp. Thereupon transpires a two-hour meeting with Murdoch, Ginsberg, and two rabbis. Ginsberg, being no fool, has evoked the two things that might always be used to counterbalance Murdoch mischief: middle-brow high-mindedness and piety, those quintessential newspaper values.)

In some sense, Ailes is a reflection more of contrariness than of politics. Everybody at the highest reaches of News Corp. shuts their eyes to Ailes. He is a piece of mischief that has gotten out of hand. Without Murdoch, there would be no tolerance for him within News Corp. But Murdoch has to live with him—because

Murdoch's odd piece of mischief, his bit of counterprogramming, has become a success.

As Fox News is rising, it is significant to point out, so is Sky News as a core part of the BSkyB operation in Britain—it is an almost comical mirror image of Fox News. In fact, if you're used to Fox News, you watch Sky News and wait for the people on air to somehow acknowledge that they're kidding around by playing it straight and reputable and agenda-free.

And that is exactly the worry at the *Wall Street Journal* editorial page—that Murdoch's politics aren't actually politics, or at least not structured, charted, formal beliefs, but some more or less picaresque adventure in which they can only look forward to becoming bit players. Indeed, he might see editorials as part of the adventure. "I'm a very, very curious person, but I couldn't sit down and write a learned article on the Middle East—but I can write a pretty good editorial about it!" Murdoch will say in one of our interviews, staking his claim to the rhetorical flourish.

**JUNE 2007**

Rob Kindler, a voluble investment banker at Morgan Stanley, believes that he and Morgan Stanley should have been hired as co-advisors to the Dow Jones board with Goldman Sachs. From early on in the process he became a negative, carping, almost jeering voice about how Dow Jones' advisors are shepherding the company to an inevitable sale to Murdoch.

He's never known a company to be sold for its first bid, he keeps saying as no higher bids emerge to challenge Murdoch.

His none-too-veiled suggestion is that Dow Jones' advisors— Goldman; Merrill; Wachtell, Lipton; Simpson, Thacher—are in Murdoch's pocket, or want to be.

The four firms, for their part, perturbed but tolerant, point to the $60—that it is just off the charts—and to the family. By bringing in every Tom, Dick, and Harry, they have demonstrated that there are no other serious bidders. So what can they do?

And yet there is something to Kindler's fulminations. A sense that ranks are closing around Murdoch. Surely, the ranks are irritated with the family—there's an underlying sense of *Good riddance* and *This is what you deserve.*

Not only are Leslie Hill and Chris Bancroft still rushing around the country, churning up all kinds of dust—duly reported as significant developments by the reporters they're blabbing to at the *Journal*—but they're dragging their heels on the editorial agreement.

The Dow Jones board is starting to call Elefante every two minutes, asking where the agreement is. The way the family has set it up, the board can't start having a substantive talk with Murdoch about a deal until they've come to terms on an editorial agreement, so the whole process is stalled. The eyes of the business world are on them (as are the eyes of the arbitrageurs who have bought up the stock—potentially litigious shareholders), and all the board can do is twiddle its thumbs.

The Wachtell, Lipton guys and Michael Elefante are now beginning to suspect that Hill and Bancroft are using the editorial agreement as a big stalling tactic.

Chris Bancroft has been contacted by Stuart Epstein, a banker at Morgan Stanley, who is acting as the chief advisor to Thomson in its merger with Reuters. Bancroft is flown to Toronto to meet with W. Geoffrey Beattie, the president of the investment vehicle for the Thomson family. (As a point of gentle irony, these are the same Thomsons who owned the *Times* of London and sold it to Murdoch.) What Bancroft is told is that Merrill Lynch, with its dire prognostications, is feeding the Bancroft family a lot of nonsense about how bad the Reuters-Thomson merger will be for Dow

Jones. In fact, Bancroft is reassured just how good it will be. If the Bancrofts can only hold out until the Thomson-Reuters deal is closed, Thomson will be back to Dow Jones with an offer a helluva lot better than $60.

Sure.

Indeed, there's a creeping sense of worry among the advisors and among some people on the board that if they don't behave themselves, Murdoch will get pissed off and lose interest. The push-pull of all this has actually forced many of the people involved with the deal to clarify their feelings: They have to admit, they're drawn to Murdoch.

For banks and law firms representing Dow Jones, as well as for the free-market dogmateers at the *Journal*, Murdoch—say what you want about him—represents the free market. He is the ultimate capitalist achievement. Everybody else, even GE, is not so ready, not so pure, not so alive. If you're actually part of the free market (even if Rob Kindler is saying this market isn't so free), you're partial to Murdoch—you *get* him. His politics, the politics of success, are your politics and the *Journal*'s politics.

On June 21, Pearson and GE, receiving little encouragement from the Dow Jones and Bancroft advisors, daunted by the Murdoch offer, and without the temperament to deal with the Bancroft family's psychological issues, end their consideration of the deal.

It's clearly only Murdoch—take him or leave him.

# ELEVEN

# The Nineties—
# The Amazing Mr. M.

**JUNE 16–24, 2007**

Sometime over the weekend of June 16, a water pipe in the ceiling of the eighth floor of the News Corp. building at 1211 Sixth Avenue—housing the management nerve center of the company—will break, dumping almost a foot of water across News' executive offices.

This is generic corporate space that reflects the News Corp.'s make-do ethos, or its patch-it-together sense, or even a bit of living above the store. (Fox News, with its fetid greenroom, is in the basement. The *New York Post* is crammed in here too. And in his mind, Murdoch is already shoehorning the *WSJ* into 1211.)

The reception area on eight has some none-too-chic furniture, a flat-screen monitor tuned always to Fox News, and a British receptionist. Murdoch's office suite is just off the reception area (he often sweeps out to pick up visitors). You go first into a secretarial area—

where seventy-something Dot Wyndoe, from Australia, who's been his secretary since 1962, sits in a frozen-in-time hairdo with two other assistants—and then around the corner into Murdoch's office proper. With its central desk and separate seating area, various television monitors, and computer sitting mostly unused on the sideboard, the office is entirely unremarkable. Now, media-conglomerate CEOs' offices tend to be pharaoh-worthy monuments to self, to power, to visualizations of strength, to seizing the day. Peter Chernin, in a new executive building erected on the Fox lot in Los Angeles, has built himself a true media-lord spread. Hushed, vast, meticulously designed, off-putting for any visitors (off-putting, in fact, to many people at News Corp.), Chernin's office implies that it's above work, beyond function, its occupant having risen to the level where will and desire alone make things happen.

A spilled cup of coffee might cause paralysis in Chernin's office, but at 1211 Sixth Avenue on the eighth floor, the flood—after it gets drained and more or less mopped up by the maintenance guys—won't be the sort of mess that anybody here can't work in. Even the mossy smell won't interrupt business as usual.

Oddly, what happened since the May 1 news of Murdoch's bid for Dow Jones is that the eighth floor has turned into not just a war room, but in some more or less unintended way a rump organiza-tion. Within a company the size of News Corp. the way a deal, even a big one, is normally conducted is that a project team is assembled, but it's sort of off to the side so that the bosses can continue their stewardship of the larger affairs of the company.

But with Dow Jones, top executives at News have *become* the project team. That is, all except for Chernin, who, out in Los Angeles, has for all practical purposes become the operator of this global company, while Murdoch and his little band—DeVoe, Nallen, Jacobs, Ginsberg—fret about their junior-size deal.

Now, again, it is instructive to compare the flow of this deal at News Corp. with how it might play out at other companies. In other companies, if a deal is perceived as being likely to have a negative effect on the share price, there are few circumstances in which it gets done.

The presumed effect of News Corp.'s acquisition of Dow Jones is that the News share price will plunge. By some estimates the cost of this $5 billion acquisition could be more than $20 billion in shareholder value. DeVoe, Nallen, Jacobs, Ginsberg, and all those whose wealth depends on stock options should rationally be less than enthusiastic about such a deal—and finally be the voice of reason in not letting such a deal happen (by force of logic, foot dragging, or general negativity). In fact, only Chernin is the reasonable figure—his neutrality is the elephant in the room. While he can't openly oppose Murdoch, he can, at least, not waste his time. In Murdoch's view, Chernin has not been *given* an opportunity to have an opinion about the deal. And why would he? He doesn't, as Murdoch often points out, even read newspapers.

The extrabusiness-like allegiance to Murdoch, the desire among the eighth-floor gang to please the boss even at your own expense, mirrors the extrabusiness-like characteristics of News Corp. itself. In a world in which corporations have long been conditioned to respond to shareholders' short-term needs, News Corp. has always been more interested in expanding its power than in getting a high return on capital. It isn't about what shareholders want; it's about what Murdoch wants.

Indeed, the guys on the eighth floor save it for him. They could let Dow Jones go, but he wants it bad, and they want him to have it.

As the cleanup proceeds on the eighth floor, the Bancrofts' draft of the editorial protection agreement finally arrives—eighteen days after the meeting in the Wachtell, Lipton offices.

Leslie Hill has solicited the opinions of lots of people on the *Journal* staff about editorial protections. In another of those extraordinary moments of helplessness or haplessness or suicidal optimism—quite similar to what had happened at the *Times* of London twenty-six years before—the *Journal* editors didn't resist at all, but helped craft an idealized framework for their theoretical editorial independence. Marcus Brauchli, the new managing editor, who had officially taken the newsroom reins from Paul Steiger on May 15, was the most active participant in designing this instrument, which would, in the end, not protect him at all. Josh Cammaker, culling the family's thinking and incorporating Brauchli's advice, drafts the agreement that is finally sent on Friday, June 22.

When Marty Lipton delivers the agreement to Murdoch in the morning, he says, "You're not going to like this."

Later, after he reads it, Murdoch calls Lipton and says, "I'm not disliking it—I'm just insulted by it!"

The insult is that it actually does what they've been discussing—it protects the paper from Murdoch's interference. It calls for a thirteen-member editorial board, for which the Bancrofts will appoint ten members, and what's more, it gives this board control over not just the editor but the publisher as well.

So . . .

"I wrote a letter," Murdoch will later tell me, "withdrawing the offer and telling them to fuck off."

There's a conclave that afternoon of the eighth-floor team—with James Murdoch calling in from London—and they get Murdoch to cool off.

While the storm and stress that Friday are genuine—there is nothing that so provokes Murdoch as someone trying to trump him—it is, nevertheless, ramped up several notches to accommodate a reporter from *Time* magazine, with whom Ginsberg has negotiated special access in return for special consideration. News Corp. is waging its campaign: Ginsberg will set up the scenes and vet the quotes in an effort to make Murdoch look like a reasonable (and, ideally, heroic) fellow trying to persevere in his dealings with the frustrating, irrational, odd Bancrofts—which is, basically, the *Time* cover story that appears the next week.

Murdoch revises the letter—there's no "fuck off," but it's still harsh, laying out all the frustrations of the last two months of dealing with the Bancroft family—and gives it to his lawyers to send. But it doesn't quite get sent. Instead, Ginsberg revises it once more. Murdoch, considering Ginsberg's draft, calls Robert Thomson at the *Times* of London, getting him to take a stab. Thomson's draft, reflecting Murdoch's continued irritation, is less equivocal, outlining all the objections to the editorial agreement and setting out an ultimatum: It's what Murdoch wants or nothing. This is on Saturday—with the *Time* reporter still sitting in Murdoch's office. The plan is to release the letter on Sunday.

But Ginsberg once again weighs in and says he'd like to take a stab at calling Dick Beattie, his former mentor at Simpson, Thacher. Ginsberg spells out to Beattie all the nonstarters in the family's proposed agreement. Without an immediate retreat, Ginsberg says, the deal is finished, over, kaput.

Now, this is, in many ways, the point: Some family members want to kill it—well, sort of want to kill it. The agreement is a passive-aggressive way to do just that. By calling Beattie, Ginsberg goes over the head of the family and puts it on the advisors' plate, knowing that the advisors will raise their voices in concert—Beattie, Lipton, Cammaker, Costa at Merrill, the guys at Goldman—to say that if they don't want to do the deal, don't do the deal, but that it has to be a choice independent of the editorial agreement, which, written this way, does kill the deal.

So, do they want to kill the deal?

No. Maybe. Not yet—still thinking.

Okay, then, in order *not* to kill it, the Bancrofts are told, they'll have to scale back on the editorial protections. So let the lawyers work out acceptable language.

By Sunday morning, the Bancrofts have retreated.

## REMAKING NEWS

The joy, the anticipation, on the eighth floor is about Murdoch, once more, getting to reinvent himself. But the irony, of course, is that he is trying to reinvent himself with a newspaper. The guys on the eighth floor, in addition to getting the deal done, somehow have to get Wall Street not to notice the fact that the deal is for a newspaper.

In developing their story, they go with Robert Thomson's digital blah-blah. Thomson, who will take command of the *Journal* newsroom if the deal gets done (no matter that News Corp. is, at the same time, saying it would not take over the newsroom), is all for the story being that the *Journal* will be the basis for an international platform of business data, sliced and diced for distribution systems and opportunities, both present and yet to be imagined. He sits down with the News Corp. PR people and dictates the digital language—and it works; people believe it, the share price holds.

Pay no attention to the fact that Murdoch doesn't get e-mail, use a computer, or even, really, know how to work a cell phone. Or to the fact that he rushes to his desk every morning to flip through the paper he is trying to buy, ripping the broadsheets back, slashing at them with his finger, delivering—as the world with more and more equanimity accepts the imminent death of newspapers—a determined and aggrieved seminar on what makes a good newspaper page.

While the eighth floor is proclaiming News Corp.'s grand design for Dow Jones, it is, at the same time, wondering if the old man has any clue at all about what he is going to do if he gets it. Meanwhile, they are pleased to baldly misrepresent the old man's real interest in Dow Jones being about digital hoopla. There is a large joke here with many nuances.

News Corp., the most retrograde, technologically resistant company in the media business—its newsrooms are outfitted with ancient computers, its Web sites are balky and cheap-looking—is, mostly by the sheer force of News Corp. people simply saying otherwise, actually thought to be technologically cunning and pre-scient and even hip (the one thing News Corp. has definitely never been).

The fact that News, in a fluke of dealmaking, has ended up owning MySpace, an au courant Internet company (well, au courant circa 2006), is amusing and baffling to most News execu-tives.

Still, while the company knows nothing, and cares less, about technology, it does know something about transformation. That it has experienced a greater level of speeded-up mutation than any other enterprise its size, that it has welcomed such constant over-haul and sudden shifts in direction, makes it, in a sense, a credible advocate for dealing with the exigencies and upheavals and revo-lutions of the information age.

This is lesson number one at News Corp: Nobody has the time, temperament, or perhaps the IQ for complicated explanations. So do it first and figure it out later.

No, no . . . that's actually lesson number two. Lesson number one is that if *he* wants it, hell, that ought to be a good enough rea-son for everybody else.

## ESCAPING HOLLYWOOD: 1990–1997

Everybody on the eighth floor will assure you that Rupert Murdoch knows all, always—except if you press just slightly, then, in an instant, you'll have everybody marveling about the luck and hap-penstance and general disorganization and ad hoc nature inherent in everything that happens at News. In fact, it is all so frequently random, so uncorporate, so seat-of-the-pants, that the only expla-nation for the company's epochal transformations—at the same time, oddly, that so many things stay the same at News—is that Murdoch must, in fact, however much the evidence contradicts this, know all. The proof is in the pudding? From 1954 until 1968, he was building a midsize Australian newspaper company; from 1968 until 1980, he was turning himself into an international publishing entrepreneur; and from 1980 to 1990, in a transformation almost as dramatic as the hand-tooled auto industry morphing into an assembly-line colossus, Murdoch turned his publishing company into an integrated multiplatform content-creation and distribution conglomerate.

Then, in 1990, along with so many businessmen of his type and period, he reaches the natural wall, the inevitable ebb, quite likely even the end, of his personal business cycle: a credit crisis. He can't meet his short-term debt obligations. He has grave troubles renegotiating his loans because of the great number of banks holding his paper—if one bank refuses to go along, likely they'll all push him into bankruptcy.

He shows up one evening in London at Prue and Alasdair's house. He's weary but calm, telling them that the likelihood is that he'll lose the company. During the months when the outcome is in doubt, his hair will turn entirely gray (as opposed to the orange it became after that). The best case is to come through with a diminished, fractional company, whose growth will be constrained by its lenders. He'll be working for the banks.

In some radical and magical transformation, though, the master of the media universe turns into a chastened hat-in-hand supplicant, and by 1991, having missed bankruptcy by a hair, he's begun to recover from the nearest-to-mortal moment of his business life.

Still, it's a funk. He's seriously sidelined.

For his sixtieth birthday, he's shipped off to a health farm in Tucson, Arizona, where BSkyB executives turn up to tell him that they won't make payroll that week. Murdoch, at 10 A.M., in his track suit, pours himself a drink.

At a conference of company executives in Aspen at this time he even allows on the agenda the topic of himself. Maybe *he's* the problem. His very inclinations and personality may be the problem—his need for constant change and new conquests. Of course, when some executives actually entertain the notion of his being a liability and see some merit in his pulling back, he immediately takes the subject off the table.

He's stuck with intractable issues: banks—and his wife.

Anna is forty-seven. She's steely, incredibly disciplined, and has been an absolutely vital adjunct to the management of his business—she's been a great corporate spouse. But you can't miss (he certainly hasn't missed it) that she's a martyr too. It's not just that he's been absent for so much of the time and that she's lived with the constant agitation and upset of him arriving and departing, but that she's had to struggle for, become so shrewish about, every little thing she's wanted from him. By 1991, Elisabeth, twenty-three, is out of college; Lachlan, twenty, is finishing up at Princeton; James, nineteen, is at Harvard. She's done the vast share of the parenting. She's even raised—with great friction—stepdaughter Prudence, now thirty-three. His contribution to child rearing has been not much more than the star turn. They adore him; they suffer her. She can take that. But now, particularly with the children gone, she wants . . . a life. A place. An acknowledgment. A reasonable plan and design.

There is actually reason for her to believe she can get this, because Rupert is henpecked—at least when he's around. He accedes to strong women—if they can catch him. He gives in, however begrudgingly. His life outside of the office—at least when he's not in transit—is what she wants it to be. She gets him out to charitable events (although he gives parsimoniously) and cultural events such as the opera (where he sleeps).

She's ambitious too. She's gone back to school, gotten a college degree from New York University. Then, in the eighties, while he's nowhere and everywhere (although not at home), she wrote two novels—bodice-ripping types. One, in fact, is about the trials of dynastic succession in a family publishing empire. This development irks him—and hurts her when he, under his breath (but not enough under his breath not to get into the papers), ridiculed her writing. Anyway, it's part of the new understanding. She'll stop with the embarrassing books if he'll be a better husband.

The bargain in 1990 and 1991 is explicit. She'll accept—and even be supportive of—his almost total emotional departure from their home life during his business crisis. She'll grin and bear it on the understanding that things will be different upon his return. He'll be a different person. He'll slow down. Begin thinking about retirement, about the transformation to a post-empire, post-work life. Anna—a precise, organized, get-on-with-it type—has begun planning for their post-credit-crisis life together, their scaled-down, depressurized, semiretired life.

If he does get through his credit crisis, he figures he'll renegotiate.

He does get through it. He's been granted a do-over. So all the energy he's spent for the last forty years on what next to buy and take and subsume, he decides now to refocus on running the businesses that he already owns. It will be a new sort of business discipline—a real, grown-up business discipline.

Focused on transforming himself and behaving himself, he moves to Hollywood, because this is where the company now has its big growth interests—the Fox network and the movie studio—and because this is where Anna wants to live. And because he no longer has the *New York Post* to hold him to New York. And because he can sell the Manhattan apartment—and, frankly, he can use the cash. While Hollywood isn't exactly the retirement Anna wants, it does feel more relaxed than New York. (Plus the house here needs to be redone. It's a tried-and-true strategy of the old-school executive husband: occupy the wife with decorating a house. He'll employ this strategy with Wendi too.)

Murdoch sees his role in Hollywood as perhaps something like that of Lew Wasserman, the CEO of MCA and Universal, and, for more than a generation, the most powerful man in the business. A force in politics and the community. A man of respect. A godfather. The world parts for him. Murdoch is vastly richer and more powerful than Wasserman ever was—so why not take the title? (Also, he and Anna live in the former home of Jules Stein, who was Wasserman's boss through the 1940s, '50s, and '60s.) This will also please Anna. Old Hollywood, the Hollywood of Lew Wasserman and the Reagans, is a place that could be home for her.

For Anna, it's almost an acceptably transformed life, in Jules Stein's hacienda-style house in the hills. She even has an office on the executive floor of the old Fox building, across from Rupert's office. They're on the lot. It's got some magic. Anna herself, with her highly structured blond coif, seems, in the commissary, almost like a retired star.

Being the new Lew Wasserman, the new king of Hollywood, is an okay plan, except that there's the Diller issue. Fox is Barry Diller. Murdoch hasn't ever worked with someone who might be as important as Murdoch himself, or as feared, or as central. At Fox, with Diller running it, Murdoch is in the way. Too many cooks. And to boot, Diller, the architect of News Corp.'s acquisition of the studio and the launch of the Fox Network, has broached the subject of his greater participation in the company, of his becoming part of the ownership structure, of being a meaningful stakeholder.

It's a collision of cultures.

Diller represents corporate America's upper managerial class with its inherent claim on equity. Diller also represents Hollywood —he's the insider. Murdoch's the outsider. If Murdoch wants in, it will cost him (it's no different from the partnerships Murdoch will shortly be making in China to smooth his acceptance).

Murdoch, for his part, is fundamentally anti-corporate; he's monarchical (pay no attention to his decades-long battle against the idea of monarchy). In his mind, it's foreign, offensive, louche that an employee, a commoner, would suggest a leveling of their relationship, a dollar-and-cents reinterpretation of their relative position and value.

Actually, in some sense, he doesn't even hear the offense; he blocks it out. In hindsight, Diller will recognize that as he himself was becoming more valuable to the company, as he became more identified with Fox, Murdoch was becoming less interested in him, colder, diffident. Diller is hardly the first News Corp. executive to have wholly misunderstood his value to Murdoch, to have assumed a three-dimensional relationship where only a flat one exists.

And, simply, Murdoch wants Diller's job: Murdoch wants to be the Hollywood boss—has got to have it if he's going to be out here.

They split relatively amicably, with Diller getting a vast pay-off—and bequeathing Murdoch, in some ultimate mischief-making scenario, the frictionless, even transparent, future king of Fox and monarch of Hollywood, Peter Chernin.

There follows a brief golden phase for Murdoch in Hollywood: a fleeting interest in stars, in accoutrements, in black-tie premieres, of him flying in newsroom guys from Australia and London to show off how glamorous he's become.

His daughter Elisabeth even gets a big Hollywood wedding— with the entire Murdoch family heading in from Sydney and Melbourne, while the groom's "brightly dressed" relations fly in from Africa, including his father, a political activist let out of a Ghanaian prison only a few months before. The bride wears ivory Christos, the bridesmaids Vera Wang, in a Catholic ceremony at St. Timothy's Church in Beverly Hills. The Reagans attend.

The problem is, Murdoch hates Hollywood. It's seldom happened, perhaps never happened, that Hollywood, with its charms and blandishments, fails to seduce (usually fleece and seduce). Even with all the reasons to accept the seduction—Anna is happy in Hollywood; it's the logical center of the business—he can't.

Hollywood is one of the great closed communities on earth. If he felt hemmed in by London, this is much worse. Hollywood business practices are set in amber. Every deviation is tectonic. And it's hierarchical—everyone has a place, and everyone has someone higher than him; there is always a brighter star—whereas

Murdoch has only ever functioned with himself on top of a leveled organization.

The state of play firms up pretty quickly. He hates the Hollywood people. They hate him. Not least of all because he gets on a roll telling them how much he hates them. It's a certain sort of Hollywood currency to be able to bring out the biggest guy you can bring out on your team—that's clout. But Murdoch, beyond even the problem of his representing some right-wing ideology that's not cool in Hollywood, scowls when stars are brought into his presence, turns sour, irritable, charmless—he keeps reminding everybody about it being *his* money. He's an inhibitor to the business—a downer.

He is, to a degree seldom seen in Hollywood, unmoved by what motivates people here. He doesn't like movie people. But perhaps more important, he doesn't like movies. Worse, pop culture itself is just strange detritus to him. He's an evident old guy. He doesn't get it. Out in the land of going with the flow and cultural relativism and indulgences of all type, he's crabby, mordant, dyspeptic—and most of all cheap. What he's watching, at Twentieth Century Fox, is *his* money potentially going up in flames. Indeed, the fact that *Titanic* will make him seem like a Hollywood genius when it becomes the biggest grosser in movie history almost won't register because it comes so close to sinking him. The $200 million that runs through his fingers on *Titanic* could well upset his careful restructuring of the company. Then, when it turns out to be a hit—analysts had reduced their profit estimates for News Corp. by 10 to 15 percent before the movie's release—he has to deal with the arrogance of these people. (James Cameron, king of the world? *Please.*)

His presence on the lot changes the whole tone of Hollywood. He's not larger than life, not acting like the royalty he should be acting like—he decidedly isn't Lew Wasserman—but is, instead, an old-fashioned headmaster, a scourge, a moralist, a grump.

He just doesn't work with other cultures—business or aesthetic. He doesn't, in any meaningful way, ever adapt. He has only ever done it the way he's done it.

"Wipe that smirk off your face!" he screams at a senior Fox executive who has not adequately covered his reaction to one of the constant not-the-way-it's-done-here ideas Murdoch offers in one of the endless meetings at the studio (e.g., to beef up advertising sales at the local Fox stations, why not just fire the man who's earned the least that month?—that's something that worked in Australia, he says). After the meeting he orders that the executive be fired.

His tone-deafness dates back to Fox's *Home Alone*, in 1990, which became the second-highest-grossing film of the year. Its $533 million earnings off a $15 million investment allow Murdoch to substantially reduce his debt to the banks. Unfortunately, *Home Alone* thereafter becomes his idea of what every movie should be. (Actually, that's an improvement of sorts: Shortly after he bought the studio, he went on a kick to do another *Crocodile Dundee* movie.)

The Fox Network doesn't make him any happier. It's a growing success, based first on the prime-time hit *Married with Children*, the scatological domestic comedy, followed by *The Simpsons*, that culturally anarchic cartoon, but it's bewildering to him. Now, there's a way to understand the Fox Network as a certain sort of postmodern tabloidism—except that Murdoch himself is never going to understand postmodernism in any context. Matt Groening, the *The Simpsons*' creator, finds it an example of almost *Simpsons*-like absurdity that such a churlish, retro, can't-get-the-joke, right-wing guy would bear ultimate responsibility for the show.

The point about Murdoch is that you can hate him as much as you want as long as you take him seriously—as long as you see him as a threat, a power to be reckoned with, a significant personage. But in Hollywood, among the poofters and cocaine addicts, he's regarded as somebody's creepy old uncle.

So he's plotting beyond Hollywood—beyond the emasculation he feels as an *entertainment executive*.

He gets his *New York Post* back in 1993. It's languished without him—as it logically would, because he's been the only one willing to sustain its great and inevitable losses. Washington, caught between causing the death of the oldest continually published newspaper in the country or giving it back to Murdoch (who has lobbied hard for it), capitulates. Without a print news operation in America for four years—during the banking crisis he's sold all his publishing properties in the United States except for *TV Guide*—he's back in business.

And he's focused on his other epochal obsession: his dynastic ambitions. In this, he's been influenced by the story of the Bingham family—the better part of the century, the Binghams have controlled two papers in Louisville, Kentucky, the *Courier-Journal* and the *Times*—and of what happens to a media empire (although to compare the Murdoch empire to the Bingham empire is to compare America to Monaco) when disparate family members have other interests and desires and different emotional axes to grind. Their downfall becomes the basis for the plot of Anna's second novel, *Family Business*.

The Bingham story becomes a point of clarity, if not alarm, for him. Control of News Corp.—especially were he to precipitously exit the stage—is a mess. The most significant voting bloc in the company is controlled by Cruden Investments, which is controlled by the family of Keith Murdoch—Dame Elisabeth and her four children, Helen, Rupert, Anne, and Janet, and their children. Any one of these principals becomes, in a fight for control, a potential turncoat or fly in the ointment or spoiler. And, he's reasoning, what have any of these others done for their supper? It's a business that *he's* singularly driven, run, imagined, suffered for, achieved—not *them*. Doing the thing that he does, narrowing his focus, hardening himself, becoming frighteningly distant—he makes it all a fait accompli, too late for argument, consideration, or sentiment—he goes in for the kill: He wants his mother and sisters and their families out. The price is arguably a fair one: $650 million. But the emotional price for his sisters and his mother is higher—to be kicked out of the empire, to be reminded that you're just a satellite.

"Rupert didn't like it one bit that any member of the family would be anything but grateful and say anything but 'Whatever you say, Rupert,'" Matt Handbury, his sister Helen's son, will say. Handbury has worked for News Corp. for most of his career, and then will go on to buy a book publishing business that News is selling called Murdoch Books—annoying Murdoch with his continued use of the name. "As an illustration of Rupert's sense of entitlement and the family being behind him, when he bought everyone out, he basically offered a future payment at a current price."

Rupert's implacable "that's the deal" position and his family's relative helplessness—although Matt Handbury tries to hire bankers and advisors, nobody else in the family wants to see this as a negotiation—culminates in a family meeting at which his mother buries her head in her arms on the boardroom table and says, "This is all a bit uncomfortable."

It is the model for dealing with family proliferation and future control: The generation's dominant member must jettison the others.

It's at this point, trapped and restless in Hollywood, and yet still with a compulsion to correct it, dominate it, even exact a certain revenge on it, that he begins to rely on Peter Chernin. It's a propitious and ultimately dangerous convergence. Chernin becomes the most successful number two or factotum in a town full of factotums—the implementer of Murdoch's revenge. This revenge—or insight, if you will—is to upend the Hollywood conceit, which is about creativity or content. That's the mark of Hollywood snobbery—the closer you are to what's on the big screen, the higher you are. Murdoch's view is the opposite: Media isn't about the media substance, it's about the media machine.

Chernin, as he begins his serious rise in the company, complements the Murdoch strategy. He doesn't bring unique experience or a substantial record of success to the table. There's nothing in his background to give him special authority, or even much of a sense of direction. He's a midlevel player. He comes from the back office, from a set of promotion and sales jobs. He's a soldier, a handler, an apparatchik. In this, except for the fact that he's not an old newspaper hack, he's a prototypical News Corp. manager—he doesn't have enough heft, or point of view, or confidence, or arrogance, to try to move the company in anything other than the direction in which Murdoch wants to take it. (At least not at this point.)

And, indeed, Chernin quickly establishes himself as a yes-man to Murdoch and a no-man to anyone who might have alternative views to Murdoch's. He's a cipher. In fact—and this is a big virtue for Chernin, as it gives him lots of operating room—Murdoch doesn't quite notice him. Although, more and more, everybody else does.

It is paradoxical that Murdoch, the control freak, likes to be taken in hand. The thing is that Murdoch rather lives in his head. For a person who is suspicious of the abstract, he himself is largely an abstraction—a media nerd, if you will, always with the mental wheels spinning, his variables, the ones he obsesses about, in constant motion: audience behavior, competitor advantages, the necessity of containing the cost of content, the complication of distribution, the difficulties of production, how to do everything more cheaply and simply, how to get the politicians off his back. He's containing this in his head, and it makes him less than socialized, isolated even. He doesn't yield easily to the world of distractions (Anna, for one, is always trying to distract him). He's grateful for anyone who can minimize the friction, who can lessen the interactions that he doesn't want to have, the interactions that disrupt his chain of thought. He doesn't want to be dealing with irrelevant details—doesn't want to have to stop and change the lightbulb. Doesn't want to have to think about what he doesn't want to think about. Murdoch just wants to move in the direction he's going and not have to stop for traffic.

He actually doesn't really consider Chernin very much. Or, to the extent he does, he doesn't especially like him. There are many of Murdoch's boys, his favorites, his pets, who have engaged him—people who have tapped into one or another of his generally passing enthusiasms. But Chernin isn't especially like that. He's more neutral. He's clearing the way. He's the hatchet man. But the secret of the good hatchet man is not at all to appear like the hatchet man—not to suggest that you've been doing the hard, thankless, dirty work. You merely want to leave the impression with your boss that it feels better when you're around, less good when you're not.

What Chernin does is cut a path so that Murdoch doesn't have to much deal with the issues that are most demanding and compelling and difficult and distracting and intractable in Hollywood —namely, talent, and the whole crap-shoot nature of the business—and let him get to the issues that he is more comfortable with: the mechanics, the true value creators, the big bold moves of the business.

Murdoch, disliking the movies, has already shifted the emphasis of Fox to television, and, in a sense, ever after, the emphasis in Hollywood itself shifts to television. And, because Murdoch isn't interested in what's on television, except for news (of course he likes having hits, but he doesn't watch them, and doesn't fetishize the process of creating them), he focuses on gaining the ground or the advantages that alter the balance of power in the business.

What you need to have is what the audience wants, and then to monopolize it.

For instance, sports.

Now, another distinguishing part of the Murdoch character is his general lack of interest in sports. This is about, likely, his own relative physical awkwardness; his impatience as a spectator; his disengagement from anything that he himself can't win; and, too, a further lack of socialization. Murdoch doesn't bond, except with a purpose. He's not one of the guys (one of the reasons he was so eager to leave Australia with its never-ending male-bonding rituals). On the other hand, contravening his psychological quirks, Murdoch is, again, a simple machine. He likes simple solutions and he likes to repeat them.

While sports has been a bedrock of television, at this point it's been a relatively overlooked one—it's niche programming. But Murdoch works the niche into the structural advantage of his networks. Sports becomes his pivotal monopoly.

Before Murdoch, soccer teams in the United Kingdom were pauper affairs, with piecemeal and poorly negotiated television deals. Murdoch locks up the television rights to soccer in the U.K., turns televised soccer into a lavishly promoted event, and turns the new Premier League into the most watched and wealthy sports league in the world—thereby making BSkyB a fixture in British life. In the United States he snatches the NFL from CBS in 1993, changing the economics of American sports broadcasting, and further re-creating his network of stations around sports rights—aligning Fox stations with rights to local teams.

But aside from his big sports play—which of course has nothing to do with Hollywood—Murdoch is still stuck out in Beverly Hills and still feels like he's a governor rather than a conqueror. He finds himself—his employees find him—wandering the building looking for anyone to have lunch or dinner with. A forlorn figure.

He's survived the debt crisis, reclaimed the *Post*—the thing that makes Hollywood bearable is that he's still on the phone with his newsrooms—but he's stalled out. He's a man heading for retirement age, with a deeply indebted hodgepodge of media companies. Worse, he's in a business he doesn't get. The business of being cool, which he is not.

So: How do you change the story—move it from coolness, which he doesn't do, to expansion, conquest, dominance, which he does do? And how do you do this without any money?

He is—and this is a fundamental entrepreneurial talent—a master illusionist. It's the essential entrepreneurial skill, to convince people you are what you have yet to become.

If the pop-culture thing eludes him, he's nevertheless on the business zeitgeist. He has a keen, even preternatural sense of how the conventional wisdom among the toughest business guys is going to shape up.

Here's what Murdoch gets—the concept that is just coming into vogue in the media business: Either you have to be big enough to control distribution, or you have to be big enough to be able to negotiate with those who do control distribution—or, ideally, both. That's about to become the 1990s holy grail.

He goes off in 1994 to see John Malone, the most powerful man in cable television and, arguably, the media business—the man who has jump-started the new era of distribution power by promising five hundred television channels (TCI, his technologically kludgy and underresourced system, has, however, been unable to deliver on that promise). Malone, to Murdoch, is the real media business—distribution, leverage, monopoly, and a vast new system undermining the old networks—whereas Hollywood is a thumb-sucking and pantywaist business.

Malone, as powerful as he is, is in a bind. His deal to sell TCI —servicing one in four cable households—to Bell Atlantic has just fallen through. With new federal regulations hitting cable earnings, Bell Atlantic tries to reduce the purchase price, and Malone walks. His stock price is in a swoon. Murdoch takes this moment of weakness to suggest that Malone should help him launch a cable sports channel and, also, a news channel—on the cheap (although Murdoch has not yet articulated his version of a conservative news channel, Malone happens to be one of the few people in the media business to share Murdoch's unreconstructed views). Or the proposal to start a news channel is a feint, and what he really wants Malone to do is support Murdoch in his bid to buy CNN—in which Malone already holds a key minority stake.

But Malone is too smart or Murdoch too poor—it's hard to control distribution without cash on your books—or they're just too suspicious of each other. Malone is not going to be Murdoch's advantage or savior.

Enter (or, actually, reenter) the Houdini of business machinations: Michael Milken, the junk bond promoter.

Years earlier, Milken set up the one-two punch that got Murdoch the Fox studio and then the television stations that would form the Fox network. Not long afterward, he was convicted of various far-reaching fraudulent practices, sent to jail, and banned from the securities industry for life. This did not, however, lessen his acumen or even his reputation. He was, upon his release, just two years into a ten-year sentence, back to advising Murdoch.

In 1994, he gets Murdoch together with the financier Ronald Perelman. Perelman, like Murdoch, is an alumnus of the exclusive club of entrepreneurs lucky enough to have been financed by Milken and to not have been indicted or gone broke. Perelman, a publicity hound and would-be media entrepreneur himself (although he will make most of his reputation from the Revlon Company, which he took over in 1985), controls a company called New World Communications, which produces television shows (notably, *The Wonder Years*) and owns fifteen television stations in good markets (among them Atlanta, Austin, Cleveland, Dallas, Detroit, Milwaukee, Phoenix, and Tampa)—all affiliated with networks other than Fox. Milken's idea is a nifty one: Murdoch will invest $500 million in New World and Perelman will forsake his existing relationships and switch his stations' affiliations to Fox—the "greatest realignment of affiliations in the sixty-year history of American broadcasting," according to *Time*. This deal essentially makes Fox and profoundly diminishes CBS, which the lion's share of the New World affiliates carried and which has just lost the NFL rights to Fox. Murdoch isn't doing an acquisition, so he stays out of trouble with the banks; he's not buying more stations, so he stays out of trouble with the FCC; and, at the same time, he turns Fox into a bona fide fourth network. (In 1997, he'll buy all the New World stations outright. Four years after that, having worked the regulatory obstacles, he'll add ten stations by acquiring the Chris-Craft group of stations, which seventeen years before had helped thwart his takeover of Warner Communications, giving News Corp. the largest stable of O&Os, owned-and-operated stations, in the nation, and making it, effectively, the most profitable television network.)

Now, something is happening in the business zeitgeist that must have surprised even him. Instead of Murdoch and News Corp. representing all that has gone wrong with media concentration in the 1980s—just do a deal, any deal—it turns out to represent what's inevitable. Time, Inc., has followed News Corp. into conglomeration in 1989 by merging with Warner Communications. In 1993, Sumner Redstone at Viacom, aping Murdoch, buys Paramount. In 1995, Disney joins in by buying ABC. The Murdoch hypothesis, or the Murdoch opportunism, or the Murdoch way, has been accepted. News Corp., which in the harsh year of 1990 seemed to be nothing more than a collection of deals that would have to be unwound and undone, is suddenly emerging as a state-of-the-art media play.

Still, he has no money. At least, not enough for the geopolitical business moves he wants—*needs*—to be making.

He is, all of a sudden, oddly, thinking about technology. Or not so much thinking about technology as thinking big. In this instance, the entertainment and information marketplace is going to be transformed by unprecedented shifts in distribution control thanks to technology.

Perhaps right here it is most necessary to address the central question of his intelligence, of its nature, and of its depth. Does he understand? What does he understand? How does he put two and two together? How has he figured this out? What has he figured out? What are his analytic abilities? His perceptual apparatus?

He ain't conventionally smart. His war against intellectuals is, in part, to level the playing field, because he lacks their advantage (so he demonizes them, belittles them). He doesn't have the kind of mental patience to work through the analysis. His is a short attention span. Also, he doesn't much like information, or, at least, to qualify information. Or if he does, he sees it as binary: Is it useful, is it not? All information is gossip: Does it appear, if only in the moment, to be true or believable? He doesn't believe in, or see the point of, objective standards or values. He eschews the long term. It's a minute-by-minute mind. Animalistic. Eat what you kill.

He has enormous respect for the transformative powers of technology without knowing, in the slightest, a thing about it. He's surprisingly open to technological solutions while being, at the same time, altogether incurious about them.

To the degree that new technology could merely replace an existing function, he gets it—or at least gets the big picture. Satellites. Mmmm. Satellites, like cable, could put stuff on your television in your house. If Murdoch could control the satellite, he could control what's on your television. He *gets* that. And satellites complement his global reputation.

Suspicious of cable because of its massive capital costs, he'd started making small, frankly ill-advised satellite investments in the early eighties. In hindsight, this will come to seem like prescience on a grand scale. Truthfully, it was just cheapness. And competitiveness—his doing something that he thought others might do (and trying to do it cheaper). Also, in the pell-mell 1980s, it was easier for him to make an investment than it was to actually pay attention to something—or he needed to invest in order to focus (however superficially).

If you invest, things get rolling. Which might be, all in all, the explanation for how he got into the middle of Sky Television, which almost brought him to bankruptcy. That is, he invested, as cheaply as possible, and then there was a competitor—a rich, powerful consortium of his enemies, Richard Branson, Pearson, and Granada among them, who had started British Satellite Broadcasting—and he got competitive. A race began: Who could launch first? The establishment (the adversary is, with Murdoch, always the establishment) or Murdoch?

It's all Keystone Kops–ish, this technology race, and it comes to depend, for Murdoch, on an Israeli company, run by one Michael Clinger. Charged in 1987 for fraud and insider trading in the United States, he's fled to Israel, where's he's taken over a company called NDS, which makes the chip that Murdoch needs to encrypt the pay movies he wants to sell. In a pretty typical example of News Corp.'s ad hoc, haphazard methods and relative openness to wild-side types—"There were crooks, there were all sorts of things," Murdoch will note with nonchalance in one of our interviews—News is in partnership with Clinger and NDS long before it knows he's on the lam. Indeed, Clinger commences a methodical campaign of robbing News Corp. blind. Even when they get rid of him in 1992, they still find him three years later operating NDS through a set of shell companies he controls. Oh, and NDS, it turns out, is allegedly hacking into other companies' encryption systems. All this will result, for News Corp., in twenty years of litigation. (NDS is exonerated of hacking.)

No matter. Murdoch wins by being first to launch his British satellite, with his screwball and seriously problematic encryption, which, because nobody has the damn dishes yet, means horrific cash outflows, which help to precipitate his huge cash crisis, which is bad for him, but worse for the other guy, his weak-willed establishment competitors. The upshot is a merger of the two systems, which he comes to control and which, by the early 1990s, is very clearly a huge success for him. (Were it not for his debt crisis, if he could just have eked out a few more months, the other guys would have collapsed, leaving him with 100 percent of what is now a $14 billion business, instead of 39 percent.)

That's technology—it helps to unsettle things, and then, if you're a tenacious son-of-a-bitch, you can maybe grab an advantage.

In his continuing effort to escape his boring life in Hollywood, and to control the distribution heavens, he makes his investment in Star, a satellite network in China, in 1993.

In the annals of business flops, his foray into China, whose government blocks almost every Murdoch initiative, will be a humdinger. (Shortly after he makes his Star TV investment, he gives a speech implying his satellites will bring down the Chinese regime—which, even though he then madly tries to curry favor with the Chinese political establishment, is pretty much the kiss of death to his Chinese ambitions). There's a moment, in his yearning to get out of Hollywood and for zeitgeist transformation, where he actually considers moving to China. He and Anna even buy and decorate a house on one of the highest peaks of Hong Kong—only to discover that it's shrouded in fog for half of the year.

His global satellite vision would, of course, be so much more, well, *global* if it could involve the United States.

Except he can't afford to be in the satellite business in the United States, so once again, enter Michael Milken. The match Milken makes is with Bert Roberts at MCI, the fastest-growing long-distance telecommunications company. It's a felicitous match in that both men and both companies are trying to be something they are not. The fashion of the moment is that telecommunications companies ought to be media companies. Likewise, Murdoch wants to be a distribution company. Or, at least, both companies want it to look like they're becoming this other sort of company.

The introduction to Roberts is also a way to poke at John Malone—Murdoch is still looking for his soft spot, still thinking he ought to be able to find the point of leverage that will get Malone to give him an advantage, even, perhaps, to give him CNN.

Malone, at this time, believes he's locked up a deal that will give him access to choice satellite spectrum. Confident, he's already gone out and bought $100 million worth of satellites. But, in Washington, there are other powers—including Murdoch's partner-in-waiting, MCI—urging the Clinton administration to look askance at the deal. The FCC in fact rules that the license for this cable spectrum can't simply be transferred but must be auctioned—an auction that, when it is held in 1996, is won by MCI.

MCI thereupon enters into a $2 billion joint venture with News Corp. MCI will become the biggest News shareholder, and together the two companies will build an American satellite network, ASkyB.

Understand: Having no cash himself, Murdoch nevertheless makes a deal that appears to give him the wherewithal to dominate the heavens, and which, too, appears to have put $2 billion onto his balance sheet. He's gotten a major cash transfusion along with the transformational potential of a massive new media distribution system—or, at least, the illusion of same.

"MCI Communications Corporation and the News Corporation Limited, two companies that have radically changed the telecommunications and media industries, today joined forces to create and distribute electronic information, education and entertainment services to businesses and consumers worldwide," begins the press release announcing the venture.

"The companies said they will create a worldwide joint venture that they will own equally, leveraging the best broadcast, satellite, programming and publishing resources of News Corp.; and the marketing prowess, customer base and intelligent networks of MCI and its global partner BT [British Telecom]."

Murdoch himself adds: "Until today, no one has put together the right building blocks—programming, network intelligence, distribution, and merchandising—to offer new media services on a global scale."

In other words, reading the MCI and Murdoch statements more clearly, nobody here has the faintest idea of what, practically speaking, they are going to do.

Now, this is bad, and it will end unhappily. Indeed, the only real material development of this partnership is something called iGuide, which opens fabulous offices on West 17th Street in Manhattan, instantly becomes the leading technology company in New York, meant to compete with AOL and Prodigy (its true competitor will be the barely imagined Yahoo!—that is, News Corp. is inventing the search engine, though it has no idea this is what it is doing), and closes within a month.

This much-vaunted MCI–News Corp. joint venture never actually comes into existence; the people who are involved with it all work for one or the other of the companies; no new company takes charge. What MCI suspects is that Murdoch is continuing to search for a better way to build his satellite empire. Hence, MCI pulls out of the deal.

Murdoch, stuck with all this serious and costly satellite spectrum, and dubious financial wherewithal to use it, now turns to EchoStar, the U.S. satellite company, started by former CPA and card counter (before he's banned from Vegas) Charlie Ergen ten years before. The reasonable supposition is that Murdoch *really* doesn't want to be in business with Ergen, and even that he's gotten cold feet about the satellite business in the United States. He's getting lots of conflicting information at this point, not least of all from his son, James, an implacable advocate of whatever he's advocating—it's the Internet.

Also, Murdoch has the serious China bug—forget the U.S. market, he's seen China. Murdoch lets the new proposed joint venture with Ergen—also heralded by major and dramatic press drumrolls—stumble on whose encryption technology to use: EchoStar's or the technology Murdoch's gotten from the bunch of crooks and hackers he's funded in Israel. On that point the prospective joint venture with Ergen collapses. Ergen sues for $5 billion—prompting a settlement in which Ergen gets the satellite spectrum and Murdoch gets some 8 percent of EchoStar.

Meanwhile, having failed to persuade John Malone to help him make a run at CNN and having watched CNN get bought by Time Warner, he's got a bug up his ass. He gets that cable news is remaking the news business and is unhappy about not being in it—and understands that it's his own fault for doubting cable. And he gets that you can't be a major media player if you don't have major cable assets. That having major cable assets is the only way to bully your way into the evolving media business. Indeed, at this juncture—where the obsession is on how to get carriage (i.e., distribution) on monopoly-controlled cable systems—it's all about bullying tactics, which he is good at.

And then, the birth of Fox News. As with so many News Corp. projects, nothing is initially intuitive about the Fox News success. He tries to hire Roger Ailes, the former political operative, who helped start NBC's cable stations. Ailes won't run Fox News unless Murdoch can provide carriage (Murdoch at this point is desperate to get Ailes, so Ailes has unusual leverage). The only way to get carriage is to buy it—which has never been done before. But Murdoch does it and, in so doing, runs up against Time Warner and the enmity of CNN's Ted Turner, who tries to keep Fox off the air, which creates the kind of us/them ruckus that makes Murdoch Murdoch, and launches Fox News with more attention and identity than it deserves.

Indeed, like so many Murdoch products, it is launched on the cheap (except for the investment in buying distribution), and looks it. This is an economic necessity, but Ailes, an old-time broadcasting pro, understands a television virtue: Cheese sells. It's as much the trashiness—the exaggeration, the vaudevillian nature, the broad joke—as the politics that works here. And beyond the politics and the tabloid appeal, it is also the distribution—they muscle in.

Murdoch gets the premise: Success in television, cable or network, is not about the programs, it's about the homes. If you are in the homes, something will work. If you're not in the homes, nothing will work.

The guys at the networks have forgotten this lesson and come to believe it's about programming, even about quality, or some such nonsense—more Hollywood baloney—rather than about monopoly. They're the modern marketers, trying to convince and seduce, while Murdoch is the old-fashioned street vendor trying to control the neighborhood.

Just as Murdoch, in his efforts to escape a stultifying Hollywood, is rushing into the slipstream of technological grandiosity, and distribution paradigm shifts, and charlatans of all varieties, Dow Jones too is entertaining possibilities of a change in its nature.

It does this, however, in a wary, stern, skeptical, altogether conservative frame of mind—all values central to its identity. It does not, as Murdoch is doing willy-nilly, speculate. In the mid-eighties, it passes on an offer to acquire 25 percent of Apple. When index options come into vogue—you can buy securities pegged to where the S&P 500 will be at some future date—Dow Jones, after considered thought, decides that it will not create a similar product referring to the Dow Jones Industrial Average. The conclusion is: *That's gambling, and we don't want to be involved in gambling.*

Nor does it want to deviate from, or be loosey-goosey about, its central purpose. Matt Winkler, a rising star at the *Journal,* tells Norm Pearlstine in 1989 that he is quitting the *Journal* "because there's this guy Mike Bloomberg down at Solomon Brothers who has decided to start this new trading service and on his terminals he wants to have news and I'm going to be his editor." And if the loss of Winkler is a sign, to be compounded again and again in the coming years, that Bloomberg is a vast new business in Dow Jones' traditional space, the feeling remains that what the *Journal* does is news and what Bloomberg does is, somehow, mere statistics and quotes—*not of our class.*

Along with other media companies late to the game, Dow Jones, during the late eighties, begins tentatively to invest in cable systems. In an uncharacteristic moment of ambition, it gets into a negotiation about buying Comcast, already a significant cable provider (it will become the largest in the United States), but still a much smaller company than Dow Jones. And while it gets cold feet about the acquisition, it ends up with 25 percent of Comcast—which, however, it stays nervous about and sells within a few years.

And there is CNBC. Pearlstine proposes a deal that would have Dow Jones supplying eighteen hours a week of programming with an option to buy, at start-up cost, 49 percent of the news business channel—which is worth now more than $5 billion. But senior management turns this down, and Dow Jones ends up supplying content on a fee basis and without an equity stake.

Dow Jones, through the late eighties—when CEO Warren Phillips is posing for his annual report photograph in front of a typewriter—and through the nineties, is seeing as many opportunities for technological transformation as Murdoch. It responds in the best business-like fashion—with seriousness and restraint. The truth is, it doesn't want to be transformed. Or it is so respectful of the power of transformation that it proceeds with the kind of caution that precludes transformation. In the end, it is so temperamentally unsuited and resistant to the ad hoc, impromptu, make-it-up-as-you-go-along, adventurous, crafty, and flimflam aspects of transformation that when it decides, ever so tortuously, to take the plunge, it screws itself in its bet on Telerate.

## TWELVE   Rupert in Love

JUNE 16, 2007

The best gut estimation of which way the deal will go occurs on June 16 when John Lippman, after eleven years as a reporter for the *Wall Street Journal,* announces he is leaving. The point here is that if Murdoch is going to clinch the deal, Lippman can't very well stay. While News Corp. has its share of greater and lesser enemies upon whom it would, given the opportunity, take its revenge, a special place on that list is reserved for John Lippman.

It may be that the worst thing that can happen to a journalist is about to happen to Lippman. His paper is being pursued by a man whom he has written about in derisive, cruel, scathing, innuendo-laden terms. Even worse: He has written about the man's *wife* in derisive, cruel, scathing, innuendo-laden terms.

In all the bad press coverage of Rupert Murdoch over so many decades, nothing has hurt him so much as the piece by Lippman and two colleagues that appeared on the front page of the *Journal* on November 1, 2000. Charting Wendi Deng's path to Rupert Murdoch, it was an extraordinary piece of journalism about ambition, guile, and the special abilities of predatory women—specifically, predatory Chinese women. In Lippman's telling, Wendi Deng *was* the yellow peril.

What's more, it is believed by some at News Corp. that Lippman holds a stash of compromising (as they say) pictures of nineteen-year-old Wendi taken by her fifty-year-old, soon-to-be first husband.

Lippman is not going to wait to see what his potential new boss's mood might be.

## RUPERT AND WENDI

Of all the office affairs in history, Murdoch's may be the biggest cliché, both silly and sweet. This monster, this control freak, this cold bastard, is as blissfully helpless in the face of a determined woman of lowly rank as any lonely, erotically deprived, death-fearing man would be.

To the business world in 1996, his marriage to Anna has long appeared elemental to his success and identity. Anna, who seemed to change her outfit six times a day, gets the Aussie bloke who so often looks like an unmade bed to act at least a *little* like royalty—although never quite enough (to her taste, anyway).

Barry Diller, who saw them frequently in Los Angeles during the eighties and early nineties, will say, "Rupert and Anna are a modern love story . . . *were* a modern love story."

By the mid-nineties, however, Rupert and Anna are barely speaking. News Corp. executives start to notice that they live in separate parts of the big Beverly Hills house. "They passed like shadows in the night," one former News Corp. executive will say, adding that he believes that, in the seven or eight months before Rupert met Wendi, "he never spoke a word" to Anna.

It's a portrait of a solitary existence: He gets up at four or five in the morning and has a bowl of porridge—"A horse," he says, "has to have its chaff"—and then after a shower and shave drives down the hill to work. He works all morning, and then goes to lunch at the Fox commissary, where every day he intently scans the menu and then every day has the same damn thing: grilled chicken, vegetables, and a Diet Coke. It's practically a Monty Python sketch. Then he goes home at about seven and stays on the phone until bedtime at eleven.

If he's not following this routine, he's traveling.

China has become a sort of liberation. There's both a messianic sense to this adventure—that he can use modern media to somehow transform China while at the same time making billions—and too the typical News Corp. ragtag, throw-it-against-the-wall-and-see-if-it-sticks business plan. It's just a bunch of wild Aussies trying to make a killing (and make Rupert happy). Although, as it happens, the Aussies have so far lost several billion dollars on Rupert's Chinese dream.

It's one reason Wendi's arrival at the Star TV offices in Hong Kong in 1996 is so memorable: She's actually Chinese.

In John Lippman's account in the *Wall Street Journal,* Wendi Deng is an amoral Chinese girl, without prospects, who uses sex and various manipulative skills to seize convenient opportunities—opportunities that she jettisons as soon as better opportunities become available. By dint of coldness and calculation she navigates up the social trajectory of both the United States and China to marry the world's richest and most powerful media magnate and, by promptly producing two children, ensures herself a central position in all future dynastic developments.

There is great poetic justice in this tale, because of course the media magnate brought low by the amoral Chinese girl's coldness and calculation and preternatural manipulative talents is himself one of the world's most famous cold, calculated, and preternaturally manipulative sons of bitches. This daughter of a manager at a machinery factory in Guangzhou insinuates herself, in the *Journal* version of the story, predator-like, into the family of Jake and Joyce Cherry. Jake Cherry is, in 1987, a fifty-year-old engineer working in China. His wife, having met eighteen-year-old Wendi through their interpreter, starts helping the young girl with her English studies. Joyce Cherry returns to Los Angeles to enroll her two young children in school. Wendi and Jake, left to their own devices in Guangzhou, are shortly, according to the *Journal*, intertwined. Joyce will tell the *Journal* she eventually finds a cache of "coquettish" (in the *Journal*'s words) pictures of Wendi taken by her husband (these are the pictures that News Corp. officially denies exist). But before Joyce finds the smoking gun, Jake convinces Joyce that they ought to help Wendi get a student visa to the United States and, also, to invite her to stay with them in Los Angeles.

Wendi arrives in Los Angeles in February 1988. Underlining her duplicity and meretriciousness, the *Journal* points out that Wendi shares "a bedroom and a bunk bed" with the Cherrys' five-year-old daughter. Anyway, evidence and emotion will out and Joyce, according to the *Journal*, gets wise to the situation, forcing Wendi, now a student at California State University at Northridge, out of the house. Jake soon follows her and the two marry in February 1990. But in no time at all, she moves on. "She told me I was a father concept to her, but it would never be anything else," the *Journal* has Jake saying, adding, "I loved that girl." She does, however, stay married to Jake for two years and seven months— long enough, the *Journal* archly notes, to get a green card.

Her next alliance, begun while she's still involved with Jake, is with a more age-appropriate suitor named David Wolf, a business-man with an interest in China who speaks a bit of Mandarin. She's involved with Wolf for at least the next five or six years. The *Journal*, with evident satisfaction, identifies a source who says that Wendi on at least one occasion referred to Wolf as her husband.

The *Journal* allows as how, at the California State campus, she is regarded as one of the most talented students to pass through the school's economics department. She departs California for Yale's MBA program. The relationship with Wolf cools, leaving her free to reel in bigger fish. After her first years at Yale, she shows up for her summer internship at Star TV.

But let's recast the story as a triumphal, even uplifting tale of pluck and achievement. She's not Becky Sharp, she's Pip in *Great Expectations*.

She's the third child in a provincial family of average station, meaning she's hungry most of the time in 1970s and '80s China. Her two older sisters are away (dislocated by the forces of the Cultural Revolution). Wendi is called "number three." A third girl, another deprivation. Her parents try again and, finally, produce a boy.

Having learned, having had to learn, how to get attention, she emerges as a young woman of uncommon directness—engaging people with great efficiency and insistence. She's smart; she's flirty; she knows she has to look for an advantage. She's a young person who likes to talk to older people; she's a young person whom older people like to talk to.

And then she meets the American family.

The Cherrys, likely in the thrall of the Chinese zeitgeist (it's just getting under way in the late eighties), undoubtedly find her to be an energizing and beguiling young woman. She's their discovery. Wendi, in her turn—intent on expanding her own horizons, taking pleasure in the pleasure they're taking in her, caught up herself in the romance of the American zeitgeist—is equally smitten with them.

The fact that she's been swept up into what is a problematic marriage, that she's been appropriated probably in part *because* it is a problematic marriage, is a circumstance that only an omniscient narrator gets to see. Likely, the nineteen-year-old isn't aware of it at all; if she does have some awareness, it's inchoate, or in a constellation of factual and emotional variables. The idea—the *Wall Street Journal* idea—of her as the nineteen-year-old emotional cat burglar is pure construct.

She arrives in Los Angeles as the guest of the Cherrys at least half a decade before Chinese students in America are a routine part of campus life. She speaks little English. She goes to work in a Chinese restaurant. She registers at the nearest state university campus.

Almost immediately, the Jake Cherry situation blows up. Here's the narrow view of even the most sensitive nineteen-year-old, not to mention one remote from family, country, language: *This is just my life happening to me*. Obviously—judging from the story's outcome—she takes on new roles with some ease. The new adventure begins, and she's open to it—she gets into it, she conforms to it.

The problem may be that she romanticizes each adventure, so after the initial exhilaration, she's bound to be disappointed. It is not craftiness and duplicity and avarice that is her character weakness but, after she cycles through a few adventures, her constant need for excitement, for drama, for change, for the new. For further opportunity.

At the same time, she's getting educated. And because she's naturally smart, with a type of studiousness not necessarily common to the adventurous, she's forging another sort of narrative. While her strained personal life is going on, she's starting to design another life, envisioning a career, understanding its direction, demands, logistics, exigencies. The adventuress begins to conceive of a different kind of adventure.

Where the *Wall Street Journal* assumes an imbroglio of certain moral turpitude—because we know the outsize end of the story, that makes her all the more dubious—it is both more and less dramatic to see Wendi's progress as a set of sequential, evolving, and to some large degree random relationships. Her story, with its

domestic dramas, evident personal miscalculations, thoughtless-
ness, and immaturity, isn't particularly extreme or more chaotic
than that of a great proportion of striving young people—she's just
traveled farther.

Indeed, having gotten a business degree from Yale, we may
assume that her life is considerably less chaotic and more focused
than most. She's making her way.

It is just because, out of all the women in the world, it is she
who ends up married to Rupert Murdoch that we—or the *Wall
Street Journal*—impute Machiavellian method, and systematic
amorality, to her upwardly mobile progress.

But, okay, let's assume that there *is* design.

She is ambitious, after all. She understands that she has a specific market advantage: She's a Chinese national with an American
MBA.

She has an interest in power, in who's who in the room. There
are numerous stories of her at cocktail parties and other gatherings
doing thumbnail descriptions of the various men and their
achievements, of wittily assessing the playing field, of knowing the
gossip. On the one hand this is avariciousness, on the other astuteness. Vulgarity or discrimination.

It's logic as well as design that takes her after her first year in
business school to a summer job with News Corp.'s Star TV in
Hong Kong. She is, of course, an extraordinarily good candidate,
given her background and education.

Almost immediately she distinguishes herself at Star. She's a
presence. A sui generis presence. She has instant stature because
she's a Chinese woman who behaves like an American woman. A
Chinese woman who isn't in the least bit indirect. Every man in the
office has a Wendi crush or fixation. She's both a breath of fresh air
and an office fantasy. She's mascot and fetish. She's aware of her
power if not exactly in control of it. She speaks constantly, has
opinions about everything, eschews self-editing. She has no accu-

rate sense of her place—or, anyway, no compunction about ignoring it. She's the one person able to turn the hierarchies of a Chinese office—and even an American company in China assumes such hierarchies—into a level playing field.

Likewise, she's in love with the office. She's not eager to go back to Yale, would rather begin her career there and then. Several would-be paternal figures in the Star office take credit for sending her back for her degree. She's not only the office infatuation but its project. The great Chinese hope. People want her to succeed. There's a vested interest in her.

"To be honest, a lot of the young Chinese executives we were developing," Star CEO Gary Davey, one of those who encouraged her to go back to Yale, will later recall, "often lacked the courage and initiative that it takes to persistently pursue an opportunity. Very smart people, but there's a natural shyness to them, whereas Wendi, I mean, she had no fear of anything."

A year later, in 1997, her degree in hand, she's back. She's just a junior staffer. And yet she's almost immediately elevated (well before Rupert elevates her). There are guilty explanations about her rise.

It is obvious then, when the boss suddenly announces he's coming to town and needs to be accompanied, needs a guide and translator and aide, that it will be Wendi (in a classic setup, the regular translator is away from the office). She'll make the office seem sharp, top of the class, cool—indeed, sexy. She'll make everybody else look good.

So, the circumstance: Rupert, bogged down in a long and tortuous negotiation to get a satellite network off the ground in Japan, decides on the spur of the moment he wants to go to Shanghai and see what he can get going there. He calls Gary Davey and tells him to get to Shanghai too. It turns out that Davey and the other top people from Star are in Delhi. But Rupert still wants to go and needs a guide, and so Davey says, "All right, I've got an MBA for you. She's really smart." And Chinese. He calls Wendi and says,

"There's somebody coming to Hong Kong who you've got to take to Shanghai. It's Rupert Murdoch."

Davey later narrates, "That's when the flame was ignited. To what extent it was consummated, that we can have no idea of."

One of the richest and most powerful men on earth, believing he's about to age out of his reason for being—at the same time he's looking desperately, inchoately, and not necessarily successfully for new worlds to conquer (China, the heavens, mortality itself)—finds himself with a young woman. And not just a young woman, but a young Chinese woman with impeccable American credentials, who, in addition, is fearless, beautiful, flirtatious, and fundamentally interested in exactly what he's interested in: power, media, China, getting from point A to point B in this world.

In fact, they talk about business all the time. He's suddenly not feeling guilty about talking about business all the time. He's sexy to somebody exactly *because* he's talking about business (Anna, on the other hand, has always wanted him to be cultured). And this is a smart person—she's sparring with him; she keeps his attention. It's all so immensely exhilarating to a stuffy old singlet-wearing man. (Let us pause for a moment to consider the first moment when Wendi sees the singlet come off.)

What are the chances? The sense of this being a long shot increases the feeling that a kind of miracle has happened. Soul mates and all. As in so many other points in his life when all is hanging in the balance, the game seems to change in Rupert's favor.

There's something else: Rupert likes a woman with a status discrepancy. Each of his wives to date has been an unequal match—the airline stewardess, and then the office intern. Rupert has Henry Higgins aspects.

At the Star offices, it will be a moment for great marveling and sheepishness—and disbelief. Indeed, one morning Rupert calls Davey, who has no idea that a relationship has begun—or even that Rupert and Wendi have seen each other after the Shanghai trip—

and says, in a businesslike manner, "You're probably wondering now why Wendi isn't back from vacation. Well, she's with me and chances are she won't be coming back to Star TV." (It's the stuff of romance novels.)

He may not handle it worse than most other departing spouses at home, but it's not good. He denies, he prevaricates, he blocks from his consideration the hurt he's caused or is about to cause. He leaves a confused and devastated family. It is at first, before Wendi's entrance, just a pained, sad, inexplicable situation, with adult children trying to soothe, mediate, mend, understand. It's a long-married couple whose grievances, till now held mostly in check, are suddenly heated. Anna's hurt; he's hurt. Nobody's speaking. The whole situation, beyond logic or apparent reason, is unraveling quickly.

First, however, they have to tell his mother. They each go to Cruden Farm and take long walks in the garden with Dame Elisabeth—unaware of Wendi—trying vainly to act as marriage counselor.

Suddenly, there are separate residences. News Corp. legal is going round the clock. And then there is the strange, final announcement through Liz Smith, the *New York Post* gossip columnist, that Mr. and Mrs. Rupert Murdoch . . . amicably . . .

After thirty-one years of a marriage during which there is practically nobody who suggests he's anything more than a suitably repressed, preoccupied, workaholic, henpecked husband, he's gone.

He continues to deny that there's anybody else. He *will* continue, officially, with great difficulty, to deny that Wendi precipitated the split.

Two months after the split from Anna, and three weeks after his daughter Prudence and her family accompany her forlorn father on a sailing holiday where he keeps slipping off to take his behind-closed-door phone calls, he calls Prue, as he'll call the three other kids, and says, "I just wanted to tell you—hmmm . . . humm . . . ahhhh—I've met a nice Chinese lady."

Prue, in the kitchen, gets off the phone and races upstairs, eyes blazing, shouting to her husband, Alasdair: "My God, you won't believe it!"

Given the billions at stake, the influence at issue, and the dynastic preparations that have been made, not to mention a certain antediluvian and strong-willed matriarch—Dame Elisabeth—who will not be so easily appeased, this is a domestic cock-up of epic proportions.

While such action may seem radically out of character, this is mostly because it involves a woman. Otherwise, it's very much in character. He closes things off. If he has to sell a business, it's gone and forgotten. When it comes time to fire a close associate, it doesn't leave an emotional hole. If he fastens on some new notion or approach or point of view or direction or opportunity, he doesn't look back. It is, in fact, as though he has some short-circuited or retarded historical mechanism: He instantly loses interest in the past.

So he's not contrite in the slightest. In fact, he gets his back up.

His mother is uncomprehending and furious. She insults him and belittles Wendi—before even meeting her. Raging and pitiless, she says she will never meet Wendi. *Never*. Closed subject. He, in his turn, storms off and says, well then, he won't speak to his mother.

With Anna, he is, in her view, "hard, ruthless, and determined" as they discuss a settlement. He refuses to entertain any efforts to salvage the marriage (it is hard to imagine Rupert Murdoch in couples therapy). "In the end, it was not I who got the divorce," she will tell an Australian interviewer. "He was the one that got the divorce."

Rupert martyred her, she will claim. "I believe that when you take a vow to be loyal to someone and look after someone all your life, you try to stick to that. You don't hurt other people for your own happiness."

This is the view—the greatest sense of moral umbrage and betrayal—taken by Anna's children. It turns out that Rupert

Murdoch, who everyone has always said is a monster, *is* a monster. "I began to think that the Rupert I loved died a long time ago," Anna will comment in the interview. "The Rupert I fell in love with could not have behaved this way. It was so ruthless."

In the fall of 1998, Murdoch forces Anna off the board of News Corp. At her last board meeting, she delivers, in the presence of her soon-to-be former husband and her son Lachlan, a scorned-woman valedictory. She says that she has worked for the company since she was eighteen years old and this is not just the end of a marriage but the end of a whole life. Lachlan walks her out after her good-bye, deeply angered by what his father has done.

Prue, on the other hand, whose own mother was done in some thirty years before by Anna, finds herself secretly rooting for Wendi.

The children show up for Rupert and Wendi's wedding on June 25, 1999, seventeen days after his divorce, but it's strained, even coerced. The wedding is on *Morning Glory*—the 155-foot yacht he and Anna bought, which Anna thought would be their retirement boat—as it circles Manhattan.

It's only after the wedding that Wendi tells her parents she's married Rupert Murdoch: "They don't know who he was. I showed them a newspaper," she will later recall. "Power of media!"

To the extent that it is possible to change one of the world's least uncertain and self-doubting men, Murdoch is, in fact, changed, or rehabbed, by his marriage.

The vanity that he's been discouraged from indulging—by self-consciousness, by Anna's staid ideal of elegance, by his own views about conspicuous consumption—is suddenly on display. The new suits—"the man went from being a conservative to suddenly wearing Prada suits," his daughter Prue will say, in continuing disbelief—the fevered workouts, the hair. The urgency and, to many, the ridiculousness of it, can't be missed.

It is, at News Corp., an incredibly awkward emperor's-new-clothes situation because the new look, the new joie de vivre, the new living arrangements—he's temporarily living in the Mercer Hotel in SoHo, like a rock star—can't be mentioned. Or isn't, at any rate. There's nobody who's that easy with him. What's more, he's not acknowledging it. His hair, although suddenly bright orange, is not an acceptable subject of discussion. (It's only Prue who chides him.)

And then China. It's another reason, inside News Corp. and his family, that Wendi represents such a threat: She represents China. In fact, it becomes a bizarre and active piece of speculation within News Corp. about Wendi's real provenance. Where *really* does she come from? Whom might she be reporting to? And just how is it that she knows Jiang Mianheng, the son of China's president, Jiang Zemin, so well? Hmm?

Even within the Murdoch family, China and Wendi join together as the wedge issue. In 1999, he sends his son James, then twenty-six, to run Star TV. James, in his conscious or unconscious (but ultimately successful) end run around his brother, bonds with Wendi in China. James is Wendi's first real ally within the family and within the company. They conspire together over how to take China—or, actually, how not to get taken by China. Because there is a growing understanding—a long time in coming, this under- standing—that News Corp.'s China adventure has been a huge dis- aster. It quite seems that it has been Murdoch, with Chinese stars in his eyes, who has been blind to his ceaseless lack of success here, and his new wife and son who are vastly more realistic.

It's simple: The Chinese government holds a monopoly on the broadcast business and sees Murdoch as a competitor. It therefore uses all its regulatory might—which is absolute—to frustrate him. Indeed, they allow him in only in ways that will drain and dimin- ish him. It's a bloody disaster for News Corp.

James' emphasis becomes shifting the attention of the business from China to other Asian markets. Wendi's emphasis becomes shifting the business away from broadcast toward striving for some- thing that News Corp. has never done very well: a lighter touch, a greater sense of social nuance. It's what Wendi does. Her charm, flirtation, and guilelessness (at least the appearance of guilelessness) are put in service to News Corp.'s new China strategy: partnerships. Indeed, Wendi and James, before the Internet bubble blows, become on News Corp.'s behalf, among the largest investors in China's Internet business. Likewise, News steps back from its historic need to control and becomes an investor in backing other entrepreneurs. Rupert, for fifty years, has gone it alone, whereas Wendi meets people and collects them and introduces them and assembles a very un-News-like mutual admiration society.

In fact, the late 1990s are a relatively down moment for News Corp., as Internet mania is in full swing and News doesn't have a play. It's a small irony. The Internet business arguably gets going in the first place—becomes the focus of big media—because of Murdoch. In 1993, one of Murdoch's longtime retainers, John Evans, a former classified ad salesman at the *Village Voice* who has developed a quirky interest in technology, gets Murdoch to buy a Massachusetts company called Delphi, which is the first and, at the time, only national Internet provider—a concept that Murdoch, rest assured, does not grasp. Nevertheless, if Rupert is buying "the Net" (in 1993 parlance), then everybody else in the media business better damn well be buying it too. Murdoch's Delphi buy is essentially the first big investment in the Internet by any major media company. But within the year it's floundering—not least of all because he's put Jaan Torv, Anna's brother—"the idiot brother-in-law," as he was known semiofficially around News—in charge. It is Delphi that, in 1995, is rolled into the brief, and much heralded, joint venture with MCI called iGuide, which shuts down a month later. The truth is, Murdoch has little patience with computers—they bore him.

By the end of the decade, and at the height of the greatest boom in the communications business and the evidence that the media world is about to be massively transformed, Murdoch, or the Murdoch vision, is looking pretty worn.

In the first days of 2000, the business world is rocked by Time Warner's radical Internet strategy—its merger with AOL. News Corp.'s Internet strategy is, for what it's worth, Wendi and James. Which, by whatever dumb luck, turns out to be—considering the fate of AOL Time Warner—a reasonable strategy.

Wendi, personifying both China and the Internet at News, is riding very high. Obnoxiously and presumptuously high, in a lot of people's minds. Then, in March 2000, just as the Internet bubble is about to burst and everything's about to change, she gets a phone call from Rupert. He says how very important it is that she not tell anyone this: He has just gotten back from the doctor and he has prostate cancer. No one must know, not even his family. Wendi doesn't quite understand what prostate cancer is. The only other person outside of his doctors who knows he's sick is his friend and longtime financier Michael Milken, who got prostate cancer in the early nineties and who's since invested a fortune in research on and treatment of the disease. Milken, at Rupert's request, ends up explaining it to Wendi.

Suddenly there's a series of assumed names and furtive appointments. And then, in April, after a visit to Memorial Sloan-Kettering Cancer Center in New York, there's a leak and News Corp. has to rush out an announcement, which sends the share price down; News' market cap plummets $10 billion. Murdoch also has to deal with frantic phone calls from his children, whom he has not told about the cancer.

Milken takes over the supervision of the treatment. In fact, it shortly becomes a support group of businessmen of high rank who have survived their prostate cancer bouts—Italian media mogul (and once and future Italian prime minister) Silvio Berlusconi and Intel's Andy Grove among them—offering advice.

Two weeks later, New York City mayor Rudy Giuliani is diagnosed with prostate cancer too. Murdoch feels he's suddenly in strong company. He sees the PR issue: The fight is as much against the appearance of mortality as against mortality itself. The game changes if they think you're mortal.

His reaction to the treatment is dogged and competitive. Exhausted though he might be, he's got to keep going, show strength, willpower, normalcy—that's his prescription. He sees himself in something close to presidential terms. The eyes of the world are upon him, trying to judge his weakness. Not just will he or won't he make it, but by what measure has he been diminished? He becomes oddly bluff about the disease. "Never felt better," he says, punching the air. The program is not to miss a day of work, stay tanned, and make a series of bold, forward-looking statements. In fact, it's in this period that he becomes, or says he's become, a true Internet believer.

Wendi, however, is isolated, confused, depressed. She is, also, at thirty, confronted with the question of children, which they've managed to never explicitly discuss before. It is far from clear to her whether she wants to be a business figure herself, the Murdoch who will take over China, or to step back and be a mother. The option, she glumly tells people, is "in the fridge." "Before, we hadn't thought about when, but after that happen, we say, if I want to have children, we have to do this," she will later tell me.

John Lippman's *Journal* story about Wendi's ignoble climb happens to appear just as she is having IVF treatment.

In some sense it turns out to be the boldest statement of his recovery and renewal: Nine months after his diagnosis, in February 2001, the announcement is made that Wendi is pregnant. Murdoch, at seventy, is having his fifth child. (The daughter of Wendi's IVF nurse gets a job at the *New York Post*.)

The simple message is about life, confidence, seizing the day, a man still in his prime. A certain generosity on the part of other media owners (themselves undoubtedly fearing prostate cancer) buffer him from a there's-no-fool-like-an-old-fool critique. The questions that are obviously prompted by a man in treatment for prostate cancer having a child are, willfully, not asked. He's spared public mockery and pity as well as even curiosity.

In one sense, it solves News Corp.'s public problem with Wendi too—she's no longer taking over the world; she's going to be a mom.

It changes the game in another unintended way. There is, after the announcement of the prostate cancer, a moment at News Corp. when people feel they can talk about succession. There's a deliberate effort to position Chernin out front. The line about Lachlan taking over is suddenly revised (with almost a clearing of the throat) to say, *Well, of course, until the appropriate day, Peter would be in charge.* Chernin is positioned as the regent. It's a nice piece of corporate legerdemain, but, nevertheless, for Chernin, the never-to-rise-above-number-two, it's a virtual promotion. Murdoch, however, recognizes the costs. For the first time, at News Corp., there's a successor. Except that, after he finishes his radiation, gets a clean bill of health, and produces in quick succession two children, he believes, as much as ever—more!—he's immortal.

The life he emerges into is the result, most of all, of Wendi's role change—she reinvents herself as an extraordinary wife. Superachieving yuppie wife. The brand-manager wife of Brand Rupert Murdoch.

As she will put it to me, "I quit work to work at home. To care for Rupert, slaving, don't get paid. Construction, chef, and cooking and housecleaning!"

In the space of seven years, she will have two children, redecorate (on a grand scale) seven homes, and entirely revamp her husband's social life—in the process meeting everyone it is useful to meet in the world.

It's not just that she is a celebrity hound—that's actually the wrong emphasis. What she has is a remarkable capacity to keep all the working characters in her head at the same time—and most of the characters turn out to be celebrities. And while they may be celebrities, she levels them—partly out of guilelessness, and particularly because there are so many of them (if you have access to all the world's celebrated people, they quickly become less than they seem), and partly because she somehow finds herself as the ultimate celebrity. Everybody wants to know Wendi—because she's Murdoch's wife, but, in addition, because her own story is so fantastic and unlikely.

The interlocking circles that she finds herself in the center of include the haute monde of Hollywood, the new figures in the technology business, the business elite of China, international heads of state, and the wife of every important person everywhere—she is the CEO of the worldwide famous husbands' wives club—as well as anybody who is anybody at News Corp. (She has a much quicker recall of who's who at News than Murdoch does.)

Here's a random selection of the names that pepper a few hours of conversation with her—people she's talking to, visiting with, or with whom she's discussing business opportunities:

Larry Page
Edward Tian
Zhang Ziyi
Sergey and Anne Brin
Tony Blair
David Geffen
Barack Obama
Mark Zuckerberg and Priscilla Chan
Tom Perkins
Tom and Kathy Freston
Graydon Carter
Barry Diller
Michael Bloomberg
John McCain
Anna Wintour
George W. Bush
Mick Jagger
Bono

Christian Louboutin

Diane Von Furstenberg

Natalia (the Russian model)

Justin Portman

Brad Pitt

Gordon and Sarah Brown

David Cameron

Pan Shiyi

Robin Li

Jiang Zemin

Jiang Mianhang

Steve Bing

Cherie Blair

Hamilton South

Michelle Obama

Karl Lagerfeld

Mike Milken

Silvio Berlusconi

Richard and Lisa Perry

It's a marked, odd, and possibly transformative shift for Murdoch: He's become an official member of the glamour establishment. He says, when I ask him about Wendi's politics, that she has no politics, really—that growing up in China has made her suspicious of politicians. But that's disingenuous. She's profoundly liberal-ish. Arguably, the exact thing that Murdoch has always stood against—the self-satisfied people, the elite people, the fancy people—she's fallen in love with. She gets him to go to Davos (where she's arranged for Rupert and Bono to act as the waiters at a dinner for the wives of world leaders and assorted queens and princesses—Rupert serves the after-dinner vodka shots), and to Cannes (and on to Barry Diller's boat on the Riviera).

Indeed, most strangely, he's suddenly, through Wendi's good offices, rather at home in Hollywood. Through Wendi, David

Geffen—the gay, über-liberal former music executive—becomes Rupert's frequent confidant.

Also—and this is just *barely* visible to the naked eye—Wendi begins to replace Rupert as the center of attention. She's the shock of the new; he's a dimmer figure.

She's living the life. With intense enjoyment.

Having, for instance, embraced the Google guys, Larry Page and Sergey Brin, she invites them to come out to the Murdoch ranch in Carmel, California. Later, trying to explain the unlikely interaction of Murdoch and the Google boys—as diametric opposites in temperament and interests as you might find—she will paint an enthusiastic portrait of Murdoch's curiosity: "He's so interested. He always asks questions. He want to know everything. He asks so many things . . . like . . ." (erupting into laughter) "'*Why you no read newspapers?*'"

There's a stoic and slightly puzzled tolerance of her inside News Corp. Or sometimes it seems more like controlled alarm. This is partly because she is so obviously changing him. And partly because she is, potentially, a loose cannon. And partly because the success of this marriage means so much to him. Hence, everybody at News Corp. is invested in it too. (When the *Los Angeles Times* suggests that it is investigating a rumor about Wendi having a relationship with another man at News Corp., dealing with the story becomes a high-level priority in the company, with Murdoch, Wendi, and the employee all supplying statements of absolute denial and no one at News giving it any credence at all. The *Los Angeles Times* doesn't run the story.)

While she's busy being superwife, she becomes a director of News Corp.'s MySpace operation in China in 2006. She makes plans to carry the torch in the 2008 Beijing Summer Olympics. She's producing a movie with Zhang Ziyi, China's most famous actress and the fiancée of Vivi Nevo, the jet-set financier who has invested heavily in media companies, including News Corp. (and who is the godfather of Lachlan Murdoch's son). She's hustled the old biddies at

Brearley, the staid Manhattan school at which her older daughter is now enrolled, and had the school implement a comprehensive Chinese-language program. She's relocated her elderly parents from Shandong to Forest Hills, Queens, and made Murdoch take her mother to Balthazar, a fashionable SoHo spot, for Mother's Day brunch. "They get along very well because they don't understand each other," she says in a fit of laughter. "I control the conversation."

She's at the center of the center. Every after-hours e-mail to Rupert Murdoch about the Dow Jones deal comes through her. Because her husband still doesn't get e-mail.

# THIRTEEN

# The Ecology

It is the *New York Times* Murdoch is really after, more than even the *Wall Street Journal*. He is a man with almost no sense of, or interest in, historical context, but things stick in his head. Meaning accrues. Sore points persist. Issues fester. Enemies remain. Don't get mad, get even. To persist, to justify, to avenge, to have his way, maybe to even impress someday—this is his long-term game. His takeover of his father's old company in 1987 was such a resolution. Now there is the issue of the *New York Times* to resolve.

Keith Murdoch set it up. Rupert was nineteen when father and son made a Sunday pilgrimage out to Hillendale, the Sulzberger family estate in Connecticut, on a visit to New York. His father was making the clear point: The Sulzbergers were the First Family of newspapers. There was a further, subtler message about measuring up, a way of establishing what it means to be a newspaper proprietor family, a setting of horizons. (His father, he came to understand, did not actually own newspapers—and the Sulzbergers did.)

There was his first business hash with the *Times*. During the 1978 New York newspaper strike—little more than a year after he'd taken over the *New York Post*—he came to believe that the *Times*, with vastly more economic muscle than he had, was prolonging the dispute with the unions precisely to put *him* out of business. (He broke from the publishers' association and made a separate labor deal—getting the *Post* back to press before the *Times* and the New York *Daily News*.)

Then there was the *Times'* earliest personal attack on him (its first profile of him, on the other hand, was a laudatory item in 1969—the *Times* called him a "boy wonder"—which appeared in a special editorial section about Australia and New Zealand clearly designed to pick up some targeted advertising). He had acquired a controlling interest in an Australian airline, Ansett, and, to increase his clout in U.S. business and political circles, decided to switch a big order for new planes from Airbus in Europe to Boeing in the United States, but he needed the U.S. Export-Import Bank, which was to provide the financing, to give him the same rates as he could get in his Airbus deal. The *Times* revealed that, as a precursor to getting the favorable deal, he'd had lunch at the White House with President Jimmy Carter and met with Ex-Im Bank president John Moore, a Carter appointee, on the same day; what's more, shortly before the deal was approved, the *New York Post* endorsed Carter over Teddy Kennedy in the hotly contested New York presidential primary. The *Times* story landed Murdoch in front of a Senate investigating committee (which absolved him of any conflict or impropriety). The *New York Times,* he told Thomas Kiernan, an early biographer, was out to get him. "I'll have my day with the *Times*" was his promise to Kiernan.

There has been, over more than thirty years, very little respite for him from the *Times'* treatment. First he was characterized as a guttersnipe, then as an outlaw and pirate, and finally now as a threat to our way of life—culminating during the battle for Dow Jones, on June 26, in the first part of an "investigative" series meant to demonstrate his unsuitability to own the *Wall Street Journal*.

One of the severest charges against Murdoch is that he runs a pitiless attack machine whose primary purpose is not journalism but the defense of his own interests—that not since the heyday of the Hearst organization, with its vendettas and passionately vindictive columnists, has there been a major American news organization so willing to prosecute its opponents as Fox News. The irony, therefore, cannot be missed that the people on News Corp.'s eighth floor are as outraged by the *New York Times*' naked attack on Murdoch as Fox's opponents are by *its* naked attacks.

The first part of the series goes after Murdoch for his regulatory dealings. The *Times* is partisan enough in this campaign not to mention that in the specific instance of lobbying for the relaxation of television ownership rules the *Times* has also been lobbying the government to relax those same rules.

The next part is about Murdoch's dealings in China:

> Many big companies have sought to break into the Chinese market over the past two decades, but few of them have been as ardent and unrelenting as Rupert Murdoch's News Corporation.
>
> Mr. Murdoch has flattered Communist Party leaders and done business with their children. His Fox News network helped China's leading state broadcaster develop a news Web site. He joined hands with the Communist Youth League, a power base in the ruling party, in a risky television venture, his China managers and advisers say.
>
> Mr. Murdoch's third wife, Wendi, is a mainland Chinese who once worked for his Hong Kong-based satellite broadcaster, Star TV. Her role in managing investments and honing elite connections in China has underscored uncertainties within the Murdoch family about how the

family-controlled News Corporation will be run after Mr. Murdoch, 76, retires or dies.

The *Times* turns out to be quite an inept attack dog. Its team of reporters has, at great expense, failed to turn up anything new. What's more, News Corp.'s own response—in a statement drafted by Ginsberg—so cows the *Times* that it cancels the rest of its planned series. All this supports Murdoch's view of the *Times:* While it is, in this attack, "using its news pages to advance its own corporate business agenda," it cannot even do that well. So what will become of it?

Murdoch, after all, is promising the greatest and perhaps final newspaper war. He is going to take the *Times* down—or, not impossibly, he is going to take the *Times* over. If he is to actually become the dominant news proprietor in America, he has to unseat the *Times*.

And now seems to be the moment to do it.

## 2007: THE *TIMES*

By late June 2007, the New York Times Company share price has fallen by more than half since 2002. The *Times* seems only marginally less weak than Knight Ridder, the second-largest U.S. newspaper company, which was forced into a sale by its disgruntled shareholders, or the Tribune Company, the country's third-largest newspaper company, owner of the *Los Angeles Times* and the *Chicago Tribune,* which will also shortly go on the block. The *Times* is having not just a business crisis but a full-scale identity blowout. The familiar *Times* reader, the Eastern establishment reader—as dedicated and loyal and homogeneous an audience as few newspapers have ever had—has, in some sense, disappeared, or, growing old, has been abandoned by the *Times*.

The *Times'* strategy—a doomsday scenario, foreseeing a one-newspaper nation, a last-man-standing paper—has been to make the paper national. Hence, the *New York Times* is no longer principally a metropolitan paper. With a daily circulation of 260,000 in the five boroughs, it is no longer even credibly a New York paper. (Its two tabloid competitors, the *Daily News* and the *New York Post*, sell a million more copies between them than the *Times* in New York City.) It has become a second-read paper across the country—if you are among that fast-shrinking population of people who actually read a newspaper, then you read your local paper and, after that, the *Times*. It has become an add-on.

The *Times* is a jittery place—far from sure about its own standing and virtue.

Its two big scandals—the first in 2003 about Jayson Blair, the reporter who made up an impressive catalogue of vivid stories, and the second in 2005 involving Judy Miller, who, with the *Times* urging her on, went to jail for protecting her sources in the Valerie Plame affair, whom the *Times* subsequently decided she should not have protected so much—were notable not just for the structural weaknesses they revealed in the *Times'* journalistic operation but also for what they revealed about the *Times'* tendency to panic under pressure. Howell Raines, the *Times* executive editor whom the publisher, Arthur Sulzberger Jr., appointed to turn the *Times* into a national paper—it was on Raines' watch that Blair wrote his fabricated stories—had the publisher's absolute support until the day he didn't and was forced to step down. Judy Miller likewise had the publisher's absolute support until it was clear that PR considerations and the court of public opinion called for the opposite position.

Murdoch has been watching the *Times'* strange behavior and spastic reactions with as much interest and appetite as he has for anything in the media business. The *Times* is his favorite train wreck—as well as, perhaps, his ultimate opportunity.

The *Times'* own insecurity about itself encourages Murdoch's own tenacity in pursuing the *Journal*—and, through it, the *Times*. Murdoch, as it happens, is no small cause of this insecurity. The rattled, humiliated, second-guessing *Times* has become a leitmotif at the Fox News Channel. Fox News has helped turn the *Times* into a caricature, a joke.

There may be something more that bothers Murdoch about Sulzberger. While he tends to associate the boyish Arthur (even though he is, at fifty-five, far from a boy) with his own children—taking great satisfaction in this comparison—Arthur in fact resembles Rupert himself. Like Murdoch, Arthur has been desperate to emerge from the shadow of his father; he is determined to speak his mind (at any cost); he is determined to be in personal control; and he is desperate to be larger than he is—to be bigger than fate has made him. Arthur is the cautionary tale—what Rupert himself, with just a slight alteration in tone and mettle, might have become.

Indeed, the Murdoch family's control over News Corp.—with its voting and nonvoting shares—apes the Sulzbergers' corporate model. Arthur—attention-seeking, immature, verbally out of control—is a vivid example of what can happen with such no-recourse governance. That worries Murdoch.

Oddly, it is Arthur himself who has most consistently, and, to Murdoch, pathetically, articulated the fragility of the *Times*—its being-and-nothingness struggle in the changing media world. Arthur seems to want something more than the *Times*, wants to make it into some new information age contrivance. It isn't a newspaper, it's an information brand, blah blah.

There is a sense, actually, in which Arthur seems to see himself as a would-be Murdoch—which, even in Murdoch's eyes, makes him all the less dignified and credible.

Arthur wants to be some New Age media mogul; Rupert wants to be a newspaper proprietor.

## FOX NEWS

In its panic about Murdoch, the *Times* is quite possibly missing the larger story about him. The epochal tale may not be, as he pursues the *Journal*, about Murdoch's bullying, but about his growing squeamishness about bullying. The *Times* is continuing to champion the case that Murdoch is a corrupter of journalism, just as Murdoch is trying to make himself, relatively speaking, its upholder. Indeed, Murdoch may be the last guy to believe that he can actually make it as a respectable journalist—whereas at the *Times* more and more people are doubting that respectable journalism is a viable profession.

Murdoch's dream of the *Wall Street Journal* and of supplanting the *Times* as the nation's blue-chip news organization is not so much (or not merely) about the *Times* as it is about Roger Ailes. Murdoch may be pursuing the *Wall Street Journal* to deal with Fox News.

Everybody else's Fox News problem, is, as it happens, his too.

Ailes is Murdoch's profoundly mixed message—one that he sometimes despairs of making any sense of.

He might be television's deftest practitioner, but Ailes is also its strangest. Using the lessons he learned as a political operative for Nixon and Reagan, his basic tactical philosophy continues to be about how to devastate or at least neutralize his opponents. Arguably, this is exactly what enlivens his network. Personally, he is a man of overriding obsessions, including his belief that he has been earmarked by Arab terrorists, which costs News Corp. a considerable premium for his 24/7 security apparatus. Delivering Ailes to work, his driver and bodyguard call from the SUV so that a second security team can fan out on the plaza in front of the News Corp. headquarters for Ailes' arrival. (This too, this paranoia—even a sense of approaching Armageddon—has arguably turned out to be a programming plus.)

Ailes, no matter how strange he may be, has created one of Murdoch's greatest successes. In the end, so much of News Corp. is just not very memorable. It is a company that has refined the profit margins on the third-rate. But Fox News is original. It has taken the News Corp. formula of the on-the-cheap and the third-rate and turned it into a culture-changing, paradigm-altering, often jaw-dropping spectacle. About this, Murdoch is proud.

Ailes is Murdoch's monster—but a very profitable one. If media success is its own justification—the essential principle Murdoch's own career has been built upon—then Ailes is not only justifiable but untouchable.

He is the one person within News Corp. whom Murdoch will not cross.

And this is not because he's blind to what Ailes is doing, or to what Fox News is. In steady, constantly discomfiting ways, Murdoch shares the feelings about Fox News regularly reflected in the general liberal apoplexy. Everybody outside Fox News and inside News Corp. suffers Fox News. Everybody outside Fox News and inside News Corp. is afraid of Roger Ailes. Further, everybody outside Fox News and inside News Corp. thinks that there's a bit of *insanity* at Fox News. Murdoch, Chernin, and Ginsberg are routinely—as often as every day—peppered with complaints by friends, family, business associates, and people of great influence about Fox, and none of them can do anything. It is some bizarre testament, really, to editorial freedom. It is uncontrollable.

Even within Fox News, under Ailes, there are people who have become so powerful that they can't be controlled. It is not just Murdoch (and everybody else at News Corp.'s highest levels) who absolutely despises Bill O'Reilly, the bullying, mean-spirited, and hugely successful evening commentator, but Ailes himself who loathes him. Success, however, has cemented everyone to each other. Within Fox News, the two PR executives Brian Lewis and Irena Briganti—famous through the media business for the violence with which they attack anybody who attacks Fox News—are themselves feared by everybody else, even the most senior people at Fox and at News Corp. Lewis is one of the few people who scares

Ailes because he has notes of many conversations that should never have occurred.

Murdoch—and this is not a point lost on Ailes—has come to occupy two opposing worlds. There's the world to which he has largely been introduced by Wendi; if this world has any one guiding cultural agreement, it's stark antipathy to Fox News. And then there's the world in which his most significant brand association is with Fox News.

What's more, the wind is changing. Democrats, who in 2006 took both houses of Congress, have started to refuse to appear on Fox. As the *Journal* battle is getting under way, so is the presidential primary season—the most closely watched in history. The Democratic candidates in March 2007 all refuse to participate in a Fox-sponsored debate because of a joke made by Ailes to a group of radio and television producers: "It is true that Barack Obama is on the move. I don't know if it's true that President Bush called Musharraf and said: 'Why can't we catch this guy?'" Indeed, at the same time that Ailes and Fox are pretty steadily portraying Barack Obama as a possible Muslim terrorist, Wendi Murdoch is having dinner with him.

Even Murdoch's desire—a long-held one—to launch a business news network has been frustrated by Ailes' own agenda.

He needs Ailes to take charge of the business news channel because he believes that nobody else is as good at cable television as Ailes. But Ailes has been vastly ambivalent about, even resistant to, doing it. There is the elevation of Ailes within News Corp., as part of his negotiation, into the office of the chairman with all the other top News Corp. administration executives. He even got Lachlan Murdoch's office on the eighth floor as soon as he left the company.

It should not be underestimated how much Murdoch does not want himself or News Corp., in his or its legacy, forever yoked to Ailes and Fox News. It is not just that he wants respectability—that is some of it, but perhaps the least of it—but that he doesn't want to give up authorship.

Ailes and Fox News have, unexpectedly and disproportionately, come to be the voice and identity of News Corp. Clearly, the way to balance it, to reassert Murdoch's own primacy as the grand designer, as the maker, is to buy something else that outweighs what he wants to diminish.

Hence the *Wall Street Journal*. That, as a point of identification for News Corp., will rival Fox News.

And Robert Thomson. Thomson is the new Ailes. He's the new Murdoch alter ego. He's the new instrument through which Murdoch is going to make his mark.

And the *New York Times*—either to supplant it or buy it.

## THE *POST*

If Ailes is going to be diminished in the balance here, so might Murdoch's beloved *New York Post*. The *Post* is sidelined during the *Journal* pursuit. In some sense, virtually silenced. There is something like an eerie quiet. And, too, there is the growing question about what the value of the *Post* will be to Murdoch if he has the *Wall Street Journal*.

This is the most confounding part. Of all the businesses and past lives that Murdoch has jettisoned, it seems that, suddenly, he might be getting ready to shed his most elemental identity: his tabloid soul.

## EARLY JULY 2007: THE DUE DILLY

The collapse of the newspaper business, which is having devastating consequences for every other proprietor, is in fact turning out to be great for Murdoch. It is giving him the opportunity to buy a blue-chip news organization that would never before have considered selling to him.

The logic here is clear to him, if not to anyone else. Indeed, there is a strange disconnect among the economic views in play. There is Murdoch trying to pay as much as he can possibly pay. There are the people at the *Journal* hoping that he will find out how little they're worth. And there is Wall Street, which, oddly, is thinking he's buying something entirely different from what he is so obviously buying.

News Corp.'s due diligence at Dow Jones begins in the first week of July. Now, News Corp. could well get into its due diligence and find enough of a deteriorating situation to knock back on the offer, not even losing much face at all—this is part of the art of the deal. Factions at News Corp. are counting on such a cold view to give them the leverage to save a few bucks a share. Likewise, factions at Dow Jones and in the Bancroft family are hoping for just this reaction—that Murdoch, the unsentimental business guy, won't want the *real* Dow Jones, as opposed to the storied myth of Dow Jones, when he gets to see it up close.

But the truth is that News Corp.'s Dow Jones due dilly is not meant as a real measure of the company's value, or even as a reasonable reality check. It is not meant to challenge the assumptions that News Corp. has already made. It is just a point of procedural follow-through, or even benign curiosity. Beyond some slight worry about pending lawsuits (nothing, it turns out, to worry about), News Corp.'s primary point of interest is about how easy or how complicated it will be to convert the existing presses to full color (fairly complicated). The basic business of Dow Jones isn't the issue.

What Murdoch is buying, his idea of value, cannot, finally, be explained to anyone else. It has to be taken on faith.

To buy something that you have always wanted but could never buy before (like his father's old company) has special value. If you can buy it and then it helps you conquer something else that stands in your way—well, a further premium. If you can buy it and it throws other people off balance, messes with their power base (e.g., Ailes and Chernin), well, the deal just gets better and better.

# FOURTEEN

# Dynasty

Toward the end of June 2007, Rupert and Wendi get away. Jamie Packer, the son of his historic Australian rival, Kerry Packer—Jamie has become Lachlan's best mate—is getting married in the south of France. It's a $6 million part-Scientology wedding at the Hôtel de Ville in Antibes. Rupert and Wendi anchor their yacht, *Rosehearty*, not far from Lachlan and his wife Sarah's yacht, *Graziella*. All the Aussie men—and Tom Cruise—in town for the big event spend the night before the wedding slamming down tequila shots at Paloma Beach.

Rupert and Lachlan discuss Jamie Packer's recent announcement—eighteen months after the death of his father—that he's decided to sell off the last vestiges of his father's media empire and put more money into the much more profitable casino and gaming business. On one hand, this is an intimation of the kind of transformation that might—or even inevitably will—happen to the Murdochs' business. Certainly, it becomes harder and harder to imagine News Corp. as forever being a newspaper-based company. On the other hand, in a development that will be unsettling to Murdoch for exactly the opposite reason, Lachlan fails to tell his father that he's thinking of buying parts of the Packer media business—which could mean he might someday be a News Corp. competitor (indeed, Lachlan's non-compete agreement with News Corp., which came with his generous payout when he resigned from the company in 2005, is just ending).

It is hard, to say the least, for Murdoch to fathom why his son, who has Australia's most powerful media enterprise at his disposal, would want a lesser one of his own. This has long been the *duh* conclusion of the entire Murdoch family: Lachlan, the New York–raised Murdoch who discovered a great love for Australia, who from 1997 to 2001 ran the company's Australian business with distinction, and who has continued to cast about for opportunities and challenges since he left News Corp. two years ago, should run Australia. This is evident to everybody, including, most obviously, father and son. But emotional negotiation is not the chief skill of the father. So, everyone agrees, it will be a while before the son comes around.

The Murdochs are in many ways an awkward dynasty. Not just because the empire builder is so sui generis as to be irreplaceable, and not just because he is so evidently determined not to be replaced, but because, relatively speaking, the members of the dynasty are so capable—even, given the circumstances, normal. Dynasties are dependent on dependence. It complicates dynastic tradition and succession if the succeeding generation has compelling options outside of the dynasty.

The further twist of the knife is that Murdoch, a naturally cheap patriarch, finds himself financing his children's independence.

It really was not supposed to be like this. After his awkward start with Prue—the early separation from Prue's mother, Prue and Anna's difficult relationship, his disinclination to see a girl as having professional potential—he got with the dynastic program. Elisabeth, Lachlan, and James were raised in a family-business hothouse. The Murdochs were not about to produce doctors or lawyers or investment bankers. Everybody was instilled with a grand media vision as well as a profound yen to please the old man. Everybody was put to work in the business at the earliest opportunity. And any effort to break away—Elisabeth getting into Stanford business school, James starting a record label—was quickly nipped in the bud. He wants them in *his* business.

But at the same time, he raised his kids in Manhattan, which is a hothouse of a different order. They were serious yuppie kids. It was the world of super-ambition. It provided a leveling effect, even. Everybody was super-rich. You were surrounded by expectations of extraordinary achievement and status. It might even have seemed, in the new age of financial derring-do, a bit bush league, a bit played out, this dynasty business.

And their particular dynasty further encumbered them. In the world of great fortunes in which they lived, the Murdoch kids always had a singular problem: They personally didn't have a lot of dough. Since they were on their own, they all worked for their upkeep. And if they did quite well—especially the boys on the News Corp. payroll—they still essentially lived paycheck to paycheck. They really weren't able to compete in the international heirs-and-heiresses set or with the heavy-hitter entrepreneurs.

The prospect of cash—liquidity—suddenly, though, became a softening agent in the intractable issue of Murdoch getting his older children to admit his young children to the family trust. It became Murdoch's reluctant—very reluctant—leverage. He really didn't want to give his children money. He didn't want to sell News Corp. stock and, too, he didn't want to give his children this kind of independence. But it was really a rather bad situation. Elisabeth and Lachlan, especially, were intent on defending their mother's settlement agreement. Prue was inclined to side with her father. James, trying to be the family diplomat, went back and forth. It was Elisabeth's husband, Matthew Freud, an inveterate middleman, and a practiced mollifier, who helped ease the group toward a solution. The older children were adamant about not giving up control over the trust but were willing to allow their new siblings equal economic participation in the family fortune (the subtext here was that giving them voting participation would effectively give Wendi, the guardian of two votes, more weight than the others). At the same time—although this was not explicitly stated as a quid pro quo—Murdoch stumped up $150 million in cash and stock for each of his kids (including Grace and Chloe, to mollify Wendi); and the Murdoch family trust started distributing annual income for the first time ever.

It is this $150 million (paid in two separate disbursements—$100 million in stock in January 2007, and $50 million in cash in October) that is giving everybody the wherewithal to be significantly less bound to him. It's letting Lachlan pursue his own search for a business and letting Elisabeth expand hers.

But there are two other elements of the trust that make for an eventual, and inevitable, tale. Quite unusual for a trust arrangement that holds sway over a large business and that must accommodate a decision-making framework, in this one there is no way to break a tie.

A two-to-two vote means absolute deadlock in the affairs of one of the world's largest companies. Already, Prue and James, inclined toward their father's view, form one bloc, and Lachlan and Elisabeth, continuing their mother's grudge (as well as their own), another.

The next potential complication of no small significance is that Murdoch himself does not accept the exclusion of his two most recent children from participation in the trust voting.

When I ask him about the mechanism to break a tie, Murdoch responds: "There are four votes now, but when my little kids grow up, they will get votes when they are twenty-five or thirty or something. All right?"

Except that this is absolutely untrue. His eldest children as well as his longtime lawyer, Arthur Siskind, are clear on the point: Grace and Chloe will be treated as financial equals—but will never get a vote.

Murdoch may have signed off on the agreement. But denial, or willfulness, or a lifelong belief that no negotiation is ever truly over, is bound to complicate things.

Meanwhile, Murdoch remains very much the main character in the story. His children, as much as anyone, are always waiting to see how he'll react. It's *his* drama. They may be angry, hurt, or confused, but the greater story is how *he* will deal with their anger, hurt, or confusion. That's what most captivates them. He even manages to turn his difficulties in dealing with personal issues into an advantage: He's so awkward about it that he earns, rather in spite of himself, an amount of sympathy.

His family, like the rest of the News Corp. universe, is under the spell of his immortality. His children can't think beyond him—don't want to think beyond him. It requires not just emotional fortitude but an exceptional imagination to envision a post-Rupert world.

And yet . . .

They will ultimately take over this company and family fortune and, as it stands now, have to agree or risk paralysis. What's more, they have yet to anticipate what moves and mischief he might make before he can no longer make moves and mischief. And they have to figure that there's a good possibility that at least one of them will want to try to take his mantle and force out the others (as he forced out his siblings and mother).

My interviews with the Murdoch children for this book are curious affairs. They are each reluctant or deeply wary—perhaps more about why their father is having them talk to me than about the interview itself. They are wary too about his wisdom in offering *them* up to scrutiny ("Why is he doing this?" is a question each of them asks me—as well as one of the questions I ask them). And then, having acceded to his instruction to cooperate, each lays out a separate agenda for what they want from this book. Their message, however, is not so much for readers as, seemingly, for their father.

It would be incorrect to imply that they are a divided group. They're much too controlled or impacted for that. But certainly, given the stakes, it's not any wonder the fault lines can't be missed.

And while on one hand his regard for them, and even sensitivity (in his fashion), holds them in thrall if not harmony—the flotilla of Murdoch boats often gathers for a family holiday—he also can't seem to keep himself from applying a Murdochian view to their futures.

In a rare rumination about life at News Corp. after he departs, Murdoch speculates that Elisabeth "would like to build a big company and sell it on her own, spend all the money and buy News Corp. shares and give James trouble." When Gary Ginsberg jumps in with "He's kidding," Murdoch responds: "I'm not altogether kidding in the sense that she would then be in the position to buy out one of her siblings." Ginsberg adds, "Right, but for the book you're kidding."

## PRUDENCE

While fixing it with his eldest daughter to meet with me in Australia, Murdoch explains that Prue, the housewife who has had relatively little exposure to the press, will be extremely nervous about being interviewed and will probably not be too helpful. Lachlan, on the other hand, whom I will also be seeing in Sydney, is of course a pro, he says, and will be able to offer valuable insights into News Corp.

Prue has a sprawling, comfortable house overlooking Sydney Harbor in Vaucluse, one of the most expensive neighborhoods in

Australia. It's a house filled with teenage children and their friends—lots of tracking in and out of the kitchen. (On the day I see Prue, her husband, Alasdair MacLeod, one of the seniormost guys at News Ltd. in Australia, is upstairs, home sick in bed.)

"Dad said say whatever you like," says Prue—the daughter Murdoch portrays as nearly reclusive. With a glint in her eye, she begins to dish.

Her message to her father is that, as the odd duck out—the half sister and the one who's not a media professional—she possesses a unique and perhaps powerful perspective. She exists as, if not a threat, then a potential spoiler or leveler—a loose cannon. A truth teller, albeit an entirely good-natured one. Indeed, while her siblings display a certain forced and watchful attention, she is easy, unconcerned, eager to throw caution to the wind. (Her father's perception of her is, in fact, an odd inversion. He must see her openness as nervousness and her siblings' control as being relaxed.) Her further message is that she's owed something more for being excluded from the family's ring of accomplishment. There's no bitterness here. In fact, it's sort of that she's owed something for *not* being bitter. And what she's owed has nothing much to do with anything material—although she is mother-hennish when it comes to her husband's and her children's futures in regard to News Corp.—but rather some further relationship with her father, some deeper level of rapport and understanding.

In this, she has also established herself—or sees herself—as her father's most reliable ally among his adult children. This is the Prue narrative, which she tells with relish, and which seems clearly to be a guiding theme of her position in the family and, ultimately, her vote: She's her father's daughter, and hence different from Anna's children.

She gives the story a neatly Dickensian spin: "I had a stepmother and they had a mother."

Prue says this about Anna: "She's very strong, she's highly intelligent and very manicured and perfect, and I was just always this sort of ragamuffin and always wanted to ride my horse and never brush my hair."

Her siblings she sees as continuing to represent the intelligent and the manicured—both of her brothers with their former model wives and her chic sister.

While her siblings have become more and more self-conscious about being Murdochs and increasingly see themselves as living inside a bubble—and it's lonely in there—Prue has cultivated her outsiderness with self-denigration and reverse mythologizing. As the Murdochs prepare to spend Christmas together in 2008, Prue is adamant that she won't be buying a yacht to join the family flotilla wherever it will dock. No, she plans to *rent* one. She will come to this conclusion after taking her son James during the last Australian summer to vacation with her family as they sail around the Aeolian Islands.

"They have massive boats, all of them. My son James completely had his head turned. He was like, 'We're not like this, are we?' I said, 'Don't be like that, that's my family. Yes we are, yes we are, we just don't have a boat.' I was quite hurt that he didn't think his mother was sophisticated enough to be on this big boat. I never feel sophisticated enough to be on this big boat. They are all taller than me, that's the worst thing, so they all look chicer wherever they are, but especially on a boat, where everyone is in shorts or a swimsuit and I'm the short fat one."

As the outsider, she's given herself a pass to say and think what she wants.

She reports telling her father, "'Dad, I understand about dyeing the hair and the age thing. Just go somewhere proper. What you need is very light highlights.' But he insists on doing it over the sink because he doesn't want anybody to know. Well, hello! Look in the mirror. Look at the pictures in the paper. It's such a hatchet job."

She further reports his response: "Well"—sputter sputter—"you need a face-lift."

Also, her father's divorce from Anna and marriage to Wendi have given her a kind of leveling confidence when it comes to her siblings: Nobody understands better than Prue.

On the birth of Grace and Chloe: "Elisabeth and I discussed it at one point in the very beginning when everyone was hurt. It was interesting to me because I was just sitting there thinking, 'Well, hello, I've done this'—and when I said that they said, 'Yes, but it wasn't like this for you.' I said, 'It was kind of *worse* because I had to live with you!'"

And yet the bond here is real and obviously fierce. When Liz married Matthew Freud—"dodgy" Matthew Freud, whom everybody was deeply wary of—Prue took it on herself to deliver the family ultimatum: "If you hurt her, I'll kill you." (Freud pointed out that James had just told him the same thing.)

But there's business too. Prue's most direct point of competition is with Lachlan on the other side of Sydney. This is partly territorial: If Lachlan comes back into the business (and it is hard to believe he won't) and if he takes the job most obviously suited to him—running News Corp.'s Australian operations—that will mean he's blocked her husband, Alasdair, from getting to the top.

But it is also temperamental: Prue is a self-styled frump, and Lachlan is a self-styled cool dude. Prue is anonymous—"I've always been low-key and not many people know about me in a way, and I like that, I just love that"—and Lachlan, to Prue, is the "king of Sydney." Lachlan lives in a $7 million home with meticulous design detail overlooking Bronte Beach, the most fashionable address in this most fashionable of cities, and Prue lives, in Lachlan's dismissive description, with the uptight people overlooking the harbor. Lachlan is outdoors and free, with his views of the wild Sydney surf; Prue is closed up and repressed, looking out over the staid bay with its moored yachts.

This is all also primal: Prue grew up as her father's least loved child, Lachlan as the most loved. What's more, Lachlan, having received that love, then petulantly turned his back on it—hurting the father whom Prue adores and will always defend.

## LACHLAN

Lachlan's turf, in addition to Bronte, is Surry Hills in Sydney. Surry Hills is where News Ltd. has its headquarters and where, in its new gentrified incarnation, Lachlan has opened offices for the mostly as-yet-to-be-determined activities of his new company. The office he's set up in a converted warehouse building resembles all self-consciously uncorporate offices in recently gentrified areas of cities around the world.

Once famously handsome and fit—the striking good looks of both Murdoch sons help account for the gay rumors attached to both of these complacently married men—Lachlan, when I visit him in Sydney shortly after the Dow Jones deal is completed, is a contented thirty pounds overweight. At thirty-eight, he now has the same boyish chubbiness that his father had at that age. (Rupert, says Prue, desperately tried to lose weight when they lived in London by trying all manner of faddish diets, grapefruit diet included.)

People mostly comment on the differences between father and son, but the similarities are as pronounced. They both, in one sense, have an odd lack of presence. They're both standoffish or even shy—making eye contact isn't their first move—and unexpectedly inarticulate. They both need someone to finish their sentences. (So much for Murdoch's view of Prue as the inarticulate one and Lachlan as confident and surefooted.)

In our interview, Lachlan is skittish and put-upon. He is talking only on his father's request. Would rather not be. Except to the extent that he, like Prue, seems clearly to regard this as a dialogue with his old man. The point he wants to make is about being infantilized.

He makes the point without obvious recrimination but with a sense of great burden. Weariness almost. Lachlan, whose career has, in a sense, yet to start, has already experienced a great roller-coaster ride in his professional life. He has been tutored, then been elevated, then been anointed, then been thwarted by his father's courtiers, then been overtaken by his brother—and then he turned his back on it all.

It's important to understand how much the Murdochs' business is suffused with emotion—how deeply involved the children have been with the affairs of the father:

"We walked back to the apartment, I remember—that was when we did the deal [the merger of Sky with British Satellite Broadcasting, which kept News Corp. afloat in 1991]—with the company being at that stage, you know, near, um, dissolvement, I think really, that, um, you know, shook him more than I've ever seen. He was—I remember, like, almost like putting him to bed. I mean, I was only whatever—what, sixteen or fifteen or something—but I remember really being worried about him."

It was a life immersion too:

"You have to understand, my dad never said to us or my mother —my mother didn't even want us to be—work in the company or be in media, like it was never a—it was never a suggestion that we should be or what we should do, but I think it was, you know, I think obviously as kids growing up, you, you expect that that's what they want, right, um, but, from the—I think that what people maybe who aren't in these situations don't believe—realize—that, and I think also my dad's being um, being um, uh—and my mother were so involved in the business from like every minute of every day, so growing up around that, right, it wasn't a business— it wasn't like Dad goes to work and he works in the media and he comes home, and you know, he's just Dad. Every breakfast was about media. My dad was, you know, we went through the news-papers every breakfast, through things, we, we would, we—when we got home, Dad would come home usually with, um, business-people—every night would be, um, um, be either someone come over for a drink or dinner, usually dinner, then there'd be people in business or in politics around all the time, so he had a constant, you know—even on weekends, right."

Now, in its way, all this living over the store added up to a stellar upbringing. From an early age each of the professional Murdoch kids was good at what he or she did, certainly far advanced beyond their age and beyond their peers. Rupert Murdoch, focused by his then-wife Anna, set his mind to combining his business interests with proper family life, and raised a coven of media managers.

Which is bound to be a problem: You empower, but then don't want to cede power. You train, but then don't let go. It didn't even cross your mind to, say, let any of the kids get an outside job. Gain a little experience on his or her own. Work for someone else. Nail down a few professional credentials, which might have given a bit of cred beyond the last name. You didn't encourage that or allow that mostly because it didn't occur to you that anybody could give your kids a better idea than you could give them. And, too, of course, because you're nature's most consummate control freak.

In Lachlan's case, the father tried to re-create his own history by sending his son to retrace his steps. Lachlan at twenty-two (Rupert's age when he took over the *Adelaide News*) was sent like a viceroy to Australia—not so much the boy publisher as the boy governor-general. And he was received, in the land Murdoch departed a quarter century before, like a piece of the cloth. He was fathered by everybody at News Ltd. Everybody took pride in his least accomplishments. Not only was he raised to be a media manager at a very young age, he actually became one. And he became the prince of Australia—learned, in fact, how to be an Aussie!—and married a girl who is just like (or at least looks just like) the girl who married dear old dad. He learned the newspaper business and pretty much did everything he was supposed to do that Dad did, and then he was brought back from the provinces to take his rightful and inevitable place at HQ.

What must the old man have been thinking? He must have been thinking in novelistic rather than business or managerial terms. It was some fine fantasy: The beloved son at his side. The beloved son taking over his beloved *New York Post*. The prince being schooled by the regent, Peter Chernin. And, most of all, the son patiently, admiringly, dutifully, loyally, lovingly watching the father as the years ran out, in this way being passed all the secrets of the Murdoch line.

There is no misunderstanding this story line among his father's retainers. As a name throughout News Corp., Lachlan is almost as redolent as Rupert. Still, if there is within the company an absolute belief in a forthcoming succession and in the Murdochs as royalty, a people apart, there is, too, an obvious and constant comparison between once and future.

If in Australia Lachlan was regarded as a clever and sophisticated guy—a tastemaker—and a good manager who built a strong rapport both in the Australian newsrooms and with his executives, in the United States he was a weak, even pitiable, version of his dad. He was too sensitive; he was petulant; he lacked charm; he was not sharp.

The father in small but constant ways humiliated the son, which made him a joke to everybody else. In every meeting the father was the impatient, domineering, fussing presence. He couldn't stop calling attention to himself and away from the son. At the same time, the son, stamping his foot, was trying to call attention to himself. He started marketing campaigns for the *Post*—tried to bring a little class to a notoriously unclassy operation by throwing functions and parties in the tabloid's name. Over on the West Coast, he hung out with movie stars and insisted his dad make smarter and hipper movies (*Fight Club*, which Murdoch detested, was a Lachlan-supported project).

There it is. As devoted a father as Rupert was, as determined as he was to foster a great dynasty, as proud as he might be of his son (and it was a huge pride), as absolutely delighted (inner-peace-type delight) as he was to have Lachlan close, it was still a story about him. He's not going to give up—is not capable of giving up—an iota of real control. And what control he does give up, he'll take back as soon as he needs it.

It's a bloody mess.

Lachlan: "Family businesses are great businesses, but they're, they're also fraught with difficulties, so um, so the, uh, you know, so they're more complex than meets the eye, and in some ways they're great and simple but . . . they get complicated, and again, because, um, I think because you go back to that fundamental character trait which has served Dad so well, which is forward thinking out here and always driving forward, I think he, um, misunderstood—doesn't understand or doesn't appreciate sometimes, or he does, but doesn't think about how complicated they are, um—I'm not really answering the question, but, uh, don't you know my dad's never going to die?"

The curious thing, the unexpected thing, the thing that doesn't happen in such a story, was that the son upped and resigned. Other than the fact that his sister Elisabeth had also a few years before been given a similar back of the hand, this really seldom happens in dynastic settings. In dynasties, you get heirs who are squashed or denuded, but you don't much get resignations. What's more, Lachlan, like Elisabeth, gave this up without having any money. Until recently, the old man had carefully held that card.

And yet here, in the old man's defense, is the other elemental point: If he tried to hold them and dominate them, he also apparently raised them to be able to say *Fuck you.*

The exit couldn't have been more painful for both father and son. Not only was the father embarrassed, but it showed his relative corporate vulnerability—Chernin and Ailes made life difficult for Lachlan and openly took credit for pushing him out. What's more, the father lost his closest confidant as well as his perfect dynastic dream.

But never mind. The Murdochs are sentimental only up to a point.

Before his chair was cold, Lachlan was eclipsed in his father's, and certainly in the company's, estimation by his brother James, who had been hounding his back since childhood. In the blink of an eye, Lachlan went from the chosen one to the fallen one. Harsh.

And then there was the issue of having no money. Oh, Lachlan had cash flow—his payout from News Corp. was certainly generous. He didn't want for relocation expenses to Australia and an appropriate gilded exile lifestyle. But he didn't have enough money to be somebody else. To make himself into something other than Murdoch's son. It has become one of Lachlan's own parenting mantras: When *his* kids turn eighteen, he's giving them personal control of their dough.

It is for him, then, a significant development that the sensitive trust issue with his half siblings was settled with $150 million payouts. Because at the same time his father is considering whether the *Wall Street Journal* might not be a strategic way to bring him back into the fold, Lachlan is finally in a position to make other plans.

And he's not telling his father—or at least he's sharing as little as possible. And driving his father crazy in the process.

When Lachlan finally phones his father in early January 2008 to tell him he is looking to do a deal, Murdoch says he is left with the understanding that Lachlan is buying the *Bulletin,* a serious and unprofitable newsmagazine in Australia that was propped up by the goodwill of Kerry Packer until his death in 2005. "A great magazine," Murdoch tells me after speaking to Lachlan. "It's not something he will get rich on, but he's hoping it will give him a bit of a presence there."

In fact, Lachlan's larger plan is to go into business with Jamie Packer, whom he seems to admire for being truly Australian and actually having control of his family and fortune, and with SPO Partners in San Francisco, which has made a name financing deals for the children of moguls. The idea is to get himself his own media empire in Australia by gaining control, in a leveraged $3.3 billion deal, of a company that has stakes in broadcast, satellite, and publishing companies.

As Murdoch starts to get inklings of what his son is planning, he dispatches James to find out what the hell is going on. James reports that the deal involves huge debt and would only give Lachlan minority stakes in media assets (many of which turn out to be businesses that News Corp., with its minority investments, technically has first dibs on).

There are tense phone calls between the father and first son.

"It's just a deal and he's not a deal person," the father fumes. "He's a very, very good executive. He works hard. He makes good judgments of people; people who work for him love him. I've been urging him, 'Get something to run.'"

Then Lachlan announces the deal to the public with a front-page story in the *Australian* on January 22, 2008, just weeks after U.S. bank stocks have tanked as the carnage of subprime mortgages spreads to general credit. SPO abruptly pulls its financing in March. Murdoch is sure that's the end of it, but Lachlan finds a savior in an old friend of the family, Michelle Guthrie, who used to help run Star in Asia and now has a finance gig with Providence Equity Partners.

People from Providence arrive in Sydney on April Fool's Day, ready to do the deal, Lachlan believes, at the price he and Packer agreed on. But Providence ups the cost, and his best mate, Packer, pulls out, humiliating Lachlan.

"I don't understand it, his brother doesn't understand it," Murdoch tells me. "Lachlan, from the age of four, was a stubborn bastard. He always was."

## ELISABETH

Lachlan and his sister Elisabeth form a special Murdoch club, the resignees—and indeed, Lachlan's exit from News Corp. in 2005 and the substantial press surrounding it were managed by Elisabeth's husband, Matthew Freud.

Like Lachlan, she is also bound to their mother. For both Lachlan and Elisabeth, there's a fierce defensiveness when it comes to Anna, and, indeed, defense: *She* didn't louse up the marriage, their father did. And like Lachlan, Elisabeth has set up on her own, not just in business but in identity—even brand. She's a powerhouse. She's a *macher*. She's hot media stuff. Both Lachlan and Elisabeth, in Australia and London, have allowed themselves to become personalities (something their father really never was). Indeed, this is the context in which Elisabeth falls in love with Matthew Freud: He's her image consultant. This in itself is something of a rebellion against her father. It's a kind of insiderness that their father finds gauche (although it's the same insiderness, in fact, that their stepmother is courting). His son and daughter are the kind of people his tabloids would naturally ridicule.

Elisabeth is, arguably, his most successful child—and his angriest. When I see her in London in the inauspicious offices of her company, Shine, which is now one of the largest independent producers of television in the world, she is as wary as Lachlan about speaking to me, and as concise in her message to her father: He's created vast emotional turmoil and ought to thank his lucky stars he's also produced children strong enough to survive it.

Which is, quite precisely, her own character note.

On one hand, she is the emotionally fragile woman with the difficult personal life whose relationship with Matthew Freud is likely the product of a major daddy complex. On the other hand, she's the super businesswoman, the dealmaker, and, as well, the person who can probably best articulate her family's dysfunction.

"It hasn't been an easy couple of years," Elisabeth tells me. "He still falls into stupid old habits. I mean, he's impossible to figure. He's weirdly awkward about things sometimes, but his heart is in the right place. He's very old-fashioned sometimes. He finds it hard to talk about emotions. He finds it hard to say. . . . If somebody doesn't know it he finds it hard to say. . . . He will say sorry if you call him on it, but he walks straight into it."

It is a curious new reality: the dynastic patriarch subject to the modern language of behavior and relationships.

Part of the wherewithal to critique their father comes not just from the psychological predicament the Murdoch children have shared—in this Elisabeth sounds a lot like any well-analyzed forty-year-old woman—but also from the fact that they share his professional world. Talking about their father is shop talk—which they've learned from him.

Indeed, they've often conspired together in the workplace—they know his moves. When Elisabeth first came to London and was given a job at BSkyB under Sam Chisholm, Murdoch would have had Chisholm believe she was an underling, but then he was on the phone with her constantly and she became his back channel. He promoted his inexperienced offspring, in his stealthy ways, into his formidable tool. His children know better than anybody else how he works.

This is one of the odder aspects of the Murdoch dynasty—its relatively clear awareness of itself, and its analytic regard for the patriarch. There's a sense that the children are intent on not being played the way he's playing everyone else—desperate not to be his fools. Trying to figure out every step he takes.

The addition of Matthew Freud added a further ironic twist to this analysis.

After the birth of Matthew and Elisabeth's first child, Charlotte, it was Anna Murdoch who marveled in the interview she gave in 2001 in Australia: "I thought what on earth is this baby going to be like with the blood of Rupert Murdoch and Sigmund Freud running about its veins."

Freud added another level not just of modern personal astuteness but of media consciousness. At times, Matthew Freud almost makes Murdoch seem like an innocent when it comes to using the media. Into the world of Rupert Murdoch came a man of unspeakable craftiness, lounge-lizard smoothness, deep connectedness, superb analytic abilities, and possibly dynastic ambitions of his own. Indeed, Murdoch initially was rather horrified by him. (News Corp. executives were so suspicious of Freud that for a time they called him "Matthew Fraud" behind his back.)

Freud too has been a factor in this book—with a calculated helpfulness and a talent for insinuation. He's contributed his own message—directed in part to his father-in-law—which is that News Corp., as it exists now, bullying and irascible, is old-fashioned, in its way a dying animal, and will inevitably have to transition to a different, cleverer, defter MO.

Variations on that are what Freud has been whispering into his father-in-law's ear—and Murdoch has begun to listen. In fact, Murdoch has come to quite like his dodgy son-in-law, something that the dodgy son-in-law seems to take enormous pride in. In the summer of 2007 when the family is sailing around Sicily, just after the Dow Jones deal is done, a photo is taken of Murdoch and Freud arm in arm, hanging off the top of the boat. Freud gets a framed copy as a keepsake.

Freud, who grew up in the London media scene, has even drawn his father-in-law into this club (membership in which Murdoch has always been strongly averse to). Freud makes it all so . . . symbiotic (the one thing News Corp. has never been).

He just happened to know Prue back when she was a researcher for the *News of the World*'s "What's On" column; he kept calling to offer her tidbits. And he happened to know *Sun* editor and News Corp. star Rebekah Wade from when she was nineteen. And Rebekah Wade happened to be introduced to Elisabeth when Elisabeth first came to London, and then . . . well, the three became best friends when Matthew started to get to know Elisabeth better as the BSkyB PR rep.

In short order, Elisabeth publicly fell for Matthew while she was married and with two small children (including a newborn). Then, after she left her husband, she went off with Matthew, and got pregnant by him, with Freud leaving her not long after she had their child. (This against the backdrop of Murdoch's own marriage falling apart.)

But then Freud returned and married her before her very unwelcoming family at a very public wedding. Made all the more tense by a very pregnant Wendi. (Since their divorce, Rupert and Anna have had to see each other three times: at the weddings of Lachlan, James, and Elisabeth.)

And they started a business together. It's an example, finally, of true media synergy: Her name and his connections jump-started a scrappy television production company. If in the begin-ning it was more a hobby or statement, Liz, who in theory wanted a business that would let her be a mother of (eventually) four, threw her all into it and, by dint of family cheapness and toler-ance for the mechanics end of the business—its main focus isn't making hits but licensing "formats" (e.g., reality shows) into niche markets around the world—built a significant business. Indeed, as her father pursues the *Wall Street Journal*, she's getting ready herself to make a dramatic acquisition that will position her company among the biggest independent television produc-ers in the world.

She has managed to build a media company apart from her father's media company. This confuses him as much as it impresses him. He frequently imagines her moving back to New York or to Los Angeles, and he solicits suggestions for business opportunities in the United States for his son-in-law.

Elisabeth so clearly is keeping herself at bay. Of course, the very process of denying him makes her all the more alluring to him. She seems pleased with having achieved this tension.

Not too long after the Dow Jones deal is completed, Elisabeth and her father are riding horses together. Her seventy-six-year-old father is thrown and lies there motionless for a terrifying moment. Elisabeth thinks (as she will later relate to Prue): *I've killed him.*

## JAMES

James, now destined to take over the empire (and the Murdoch children do call it "the empire"), may be the kid his father understands least of all. On James' part, this might be calculated. A certain cat-and-mouse game with the old man. You can dodge him by talking over his head.

His record label was either a conscious or instinctive move into the one area of media that his father has no interest or experience in. Music hadn't ever been among the Murdoch media businesses. But suddenly he had a son full of A&R talk. A semi-hipster son with his hip-hop acts and bleached blond hair, which would soon be traded in (as soon as Pop bought the record label) for sharp suits and black, thick-rimmed glasses when he got into the Internet business.

James grabbed the Internet business at News Corp. during the boom, setting himself up, in his mid-twenties, as technologist and futurist and digital leader. His father had no idea what he was talking about—but was pleased someone was doing the talking.

And then satellites. James took over the Asian satellite operation in 2000, just months after he was married. Satellites were a business his father had been successful in but which, in essence, he didn't know beans about. The satellite businesses in the United Kingdom and Asia had been run by strong-willed managers and technical people. Murdoch had supported them from afar. Hence once more, in James' canny appreciation of his father's MO—dominate what he understands, find someone to trust when he doesn't—he put himself out of harm's way. His brother, running newspapers, was bound to be second-guessed by his father in every decision he made; James, dealing with satellites, had a much wider berth (not to mention he was six thousand miles away). Of course, James himself knew nothing about the satellite television business—except that he had taken for himself, at News Corp., the technology portfolio. On virtually any issue involving technology, from the mid-nineties on, Murdoch would seek his son's counsel, regardless of his having no established technological expertise.

But, like so many people in the early Internet boom, James sure could talk the talk.

His father has, curiously, come to believe that James is not just so much smarter about all this stuff than he is but better educated too—which is, Oxford graduate to Harvard dropout, not exactly true.

Certainty comes naturally to James. He is the most articulate member of the family—really the *only* articulate Murdoch (the underrated Prue is his only rival). He's all about constant, declarative conversation (although he is the only one of his siblings to put direct quotes from our interview off the record). It's all challenge and menace. He wants to joust, clash, correct, instruct, prevail. He's emphatic. Contrarian. No niceties.

This became a terrible problem for his brother and father during board meetings in the late 1990s and early 2000s. James, the polemicist with absolute confidence in his analytic skills, didn't let up on Lachlan (whom he has not let up on since childhood), who, in his markedly less articulate turn, tried to keep up and defend himself. Neither their father nor the other board members ever figured out quite how to deal with these sibling rivalry events.

His powers of certainty and emphasis are directed not just at his brother; his father, among others, takes it too, with not just good grace but something like pride in his take-no-prisoners son.

Alastair Campbell in his diaries described a dinner with Tony Blair, Murdoch, James, and Lachlan early in 2002. "Lachlan," noted Campbell, "seemed a bit shy of expressing his views whereas James was anything but." Murdoch gave his usual, and deeply felt, defense of Israel, and James, from across the dinner table, told his father that he was "talking fucking nonsense." Murdoch went on, saying that he failed to understand the Palestinian complaints, and James replied, "They were kicked out of their fucking homes and had nowhere to fucking live." Murdoch then said he didn't think James should be talking like that in front of the Prime Minister— who said later how impressed he was that Rupert let his sons do most of the talking.

James' certainty has become part of a signature aggressiveness that he seems to think mimics, or extends from, that of his father. When I see him in London at the BSkyB offices, not long after he flew back from meeting with his father and the Bancrofts, he discusses the advantages of his father's menacing reputation—with a pleased glint in his eye. "A little menace isn't a bad thing."

But his father's menace, which is cowboy- or outlaw-style menace, has mutated in James into a sort of programmatic, techno-manager, automaton-like cultishness. He surrounds himself with a coterie of same-age, same-look (short hair, dark suit, open-necked white shirt) fellow automatons. And from his mouth comes paragraph after paragraph of super-abstracted business-speak.

His sister Prue, with whom he forms a likely voting bloc of two on the Murdoch family trust, refers—half affectionately, half mockingly—to his OCD. (The first to have children, Prue noticed James' horror one day as they ate dinner on his yacht and her youngest child, Clementine, then age five, ate her spaghetti with her hands. "Because James is almost obsessive-compulsive, he started having contortions," Prue recalls. "I had hoped that he would learn the lesson about children when he had his own. But no, James' children are perfect. Elisabeth's children are perfect. Lachlan's children are perfect. And I have got the ragamuffins.")

Each of James' siblings, and perhaps his father too, seems to view him as having particular Martian qualities—which may complicate things when he needs their support on the trust.

For one thing, he's not much fun. Lachlan and Elisabeth are highly social creatures, if not glamour-pusses, and Prue is relaxed and insistent that what you see is what you get, while James is . . . remote. Harsh, intense, judgmental, deeply involved with his own perfection.

He seldom goes out. (When he does, his hosts are apt to worry about whom to seat him next to.) He avoids press. He leaves the people with whom he does interact feeling invariably lesser and one-upped.

And, truly, he is rather fearsome.

His arrival at BSkyB, which was met with some serious opprobrium, required a special brazenness. This was, after all, a major independent public company, and here he was, the inexperienced, barely adult son of the chairman of the controlling shareholder being handed the top job. True, his arrival was carefully orchestrated by his father (there was Murdoch's deal with Conrad Black that his papers would go easy on Black's legal problems if Black's *Telegraph* went easy on James' appointment at BSkyB), as well as Murdoch calling in favors from investors in London's financial community. But what finally carried the day was James' own relentlessness. He stared everybody down. As British investors were wiping 19 percent off BSkyB stock on one day in 2004, James was adamantly telling them that he would make the outrageous target of eight million subscribers by 2006. By the time his brother announced his resignation in July 2005, it was clear James would exceed all of the company's goals—and suddenly the non-Murdoch British press seemed happy to call him the deserved heir apparent.

And then he *really* made his bones: He faced down Richard Branson.

The Virgin chief has long bedeviled the Murdochs. He's been an occasionally irritating force in the media world—Virgin was one of the early partners in BSB, the Sky satellite rival—and has for years tried to insinuate himself into media significance. But more annoyingly, he's confoundingly taken the entrepreneurial outsider role and fashioned himself into a cultural hero. And if Murdoch has never needed to be or even wanted to be a hero, it is nevertheless galling that this imitation rebel gets the role—and then uses it to bother the Murdochs.

Branson was looking to invest in satellite's nemesis: cable. Now, BSkyB had beaten out cable before, introducing digital television in 2002 and tying up key sports rights, in the process flattening dominant U.K. cable operator ITV. But, by 2006, ITV was back in the game, offering broadband service to its U.K. customers. BSkyB understood it needed a broadband option, too, but that would take some time to roll out, time it believed it had because the U.K. cable industry was so inept at marketing itself.

But then along came master marketer Branson, whose Virgin Media might give cable what it didn't have: a consumer brand and entertainment razzmatazz. Branson proposed merging Virgin Media with ITV, which would give him control. BSkyB—and James Murdoch, if not Rupert Murdoch—saw this as a threatening alliance of two organizations it had previously defeated.

In 2006, as Virgin Media and ITV were negotiating their merger, James Murdoch swooped in, dead of night and all, and bought 17.9 percent of ITV, seriously lousing up the Virgin Media deal.

It was so Murdochian: the suddenness, the secrecy, the game-changing aspect of it, the eight-hundred-pound-gorilla-ness of it, the lack of manners and civility, the audacity. Actually, it was audacious, in part, because it was such a crummy deal. News Corp. would never be allowed to buy the whole company (it probably wouldn't want it anyway), it paid way above market value, and it would probably be forced at some point to sell its position (and, in fact, it is eventually ordered to do so), prompting losses of more than a billion dollars.

On the other hand, this bad deal bought BSkyB probably three years to get its broadband play in place without a serious competitor. But it doesn't really matter whether the three-year lead is worth the billion or so it costs—what matters is that the Murdoch kid did something his old man might have done.

Throughout the Dow Jones deal, James is his father's constant confidant. In James' telling, everybody else—Chernin and Ginsberg not least of all—is resistant. It's he and his father toughing it out. Dow Jones is *their* move.

They're in it together—on the same emotional wavelength.

Indeed, on July 4, when James and his father, having traveled from Jamie Packer's wedding in the south of France, are at the America's Cup in Valencia, when it looks like the Dow Jones deal is heading south, when everybody else is trying to calm Murdoch down, James proposes the series of ads that will later appear as the valedictory announcement—the "agent provocateur" ads—but which now James suggests as the way to tell the Bancrofts to fuck off.

The father is saying, "No, no, no, they'll come around—we'll just hold the line." The son is saying, "Pull the deal—that's the way to get them to be serious."

His father, perhaps most of all, is wowed by the boy's pure aggression, by his fight, by his fearsomeness. Which is why the old man figures that, as he chases the *Journal*, it's time to move James up. Having proved his Murdochness, he'll get, in addition to BSkyB, all of Europe and Asia too—making him number three in the company.

# FIFTEEN

# Putting the Deal to Bed

**JULY 2007**

The message being sent about the Dow Jones deal after July 4—
that Murdoch is ready to walk away from the deal—is entirely
wrong.

It's true that he's pissed off—pissed off by the hand-wringing
of the Bancrofts. But it isn't true that he's going anywhere. This is
just dealcraft: the walking-away gesture. Actually, by this point, it
ought to be clear that, having so publicly endured such a bizarre
and dysfunctional deal process, it ought to have been clear he's not
going anywhere. That he is as sentimentally and as fatally attached
to this deal as the Bancrofts are.

But for the Bancrofts, the image of Rupert Murdoch slamming
shut the iron door and pulling up the drawbridge is suddenly a very
primal and threatening one. It begins to feel like an existential
moment to them—to be or not to be sellers.

This figure of a mercurial and threatening Murdoch is drawn most clearly from the reporting in the *Wall Street Journal* itself and, to a slightly lesser extent, in the *New York Times*. Both papers have quite misunderstood the reality of the situation and of Murdoch's desires. In the dominant narrative in both the *Journal* and the *Times*, the Bancroft family is resisting the deal and Murdoch is getting closer and closer to taking a hike. The real narrative is the opposite: Key Bancroft voting blocs are favoring the deal (while this represents just a handful of Bancrofts, it also represents enough votes to do the deal) and Murdoch understands that, in fact, it's all going quite in his favor. Indeed, it's going so much in his favor that he's suddenly thinking he can save the sweetener he had been prepared to offer Dow Jones on the $60 offer—if need be, as much as another dollar or two.

In fact, he's able now to use Dow Jones' and the Bancrofts' sudden, late-inning bid for a little more money as a pretext for his contempt and mounting annoyance—and as a rationale to walk away (or pretend to). Murdoch, with his $60 bid, is the righteous one; Dow Jones and the Bancrofts are the greedy ones. They don't deserve him.

Such is the predicament that most of the Bancrofts, or at least the Bancrofts not directly involved with the deal process—which is most of them—come to understand: Their family's greed and bad behavior have made Murdoch mad.

At the *Journal*, the main reportorial sources are the most resistant, and most vocal, Bancroft family members: Christopher Bancroft and Leslie Hill, two of the four Bancroft family board members. The third family board member, Lisa Steele, who controls one of the most significant voting stakes, isn't talking much; nor is Michael Elefante, the trustee with the most clout, who favors the deal. Reporters at the *Journal* and at the *Times* are also talking to the bankers and lawyers, all of whom are pushing the deal and, accordingly, the idea that Murdoch will walk away if it doesn't happen soon.

The family "farted around, they were dysfunctional." Nobody "could corral the cats, and it dragged and it dragged and it dragged, and Rupert got pissed. We started losing Rupert's goodwill," one of the Dow Jones lawyers will say after the deal is done, in a reasonable précis of the message that the professionals are spreading.

And then there is the Denver Trust. The Denver Trust represents Hugh Bancroft, Christopher Bancroft, and Kathryn Kavadas, with 9.1 percent of the voting shares, but it has no family members as trustees. Its trustee, Lynn P. Hendrix, a Denver lawyer, believes he has to act in the best interests not of the family, or Dow Jones, but of the trust itself. His job, in other words, is to get the highest return possible on capital. In this pursuit, he is aided by Rob Kindler from Morgan Stanley, who, when he was at JP Morgan Chase, had represented Dow Jones, and who has struggled since the early days of the offer to get in on the deal, finally snagging the Denver Trust as his client. Hendrix and Kindler, by early July, are taking an unreconstructed financial view: The controlling shareholder should get a premium. That is, if the Dow Jones shareholders get $60 for the shares, the controlling shareholders should get more because their vote is worth more. Or if $60 a share is the total price, then the common shareholders should get less of it and the controlling shareholders more of it.

While a control premium is illegal in some states, it's not illegal in Delaware, where Dow Jones is incorporated. Rewarding shareholders inequitably is, however, a lesser practice, a gaucherie, not a blue-chip way to go. The Dow Jones board—including the Bancrofts on the board—says it won't approve a control premium deal. The Denver Trust's initiative rattles many of the Bancrofts, highlighting the conflict between their ideas of fairness and their desire for more dough. In some sense, fairness wins out. In an inversion, not asking for a control premium and just selling the company for $60 a share actually begins to feel like a virtuous thing to do.

Inside News Corp. they're counting votes. Murdoch has his only off-the-record meeting with a Bancroft family member. Billy Cox, accompanied by his wife, Beatrice—who are, via Andy Steginsky, News Corp.'s most prolific source of information about the Bancroft family—stop in at Murdoch's office. Murdoch, dressed in a tux, is in an ill humor not because of the Bancrofts but because he has to go to the opera.

After seeing Billy, Murdoch calls Tom Hill in Boston—because Murdoch understands, through Billy, that the Hill brothers are in favor of the deal. He tries to get Hill to put him in touch with his mother, Jane Cox MacElree, whose vote controls her family's trust, and who is still stubbornly resisting the deal. Tom Hill says he doesn't think this is such a good idea and that he'd be uncomfortable in the middleman role.

News' due diligence at Dow Jones winds up. One of the key rationales of the deal—that the *Wall Street Journal* could become an important pillar of the new Fox business channel—falls apart during the due dilly. It turns out that the *Journal*'s content-sharing deal with CNBC is much tighter than anybody at News Corp. thought (there's a lot of oohing and ahhing at News at the legal drafting that went into the agreement). The *Journal* as an advantage to a television network, it turns out, is effectively owned by News' competitor until 2012. But pay no attention . . .

The other problem element that the due diligence foreshadows is the fundamental nature of Dow Jones—it's a vastly encumbered, bureaucratic, hierarchical organization, whereas News Corp. thinks of itself as a cowboy shop. "It's run like an old Detroit car company," John Nallen, the number two News Corp. financial guy, will conclude about Dow Jones. "There are twenty-six grades of people. Your aspiration as a grade thirteen is to become a grade eleven. That's just not the way a News Corp. company operates."

Oh, and the printing facilities. It's not only that full color is going to be difficult, but the entire structure of the print process at the *Journal* is obtuse and antiquated—designed, in fact, for a business newspaper rather than for Murdoch's dream of a national beat-the-*Times* paper. "There are seventeen printing sites," Nallen will sigh. "The fact that you have to go to bed at eight o'clock, you can't get any breaking news. There's an election tomorrow night and you're not going to read about it in the *Journal* on Wednesday."

But no matter . . .

On the morning of July 16, there's the first of several ritualistic assemblies that happen that day at the News offices. Mike Costa from Merrill Lynch (representing the Bancroft trusts), Greg Lee from Goldman Sachs (representing the Dow Jones board), and Rich Zannino sit down with News Corp.'s two top financial executives, Nallen and CFO Dave DeVoe. Costa, Lee, and Zannino have a clear message: *We can make this deal happen, we really can, if you give us more than sixty bucks.*

As a negotiating position, this one is about two months overdue.

DeVoe, giving the on-script negotiating response, says, *Sixty bucks, that's the deal.* (Even if you're going to fold, you don't fold right away.)

Costa, Lee, and Zannino cool their heels while they wait for a lunch meeting at News Corp., where Murdoch and Lon Jacobs are due to join DeVoe and Nallen. Dow Jones chairman Peter McPherson will also be joining them, along with board member Lewis Campbell.

At lunch Nallen detects clear tension between Campbell, who the News Corp. people believe has been a consistent "reasonable" voice, and McPherson, whom the News Corp. people don't trust. McPherson takes up the negotiating position, asking Murdoch if he'll consider raising the bid. There is something too ritualistic about it all—it's a going-through-the-motions move. It's people exercising their "fiduciary responsibility"—a term McPherson seems to utter in almost every sentence. Murdoch says no, the offer is the offer. McPherson asks him to think about it. Murdoch, ritualistically, agrees.

The Dow Jones group returns, in something like slow motion, later in the afternoon to receive Murdoch's formal response.

Murdoch gives a little talk about the process, about Dow Jones, and about how $60 is a full and fair offer.

And that's it. The Dow Jonesers, in a good mood, thank Murdoch and leave. On the way out, Lewis Campbell tells Murdoch they're there—basically there.

The next day, the seventeenth, the Dow Jones board votes to approve the offer and recommend it to its shareholders—with the understanding that if there is a "satisfactory" level of support from the Bancroft family, the board will review a definitive merger agreement. Leslie Hill and Dieter von Holtzbrinck, a board member since 2001, abstain from the vote (an outright "no" vote, they have been advised, might subject them to shareholders' suits). Christopher Bancroft, still on the hustings for alternative buyers, recuses himself from the vote.

On July 19, von Holtzbrinck, while agreeing that the economics of the deal are very strong, says he can't support the journalistic ethics of the deal and asks if he can disregard the economics and cast a no vote on the basis of the ethics. He's advised that this would not be the appropriate, fiduciarily responsible thing to do. He resigns rather than cast a yes vote.

On July 20, having received the board's approval, and by now confident that he has the minimum support he needs from the family, Murdoch sets a deadline: July 31.

At the seashore in Maine, Peter Kann has lunch at Martha Robes' home. He's there with his wife, Karen House, and their children, and with Robes and her sisters, Lisa Steele and Jean Stevenson, and their husbands and children. The elder Bill Cox is there with his wife. It's a social and sentimental occasion. The old days of the *Journal* are the subject. It's a valedictory moment: "Be proud of what your family did for all these generations," is what Kann says, knowing the likelihood that Lisa Steele will carry her sisters into a vote for Murdoch. "All of us who worked for the company were appreciative—are appreciative—so whatever happens, don't, you know, feel bad. Life goes on, or something like that," is the substance of what Kann will recall he told the family members.

On July 23, the three branches of the Bancroft family assemble in Boston at the Hilton Hotel on Broad Street. It is to be their final meeting as shareholders in a family business—it is, too, quite likely their final meeting as a family. There are dozens of reporters in front of the hotel, creating a circus-like atmosphere that most of the Bancrofts find embarrassing and which adds to the levels of anger, emotionalism, and encirclement. This is a last stand. Chris Bancroft shows up wearing a hat that says "Bite Me."

Murdoch is as well versed on the leanings of the various blocs within the family as anyone in the family. Indeed, by mid-July Andy Steginsky, whose Bancroft sources, not least of all Billy Cox, have continued to keep him closely informed, and who proves to be an astute vote counter, is speaking to Murdoch almost hourly. At this moment, as the Bancrofts begin their meeting, Steginsky's in India, on a trip with his twenty-one-year-old son. As his son sleeps—it's the middle of the night in India—Steginsky is locked in the hotel bathroom, listening in on the Bancroft conclave via an open cell phone. He's reporting to Murdoch on a blow-by-blow basis.

Almost nothing has changed in the family's fundamental discussion of the deal. For two months the argument has remained fixed. On one hand, there is the intractable financial picture of Dow Jones and the panacea of the $60 offer. On the other hand, there is Murdoch and the sense among many of the most vocal and most august members of the family that there must be an alternative—because what is the world worth without an alternative to Murdoch? If that's *it*, if there is *only* Murdoch . . .

What has changed is how tired the family is, not just of the argument but of each other.

The meeting lasts for eight hours.

Merrill Lynch, once again, makes the main presentation. In many ways, it is simply a review of what has been, by now, reviewed over and over again. The presentation has hardened into something of a no-exit scenario. Once again: Not in anyone's wildest imagination is there a way the company will ever return $60 a share in value. The Merrill Lynch presentation reviews the various alternatives to the Murdoch offer and explains why none of them is a realistic option—leaving only Murdoch's offer.

Still, there is an odd hope. Or a stubborn hope. "Maybe there is some other scenario that is real, that we can say, 'Okay, we can say no to Murdoch because there is this other alternative that is plausible,'" thinks one family member plaintively, going into the meeting. Even an offer with fewer dollars.

Lewis Campbell, representing the Dow Jones board, explains to the family why the board has decided to support the offer: In his business career he has never seen such a gap between price and value. In other words, it's a no-brainer.

Michael Elefante gives a tortured rationale from the point of view of the trustees that combines both an argument about fiduciary responsibility—making the implicit point that he and his firm could be held accountable for making a bad economic decision and that, to be sure, Murdoch's offer is the right economic decision—and another, more nuanced argument about the nature of the trust. While, certainly, one of the purposes of the trusts is to protect the independence of the *Wall Street Journal*, the trusts also make mention of the continued prosperity of the company. The family's continuing relationship to the company might, in fact, be hurting the continued prosperity of the company. See?

Elefante's partner at Hemenway and Barnes, Michael Puzo, reviews the terms of the editorial-protections agreement to which the family and Murdoch have agreed.

"How can you stop Rupert from interfering?" the elder Bill Cox demands to know. "Why would you sell a company to an owner where you need this kind of protection?" asks Cox's sister, Jane MacElree.

Puzo says he believes, as do the *Journal*'s editors, that the agreement has "teeth." Chris Bancroft makes the anti-Murdoch case, saying there's just no pressing need to do this deal now, and, in fact, arguing that it isn't a very good deal. He suggests that the premium isn't such a great premium after tax. Leslie Hill then says that she had prepared a talk about why they shouldn't sell, but that she's decided not to give it. Instead she reads letters from reporters at the *Wall Street Journal* who have written her about their fears of what Murdoch will do to the institution.

Then Leslie's mother, Jane McElree, the last matriarch, gives the day's most emotional appeal. She brings up the terrible things she believes Murdoch has done in China, how he would do anything for business reasons (she's gotten this mostly from reading the *Journal* and the *Times*), and then evokes Danny Pearl, the celebrated *Journal* reporter who was beheaded by terrorists in Pakistan in 2002, suggesting both that there won't be any more fearless reporters like Pearl under Murdoch and that selling the paper is somehow a betrayal of Pearl's memory and of his sacrifice. (Her sons are rather annoyed by their mother's use of the Danny Pearl card.)

Michael Elefante distributes the voting agreements and establishes a deadline of a week hence, July 30, for their return.

The meeting finishes at eight o'clock that evening. Andy Steginksy, from India, tells Murdoch that it's all gone rather well.

On July 27, as the Bancrofts consider their votes, one of the Hill brothers, Crawford, a biology teacher, sends an e-mail to each member of the Bancroft family, which reads in part:

It was I who jumped into the back seat of the limo that we grabbed to rush Gay [Jessie Cox] to Lenox Hill Hospital after her renowned collapse at the family dinner at "21" in April of 1982. In that back seat, next to Uncle Bill, I attempted CPR on her, but sadly, it was too late and she had taken her last breath.

What most of you do not know however is that the very same Jessie B. Cox that is mentioned at every turn as "family matriarch" and to whom many of us owe "the legacy" forced her incredibly talented husband, William C. Cox, top student at Milton and Harvard luminary, to retire prematurely from Dow Jones at age 40 so he could be full time in the social swirl of Cohasset. He was a star at the company! My firstborn child—Hadley—has that "C." in her name— Coburn—to honor the talented and caring Bill Cox, Gramps to his grandchildren . . .

It's four thousand words recapitulating Bancroft family wounds, missteps, slights, and betrayals, as good a piece of evidence as any that it's time for this odd, insular, and out-of-it-family to give up the ghost.

On July 29, Michael Elefante tells the Dow Jones board that 28 percent of the family's voting shares favor a deal. This, combined with the 36 percent of the voting shares controlled by the common shareholders—with the assumption that because the common shares are now overwhelmingly owned by arbitrageurs, they will vote for the deal—likely means that there is enough support for the deal. Murdoch, however, is looking to hedge his bet.

The News Corp. concern is that proxy solicitors have advised that while 100 percent of the common shareholders might be for the deal, News shouldn't count on more than 80 percent of the common shareholders actually casting a vote. Still, with the support of 28 percent of the family's votes, this should put them just over 50 percent. But this, while giving News a victory, is hardly a PR coup. Murdoch continues to suggest that he won't do the deal unless he gets the backing of family representing 50 percent of the vote.

Beginning on the night of the twenty-ninth and running throughout the day of the thirtieth, Murdoch's inner circle works the phones, looking to move the vote in News Corp.'s favor. One focus is Christopher Bancroft, who controls approximately 15 percent of the voting shares and who has flip-flopped on the deal (initially for, then against) for either moral or financial reasons or both and pursued his own, often grandstanding agenda. As it happens, his brother, Hugh Bancroft III, his sister, Kathryn Kavadas, and their niece, Lizzie Goth, whose trust he controls, favor the deal—but his no vote will withhold approval. After extended discussion—involving possible financial sweeteners—he agrees to abstain, meaning the trusts can approve the vote. But then it turns out that under Massachusetts law, where these trusts have been constituted, a trustee can't abstain in such a vote. There's a sudden rush to reconstitute these trusts in another state where this would be possible—except this would probably require an extension of the deal, which Murdoch absolutely doesn't want to do.

Meanwhile, a discussion has been going on with the Denver Trust, with its 9 percent of the vote, and its trustee, Lynn Hendrix, who has for almost a month now been holding out for the control premium. After a series of conference calls that run through the night of the twenty-ninth, News Corp. relents, giving them the premium in the form of an agreement to pay all the legal and banking fees for the entire Bancroft family. The Denver Trust signs on to the deal, meaning family representing 37 percent of the voting shares approve—meaning the deal, albeit falling short of Murdoch's 50 percent wish, will be approved.

On August 1 in the afternoon, Andy Steginksy, in the habit of speaking to Murdoch several times a day to talk about the deal, calls in, even though the deal is done. Murdoch's secretary, Dot Wyndoe, patches Andy through to Murdoch, who is at home and getting into bed. Murdoch's exhausted. He tells Steginsky he should go to bed too.

**The Proprietor**

Here's an up-close of Murdoch as a newsman:

One morning when I arrived at his office with my research assistant, Leela de Kretser, for another interview session with the seventy-seven-year-old chairman, he was hunched over the phone reporting out a story. He'd been out the night before and gotten a tip. Now he was trying to nail it down. His side of the conversation was straight reporter stuff: Whom could he call? How could he get in touch? Will they confirm? Barked, impatient, just the facts. Here was the old man, in white shirt, singlet visible underneath, doing one of the same basic jobs he'd been doing since 1953, when he took over the *Adelaide News* in Australia from his father. And he was good at it. He was parsing each answer. Re-asking the questions. Clarifying every point. His notepad going. He knew the trade. Of how many media company CEOs could that be said? This wasn't a destroyer of journalism, this was a practitioner.

On the other hand, he was trying to smear somebody. At the dinner party he'd attended—now that he was an unlikely fixture at fashionable tables—he'd heard that a senior Hillary Clinton operative was a partner in an online porn company. He didn't like the operative, and he didn't like—no matter how much he had tried—Hillary. So it didn't much matter that the story itself seemed far-fetched and tenth-hand, it was juicy and would slime somebody he thought was... a slime.

True, it didn't pan out—and that was the end of it. Well, sort of. Because he kept recycling it. It became a staple in Murdoch's repertoire of whispers and confidences and speculations. (He also had a *New York Post* reporter chasing, unsuccessfully, the story.)

Rupert Murdoch doesn't necessarily need to print or broadcast the news to make it news. He may be among the biggest gossips in New York. In my many months of interviewing him, I found that the most reliable way to hold his interest was to bring him a rich nugget. His entire demeanor would change. He'd instantly light up. He'd go from distracted to absolutely focused. Gossip gives him life (and business opportunities).

This is, I believe, how the rumor about Michael Bloomberg buying the *New York Times* got legs. I offered it to Murdoch as a bit of speculation, conflating two of his favorite subjects— Bloomberg, whom he greatly admires, and the *New York Times,* which he does not—in suggesting that a Bloomberg Times deal could be possible. He paused, considered, opened his mouth, seemed blissed out for a second, processed this information against his own needs and interests, and then said, "I think it makes sense. I'll ask him." And suddenly the rumor was everywhere—he was telling everybody, which made it "true." In fact, the mayor's people seemed to like the rumor so much that they began to talk it up themselves. Bloomberg himself seemed to fancy it (offering only a tepid denial), and Murdoch thought he might act on it.

Murdoch is a troublemaker—one of the last great troublemakers in the holier-than-thou, ethically straitjacketed news business.

In August 2007, after News won Dow Jones, Gary Ginsberg told his boss that he was planning to go to Paris for the wedding of his friend Doug Band, Bill Clinton's chief aide, to the handbag designer Lily Rafii. Ginsberg reported to Murdoch (Ginsberg too knows that Murdoch likes—*needs*—gossip) that the wedding was going to be a party-hearty affair with Ron Burkle, Steve Bing, and of course, Clinton himself. So Murdoch, onto not just a good story but also a way to annoy Ginsberg, called *New York Post* editor Col Allan and, busting the expense budget, had "Page Six" send a reporter to Paris. Headline (to Ginsberg's consternation): "Bill and Pals Do Paris (The City, Not the Bimbo)."

Eight months after he had taken over the *Wall Street Journal*, the paper arguably was a better one. On a daily basis it seemed to metamorphose in the subtlest of ways into a sharper, less fussy view of business and of the events shaping markets and economies. The *Journal*'s foreign coverage was, suddenly, as good as any paper's in the United States—as good as the *Times*. Within a few months of his takeover—even after Murdoch forced out the editor, thereby doing the one thing he'd agreed with the Bancrofts he wouldn't do—most of the talk of his tabloidizing the paper, undermining its credibility, or bastardizing the brand went quiet. (As a further poke at the Bancroft family, in fulfillment of his agreement to appoint a Bancroft family representative to the News Corp. board, he selected Natalie Bancroft, a twenty-eight-year-old would-be opera singer who lives in Europe—who'd contacted her family only twice during the takeover drama.) Suddenly the only debate that remained was the business issue: Might his stated plan to turn the *Journal* into a national paper mean it would lose its focus on business? Was that really a good idea, to go from a specialized publication to a general-interest one?

And, actually, was that even the true plan?

Murdoch might be talking about a national paper covering politics and foreign news, but his editor, Robert Thomson, was hurrying to assure the *Journal*'s readers and advertisers that it would remain a business paper, that there would be no dilution of its focus. In separate discussions they were describing separate papers.

Part of the curiousness of the takeover was not just that Murdoch seemed to have no immediate Murdoch stamp to put on the *Journal* but also that he seemed in fact to have no specific plan at all for it. Not that he was adrift, but more in the sense that it was a new day. The world was fresh. He was marveling at what he held in his hands.

The truth was that he had strikingly little idea about what he had bought. He was uninformed about Dow Jones' businesses—comprising more than half of the company's revenues—beyond the paper. He had a vague and mostly incorrect idea of what Factiva, Dow Jones' news database, did. He was all for making the *Journal*'s subscription-supported Internet business free until someone pointed out the immediate P&L hit that would cause. His idea was to sell Dow Jones' chain of smaller newspapers until he found out there were no buyers (News Corp. quietly put the Ottaway papers on the block, and then, with no interest above their minimum asking price, announced that they had decided how wonderful it was to own these papers and what a strategic fit they were). And he and everyone else at News were gobsmacked by the sorry state of the U.S. newspaper business—especially in the face of a sudden economic downturn, which Murdoch was particularly gloomy about. (His vision of a great new News Corp. Center dominating midtown Manhattan was, as a result of the real estate meltdown, taken off the table.)

If *panic* was not the right word to use, *concern* certainly was. Murdoch, whose playbook for buying a newspaper was invariably to cut its price, thereby boosting its sales against the competition, upped the newspaper price of the *Journal* from $1.50 to two bucks—50 cents more than the *Times*. (And he doubled the price of the *New York Post* to 50 cents.)

Eight months after Murdoch & Co. walked in the door at Dow Jones, the News Corp. share price was down by 35 percent, with News executives putting the blame directly on Dow Jones. Indeed, not only was Dow Jones a certain culprit, but blaming Dow Jones made everybody else's business less responsible. It was, although no one would have quite said it this way, Rupert's fault. Indeed, at the rate the newspaper business was imploding, if he had waited six months News Corp. could have saved a billion or more on the deal. Ginsberg and Chernin, with gallows humor, sat on the phone together discussing the relative fortunes they'd each lost on their News Corp. options.

The question remained: How come? Why the *Journal?* What was the point? His children and some of his executives had begun to speculate that it was a sort of retirement move. That Murdoch wanted to stop traveling so much; that he wanted to spend time with his wife and youngest children and needed an excuse to stay put in New York; that the *Journal* was a place he could go to in the afternoons. As much to the point, he had effectively divvied up the rest of the company. Peter Chernin ran the U.S. entertainment assets; his son James ran the European and Asian assets; Australia, specifically carved out of James' purview, awaited Lachlan's return; Roger Ailes ran Fox News. Murdoch himself was left, in a manner of speaking, with only the *Wall Street Journal* and the *New York Post.*

And yet this view seemed likely to be about his children's wishfulness—to see their father content and to have him understand his natural, compartmentalized place in the world. Too, it seemed to buck more than fifty years of evidence about how Murdoch used newspapers.

From the *Adelaide News* to the *News of the World* and the *Sun* to the *New York Post* to the *Times* of London to his father's old company, the Herald and Weekly Times, each of the newspapers he'd bought had been a transformative catalyst, turning him into something beyond what he was. Indeed, one central criticism of Murdoch—that he uses the clout of his newspapers to further his personal agenda—misses the larger point: He uses his newspapers to change *himself.* It's as though he can't quite express himself without one—or can only express himself with one. Nor, accordingly, can he truly see a paper as separate from himself.

What he got, what the shareholders of News Corp. got, for $5.6 billion would be a newer, fundamentally transformed Rupert Murdoch.

It's even possible to say that we really might not have the old Rupert to kick around anymore.

The change in Murdoch could not be missed. At the same time, nobody acknowledged it. You couldn't say he had changed, because that might imply that he'd needed to be changed before—that, for instance, he had long been among the must obdurate and knuckle-headed of right-wingers. Another reason you couldn't say he had changed was that Murdoch didn't do or understand that kind of talk—that psychological stuff. And finally, saying that he'd changed might imply he was mellowing—which might imply he was getting old.

But he *had* changed.

This was about Wendi. While Murdoch says she has no politics, what he means is that she has no bias, no prejudice. She does not think in the binary ways in which Murdoch had always thought. She has had to be so open and so plastic and so take-what-may in her own life's adventure that her natural disposition has become enthusiasm, satisfaction, joie de vivre, and a big embrace of the opportunities and pleasures of the world. In other words, just the opposite of the disgruntlement, antipathy, and embattlement her husband cultivated for so long.

The girl whose American adventure started, before she could speak English, in a kitchen of a Chinese restaurant and took her to the Yale School of Management and then into the arms of Rupert Murdoch is a compelling heroine. Her adventure, in a way, may be as great as his. And he's obviously captivated by it and by her ambition (their pillow talk, one might suspect, is business talk). You can see this as comic: no fool like an old fool—his gray hair bursting into colors not found in nature. But I think that misses the true

quality of the change. Of the plot twist. Rupert Murdoch is, characteristically, seizing an opportunity. The zeitgeist is changing and
he's after it.

She has turned him into . . . well, almost a liberal. At least she
has introduced him to liberals. The angry outsider, the anti-elitist,
the foe of airs and pretension has become part of the achieving,
glamorous, clever, socially promiscuous set. Davos, Cannes, Sun
Valley, Barry Diller's yacht—this is now Rupert Murdoch's world.
The people around him debate how much this is real, how much
he might have gone over to the other side; and how much of it is
for Wendi—how much he's just the put-upon husband.

Surely he remains a militant free-marketer, is still pro-war
(begrudgingly—he's retreated a bit) and uncompromisingly anti-
Europe. And then there are his views on the inbreeding of Muslims.

And yet he's come to like the liberals more than the conservatives—and many of them have come to like him too. Bono and Tony
Blair and the Google guys and Nicole Kidman and David Geffen are
his and Wendi's circle. Liking Wendi's friends so much better than
his own (indeed, never really having had friends of his own), he
finds himself with an increasingly conflicted temperament.

Along with Wendi, it is also his four adult children, all more or
less liberal, certainly more liberal than he has ever been, pulling
him in new directions. It's very simple: Going his own way, he
seems to sense, however ruefully, is the way of being old; going
their way is young.

Like Wendi, his children are perfectly integrated into a more
or less limousine-liberal world. And for all the griping he continues to do about such "values," and all the ways he eschews talking
that kind of talk, he's in another place now than he was when, in
the world's eyes (particularly the liberal world's eyes), he became
Rupert Murdoch.

His own awareness of this seems tinged with both resignation
and curiosity about the new game. One day as we spoke, he tried,

with some determination, to describe his son James' conservative bona fides. Of course then there was the problem that James is also a "tree hugger." And then too, in a kind of double political reversal, there's the situation in Britain. Murdoch continues to like Gordon Brown—he might be the Labour prime minister, but he's conservative, particularly in the Murdoch sense of no pretense, no frills. But then there is James' infatuation with David Cameron, the Tories' cool, glam former PR guy, whom Murdoch knew he was, however begrudgingly, going to have to accept.

As I was finishing this book, Wendi urged me to do one more interview. To see Tony Blair.

The arrangement with Blair to sit down with me in his office in Grosvenor Square—John Adams's old house in London, converted now into a set of minimalist conference rooms—was clearly a family affair (Matthew Freud is one of Blair's longtime PR consultants). He was doing this at the Murdochs' request and to buff the Murdoch image—and happily so. They have become brothers in arms, united not just by political wars but by longtime familiarity and even intimacy. By the time I spoke to Blair the Murdoch family was abuzz with consternation of how indiscreet Prue Murdoch might have been with me, which Blair had been fully apprised about (by Prue herself) and which indiscreetness he tried gently and generously to help smooth, "She told me what she said to you," he laughed.

The Murdoch-Blair relationship, which began as one of convenience—of Blair the supplicant and Murdoch the cynical, realpolitik manipulator—has morphed into a relationship of philosophical identification.

Blair, curiously, sees the old man in much the same way as his children see him, partly understanding Murdoch as the product of a generational divide: "For someone of his generation—he doesn't—he breaks out of traditional right-wing thinking at points and he is—he's not somebody who admires position or wealth unless it's been made by that person. You know what I mean by that?"

They like each other—and these guys are disliked by many of the same people. Over the thirteen years of this relationship, the tabloid right-winger and new Labour exponent have gone from opportunistic alliance to fast friendship—against which each, with evident humility, leavens his views. For each of them, this began in no small way as an effort to please Wendi. Tony liked Wendi and was therefore willing to get along with her difficult husband, and Rupert understood that Wendi liked Tony, so he'd make the effort too. When I asked Blair about the possibility of him going to work for News Corp., he blushed.

Just before the New York Democratic primary, when I found myself undecided between Clinton and Obama, I said to Murdoch (a little flirtation, like a little gossip, softens him): "Rupert, I don't know who to vote for—so I'm going to give you my vote. You choose."

He paused, considered, nodded slowly, then said, "Obama—he'll sell more papers."

Even though his wife had been attending fund-raisers for Obama in Los Angeles—as his daughter, Liz, and her husband, Matthew, had been raising money for him in Notting Hill—this was a leap for Murdoch. Murdoch has traditionally liked politicians to come to him. His historic shift in the 1990s to Tony Blair came after Blair made a pilgrimage to Australia.

Obama, on the other hand, was snubbing Murdoch. Every time he reached out, nothing. (At one point, Gary Ginsberg knew Caroline Kennedy was riding in a car with Obama and begged her to show Obama the *New York Post*'s endorsement.)

It wasn't until early summer 2008 that Obama relented and a secret courtesy meeting was arranged. The meeting began with Murdoch sitting down knee to knee with Obama at the Waldorf-Astoria. The younger man was deferential to Murdoch—and interested in his story. Obama pursued: What was Murdoch's relationship with his father? How had he gotten from Adelaide to the top of the world?

Murdoch, for his part, had a simple thought for Obama, which he'd prepared ahead of time. He has known possibly as many heads of state as anyone living today—has met every American president since Harry Truman—and this is what he understands: Nobody gets much time to make an impression. Leadership is about what you do in the first six months.

Then, after he said his piece, Murdoch switched places and let his special guest, Roger Ailes, sit knee to knee with Obama.

Obama lit into Ailes. He said he didn't want to waste his time talking to Ailes if Fox was just going to continue to abuse him and his wife, that Fox had relentlessly portrayed him as suspicious, foreign, fearsome—just short of a terrorist.

Ailes, unruffled, said it might not have been this way if Obama had come on the air instead of giving Fox the back of his hand.

A tentative truce, which may or may not have historical significance, was thereupon agreed.

There is, possibly, also another motive behind Murdoch's interest in Obama. Peter Chernin was one of Hillary Clinton's most significant backers. Murdoch, with his support of Obama, was putting it to Peter. He was denying him. There was something good-natured here, but there was something much less good-natured too. Murdoch's Chernin problem remained a significant one—it was just good corporate politics to get in the way of Chernin being the one whom the president owed.

And then there was Fox News. Murdoch's life is now largely spent around people for whom Fox News is a vulgarity and a joke. And if he has happily spent much of his career being regarded as a rude vulgarian, the people who feel this way about his most significant news operation have never been so close to him.

It's life with Wendi versus life with Fox News.

The embarrassment can no longer be missed. He mumbles even more than usual when called on to justify it. He barely pretends to hide the way he feels about Bill O'Reilly. And while it is not that he would give Fox up—because the money is the money; success still trumps all—in the larger sense of who he is, he seems to want to hedge his bets.

And call it restlessness, too. He has done this—done Fox. You can't do it any more than he's done it.

He needs a new chapter, a new plot twist to keep the story going.

His purchase of the *Journal* was in no small way about wanting to trade the illiberal—the belligerent, the vulgar, the loud, the menacing, the unsubtle—for the better-heeled, the more magnanimous, the further nuanced. He was looking for better company.

Also, it is, with a little critical interpretation, perfectly in character. Taking over the *Journal*, actually becoming a respectable publisher, is the ultimate fuck-you to the people who have always believed *they* embody respectability.

Characteristically, his experiment in respectability may yet become an avaricious and all-consuming one if he pursues the *New York Times*, too.

Which he will be temperamentally compelled to do.

Business exists, continues to exist, as a series of fantasies he makes come true.

There was the moment, in the car heading out to the airport in the weeks before the *Wall Street Journal* formally became his, when the news broke that Merrill Lynch was going into the tank. Its CEO, Stan O'Neal, had just been fired. Anticipating events—Merrill's need for cash, its inevitable sale of assets—Murdoch became, for an hour or so, the presumptive buyer of Merrill's 20 percent stake in Bloomberg (Murdoch cultivates obsessions, and Bloomberg is one). Soon to have the *Wall Street Journal*, now soon to have his mitts on Bloomberg, Rupert Murdoch, at least in his own mind, would control worldwide financial information. It was management by fantasy—even though this one, like so many, was shortly to pass.

There was the Yahoo! moment. Or the several Yahoo! moments. During the Dow Jones battle, Peter Chernin, on the West Coast, was trying to talk about a MySpace-Yahoo! combination with Yahoo! CEO Terry Semel (this was, in part, Chernin's effort to distract attention from the *Journal* deal). But then Semel got ousted. Then, after the Dow Jones deal, as Microsoft was trying to corner Yahoo!, Murdoch, creating a story for a day or two, put it out that News Corp. and Microsoft might have convergent interests in the deal—which would be true only in a parallel universe. But hey, you never know.

Buying the *Wall Street Journal* was surely an exercise of pure fantasy. To think he could take over a company absolutely controlled by a family that had repeatedly said it would never sell was fantasy. To think it was worth what he was paying for it was fantasy. And yet . . . now it's his, and if his shareholders are puzzled and grumpy, so be it (he'll ignore them as much as he ignores his other critics). He's in it for the long haul—even at seventy-seven.

Everybody around him continues to tell him that buying the *Times* is pretty much impossible. There will be regulatory problems. The Sulzberger family would never ever . . . And then there's the opprobrium of public opinion. But it's obviously irresistible to him. It would be the realization of his destiny. Not just because the *Times* represents the ultimate in newspaper proprietorship and he believes he is the ultimate newspaper proprietor. But because he believes he is the last person to love newspapers—the only person who is willing to treat them right. He thinks the *Times*, with its soft stories and newsless front page and all its talk of being a news *brand* instead of a newspaper—has forsaken what a news*paper* is. He is, he believes, the real white knight of newspapers.

Of course, however plausibly virtuous he's been so far as the *Journal*'s owner, he's still the same ol' Rupe. I've watched him go through the numbers, plot out a *Times* merger with the *Journal*'s backroom operations, and fantasize about the staff quitting en masse. He has conjured, too, how, in Murdoch style, he might convince the Sulzbergers to let him in if he promises to leave Arthur in charge—and how he could then make Arthur his puppet.

Shortly after the *Journal* takeover, *Newsday*, the paper that dominates Long Island, was put on the block by its owner, Sam Zell, the real estate magnate who had just bought *Newsday*'s parent company, the *Tribune*. It was a rare opportunity. Murdoch could finally, after thirty years, see a way, by combining operations with *Newsday*, to make the *Post* pay for itself. But he was ambivalent. Because he was dubious about Long Island (real estate, the economy, etc.). Or because he really didn't want to think about the *Post*—he had other things on his mind. Still, he wouldn't let Mort Zuckerman, the owner of the *Daily News*, grab *Newsday*—that would hellishly squeeze the *Post*. On the other hand, he might not have minded if Cablevision, the cable company based on Long Island and run by the Dolan family, famous New York numbskulls, suddenly and unaccountably interested in the newspaper business, got it. He went back and forth. His intermediary was David Geffen, Wendi's close friend, who'd gotten close to Zell because he was interested in the *Los Angeles Times*. It looked good. And although buying *Newsday* would exacerbate Murdoch's regulatory problems if he were, ultimately, to go after the *Times*, he suddenly rationalized this—the *Times*, after all, was really a national paper now.

But in fact, the Dolans, numbskulls that they are, bid up *Newsday* beyond reason. He didn't mind—they'd run it into the ground, so no threat. But what seemed to happen here as well was that the *Post* became further unfixed in his mind. He'd traded up. So, suddenly, coldly, his beloved *New York Post* was in an awkward position. With decisiveness and some clandestine business craft, he began a discussion with the *Post*'s number one enemy, Zuckerman. (There is an unbecoming setback with some landscaping in front of News HQ at 1211 Sixth Avenue, where, after an interview one afternoon, I spied Mort Zuckerman waiting on a bench.) Everything was suddenly on the table: a possible joint operating agreement, combining ad sales, merging, selling—all scenarios which would lessen the *Post*'s cash drain on News Corp., his identification with it (as opposed to his new identification with the *Journal*), and its regulatory drag if he decided to go after the *Times*.

His world was new—and getting newer.

But of course it was the same one, too. By the fall of 2008, having stoked great expectations among his liberal executives and family about his growing Obamaism—"He's going to do it," said Ginsberg; "He is a rock star. It's fantastic," Murdoch had said about Obama at a conference in May—he began to pull back. Obama was wishy-washy, insubstantial, lacked clarity.

Indeed, Murdoch was responding to suggestions about his nascent liberalism—in September I discussed his Obama leanings in *Vanity Fair*—with grumpiness and contrariness. *He* wasn't a liberal! Who said that? He was, stubbornly, what he wanted to be, what *he* decided he would be.

He could give. He could take. Indeed, the *New York Post* endorsed McCain in September. Everybody around him who had been reminded of this so many times, was reminded again. He was not a product of circumstances. He created the circumstances. He wasn't anybody's foil.

On the other hand, he couldn't help muttering. John McCain was so . . . *old*.

By the summer of 2008, with News Corp.'s stock sinking to a six-year low—some people in the company were arguing that this meant Dow Jones hadn't cost $5.6 billion but rather something like $25 billion, thanks to lost market cap—the unique, and perhaps ridiculous, aspects of News once again came into high relief. No other public company of its size was—or had ever been—such a singular reflection of one man. He had managed to make history's most unbusinesslike business. He had re-created the idea of monarchy. He had figured out how to monetize his deepest hankerings and whims. He had created a vast, occasionally brilliant, often incoherent, still-unfinished personal statement.

Murdoch, in August, was in Beijing—for the Olympics—when he had to do News Corp.'s quarterly earnings call with Wall Street analysts. Murdoch, treated by the Chinese with all the pomp and deference due a dictator, was perhaps at his most inflated—feeling both righteous and indestructible. And he was at his most jetlagged—hence at his most irascible and peremptory and with the most-winnowed attention span. Pure Murdoch, in other words: immortal and irritable—and not about to listen to anybody.

The analysts' call was classic Murdoch. He refused to prepare, waved away all advice, and then, on an open line to Wall Street and to investors everywhere, he got distracted, lost his train of thought, and, evidently with other, more interesting things on his mind, was impatient with everybody's questions and interrupted Peter Chernin. It was a disastrous performance, sending News shares down another 7 percent. Even his most loyal retainers were furious.

Say what you want, he'd once again made the point:

It all depends on him.

**Rupert to Internet: It's War!**

War is Rupert Murdoch's natural state. When he launched the Fox Broadcasting Company, in October 1986, he went to war against the hegemony of CBS, ABC, and NBC. With Fox News he crossed swords with CNN's Ted Turner. At Sky, his satellite-TV system in the U.K., he went up against the BBC. He's battled China, the FCC, the print unions in Great Britain, and, recently, most of the journalism community in his takeover of the *Wall Street Journal.* He relishes conflict and doesn't back down—one reason why he's won so many of his fights and so profoundly changed the nature of his industry.

Now he's gone to war with the Internet.

Two thousand nine wasn't a good year for Murdoch—the largest publisher of newspapers in the worst year in newspaper history. His 2007 purchase of the *Wall Street Journal* is widely seen as one of the worst moves of his career—News Corp. has already taken a $3 billion write-down on the purchase. His beloved *New York Post,* always a money loser for him, is suffering such great losses that Murdoch is considering a partnership with or even sale to the *Daily News,* the *Post*'s archenemy. His once highly profitable newspaper groups in the U.K. and Australia are faltering. News Corp.'s share price has been among the hardest hit of any major media company.

And yet, Murdoch, at seventy-eight, would double-down in a heartbeat: He strategizes constantly about how he might buy the *New York Times.* But first he might have to save the newspaper business itself. As it happens, he, unlike almost everyone else in the business, believes newspapers are suffering not at the hands of technological forces beyond their control but at the hands of proprietors who are weaker than he is.

After fulminating for a year about how people on the Internet should pay for news, he made it official. Announcing in August 2009 the biggest losses his company has ever sustained, he added that he'd had enough and if people wanted to read his newspapers they could bloody well pay for them.

I am not a neutral party here. Two years ago, I helped found Newser, a news aggregator that summarizes the stories of other news providers, which—along with the Huffington Post, the Daily Beast, and Google News—has become a focus of the print world's antipathy. (When I tried to explain Newser to Murdoch, he said, "So you steal from me.") The current battle for how the Internet will monetize news divides pretty cleanly between managers of established media properties and people who spend their working lives in the new-media business.

Traditional media managers, who once rushed into the Internet hoping to establish new businesses as well as their new-media bona fides, have all now been chastened by its economic realities and want to take back their free content. "Obviously we will all be closely following Rupert's efforts in this direction," said John Huey, Time Inc.'s editor-in-chief, when I contacted him—a curious throwing up of the hands from Time Warner, the world's largest magazine publisher and the world's largest media company, which has tried more strategies on the Internet than any other traditional media company.

Almost all Internet professionals, on the other hand, think that charging for general-interest news online is fanciful—"Rubbish . . . bonkers . . . a crock . . . a form of madness," in the description of Emily Bell, who has long run the *Guardian* newspaper's Web site, one of the industry's most successful—and, in fact, it has been tried before and has failed. "It's *Groundhog Day*," adds Bell. The *New York Times* tried to levy a subscription charge for its columnists but reversed course and declared itself free again. Even Murdoch's *Wall Street Journal*, the model of subscription content online, has made more and more of its site free.

I have often argued the nature of Internet culture with him to little avail. Murdoch can almost single-handedly take apart and re-assemble a complex printing press, but his digital-technology acumen and interest is practically zero. Murdoch's abiding love of newspapers has turned into a personal antipathy to the Internet: For him it's a place for porn, thievery, and hackers. In 2005, not long after News Corp. bought MySpace, when it still seemed like a brilliant purchase—before its fortunes sank under News Corp.'s inability to keep pace with advances in social-network technology—I congratulated him on the acquisition. "Now," he said, "we're in the stalking business."

Internet business strategies are often an intractable issue for media companies because they involve turf wars among contrary skill sets, business models, and corporate cultures. The result is usually bureaucratic stasis.

But News Corp. isn't like other media companies. Murdoch can cut through and level all bureaucratic confusion and inaction. If he says it will be paid, then all the voices that in other companies would tell you why this logically might not work go silent at News Corp. The logic of the situation is remade around Murdoch's logic. Whereas in another company Internet responsibilities might reasonably be given to those most enthusiastic about the medium, London is ground zero in Murdoch's Internet war because the executives there are the ones most devoted to newspapers. (His thirty-six-year-old son, James, who seems determined to do even more of whatever his father would have done, is responsible for the London operation.)

There has been, as it happens, a significant turf war in London, which might have produced a classic stasis, but which in this case became a solution. The *Times* of London and the *Sunday Times*, historically separate papers, have long shared a Web site, controlled, to the consternation of the Sunday editor, by the daily. The decision (after a long political tug-of-war) to separate the two suddenly became an opportunity in the new Murdoch logic of making people pay. Because the *Sunday Times* has not had a Web site before, it would not, by launching one with a pay wall, lose any users. Every subscriber would therefore be a plus.

In Murdoch-think, there is, too, the magic of the Sunday paper. Murdoch believes that people can't do without a Sunday paper. (Two years ago, he personally supervised the makeover of the Sunday *New York Post*.) Ipso facto, if people can't live without their Sunday paper, then they'll buy it on the newsstand or pay for it online—no matter that it comes out once a week and the Web is a minute-by-minute medium.

And then, *thelondonpaper*. Three years ago, Associated Newspapers—publishers of the all-powerful *Daily Mail*—launched the free afternoon paper *Standard Lite* (later *London Lite*), forcing News Corp. to launch its own free sheet, *thelondonpaper*, which undermined News Corp.'s other papers. Murdoch never shuts a paper and never backs down from a war. Except now, with his new war against free, there was suddenly the logic to do what everybody had been begging him to do: close the damn free thing—which he did, suddenly, in August.

Still, saying that when Murdoch speaks things happen does not mean that anyone in the company has quite figured out what exactly he wants to happen. Will Fox News charge for its online content and cede the online market to CNN and MSNBC? What happens to the *New York Post*, whose site, because of its outdated technology, is often hard to access—even for free? And whither MarketWatch, the free financial-news site bought by the *Wall Street Journal*'s parent company precisely because it wanted a free site?

It is difficult not to sound catty when discussing News Corporation's adventures with the Internet. But the litany of its failures—even more extreme than those of most other media companies that have struggled unsuccessfully online—is, I think, relevant to understanding exactly what Murdoch might really be trying to do with his pay-wall plan. From the failure of Delphi, one of the first public-access Internet providers, in 1993, to iGuide, the precursor to Yahoo and Google, which closed within months of its launch, to his son James's aborted Internet-investing spree in the late nineties, to the great promise of MySpace, which was shortly flattened by Facebook, to the second launch of Pagesix.com, which Murdoch closed this year after four months of operation, Murdoch's Internet starts and stops have engendered at News Corp., in the description of Peter Bale, who once ran the Web site of the *Times* of London and now runs MSN in the U.K., a relative "fear or abhorrence of technology."

In one of my favorite Murdoch stories, his wife, Wendi, who had befriended the founders of Google, Larry Page and Sergey Brin, told me about how the "boys" had visited the Murdochs at their ranch in Carmel, California. When I marveled at this relative social mismatch and asked what they might have talked about, Wendi assured me that they had all gotten along very well.

"You know Rupert," Wendi said. "He's always asking questions."

"But what," I prodded, "did he exactly ask?"

"He asked," she said, hesitating only a beat before cracking herself up, "'Why don't you read newspapers?'"

Murdoch's son-in-law Matthew Freud—married to Elisabeth Murdoch and one of the most well-known PR men in the U.K.—

explained to me what he believes is the essence of Murdoch's approach to business: Murdoch is not a modern marketer. He runs his business not on the basis of giving the consumer what he wants but through more old-fashioned methods of structural market domination. His world, and training ground, is the world of the newspaper war—a zero-sum game where you wrestle market share from the other guy. Curiously, his newspaper battles have most often involved cutting prices rather than, as he now proposes to do on the Internet, raising them. (Murdoch has contributed as much as anyone, with his low-priced papers, to the perception of news as a devalued commodity.)

But more than being about cost, his strategy is about pain. What he is always doing is demonstrating a level of strength and will and resolve against which the other guys, the weaker guys, cower. He can take more pain than anybody else. While others persist in the vanity of the Internet, he will endure the short- or medium-term pain necessary to build a profitable business.

He is also a scold who can intimidate the market into doing what he wants it to do. Part of his premise now is to invite and scare other publishers and content creators into a self-created monopoly. If everybody charges, consumers will have no choice but to pay. If all publishers have the opportunity to get paid, why wouldn't they take the money?

In the Murdoch view, media only really works as a good business if it achieves significant control of the market—through pricing, through exclusive sports arrangements, through controlling distribution (he has spent twenty years trying to monopolize satellite distribution around the world).

And, indeed, by announcing his all-paid-content intentions, he has, almost single-handedly, not just made the paid model the main topic of digital strategy in other traditional publishing companies but imbued it with nearly the force of a *fait accompli*. "It's a done deal," says a journalist I know who's suffered in the downturn, arguing that Murdoch, for so long journalism's great debaser, is now its last protector.

The Murdoch plan is, however, in the estimation of almost anybody whose full-time job is occupied with digital business strategies, not just cockamamy but head-scratching. It seems that Murdoch has, in a fit of pique, made certain pronouncements that may have to be humored by the people who work for him but that will be impossible to implement and will have no business advantages. Or that Murdoch, a man with something of a divine gift for acting in his own self-interest, has a plan not yet quite evident to mere mortals.

The position of Internet professionals is straightforward: while it's possible to charge for certain kinds of specialized information—specifically, information that helps you make money (and that you can, as with an online *Wall Street Journal* subscription, buy on your company expense account)—there are no significant examples of anyone being able to charge for general-interest information. Sites where pay walls have been erected have suffered cuts in user traffic of, in many cases, as much as 95 percent, as audiences merely move on to free options.

"What Murdoch seems to be talking about only has a logic if you don't introduce the behavior of the audience into the equation," says Emily Bell.

There is, alternatively, the compounding and intoxicating effect of free. While there may not yet be a way to adequately monetize free traffic, it has opened up, for many publications, great new audiences. The million-circulation *New York Times* has an audience of more than 15 million online. The *Guardian,* a U.K. paper with a circulation of 350,000, has become, online, with ten times its print readership, a significant international brand. One theory about the decline in the fortunes of the *Wall Street Journal* is that, because of its pay wall, the *Journal* is not a factor in Google searches, causing a fundamental decline in its importance, impacting its brand and standing with advertisers.

Murdoch believes that the *Sunday Times* has certain franchises so valuable that he will surely be able to capture a paying audience. Jeremy Clarkson is one of News Corp.'s strongest cases. Clarkson, who writes a column about cars, is a veritable British institution—everybody consults Clarkson before buying a car. He is, according to in-house estimates at the *Times*, now responsible for 25 percent of timesonline.co.uk traffic. The thinking is that, even if a pay wall cuts Clarkson's traffic, there are enough fanatical Clarkson readers who will pay enough to make a paid Clarkson more valuable than a free, ad-supported one. But the problem for Clarkson is that Murdoch's potential gain is Clarkson's loss. It's an almost intolerable loss—most of your readers (and their constant and addictive feedback). "When we opened the *Times* site to free international traffic," says Peter Bale, "suddenly our columnists were getting speaking engagements in Milwaukee." At the *New York Times*, it was the op-ed columnists themselves who objected most of all when a pay wall choked their readership and notoriety.

Murdoch has a larger problem still. It is, after all, not the Internet that has made news free. News in penny-newspaper or broadcast (or bundled cable) form has always been either free or negligibly priced. In almost every commercial iteration, news has been supported by advertising. This is, more than the Internet, Murdoch's (and every publisher's) problem: the dramatic downturn in advertising.

Or, in a sense, the plethora of advertising created the online problem. When Time Warner's Pathfinder launched the first ad-supported site, in 1994, it quickly created a juggernaut of wild advertising growth online. It was a simple proposition: more traffic, more advertising money—and a free site got vastly more traffic than a paid one. But the recession has, at least temporarily, dimmed advertising's promise, creating something of an end-of-the-world panic.

And no one's panic seems to be greater than that of Rupert Murdoch, who has a habit of finding himself with his back to the wall during times of recession. (In the early-nineties recession, he almost lost his company because of its great debt load.)

It's Chicken Little panic.

It is hard to imagine that when advertising growth resumes there will not once again be a rush to encourage traffic growth, but right now, the news business, supported for a hundred years by advertising, whose core skill has been selling advertising, believes it must right away, this second, re-create itself with a new business model in which advertising is just the cream on top and it's the consumer who pays the true cost of newsgathering.

But what if Rupert isn't really interested in a new business model? There may be earnest men trying to unlock the secret balance between the expectation of free content and the exceptions and the methods that might allow for micro or other incremental payments.

But what if that's not Rupert?

"Rupert isn't very nuanced about this," says Merrill Brown, the former MSNBC news chief, who is now a consultant to a venture trying to promote an online charge system. Murdoch, at seventy-eight, doesn't, practically speaking, have the time to see the online world into maturity—nor the intellectual interest to want to be part of the effort. Rather, his strategic effort may more logically be to slow it down.

The mordant joke among journalists is that, with any luck, the older among us will make it to retirement before the business entirely collapses. This may be part of Rupert's own thinking.

It is not so much that he wants people to pay to read Jeremy Clarkson online; he wants them, or a portion of them who might otherwise read a free Clarkson online, to return to the newspaper.

It is not, what's more, merely that Murdoch objects to people reading his news for free online; it's that he objects to—or seems truly puzzled by—what newspapers have become online. You get a dreadful harrumph when you talk to Murdoch about user-created content, or even simple linking to other sites. He doesn't get it. He doesn't buy it. He doesn't want it.

Every conversation I've had with him about the new news, about the fundamental change in how people get their news—that users go through Google to find their news rather than to a specific paper—earned me a walleyed stare.

The more he can choke off the Internet as a free news medium, the more publishers he can get to join him, the more people he can bring back to his papers. It is not a war he can win in the long-term, but a little Murdoch rearguard action might get him to his own retirement. Then it's somebody else's problem.

## PROLOGUE

1    *Murdoch toying with changing News Corp.'s name:* Gary Ginsberg, conversation with author, October 10, 2007.

2    *Agent provocateur ads:* Murdoch interview, October 10, 2007. The ads that finally ran, in a $2 million campaign, had the headline "Defying Conventional Wisdom for Six Decades" and contained a timeline of News Corp.'s acquisitions since 1954. "Today the greatest brand in financial journalism joins up with the world's most restless global media company," the ad read in part.

3    *James' annual report:* Murdoch interview, October 10, 2007.

3    *West Side railyards bid:* After the credit crunch hit, News Corp. dropped out of its bid. Related in March 2008.

4    *Murdoch wiped out:* He added: "It's awful, the amount of time I sat around thinking about it . . . I was very calm about it all. I was rather amazed by how calm I was through it all. When it was over I was suddenly tired and I realized just what a nervous strain it had been." Murdoch interview, September 19, 2007.

5    *Col Allan breaks cuff link:* Former and current News Corp. sources.

5    *Wanting to sack Dow Jones employees:* Murdoch interview, September 22, 2007.

6    *"Doesn't he understand it's our paper now?":* News Corp. executive in conversation with the author, December 14, 2007.

6    *Keller confronts Ginsberg:* Gary Ginsberg, conversation with the author, June 2007. This appeared in the author's September 2007 *Vanity Fair* piece about the Dow Jones takeover. In this piece Keller was described as "angrily" confronting Ginsberg; Ginsberg subsequently described Keller's manner as more edgy or mocking.

7     *O'Reilly talking dirty: Andrea Mackris v. Bill O'Reilly, News Corporation, Fox News Channel, Twentieth Century Fox Film Corp., and Westwood One, Inc.,* filed October 13, 2004, in the Supreme Court of the State of New York; settled two weeks later. The *New York Post* reported that O'Reilly had paid "multimillions of dollars."

7     *Richard Johnson takes money:* News Corp. admitted that Richard Johnson in 1997 had accepted a "Christmas gift" of $1,000 in an envelope from New York restaurateur Nello Balan, a frequent gossip subject. The company did not deny a claim by fired gossip columnist Ian Spiegelman that *Girls Gone Wild* founder Joe Francis had thrown Johnson a $50,000 bachelor party in Mexico.

7     *Jonathan Alter:* Conversation with author at Media 3 television studio in midtown Manhattan in September 2007.

8     *Tina Brown:* e-mail to author, September 5, 2007.

8     *Judith Regan suddenly taken seriously:* See Frank Rich, "What 'That Regan Woman' Knows," *New York Times,* November 18, 2007.

8     *Murdoch is a "gifted journalist":* "Rupert is a very fine journalist," Col Allan told Lloyd Graves. "You can take any person on a newspaper—anyone—and he can do their job. He's simply a gifted journalist." "Rupe's Attack Dog Gets Bitten, Keeps Barking," *New York,* September 10, 2007.

9     *Murdoch "has demonstrated a habit over time . . .":* David Carr, *On the Record* podcast, http://www.ontherecordpodcast.com/pr/otro/blog-impact-revealed.aspx.

9     *Murdoch on a New York magazine best-of list:* "Reasons to Love New York," *New York,* December 17, 2007.

9     *Marcus Brauchli talking up Murdoch:* Interviews with *Wall Street Journal* reporters.

11    *Vendetta against Primedia: New York* magazine sources.

12    *"And she believed him":* Interview with Prudence Murdoch, February 28, 2008.

13    *"Just say what you want to say":* Interview with Prudence Murdoch, February 28, 2008.

## CHAPTER 1

15    *Murdoch quits smoking:* Murdoch, swimming off the coast of Sicily in 2007, made a bet with London *Sun* editor Rebekah Wade, then thirty-nine, that he could beat her in a race around his yacht. If he won, she had to give up smoking. He told her he gave up smoking at forty-two. Conversation between Wade and the author, October 2007.

16    *"Too busy to tell you the truth":* Murdoch interview, October 9, 2007.

16    *Could have had friends:* Conversation between Murdoch and his wife in front of his children.

16    *"Married to the business":* Murdoch interview, October 9, 2007.

17    *Shyness:* Jenkins, *The Market for Glory,* 69.

17    *Crippled by shyness:* Evans, *Good Times, Bad Times,* 159.

18    *Face-lift:* "Banned by Fleet Street: Murdoch by His Butler," *Punch,* July 4–17, 1998

18    *Sending his gang back to London:* "I more or less pushed them back to London, because I could see they had no understanding, they thought they were having a good time running around New York in limousines. I wasn't happy with some of them, so . . . I kept some of them, brought some Australians in, and recruited Americans where I could." Murdoch interview, October 9, 2007.

19    *Hardy finds the Murdoch years most satisfying:* Bert Hardy interview, October 4, 2007, London.

19    *E. 72nd Street apartment:* Murdoch interview, October 9, 2007.

20    *News Corp. market cap in 1974:* Murdoch interview, October 10, 2007.

20    *James Goodale:* Conversation with author, September 13, 2007.

21    *Knows Sulzbergers, Katharine Graham, and Leonard Goldenson:* Murdoch interview, October 9, 2007.

22    *"Not just monopolistic, but growing ever more boring":* Murdoch interview, October 9, 2007.

24    *Hugh Bancroft:* After years of mental illness, Hugh Bancroft suffered a breakdown in 1932 and went to live in the blacksmith shop on his family's Cohasset estate. In the week before October 17, he checked out books from the local library on poisonous gases and then stuffed the doors and windows of the shop so he could gas himself. The *New York Times* and the *Wall Street Journal* initially reported the death as a heart attack. Tofel, *Restless Genius* (from manuscript of April 2008, 99).

24    *Bancroft family oath:* Tofel, *Restless Genius* (from manuscript of April 2008, 190).

24    *Bancroft family giving Dow Jones managers carte blanche:* Interviews with former and current Dow Jones managers and Bancroft family members.

26    *Kann avoids an offer:* Interview with Peter Kann, May 14, 2008.

26    *Keeping information from the family:* Interviews with Dow Jones management and Bancroft family members.

27    *Billy Cox:* In interviews with reporters who covered the Elizabeth Goth and Billy Cox insurrection in 1997, they said that they had received telephone calls from Dow Jones managers that attempted to smear Billy Cox.

28    *Cox and Goth blab to Fortune:* Joseph Nocera, "Heard on the Street," *Fortune,* February 3, 1997.

28    *Parade of suitors:* Interviews with Richard J. Tofel, September 14, 2007, and Peter Kann, May 14, 2008.

29    *Nothing happens:* In 1997, after the *Fortune* article came out, Bancroft scion Crawford Hill gave a speech at a family meeting, in which he said it was time to change the coach. "It was pretty well acknowledged across the family for the most part that . . . there is a lot of respect and affections for Peter Kann—he's a great guy, a great writer, great journalist, no doubt about that—but we also had the same view that this is not a great businessman to be leading this enterprise in the direction that it needs to go. That was well acknowledged—but there was this inability to do something about it." Interview with Bancroft family member, June 27, 2008.

## CHAPTER 2

32    Rupert and Anna Murdoch were married in April 1967, announced their separation on April 20, 1998, and divorced in June 1999.

33    Wendi Deng Murdoch was born in the city of Jinan, in Shandong province, on December 10, 1968.

33    *Murdoch moves to SoHo:* Rupert and Wendi Murdoch spent $6.5 million on a penthouse apartment on Prince Street in September 1999. Lachlan and Sarah Murdoch spent $3.5 million on an apartment at 285 Lafayette Street in mid-October, and James bought a $1.35 million apartment on Downing Street in

1998. Kate Kelly and Carmela Ciurara, "The Murdochs of Downtown," *New York Observer*, December 26, 1999.

33 *"His whole family like this. They so cheap":* Wendi Murdoch interview, April 28, 2008.

34 *Number of homes:* Wendi Murdoch interview, May 19, 2008.

35 *Howard Rubenstein negotiating truce with Mort Zuckerman:* Ken Auletta, "The Fixer," *New Yorker*, February 12, 2007.

35 *Murdoch paid $350,000 for a duplex at 834 Fifth Avenue:* Motoko Rich, "Make an Offer," *New York Times*, October 13, 2005.

36 *"So WASPy":* Wendi Murdoch interview, April 28, 2008.

36 *"Incomparably imperial apartment":* Tom Scocca, "Rupert Murdoch: Can the Newspaper Business Outlive the City's Cunningest Media Mogul?" *New York Observer*, December 18, 2005.

37 *Hair dyed orange and aubergine:* In interviews with each of Rupert Murdoch's older children—except James—they all commented on his hair color, as did a number of executives.

37 *The most difficult press inquiry is about Trump rent:* Former *New York Post* reporter Tim Arango reported in "Mogul Rent Control," *Fortune*, October 30, 2006, that Murdoch, under pressure from the press, had decided to pay back the $50,000-a-month rent that News Corp. had been paying for him to live in the Trump Tower while his Fifth Avenue apartment was being renovated. Murdoch had tried to defend the payments on the basis that his official address was still in Los Angeles and therefore the company should pay for his accommodation while working in New York. Claire Hoffman, "Murdoch's Pay Includes a $50,000-a-Month Rental," *Los Angeles Times*, September 9, 2006.

38 *Murdoch learning about Malone buying up News Corp. shares:* Interview with Gary Ginsberg, June 10, 2008.

40 *"I was asleep or something":* Murdoch interview, January 29, 2008.

40 *". . . nice old man":* Steve Fishman, "The Boy Who Wouldn't Be King," *New York*, September 11, 2005.

40 *Stan Shuman past his sell date:* Murdoch interview, September 19, 2007.

41 *And never misses a day of work:* "I have not missed a single day of work," Murdoch boasted in an interview with Geraldine Fabrikant and Mark Landler after finishing his radiation therapy. "Just Which Murdoch Will Become the Next Rupert?" *New York Times*, October 8, 2000.

41 *Peter Chernin and Roger Ailes ganging up against Lachlan Murdoch:* Interviews with senior News Corp executives and Hollywood sources.

44 New York Post*'s losses:* As described by senior News Corp. executives.

46 *Wasserstein and Murdoch lunch:* Bruce Wasserstein and Rupert Murdoch had a falling-out during the Dow Jones takeover when Wasserstein tried to collect a fee from Murdoch for suggesting the deal. Murdoch interview, September 19, 2007.

47 *Vernon Jordan tells Murdoch to put the money on the table:* Jordon also irritates Murdoch by soliciting a fee. Murdoch interview, September 19, 2007.

47 *Jimmy Lee urges him to look at Dow Jones:* Jimmy Lee interview, October 15, 2007.

47 *Norm Pearlstine and John Huey visit Murdoch:* Norm Pearlstine interview, September 12, 2007, and conversation with John Huey, September 11, 2007. When the author first brought up the meeting with Huey and Pearlstine, Murdoch said he couldn't remember the incident. Yet a description of the

meeting—different in some details from the one used in this book—turned up, most likely provided by Murdoch, in a *Newsweek* profile of Murdoch, "Murdoch, Ink," by Johnnie L. Roberts, published April 28, 2008.

48    *Chernin's reaction to Dow Jones:* Peter Chernin interview, January 18, 2008.

49    *Peter Chernin and his kids don't read newspapers:* Murdoch interviews, September 22, 2007, and October 23, 2007.

49    *News Corp.'s Olympic book:* John Nallen interview, January 7, 2008.

49    *Murdoch calls Elefante:* Murdoch interview, September 19, 2007. Bancroft and Dow Jones sources acknowledge the call took place, but cannot recall high fives.

50    *Blind-sourced piece:* Steve Fishman, "The Boy Who Wouldn't Be King," *New York,* September 11, 2005.

50    *Reorganizing the company around a crush:* Murdoch briefly gave up control of his European operations in the early 1990s to create a job big enough for Andrew Knight, the former head of the *Economist,* with whom he'd become smitten.

51    *Murdoch meets Robert Thomson:* "I think someone mentioned him to me. Five or six years ago, it was when he just missed the editorship, because he was the staff candidate . . . And that he was unhappy and talked to CNBC, all right. And I just called him up and said, 'Come and have a beer.' And we met at the Dervish round the corner. And we had two or three subsequent meetings there." June 2, 2008.

51    *Fart joke:* Rebekah Wade: May 8, 2008

51    *Thomson's and Murdoch's wives:* Wendi Murdoch is well aware of the rumors flying around News Corp. that her husband's friendship with Robert Thomson is based on their younger Chinese wives, who were both pregnant when they met. "People say, 'Oh, they hired Robert because he has a Chinese wife.' . . . Like we were best friends. No. I'm friendly with everybody's wife. We see them a lot. She's Chinese, so obviously we talk. Our children play together." May 19, 2008.

## CHAPTER 3

53    *Andy Steginsky's role:* Andrew Steginsky interviews, December 13, 2007 and May 23, 2008.

54    *Murdoch on the phone:* "If I needed to talk to him you could always get him on the phone . . . no matter where he was he would take the phone calls. Rupert would take phone calls from people that he has no idea who they are. I mean, he is unbelievable in this way. The shoeshine boy called him up and he would take his phone call. That is part of his makeup, but if I get him a message that it's important to speak to him, he'd either drop what he's doing immediately or get right back to me. It's never been an issue." Senior News Corp. executive, June 3, 2008.

54    *"I could make some calls":* Conversation between Steginsky and Murdoch, as recalled by Rupert Murdoch, September 19, 2007.

55    *"And so I hung up the phone":* Andrew Steginsky interview, December 13, 2007.

57    *"I would not underestimate the* Times *in that regard":* Robert Thomson in conversation with author, November 15, 2007.

59    *"She was an okay mother":* Murdoch interview, March 21, 2008.

59    *Dame Elisabeth's reaction to Wendi:* Interviews with Murdoch family sources and News Corp. executives.

60    *Dame Elisabeth interview,* February 25, 2008.

61    *Murdoch ancestral history:* Shawcross, *Murdoch,* 29–46. (Also on the Free-
churchers see: William D. Maxwell, *A History of Worship in the Church of
Scotland* [New York, 1955], 59; A. MacKay, *Cruden and Its Ministers* [Adelaide,
1912]; A. Macdonald, *One Hundred Years of Presbyterianism in Victoria*
[Melbourne, 1937]; C. McKay, *This Is the Life* [Sydney, 1961]; J. La Nauze,
*Walter Murdoch* [Melbourne, 1977]; D. Zwar, *In Search of Keith Murdoch*
[Melbourne, 1980].)

62    *Keith Murdoch's role in Gallipoli:* Knightley, *The First Casualty,* 106–10.

67    *"A newspaper is to be made to pay":* Hamilton Fyffe, *Northcliffe: An Intimate
Biography,* 83.

68    *Murdoch's childhood:* "The common theme in these stories, which are told
affectionately, is power and denial," Chenoweth, *Rupert Murdoch,* 37.

68    *Sir James Darling apologizes:* Shawcross, *Rupert Murdoch,* 54.

69    *Murdoch attempts to buy school newspaper:* "I remember one specific occasion,
a conversation I had with him when he was interested in the possibility of buying the undergraduate magazine *Cherwell.* That never came to anything,
whether it would have anyway I don't know, but I told him I thought *Cherwell*
would never get enough advertising from the sort of ordinary university advertisers to make it profitable. And he was enthusiastic, as he always is. No doubt
if he had got it he would have made it a much livelier magazine than it then
was. I think he saw me probably as a potential investor. It would have been a
very exciting project in his hands. Anyway he went down at the end of that year
after his father died and it certainly never came to anything." William Rees-
Mogg interview, August 2008.

70    *"It was very hard":* Dame Elisabeth interview, February 25, 2008.

74    *The history of the Fairfaxes:* John Fairfax—printer, bookseller, stationer, born
in Warwick, England, in 1804—arrived in Sydney in 1838, not long after the
arrival of Murdoch's great-great-grandfather George Govett. Fairfax bought
the *Sydney Herald* and quickly turned it into the most popular newspaper in
the colony, changing its name in 1841 to the *Sydney Morning Herald.* Its values were Protestantism, the British monarchy, and free enterprise. It came to
define the establishment—and was fondly called, for the next 150 years, the
"Granny Herald." It cemented its hold in the 1850s, Australia's famous boom
era, when gold was discovered. John's sons, Charles and James, joined the firm
and, in 1860, launched the *Sydney Mail.* The company passed to the first son,
Charles, who died in 1863, falling from a horse, and then to James, who ran
the paper for the next sixty-seven years and became arguably the most influential person in Australia. Certainly the *Sydney Herald* is unrivaled in its
influence. It ranks with the greatest papers—the London *Times,* the *New York
Times,* the *Wall Street Journal*—for its probity, respectability, and establishment snobbery. (It represents exactly the kind of elitism that Murdoch came
to resent and covet.) Among them there was only one heir: Warwick Oswald
Fairfax, who in 1926 become chairman at the age of twenty-five. The company's real period of expansion happened after the Second World War, when
it launched the *Australian Financial Review,* started the *Sun-Herald* and the
*Sunday Morning Herald,* and bought Associated Newspapers, publisher of the
afternoon *Sun* and various magazines after a takeover battle with Sir Frank
Packer's Australian Consolidated Press. In 1956, the Fairfaxes entered the tel-

evision business, which they would come to dominate while continuing to make print acquisitions.

74  *The history of the Packers:* R. C. Packer was a Sydney newspaperman who in 1918 lucked into a one-third interest in a new national periodical called *Smith's Weekly,* which, with a populist tone and lots of pictures, was an instant success. Shortly thereafter, Packer and his partners launched the *Daily Guardian* in Sydney, a mass-market tabloid, which aped the Northcliffe techniques, at just the same time Keith Murdoch was aping them at the *Herald* in Melbourne. R. C. Packer was a notorious son of a bitch, as was his son Frank. In 1932, R. C. Packer, having sold his interests at great profit, became the top executive at Associated Newspapers, which owned Sydney's sole afternoon paper, the *Sun.* Frank Packer, in a low-grade bit of deception, managed to make many people believe he was about to launch a competitor to the *Sun.* As it happens, he didn't remotely have the money to do this. Nevertheless, his father paid him the equivalent of almost $4 million of Associated Newspapers' money not to do what he, as it happens, could not have done. So it goes. With that dough, in 1933, Frank started *Women's Weekly,* which would shortly become the largest-circulation magazine in Australia and the basis of his empire. There followed wild and successful expansion into newspapers, radio, and television.

74  *Murdochs vs. Packers vs. Fairfaxes:* Right up until Murdoch's son, Lachlan, and James Packer went head-to-head over Super League in the nineties, the families would try to take what belonged to the other. These were battles fought for business turf, for political influence, for strategic advantage—fought by families that were as intertwined and fundamentally alike as any could be. The only reason for the ritualized enmity, ruthless competition, and instinctive backstabbing was that it was a zero-sum game: Only one would prevail generations hence.

74  See Griffen-Foley, "The Fairfax, Murdoch and Packer Dynasties"; Barry, *The Rise and Rise of Kerry Packer.*

74  *Murdoch vs. Packer brawl:* "Kerry Packer: The *Times* Obituary," *Times* (London), December 27, 2005.

75  *Banking relationships:* Chenoweth, *Murdoch,* 74–77; Shawcross, *Murdoch,* 74–76.

77  *Peter Kann lunch:* Interviews with former Dow Jones executives and Peter Kann, May 14, 2008.

77  *Sulzberger's offer reported:* Ken Auletta, "Family Business: Dow Jones Is Not Like Other Companies. How Long Can That Go On?" *New Yorker,* November 3, 2003.

77  *Bancrofts' learning of* New York Times *bid through* New Yorker, *reaction to share price, and family meetings:* Bancroft family member interview, May 28, 2008.

77  *Kann pushing up his retirement:* Dow Jones executives and Bancroft family interviews.

78  *Peter Kann wants to give his wife the top job:* Karen House denies she was interested in the job of chief executive. "I believe I was the most qualified person at Dow Jones to be publisher, and I was given that job. I had no interest in being CEO. I said that repeatedly in the presence of Rich and Gordon and Peter." Peter Kann said she had informed the special committee appointed to look for his replacement and him about her lack of desire to be CEO. Karen House interview, June 25, 2008; Peter Kann interview, May 14, 2008.

78    *Karen House, a figure of great contention:* Descriptions of House provided by Dow Jones executives and *Wall Street Journal* reporters in interviews. See also Katherine Q. Seelye, "Dow Jones Turns to Financial Side in Naming Its New Chief Executive," *New York Times,* January 4, 2006.

79    *Peter Kann's succession:* A succession plan had been knocking around the company since the Telerate debacle in 1997. Bancroft family interviews.

79    *Dow Jones directors meeting:* As described in interviews with Dow Jones executives and board members.

## CHAPTER 4

83    *Jimmy Lee introduces Murdoch to Richard Zannino:* Interviews with Murdoch, September 19, 2007; Lee, October 15, 2007; and Zannino, November 1, 2007.

84    *Perceptions of Zannino:* Interviews with Dow Jones executives and *Wall Street Journal* reporters.

85    *"shit-eating grin":* Interviews with *Wall Street Journal* reporters.

85    *"It wasn't like you should work there":* Bancroft family member, May 28, 2008.

86    *Bancroft family history:* See Wendt, *Wall Street Journal.*

87    *Jane Bancroft's oath:* Ibid., 235.

90    *Nature of Bancroft trusts:* Interviews with Bancroft family members and their representatives.

91    *Merrill Lynch presentation:* Interviews with Bancroft family representatives and Merrill Lynch advisors.

92    *Hills thinking of suing:* Interviews with Bancroft family representatives, Murdoch, and Steginsky.

93    *Murdoch on the Newhouses:* Murdoch interview, September 22, 2008.

95    *Prue:* Prudence Murdoch interview, February 28, 2008.

96    *Murdoch offers MacLeod a job:* "You tell Dad to get off my turf right now," Prudence screamed at her father's secretary, Dot Wyndoe, when she called to patch through Murdoch to his son-in-law about a job at the *Times* of London.

97    *"... dirty old man":* Australian Broadcasting Commission, *Inside the Murdoch Dynasty,* 2002.

98    *Elisabeth attends Geelong Grammar:* Matthew Freud.

98    *Elisabeth suspended for drinking:* When Prue's oldest son, James, was suspended for drinking from school, she e-mailed her sister Elisabeth to say, "He's following in your footsteps." Elisabeth lectured James, "Don't do what I did. It ruined my education. I never got over it." But as Prue points out about her sister, named Business Woman of the Year by *Harper's Bazaar* in 2008, "What a shocking life she's had." Prudence Murdoch interview, February 28, 2008.

98    *Elisabeth disappears on a Vespa:* Petronella Wyatt interview, November 12, 2007.

99    *Elisabeth gets into Stanford:* Elisabeth Murdoch interview, November 15, 2007.

99    *Elisabeth "has some things to work out ...":* Mathew Horsman, "Sky: The Inside Story: Bowing Out to the Inevitable," *Guardian,* November 10, 1997.

101   *Murdoch children in New York:* Geraldine Brooks, "Murdoch," *New York Times Magazine,* July 19, 1998.

102   *Lachlan's lack of a job:* Interviews with News Corp. executives on both the East and West Coasts.

102   *James Murdoch:* Annette Sharp, "The Diary," *Sun-Herald* (Sydney), June 18, 2000; Raymond Snoddy, "The Saturday Profile: James Murdoch," *Independent,*

August 6, 2005; Valerie Block, "The Dutiful Son: Spare Murdoch Heir, a High-Tech Kid, Waits Patiently to Rotate into New Post," *Crain's New York Business*, August 10, 1998; "A Grass-Roots Murdoch," *New Yorker*, September 16, 1996, 44; "Like Father, Like Son," *Economist*, November 8, 2003, 64; Madden Normandy, "James Murdoch," *Advertising Age*, January 26, 2004; "Young Murdoch's Asian Adventure," *Ad Age Global*, May 2001, 30; Raymond Snoddy, "Murdoch Son Attacks BBC's Global Claims," *Times* (London), August 28, 2000.

103   *Tunku Varadarajan on James:* "Bad Company Rupert Murdoch and his son genuflect before Chinese communists," *Wall Street Journal*, March 26, 2001.

104   *James is the "real thing":* Interviews with News Corp. executives.

104   *James as recluse:* James Robinson, "James Murdoch: Triumph of the Family Man," *Observer*, December 9, 2007.

104   *James' wedding vows:* Rohm, *The Murdoch Mission: The Digital Transformation of a Media Empire*, 41.

107   *Excerpt from Charlie Rose:* "A Conversation with Rupert Murdoch," *The Charlie Rose Show*, July 20, 2006.

107   *Wendi and Murdoch fight:* Interviews with News Corp. executives.

110   *$45 per share projection from Zannino:* Interviews with Dow Jones executives and Bancroft family members.

111   *Lee meets Murdoch and the boys at Sun Valley:* Jimmy Lee interview, October 15, 2007.

111   *Who's paying Lee's fee:* Richard Zannino interview, November 1, 2007.

112   *Links Club meeting:* Interviews with Lee, Murdoch, and Zannino.

**CHAPTER 5**

116   *John Nallen updates the book:* John Nallen interview, January 7, 2008.

117   *JPMorgan Chase meeting:* Interviews with Murdoch, Lee, and Zannino.

117   *Zannino as a seller:* Zannino denies he was looking to sell the company and insists that he was trying to increase shareholder value—and succeeding—on the basis of the plan he had set forth not long after he took the reins as CEO. "Jimmy calls me after that lunch and says, 'What should we do next?' And I said, 'There's nothing to do. The family's not a seller, Rupert's not a buyer, and, you know, we're not talking about it at lunch.' We're working the plan." Rich Zannino, November 1, 2007.

118   *Jamie Dimon stops by:* Interviews with Murdoch, Lee, and Zannino.

120   *Murdoch doesn't look back:* Wendi Murdoch notes: "I think also, he's not sentimental about things. Most people, if something happens, they feel depressed. Urgh. He's like, he feels bad for the day and then . . . I remember with DirecTV that was so close. He didn't get it, he did feel bad, but the next day he was . . . We didn't know until dinnertime when we saw . . . and then we went to Col Allan's house for curry dinner. Then next day he started working on the lobbying for Washington. I think he thrives on stress. Rather than feel sorry for himself, he was thinking what to do next. You know, if he didn't get it, it doesn't bother him that much." April 28, 2008.

122   *Who is the establishment:* Murdoch interview, October 10, 2008.

122   *Hunting story:* Chapman Pincher interview, July 2008: "Harry Hyams, the property developer, has a country house and estate called Ramsbury Manor, in

Wiltshire. Probably the most beautiful house that's liveable in, it's not all that enormous. He has made it even more superb by restoring it. He has a pheasant shoot there. I was a very keen pheasant shot. Harry had six shoots a year and he used to ask me to them all. You had some very interesting people there, such as Grand Prix racing driver Graham Hill, all sorts of people from all walks of life. He told me that this fellow Rupert Murdoch would be coming with his wife, Ann[a], who I remember as being rather tall and blond. She didn't have a lot to say for herself, but I thought she was very nice. He turned up in brand-new shooting suit, with knickerbockers—you could see it was absolutely brand-new—and what looked to me, as an old hand, like an absolutely brand-new twelve-bore, side-by-side gun. I wondered how much shooting he'd done, because they don't have that kind of shooting in Australia. These were driven birds and some of the drives were very special. There were a couple of drives called the plantation drives. The birds were very high and very difficult. They weren't only high but they were dropping. Rupert remembered having met me, and he said, 'Would you keep telling me what to do? I don't really know what to do. I've never done this before.' I said, 'Sure.' So we lined up and he happened to be drawn next to me, or maybe I got Harry to put him next to me. Anyway, we were next to each other. He said, 'What do we do?' I said, 'When the birds come over, you'll find they're very difficult. But the first rule is not what to shoot at, it's what not to shoot at. You don't shoot at your neighbor's birds. You don't shoot at birds that are going over me and clearly going to come to me, and you don't shoot birds that are going to come to your neighbor on the other side. The next thing is try and imagine that you're shooting slightly in front of the birds.' Well, the birds came over him, there were quite a lot of them, and we all had a rip-roaring drive. They were very difficult. He didn't disturb a feather, didn't hit one. By the end of the day he was knocking them down. He was that sort of guy. You could see right away, if he wanted to he would make a good shot. A lot of people say, 'Bugger it! I can't do this.' But not Rupert. By the end of the day he was acquitting himself quite well. We were all rather impressed. Quite honestly, I don't think he'd fired at a pheasant before in his life. The only other thing I remember about that conversation was that he bellyached to me, when we were walking together between drives, about the attitude of the British people towards him and particularly towards his wife. I don't know that he used the word 'snooty,' but whatever the Australian equivalent of that word was. I think he hinted that he would get the hell out of Britain because he didn't like the attitude of the Poms [Australian slang term for the English]."

123   News of the World *deal:* Shawcross, 103–17.

126   *Bert Hardy retained:* Bert Hardy interview, October 4, 2007.

127   *"I don't agree it's sleazy for a minute…":* Leapman, *Barefaced Cheek,* 50.

127   *Murdoch and Frost interview:* Frost, *David Frost: An Autobiography.*

129   *"We've had enough of your hospitality":* Shawcross, *Rupert Murdoch,* 117.

129   *Murdoch on Frost:* "I swore I would never, ever have anything to do with Frost on any level in any way and I made it my, for at least twenty years I never spoke to him. He'd be all over me at parties, 'Oh, Rupert . . .' I've never had a one-on-one with him since and I've always been very cold to him, but I've been in situations where I've had to have social conversation. But I thought he was such an arrogant bastard, a bloody bugger . . . I feel like saying I'll still get the bastard one day, but he'll die before I get him." October 10, 2007.

131   *Murdoch on Cudlipp and Bartholomew:* Murdoch interview, October 10, 2007.

131   *Harry Guy Bartholomew:* The *Mirror* editor was also renowned for hitting his editor Cecil Jones over the head with an eight-foot plank of wood. Few realized—until "Bart" showed them, falling over himself laughing—that the plank was made out of balsawood. "To the Niminy Piminy," *Time,* September 28, 1953.

134   *Private Eye:* "Well, they were almost a sort of Establishment in a funny sort of way, in a strange English way, with somewhat more humor, but still you know . . . I laughed at it." Murdoch interview, October 10, 2007.

136   *Anna's car accident:* Bert Hardy interview, October 4, 2007; "In Brief: Car Death Verdict," *Times* (London), January 10, 1973.

137   *Merrill Lynch's analysis of $45:* Bancroft family sources.

138   *Zannino's breakfast:* Interviews with Murdoch and Zannino.

139   *Zannino tells Dow Jones executives:* Interviews with Zannino and Michael Elefante, January 25, 2008, and Peter Kann, May 14, 2008.

## CHAPTER 6

141   *No women on News Corp. board:* Murdoch told *Sun* editor Rebekah Wade that he was resistant to putting women on the News Corp. board before appointing Natalie Bancroft because he thought women talked too much. Wade conversation with author, May 8, 2008.

142   *Murdoch dinner at Milos:* Rod Eddington interview, February 25, 2008.

143   *Bancroft family meeting:* Interviews with Bancroft family members.

143   *"What the hell's the matter with my Red Sox?":* Susan Pulliam, Dennis K. Berman, Matthew Karnitschnig, and Sarah Ellison, "Dynasty's Dilemma: For Bancrofts, Dow Jones Offer Poses Challenge—Murdoch Bid Tests Family's Cohesion; Sell 'Grandpa's Paper'?" *Wall Street Journal,* May 12, 2007.

144   *Peter McPherson:* M. Peter McPherson interview, May 27, 2008.

144   *Irv Hockaday and Harvey Golub as logical candidates:* Interviews with Dow Jones executives and Bancroft family members.

147   *Howard Squadron is a minor politico:* Howard Squadron briefly ran for a West Side seat in Congress but withdrew because he said that politics would be too demanding for him as a single father. (His wife had died in 1967 of an aneurysm, leaving him to bring up three young children.) William Glaberson, "Howard M. Squadron, 75, Influential Lawyer, Dies," *New York Times,* December 28, 2001.

148   *Ed Downe Jr.:* Ed Downe Jr., along with Marc Rich, was pardoned by President Clinton in his last days of office.

149   *Murdoch is introduced to Felker by Katharine Graham:* Murdoch interview, October 9, 2007.

149   *Murdoch on his fallout with Clay Felker:* "I met him very early on. He was a friend. And I was very sad about our falling-out . . . Looking back, I was sorry it ended up a hostile takeover and so on, which it wasn't in the sense that Clay was talking to me about me buying it. I think he was having a bet each way because he was fighting with his board. The truth was his board had over 50 percent of the shares. And they came to me, and they had bankers like Stan Shuman, the board came to me and said, 'Look, we know you've been talking to Clay because Clay's been telling us, reporting his conversations. And he won't make up his mind. But we'll tell you one thing for certain—we are going to sell. So you can

buy or miss, whichever, you know.' I thought about it for twenty-four hours and thought, 'Okay, I'm sure I could make it up with Clay. The best thing is to do it and then over time he will calm down and we can talk it over to carry it forward.' He reacted negatively, rushed to Katharine Graham. And then one evening in my apartment when it was all being signed, she called and said, you know, and then when she saw what we had it . . . and I made the worst business decision of all, it was a pretty small business decision, but a bad one. She said, 'Well, would you sell *New West?*' which was Clay's idea of doing something in California that was losing money. And I think she was buying something for Clay to go to, but everything was too far gone. And I said, 'No, I think it's gone too far, I'm sorry.' She said, 'Okay.' . . . That was a cross to bear for about two or three years before we finally sold it off." Murdoch interview, October 9, 2007.

150    *Murdoch chooses schools:* Murdoch interview, September 22, 2007.

150    *Dalton's advantage:* Murdoch would also meet Van Gordon Sauter through the Dalton School when Sauter's stepson attended that school with Lachlan Murdoch. Murdoch interview, October 23, 2007.

151    *Dolly Schiff had a crush on Clay: New York* magazine sources.

151    *Murdoch hires Stan Shuman:* Former World Bank president—and fellow Australian—James Wolfensohn was Murdoch's original banker in New York. Wolfensohn said he could no longer represent him, so Murdoch turned to Stan Shuman. Stan Shuman interview, September 6, 2007.

153    *Elaine's:* William Claiborne and Robert G. Kaiser, "Takeover in Gotham: How a Rich Australian Publishing Baron Wrested Control of *New York* Magazine," *Washington Post,* January 9, 1977; "Bacon and Eggs at Elaine's and Other Tales of Rupert Murdoch's Noisy Arrival on the New York Media Scene," *Advertising Age,* March 29, 1999.

156    *Murdoch believes Burden has a loophole in his contract with Felker:* Murdoch interview, October 9, 2007.

156    Village Voice *editors sue Clay Felker:* Ed Fancher, Norman Mailer, and David Wolf received $488,000 from Clay Felker in a settlement after suing on the basis that Carter Burden had to offer his 80 percent share to them before he sold to Felker in 1974 for $2.5 million. "Paper Route: Buying and Selling and Buying the *Voice,*" *Village Voice,* October 18, 2005.

157    *Letter to board by staff:* Deirdre Carmody, "Murdoch Seen Closer to Completing Acquisition of *New York* Magazine," *New York Times,* January 4, 1977.

158    *Luck:* Murdoch interviews, October 9 and 10, 2007; September 22, 2007.

159    *$2 million check:* Murdoch interview, October 9, 2007.

160    *Gail Sheehy article:* Gail Sheehy, "A Fistful of Dollars," *Rolling Stone,* July 14, 1977.

## CHAPTER 7

161    *The Leak:*
       From: Faber, David (NBC Universal, CNBC)
       Sent: Tuesday, May 01, 2007 10:46 AM
       To: Ginsberg, Gary
       Subject:
       I need to speak with you.
       I know.

       From: Ginsberg, Gary
       Sent: Tuesday, May 01, 2007 10:59 AM

To: Faber, David (NBC Universal, CNBC)
Subject: Re:
You know what?
Sent using BlackBerry

From: Faber, David (NBC Universal, CNBC)
Sent: Tuesday, May 01, 2007 11:00 AM
To: Ginsberg, Gary
Subject: RE:
you know what I know and I'm about to report it
WSJ

162   *Gary Ginsberg's role at News Corp.:* Gary Ginsberg conversations with author, June 2007, and interviews with Murdoch family members. "Gary's great. I see him a lot. I love Gary, Gary Ginsberg. He's so easygoing, bam, bam, bam . . . But he's like, he can make you talk. And he's fun. He can be friendly to anyone, you can take him anywhere and he will talk to your friend. That's funny." Wendi Murdoch, May 19, 2008.

164   *Elefante's delay in telling the family about the offer:* Interviews with Bancroft family members, their representatives, and Dow Jones executives.

164   *April 24 meeting:* Interviews with Michael Elefante, January 25, 2008, and Bancroft family members and advisors.

165   *Roger Altman pushed out:* Rob Kindler interview, March 7, 2008.

166   *Marty Lipton and Merrill Lynch advising the family on how to keep control:* Elefante interview, January 25, 2008.

166   *Jimmy Lee is everybody's favorite as the leaker:* Author asked every interview subject involved in the deal who they believed leaked the information. Jimmy Lee was the response 90 percent of the time. Jimmy Lee said, "I don't know. I honestly don't. I just don't know. I'm not, my style's not leaking like that. There are guys who do what I do who do that. I'm one of these sort of straitlaced kind of guys. You knew it was going to get out." October 15, 2007.

166   *". . . not the biggest deal, but a jaw-dropping one":* David Faber interview, September 2007.

168   *Murdoch writes to Steiger:* Paul Steiger interview, September 10, 2007.

169   *"Stories need to be shorter . . ."* These were recommendations Barney Kilgore made in 1958 for how to remake the *New York Herald Tribune:* As cited in Tofel, *Restless Genius.*

170   *"To the People who edit the . . .":* Deirdre Carmody, "Bullish *Wall Street Journal* Is Largest Daily in US," *New York Times,* January 13, 1980.

172   *Description of the* Wall Street Journal *in 1970s and 1980s:* Norm Pearlstine interview, September 12, 2006.

173   *Advertising in 1980s:* Newspaper Association of America.

173   *Murdoch on the queen:* "Someone had asked, some courtier, if the queen—the queen's heard that Mr. Murdoch liked the film or something, and if the queen was to ask him for a cup of tea, would he accept? It shows you how they've come down. They would have thought that their invitation to tea was absolute royal command. Death sentence if you say no to their rotten cucumber sandwiches . . . Of course I'd go. She's a nice old lady." November 5, 2007.

173   *The* Sun's *cash flow:* Shawcross, *Rupert Murdoch,* 225.

173   *Diana:* The day Princess Diana died, Murdoch met a News Corp. executive at the bar at the Dorchester and was obviously shaken by what the death would mean to Fleet Street. Murdoch proceeded to get "shitfaced" on a bottle of

French chardonnay, passed out, and had to be carried out to Harry's Bar around the corner, where he was due to meet a group of bankers. Former News Corp. executive interview, February 27, 2008.

174 *Enemas:* Gary Ginsberg points out that he has taken numerous flights with Murdoch and never once witnessed this.

177 *Groping toward a style:* David McClintick, "Publisher Paradox: Reserved, Soft Spoken, Murdoch Is Antithesis of the Papers He Owns," *Wall Street Journal,* January 7, 1977.

181 *Steve Ross' "racketeering" and mob connections:* In what was known as the Westchester Premier Theatre Affair, two Warner executives were indicted for racketeering in connecting to a mobbed-up theater in Tarrytown, New York. Solomon Weiss was convicted and fined $58,000 with five years' community service attached. Jay Emmett pleaded guilty and received a suspended sentence. The prosecutor had alleged that the execs had in fact taken the fall for Ross, which the Warner boss denied. See Roger Cohen, "A $78 Million Year: Steve Ross Defends His Paycheck," *New York Times,* March 22, 1992, and Bruck, *Master of the Game.*

181 *Harry Evans hired by Ross:* Roger Smith, conversation with author, January 22, 2008.

183 *Bill Ziff's young woman:* News Corp. advisor interview.

185 *Murdoch willing to give up citizenship:* Murdoch interview, October 9, 2007.

187 *John Kluge is a bully and vulgarian:* Bill Abrams, "Metromedia's Kluge's Moves Made Him Wealthy—And He Shows No Signs of Retiring After Sale of Stations," *Wall Street Journal,* May 8, 1985.

187 *Kluge screws his shareholders.* Kluge took Metromedia private in 1984 in a $1.1 billion leveraged buyout, then turned around and sold off the company in bits for $5.5 billion, netting him personally $3 billion. As *Fortune* pointed out in 1987, "Everybody admits belatedly that Kluge is some sort of business genius ... But how much is genius worth? $3 billion? And how much of this prescience did he impart to his shareholders? Gary Hector, "Are Shareholders Cheated by LBOs?" *Fortune,* January 19, 1987.

187 *Murdoch meets Kluge:* Kiernan, *Citizen Murdoch,* 272.

188 *"Under Australian Accounting Principles"* Johnnie L. Roberts, Laura Landro, and John Marcom Jr., "Moguls Gamble: Rupert Murdoch Takes His Biggest Risk So Far in Purchasing Triangle," *Wall Street Journal,* August 9, 1988.

188 *"I need to sell you ...":* David Schneiderman, conversation with author, May 2001.

190 *Murdoch buys a jet:* Barry Diller will buy the Gulfstream II from Fox when he resigns. Murdoch keeps the Gulfstream III.

192 *William Collins & Sons deal:* Shawcross, 288–91, 333–36.

193 *Peter Kann meets Murdoch during* South China Morning Post *deal:* Interview with Karen House, June 20, 2008.

195 *Warren Buffett takes a position:* Interviews with Dow Jones executives and board members.

## CHAPTER 8

198 *Spiegelman's vendetta:* E-mail from Ian Spiegelman that got him fired, obtained by gawker.com.
From: "Ian Spiegelman" [XXX]
To: [XXX]
CC: [XXX] [Richard Johnson]

Subject: Abigail
Date: Mon, 21 Jun 2004 21:23:05 -0400
Doug,

You picked the wrong boy to fuck with, you pussy. I am not like anyone you've come up against and I don't consider there to be any rules in this. I break aging trust fund pussies like you as a matter of course. If you think you can bring it, then bring it, faggot. Because I know that in my world you're nothing but a two-bit lame. Do you know what a lame is, Doug? A lame is an also-ran, a lame is the excuse for the person he would have been if he wasn't so fucking weak, so completely pathetic.

You're a lame and a pussy, Doug. And you should know better than to try and wage war on me. I'm better, stronger and smarter than you, you little Nancy. If I wanted to take your girl out, I would. You have nothing I can't take away from you, you non-man. Doug, you little tiny fairy, you arrested boy, I will break your back over my knee in the press and I will push your face inside-out in private or public. You've crossed a line that you are currently too insane to see that you've crossed. But I am giving you this one freeby:

Mention my name anywhere, ever, again, and we're going to find out two things: First, whose word means anything anymore in this town. Second, how many times I can slam my fist into your face before someone pulls me off you. Now I know you'll try and get a restraining order against me, you suit-happy little pussy. After all, you live in your mother's apartment. And that's fine, go ahead. I just want you to know who you picked a problem with, pussy. You picked a fight with someone who doesn't sleep until he's paid it back, you limp little woman. Now you wait for it.

Best,
Ian

198    *Stern's shakedown:* First reported by William Sherman, "The Billionaire, The *Post* and the $220G Shakedown: Page Six Writer Wanted $$$ to Stop Inaccuracies," *Daily News*, April 7, 2006.

198    *"Page Six" breaks the inside scoop on itself:* "Lies & Smears Aimed at *Post*," *New York Post*, May 18, 2007.

199    *Russell Crowe deal:* "Page Six," ibid, included the following allegation without offering a denial: "The favor banking system also extended to Murdoch's son Lachlan Murdoch, former publisher of the *New York Post*. After actor Russell Crowe purchased a house in Australia from Lachlan, Page Six was ordered to kill unflattering stories about him. Lachlan also extended this protection to famous friends like Nicole Kidman."

199    *Ginsberg negotiates confession:* Gary Ginsberg.

199    *Col Allan's worry:* Interviews with News Corp. executives.

200    *Dunleavy drunk:* Charlie Leduff, "Neighborhood Report: Bending Elbows; Absolute Dunleavy: Vodka and Tonics at Langan's," *New York Times*, October 14, 2001.

200    *Aurora:* Author visited Aurora and witnessed salsa dancing, as well as the Sydney *Daily Telegraph*'s editor, David Penberthy, arguing with the New South Wales premier (equivalent of governor) loudly down the phone over the next day's spectacular front page. February 28, 2008.

201    *"The horrible conditions . . ."* Chippindale and Horrie, *Stick It Up Your Punter!*, 42–43.

202    *"There's levels and levels of editing":* Murdoch interview, September 19, 2007.

204    *rivers of gold:* Classified advertising historically has been called the "rivers of gold" in Australia.

204    *If Murdoch had inherited Queensland Newspapers:* Lachlan Murdoch interview, February 29, 2008.

207    *Frank Costello's* National Enquirer *connections:* Erik Himmelsbach, "Book Review: 'The Godfather of Tabloid: Generoso Pope Jr. and the National Enquirer' by Jack Vitek," *Los Angeles Times*, September 4, 2008.

209    *"We voted to die with dignity"*: Shawcross, *Rupert Murdoch,* 202.

210    *"Everybody in this country wants to get ahead"*: Ibid., 201.

211    *Rebekah Wade sits in jail . . .*: Michael Seamark and Stephen Wright, "The Fiery Redhead, two 999 calls, ex-Cabinet Minister and a Husband Nursing a Fat Lip," *Daily Mail,* 9.

211    *Bill O'Reilly handled as internal matter:* News Corp. executives.

212    *Col Allan and strip joints:* Col Allan's sojourns at strip joints became an issue in the Australian election in 2007 when it was revealed that the soon-to-be prime minister, Kevin Rudd, went to Scores with Allan when he visited New York. Rudd's poll numbers went up after the story broke in a Murdoch newspaper.

213    *Col Allan misses Super Bowl moment:* The *New York Post* ran its upfront news Super Bowl coverage with the headline "Ad-Ventures in Pro Football—Winners & Losers for Commercials During Big Game," published February 2, 2004. The story began: "It was a Super Bowl to remember, for what was seen—and what shouldn't have been. The telecast featured a billion dollars' worth of new ads for 32 products, ranging from pickup trucks and Pepsi to computers and potato chips. On the field, the Patriots held off the Panthers to win the title 32-29, while Janet Jackson and Justin Timberlake unsuccessfully tried to steal the limelight with a steamy ending to the halftime show. But, as always, it was the new ads that had fans talking."

213    *Col Allan's genius:* The pros and cons discussed by News Corp. editors and executives.

213    *Allan's loyalty:* Legendary story repeated by News Corp. executives in interviews.

214    *Larrikin Rebekah Wade:* Conversation with author.

215    *Regan's alleged anti-Semitic remarks:* Judith Regan settled a defamation suit against News Corp., in which she alleged that the company fabricated the fact she'd made anti-Semitic remarks, in January 2008. News Corp. and Regan issued a statement describing an "equitable, confidential settlement, with no admission of liability by any party." News Corporation redacted its claim that she had made anti-Semitic remarks: "After carefully considering the matter, we accept Ms. Regan's position that she did not say anything that was anti-Semitic in nature, and further believe that Ms. Regan is not anti-Semitic."

216    *Judith Regan's fall from grace:* First reported in Michael Wolff, "The Trouble with Judith," *Vanity Fair,* March 2007.

217    *Murdoch's relationship with Regan:* Interview with News Corp. executive.

218    *Roger Ailes dates Regan and finds it "the scariest three hours of my life":* Ailes conversation with author, autumn 2003.

221    *Lisa Steele's feelings about Murdoch:* Interviews with Bancroft family members, representatives, and Peter Kann.

222    *May 14 and May 23 meetings:* Interviews with Bancroft family members and representatives.

224    *"An influential member of the family . . .":* Matthew Karnitschnig and Susan Warren, "Key Dow Jones Holder Cites Opposition to Murdoch Bid," *Wall Street Journal,* May 24, 2007.

## CHAPTER 9

227    *Family being informed by reporters:* Interviews with Bancroft family members, Dow Jones board members, and executives.

228 *Billy Cox's e-mail:* Matthew Karnitschnig, Sarah Ellison, Susan Pulliam, and Susan Warren, "Family Dynamics: Behind the Bancrofts' Shift at Dow Jones—Mounting Pressure from Dissident Wing Raises Odds of a Sale," June 2, 2007.

228 *May 31 board meeting:* Interviews with Dow Jones board members and advisors.

228 *Leaks:* Interviews with Michael Elefante and Peter McPherson.

233 *Evans pushed out at Random House:* Lorne Manly, "Harry Evans Leaves Random House for Zuckerman's Shop," *New York Observer,* November 30, 1997.

233 *Evans pushed out by Zuckerman:* Donald Trelford, "Harry Calls It a Day," *Evening Standard,* October 27, 1999.

234 *Weinstein gets rid of Brown:* Phyllis Furman, "Tina Gets $1M in Miramax Split," *Daily News,* July 25, 2002.

235 *Murdoch's nemesis:* Murdoch on Conrad Black, September 22, 2007; on Ted Turner, October 23, 2007; on Maxwell, numerous interviews.

237 *"Murdoch drifted in like a ghost . . .":* Morgan, *The Insider,* 19.

238 *Murdoch gossiping in business section:* Interviews with several business reporters and editors at News Corp. newspapers in Australia, London, and New York.

239 *"Old Grumpy,"* Dover, *Rupert's Adventures in China.*

239 *Uppers and downers:* Interviews with former News Corp. executives and "Banned by Fleet Street: Murdoch by His Butler," *Punch,* July 4–17, 1998.

239 *"Two-pot screamer":* Interview with former News Corp. executive February 27.

240 *". . . intemperate and disagreeable":* Giles, *Sundry Times,* 212.

241 *"in his impulsiveness":* Ibid., 203–4.

241 *"It is important here, for the sake":* Ibid., 206.

241 *"restless temperament":* Ibid., 222.

241 *"authoritarian management":* Ibid., 217.

244 *Robert Thomson under Murdoch's thumb:* Former *Times* editor, conversation with author.

245 *Havard mafia:* Jesse Angelo interview, October 29, 2007.

246 *Roosevelt Island as Aussie enclave:* Col Allan, April 11, 2008.

246 *Paula Zahn:* "I could have put a dead raccoon on the air this year and got a better rating than last year," Roger Ailes told the *New York Times* when confronted with the fact that Zahn's ratings on Fox had risen 90 percent. "That's all just the growth of our network. All our shows are up." Bill Carter, "Fox News Hires a Star Host over CNN Bid," September 6, 2001.

247 *Murdoch and Black deal:* Former *New York Post* reporter interview, confirmed by News Corp. executives.

249 *Harvey Weinstein's influence on "Page Six":* Richard Johnson, conversation with author, autumn 2003.

249 *Dubious motives and good journalism can coexist:* Jenkins, *Market for Glory,* 27.

250 *"He truly is Citizen Kane . . .":* Morgan, *The Insider,* 75.

251 *June 4 meeting:* Interviews with Murdoch, Peter McPherson, Michael Elefante, Lon Jacobs, and James Murdoch.

252 *"I brought in James":* Murdoch interview, September 19, 2007.

252 *"That was actually my idea":* Jimmy Lee interview, October 15, 2007.

254 *Grand Havana Room:* Murdoch and Lon Jacobs interviews.

## CHAPTER 10

255 *Warren Buffett calling:* Peter McPherson, May 27, 2008.

256 *Leslie Hill looking for buyers:* Interviews with Bancroft family members, Dow Jones executives, and board directors.

256 *Brad Greenspan's offer:* Brad Greenspan would later offer to lend Dow Jones the money to buy back half its stock from the family at $60 a share. Board members said they were not convinced he could source the funds.

256 *Chris Bancroft's pursuit:* Dow Jones executives and Bancroft family members and advisors.

257 *Management as true believers:* Warren Phillips was actually perceived by Dow Jones executives and staff as something of a liberal.

258 *Peter Kann's politics:* Peter Kann interview, May 14, 2008.

258 *Murdoch the preferred buyer:* Karen House, June 20, 2008.

260 *"You can't write a fifty-fifty editorial":* As quoted in Tofel, *Restless Genius,* 87.

260 *"On our editorial page . . .":* Grimes, as quoted in *Wall Street Journal* editorial, "An Independent Newspaper. The Bancrofts and a Century of 'Free People and Free Markets,'" June 6, 2007.

260 Wall Street Journal *editorial page history:* Richard J. Tofel interview, Spring 2008.

263 *Murdoch loses circulation over front-page stories about Europe:* Murdoch interview, October 23, 2007.

265 *Murdoch visits Kennedy:* Murdoch interview, March 21, 2008.

267 *Murdoch as* Star *columnist:* Jann Wenner, conversation with author, 2008.

267 *"The American Press might get . . .":* Kiernan, *Citizen Murdoch,* 145.

267 *Whitlam stops speaking:* Ibid., 141.

268 *CIA plot:* Ibid., 170.

268 *Murdoch's coverage of Whitlam's Khemlani loans scandal:* Interviews with journalists at the *Australian.*

269 Marian Faris Stuntz, now Cita Stelzer, interview, November 12, 2007.

269 *"Murdoch didn't change a word of my copy . . .":* Joyce Purnick interview, January 21, 2008.

271 *Muslim crack:* Murdoch interview, February 13, 2007.

273 *Wyatt as a diarist:* Wyatt, *Confessions of an Optimist.*

273 *"A bloody menace . . .":* Bernard Ingham interview, May 12, 2008.

274 *Petronella Wyatt's sex scandal with Boris Johnson:* "Boris Johnson Sacked for Lying over Affair," *Times* of London, November 14, 2004. Petronella Wyatt is now a columnist at the *Daily Mail.*

274 *Stelzer negotiates payout to widow Wyatt:* "I remember when Woodrow died, and Woodrow, who lived well beyond his means, had waived the company pension in order to increase his current income. So I don't know how you do that, but he did it. So now he is dead and there is his widow and I go to see her and she says I have no money, which wasn't true, because Woodrow waived his pension. So I went to Les Hinton. I said can you fix it? Give her the pension, anyhow. Talk to Rupert about it, tell him the story. So Rupert says to Les at some point, pay her the pension. Then he comes over and says, 'I'm going to have tea with the widow Wyatt.' I said, 'Don't go.' He said, 'Why not?' I said, 'Because she is going to cry and you are going to pay her more.' 'No, no, no, I won't.' But he did. But you know that is the way he was." Irwin Stelzer interview, November 12, 2007.

276 *Murdoch and the Stelzers:* Irwin and Cita Stelzer interview, November 12, 2007.

277 *Eric Breindel dies of AIDS in 1998:* Reports of Breindel's death always cited liver failure and chronic health problems. After his death, News Corp. will sponsor an annual award in his name. In 2007, as the deal with Dow Jones wrapped up, a *Wall Street Journal* columnist won. The *New York Post,* ordered to cover the event by Murdoch, runs a story the next day in which the *Journal* columnist's name is spelled wrong.

278  *Murdoch's fax on the Pope:* Alan Howe interview, March 3, 2008.

280  *"He spends a few days in Washington ...":* Frank Luntz interview, September 6, 2007.

280  *FCC closes its eyes to foreign ownership:* Chenoweth, *Rupert Murdoch,* 122–125.

280  *The diaries of Alastair Campbell:* Campbell, *The Blair Years.*

283  *Ailes' independence:* Roger Ailes, conversation with the author, Autumn 2003.

283  *Murdoch buys crèches:* News Corp. executive interviews.

284  *"I'm a very curious person ..."* Murdoch, October 23, 2007.

284  *Kindler believes he should have been hired:* Rob Kindler interview, March 7, 2008.

285  *Hill and Bancroft stalling:* Interviews with advisors and family members.

285  *Stuart Epstein and Thomson:* Bancroft family members were sent an e-mail by the banker, advising them not to accept Murdoch's $60 offer and asking them to come meet with Thomson.

## CHAPTER 11

287  *Water pipe bursts:* Author visited the eighth floor on June 18, 2007.

289  *Chernin not given an opportunity:* Murdoch's opinion of Chernin's reaction, expressed at his temporary home in a Trump building on Park Avenue on September 22, 2007.

> AUTHOR: What was the reaction inside the company, from other parts of the company, to the *Journal* deal? How did Peter Chernin react to it?
>
> MURDOCH: (*Pauses.*) He didn't.
>
> AUTHOR: He didn't oppose it?
>
> MURDOCH: I don't know, but certainly nothing's come back to me, not from anyone on the board level or anything like that. But it wouldn't have been something he liked. He doesn't read newspapers. But on the other hand, Peter is very territorial on everything out of Los Angeles . . . Not all of it to good effect, but we'll see.

290  *Marcus Brauchli's role in editorial agreement:* Interviews with Bancroft family sources and their advisors.

290  *Josh Cammaker's role in drafting agreement:* Interviews with Bancroft family sources and their advisors.

290  *Murdoch conversation with Marty Lipton:* Murdoch interview, September 19, 2007.

290  *". . . telling them to fuck off ":* Murdoch interview, September 19, 2007.

291  *Advisors reach out to Bancrofts:* Interviews with Bancroft family sources and their advisors.

292  *Robert Thomson as architect of digital blah blah story:* Interviews with News Corp. executives.

294  *Murdoch turns up at Prue and Alasdair's house:* Prudence Murdoch interview, February 28, 2008.

294  *Murdoch goes gray:* Lachlan Murdoch interview, February 29, 2008.

294  *Meeting in Aspen, where they discuss him being a liability:* News Corp. sources.

296  *Murdoch ridicules Anna's books:* "Banned by Fleet Street: Murdoch by His Butler," *Punch,* July 4–17, 1998. Butler Philip Townsend writes: "I will never forget the hurt look on Mrs. Murdoch's face as she flounced off to the bedroom when Rupert scoffed at her efforts to become a literary celebrity. They had just returned to the flat in St. James's after dinner at a smart restaurant and I expected them to be in a good mood. While they were out, I had taken a call

from a publicist in Los Angeles who was excited about the caliber of guests he had managed to get for a party to launch Mrs. Murdoch's latest book."

296 *Murdoch and Anna's bargain:* Interviews with Murdoch family members and News Corp. executives.

298 *Murdoch less interested in Diller:* Barry Diller interview, January 28, 2008.

298 *Murdoch out of it in Hollywood:* Interviews with various News Corp. executives and talent on the West Coast.

"I mean he just comes in and it's just . . . it's you know . . . he hated Hollywood. It's a place he doesn't like, so he would come in and ramp about Hollywood. This is what I chose to do for my, you know, for a living. So there was always this, like a rub, you know. He felt like people in Hollywood didn't work hard and, you know, people care about, you know, your people care more about where they go to lunch . . . and stuff like that. There is a portion of this is true, but there is a portion of every business where that is true. . . . So, it was like . . . it was very rough . . . going. You know actually, weirdly, as we got more success-ful the more he would attack. You know, 'I hate the movies and I hate the kind of excess of it all.'" Interview with former Fox studio executive.

"The base reason that he doesn't like Hollywood is because he can't actually function within it and control it. Because there are participants in it. He does not like participation. He just natively does not like it, he does not like joint ven-tures. He's a wolf. He does not like those kinds of situations. He does not like it because he thinks it's excessive and all these kinds of things and all these obvi-ous kinds of things." Interview with former Hollywood boss.

300 *"Wipe that smirk off your face!":* Interview with former Fox executive who attended the meeting.

300 *The Simpsons:* Matt Groening, conversation with author, February 2002.

301 *Bingham family:* Tifft and Jones, *The Patriarch.*

301 *Anna writes a novel:* Anna Murdoch, *Family Business,* 1988.

301 *$650 million:* Several published reports in Britain, the United States, and Australia.

302 *"Rupert didn't like it one bit":* Matt Handbury interview, March 1, 2008.

304 *Sports:* Knee-deep in his banking crisis, Murdoch battled against ITV in the auction for the Premier League rights, and it almost went the other way. At the last second before bids closed, ITV trumped BSkyB. So Murdoch's lieutenant Sam Chisholm, who ran BSkyB, called to ask for another $40 million. It was four o'clock in the morning and Murdoch, who is not the easiest guy to under-stand at the best of times, let out a roaring *mmmmmrrrhh* sound. Chisholm took that as a yes. Three hours later, Murdoch woke up and called back to ask what was going on.

CHISHOLM: Well, look, we put another forty million quid on the table.

MURDOCH: Oh, you know, good heavens. Oh, really? Good heavens. Can we afford this?

CHISHOLM: Well, look, probably not.

MURDOCH: Okay.

Six hours later, Chisholm called Murdoch. He wasn't there—he was out at the barbershop. So Chisholm got the number of the barbershop and interrupted Murdoch's haircut.

CHISHOLM: Look, Christ, we won this bloody thing."

MURDOCH: God. Congratulations. Unbelievable. You know, walking up to this phone, I thought you were gonna ask me for another forty million quid.

CHISHOLM: Would you have given it to me?

MURDOCH: Without a question, without a question.

306   *Malone and Murdoch meet in 1994:* Ken Auletta, "The Pirate," *New Yorker*, November 13, 1995.

307   *Milken as Murdoch's advisor:* James B. Stewart, "Milken File," *New Yorker*, January 22, 2001.

311   *Anna and Murdoch buy a house in Hong Kong:* Interviews with former News Corp. executive, February 26, 2008.

315   *Matt Winkler tells Norm I quit.:* Matt Winkler met Michael Bloomberg when he went to interview him for the *Wall Street Journal.*

315   *"because there's this guy . . .":* Norm Pearlstine interview, September 12, 2007.

## CHAPTER 12

317   *Lippman leaves:* John Lippman left the *Wall Street Journal* for the *Los Angeles Times.* Copy of memo sent to staff at the *Los Angeles Times*, obtained by LAObserved.com:

To: The Staff

From: Davan Maharaj, Business Editor and Sallie Hofmeister, Deputy Business Editor

John Lippman is best known for his story about how a young Chinese-born TV executive named Wendi Deng arrived in the U.S., became the wife of Rupert Murdoch and rose to become a powerful force at his company, News Corp.

When Murdoch, owner-in-waiting of the Wall Street Journal, was asked recently by Journal reporters if he had any problems with the paper's coverage of his company, the media mogul replied that he had none—with the exception of that story about his wife. Asked if he would have taken any action against the writer, Murdoch assured: "No, he's gone."

Now John is coming to Business as an editor in the entertainment group, replacing Jim Bates. Those of you fortunate to be here in the early 1990s will remember John as the television beat reporter who broke an endless string of stories and chronicled the congenial deal-making among media moguls in the pre-Internet age. He then left us for The Wall Street Journal, where he covered the movie industry and wrote the much-followed Hollywood Report column.

At the WSJ, John was known for such front-page stories detailing how "Mighty Morphin' Power Rangers" producer Haim Saban came to rule children's television—Bob "Captain Kangaroo" Keeshan said he was appalled—and how a hot Pasadena start-up called Gemstar TV run by a Cal Tech engineer nearly collapsed from its aggressive accounting methods.

After 25 years as a reporter covering entertainment and media, John will now apply those skills helping to shepherd the group's stories into the paper. Before he arrived at The Times the first time, John worked at The *Sunday Times* in London, Variety, and Broadcasting & Cable magazine. He grew up in New Hope, Pa., and graduated from St. John's College, Annapolis, Md. John has spent the past year trying his hand at public relations at Sitrick & Co.

John lives in the foothills of Pasadena, where he spends his weekend running the trails of the San Gabriel Mountains and trying to amuse his wife, Eve Zukowski, a psychologist, and his two daughters, Rose, 9, and Sonja, 4, with his knowledge of Ancient Greek. Like Murdoch, they remain unimpressed.

318   *Lippman's stash of photos:* Interview with News Corp. executives. Phone calls to Lippman not returned.

318   *Anna changes her outfit six times a day:* Former News Corp. executive, February 26, 2008. "I could never get to grips with Anna . . . I remember going up there to, to, to their house, lots of times. And Rupert would be there. I mean he looks like an unmade bed all the time . . . I'd go up on the weekend, and Rupert's there in a pair of you know, his belt on inside out, God, honestly, I know, he's amazing, sitting around, always looking at his fingernails . . . And, Anna would come out in the morning, right, and um, Rupert would be there sitting there, and then we'd have lunch, and Anna would have changed, into a, you know,

into a nice dress or something. Anna would sort of do all those things but they didn't, they didn't have any real, they never seemed to me, to have any sort of real, connection. I don't know and maybe he is, but he's very affectionate with his children, he's got a great affection for his children I mean, Anna calls him darling and this sort of stuff . . . But Anna didn't ever seem to sort of, she was always very, she always looked like a bloody contrivance to me, Anna. I didn't think there, I didn't think there was much to her. You know, and she did a lot of, she did these things, you know it was all to commit, but I'm a sort of, earthy sort of character. And she'd be better off, instead of trying to change her dress six times a day, you know what I mean."

318   *Were a modern love story:* Barry Diller interview, January 28, 2008.

318   *". . . passed like shadows in the night":* Former News Corp. executive, February 27.

319   *The* Journal's *Wendi piece:* John Lippman, Leslie Chang, and Robert Frank, "Meet Wendi Deng: The Boss's Wife Has Influence at News Corp.—Murdoch Spouse, 31, Has Come a Long Way Since Leaving China a Dozen Years Ago," *Wall Street Journal,* November 1, 2000.

320   *Wendi Murdoch early bio:* Wendi Murdoch interviews, April 28 and May 18, 2008.

322   *Wendi works in a Chinese restaurant:* Wendi Murdoch interview, May 19. "The first day I got fired from one restaurant, because they asked me if I had experience [laughs] and I said yes. And then I'm not getting it, how to carry that tray. [Laughs] Then I work in the kitchen and they gave me food for free. It was amazing. I got paid $20 and worked from eleven o'clock in the morning to eleven o'clock at night, but you get a leftover soup to take home. [Laughs] I mean for a whole month, I spent $9 for a whole month because I buy a whole bunch of instant noodles and you can eat every day. But in China it's worse because when we grow up there's not enough food so you just have like rice and water. You know, they have meat every day in the restaurant. I gained like ten pounds. I used to be a lot smaller. [Laughs] It's a great life because you have meat every day. It's amazing."

323   *Wendi gets a summer job at Star TV:* Wendi Murdoch interview, May 19. "The story say that I met Bruce Churchill on a airplane, and that by the end of the airplane I got myself a job. So what did I do on the plane, you know, in first class? [Laughs] . . . No, it's not true . . . I interviewed with Bruce in Los Angeles, on my spring break. One of the Yale alumni introduced me. And I went into the office and he interviewed me. And he also interview other people, so went through the process. So me and also Dan Goldman, the other summer intern, we both got hired—he was from Columbia . . . I was summer intern out there for two and a half months, I was traveling, doing different . . . I never met Rupert. But people have so many different stories."

323   *Wendi at Star TV:* Interviews with former and current Star TV executives.

324   *"To be honest, a lot of young Chinese . . .":* Gary Davey interview, March 1, 2008.

324   *Rupert needs a translator:* Gary Davey interview, March 1, 2008. Dover, *Rupert's Adventures,* 134. Bruce Dover argues that Wendi had actually met Murdoch at a cocktail party just before the July 1, 1997, handover of Hong Kong. Dover said Murdoch told him after the party how "impressive" he found the young Chinese woman. Wendi denies this meeting.

325   *Wendi and Murdoch talk business:* Gary Davey and other News Corp. executives.

325 *Wendi chronology:* Wendi Murdoch first directed the author to use Gary Davey's account of how she and Murdoch first met. But in a follow-up e-mail, she said, "I met Rupert at a business meeting in HK, Spring 1998." News Corp. executives and family members say they believe the relationship started before the separation.

326 *Murdoch calls in sick for Wendi.* Gary Davey says the phone call occurred months before Murdoch told Anna. Bruce Dover says the phone call occurred in late 1997, Dover, *Rupert's Adventures.*

326 *marriage counselor:* Dame Elisabeth interview, February 25, 2008.

326 *Separation announcement:* Liz Smith, *New York Post,* April 20, 1998.

326 *"I've met a nice Chinese lady":* Prudence Murdoch, February 28, 2008.

327 *"hard, ruthless and determined.":* David Leser interview with Anna Murdoch, *Australian Women's Weekly,* published July 25, 2001. Copy of interview transcript provided to the author.

330 *". . . idiot brother-in-law":* Interviews with News Corp. executives.

331 *Prostate cancer:* Wendi Murdoch, May 19, 2008.

331 *Wendi confused:* May 19, 2008.

WENDI MURDOCH: I didn't know what is prostate cancer. It was a really scary experience. Thank God everything came out fine. Mike Milken really helped, though.

LEELA DE KRETSER: Do you remember finding out?

WENDI MURDOCH: He called me. We have to keep it a secret, don't tell anybody else. But then when we came to Sloan-Kettering hospital, someone leaked from the doctor's office and the stock price went down.

DE KRETSER: Shit.

WENDI MURDOCH: It was a really scary experience, he was so helpful. He was talking to me, explaining it to me, because he had himself. Rupert found out early, so. Every morning he'd go for radiation with the same person at St. John's Hospital, I'd go with him. Just a really, umm, that's why we started having children. Before, we hadn't thought about when, but after that happen, we say, if I want to have children, we have to do this . . . So . . . It's a big decision. Are you going to have kids?

DE KRETSER: Yeah. Is that what happened?

WENDI MURDOCH: Yeah. Because you have no choice. Because after radiation you're not so sure. Then, I think compared to other people, at the time we couldn't talk about it, we had to go to the hospital under a different name and everything. And I was very isolated, and a bit down, depressed. Once you open up to people, a lot of people go through the same thing. So many people. I never thought. I thought it just happened to us, but it's not true.

DE KRETSER: What about Lachlan and James and Elisabeth, were you able to talk to them about it?

WENDI MURDOCH: In the beginning, Rupert didn't want to say anything, but later on when it came out in the press, they all worry, duh, duh, duh. Like me, they were so shocked in the beginning. But then, they found out already during this process. Also, he stopped the radiation for one week, every day he did it from Monday to Friday, every day, right, but that one week we went to James' wedding, the radiation. I think it bring the family closer and it was nice.

AUTHOR: What kind of treatment? Did he have that pellet treatment, where they—

WENDI MURDOCH: No. Radiation only.

DE KRETSER: Was it the external beam, where they—

WENDI MURDOCH: Yep. You go there, that machine. He go first in the morning, he had a different name, he'd go there get the key. Michael Milken helped with everything, just amazing. But also he just realized that all his friends have it, from Silvio Berlusconi to, umm, Intel, Andy Grove, everybody called and "I did this, I did that, you should try this." A million people had it. It's very common.

AUTHOR: Yeah, totally. It's the old man club.

DE KRETSER: It's one thing for the guys to talk, but if you're the wife, though, you are going through your own special—

WENDI MURDOCH: I didn't talk to anybody. I don't talk to anybody. I just remember it was very isolating. And I just feel like you want to be secretive, you don't want to tell people, duh, duh, duh, that's hard. [Laughs]

336    *Murdoch and the Google guys:* Wendi Murdoch, April 28, 2008.

336    *Rupert is dimmer figure than Wendi (and submissive):* Prudence Murdoch, February 28, 2008. "I think he says yes to have a peaceful life, and does what he wants, like most men. 'Yes, dear. Yes, dear,' but just do what you want. That's not the same as being submissive. That's *appearing* submissive. But I think Wendi, in a way, is almost the strongest woman he's ever had . . . Because she seems to get away with more than anything. She goes on and on and on. And she's quite violent because she handles the language not very well. And her intonation is not quite right. And so sometimes she really—it's kind of like whoa—there's no mucking about. I really like that about her. 'Oh, Rupert!' Rolls her eyes in front of everybody. And he'll go, 'Oh, I know.' Then he is submissive. He's kind of taken on more than he can handle in a way. But he's got better at telling her to be quiet. Not that she listens."

336    *Wendi accused of an affair:* News Corp. executives did not—and do not—believe that Wendi was having an affair with the employee. Most were disgusted that the *Los Angeles Times* had made the phone call and told the story to demonstrate the types of attacks Wendi has suffered while an employee.

336    *Wendi making a movie:* Wendi Murdoch and Zhang Ziyi have bought the production rights to Lisa See's *New York Times* best seller, *Snow Flower and the Secret Fan.*

## CHAPTER 13

339    Times *first covers Murdoch:* "Working to Upgrade Masses," *New York Times,* January 17, 1969.

339    *Murdoch wants to get the* Times: Kiernan, *Citizen Murdoch,* 236.

340    Times *attack 1:* Jo Becker, Richard Siklos, Jane Perlez, and Raymond Bonner, "Murdochracy: Murdoch, Ruler of a Vast Empire, Reaches Out for Even More," *New York Times,* June 25, 2007.

341    Times *attack 2:* Joseph Kahn, "Murdochracy: Murdoch's Dealings in China: It's Business and It's Personal," *New York Times,* June 26, 2007.

343    *Circulation:* "Up, Up, Up, Again for New York's Newspaper," *Daily News,* May 1, 2007.

345    *Roger Ailes' terrorism fears:* Roger Ailes, conversation with the author.

346    *News Corp. hates Bill O'Reilly:* News Corp. executives.

346    *Brian Lewis notes:* News Corp. executive.

347    *"Is it true that Barack Obama is on the move . . .":* Celeste Katz, "Fox Prez 'Obama' Crack Ends Debate," *Daily News,* March 10, 2007.

347    *Wendi Murdoch dines with Obama:* Wendi Murdoch interview.

349    *Due diligence:* John Nallen and Lon Jacobs interviews.

## CHAPTER 14

351    *Packer gets married to Erica Baxter:* Jamie Packer's wedding was part Scientology. The reception was held at the Hotel du Cap–Eden Roc.

352    *Murdoch worries about Lachlan:* Murdoch interviews, January 12, March 21, and June 2, 2008.

354    *Murdoch children negotiations on trust:* Interviews with Murdoch family members and News Corp. executives and advisors.

355 *Interviews with children:* Prudence Murdoch in Vaucluse, Sydney, February 28, 2008; Lachlan Murdoch in Surrey Hills, Sydney, February 29, 2008; Elisabeth Murdoch, November 15, 2007; James Murdoch, Wapping, London, May 1, 2008.

363 *Lachlan is weak in the United States:* News Corp. executive interviews.

363 *Lachlan supports Fight Club:* Interview with former Fox executives.

364 *Chernin and Ailes take credit for pushing Lachlan out:* Interviews with News Corp. and Hollywood executives.

365 *"A great magazine":* Murdoch interview, January 12, 2008.

366 *Lachlan and Jamie Packer's deal:* Miriam Steffens, "Nothing Joint-Ventured, Nothing Gained," *The Age,* April 12, 2008.

366 *"I don't understand it":* Murdoch interview, March 21, 2008.

368 *Anna Murdoch on Charlotte:* After wondering about the blood of Murdoch and Freud running through her granddaughter's veins, Anna Murdoch added, "But Charlotte is the most happy, sanguine child that you could ever imagine." David Leser, *Australian Women's Weekly,* July 25, 2001.

369 *Freud and Murdoch become friends:* Interviews with Murdoch family members and News Corp. executives.

369 *Sailing anecdote:* Rebekah Wade interview, October 2007.

369 *Freud knows Prue:* Prudence Murdoch interview, February 28, 2008.

370 *Shine: Are You Smarter than a 5th Grader, Ugly Betty,* and *The Office* are among the shows licensed by Elisabeth Murdoch.

371 *James:* Steve Hemsley, "Murdoch Clinches Mushroom Buyout," *Music Week,* September 19, 1998; Jane Martinson, "James Murdoch Sets Net Aims," *Guardian,* July 10, 1999; David Lieberman, "Murdoch Grew Up in an Atmosphere of Ritual Feuding with Other Media," *USA Today,* August 1, 2007; Steve Clarke, "Murdoch, a Chip Off the Old Block," *Variety,* December 17–23, 2007.

372 *James and Lachlan fight:* News Corp., Murdoch interviews.

372 *James and Lachlan visit Blair:* Campbell, *The Blair Years,* 603.

373 *"a little menace":* James Murdoch interview, June 2007.

373 *James' personality:* Prudence Murdoch interview, February 28, 2008. "I love James. He's very smart. James . . . got so much responsibility that he's become quite formal. He's had to grow up very quickly. The way he's handled that is he's become quite formal in his ways. He's always been quite like that, but I think more so recently."

374 *Deal with Conrad Black:* Former *New York Post* reporter, confirmed by News Corp. editors.

375 *James and ITV:* Barry Flynn and Chris Whynn, "BSkyB's Long-Term View Bets on US Pay-TV Model," *New Media Markets,* August 13, 2004; Maggie Brown, "Are Branson's TV Plans Virgin on Ridiculous?" *PR Week,* February 9, 1996; Simon Goodley, "BBC Breaks Ranks to Join BSkyB in Digital TV Bid," *Daily Telegraph,* June 13, 2002; Robert Lea, "Branson the Star in ITV Merger Plan," *Evening Standard,* November 10, 2006; Chris Tryhorn, "Branson Rages at Sky as ITV Rejects His Offer," *Guardian,* November 22, 2006; Daniel Farey-Jones, "Sky Ordered to Reduce Stake in ITV Below 7.5%," *Brand Republic News,* January 30, 2008.

376 *America's Cup:* "It's All Over," *New Zealand Herald,* July 4, 2007.

376 *Agent provocateur:* James Murdoch interview, May 1, 2008.

## CHAPTER 15

377  *Murdoch is ready to walk away:* Interviews with Dow Jones executives, board members, and Bancroft family members and advisors.

378  *Sweetener:* News Corp. executive, conversation with the author, June 2007.

378  *Bancrofts out of the loop:* Interview with Bancroft family members.

379  *"farted around and were dysfunctional":* Dow Jones advisor interview, January 10, 2008.

379  *Denver Trust:* Interviews with Dow Jones board members and Bancroft family members and advisors.

380  *Billy Cox visits Murdoch:* Andrew Steginsky, May 23, 2008.

380  *Murdoch calls Tom Hill:* Bancroft family members.

380  *Due diligence:* John Nallen interview, January 7, 2008.

382  *Dow Jones wants more:* John Nallen interview, confirmed by Dow Jones executives.

382  *Board approves the deal:* Interviews with board members.

382  *Kann meets with the Cook branch:* Peter Kann interview, May 14, 2008.

383  *July 23 meeting:* Interviews with Bancroft family members and their advisors.

385  *Crawford Hill e-mail:* "Bancroft Cousin's Letter: 'Paying the Price for Our Passivity,'" *Wall Street Journal,* July 27, 2007.

387  *News Corp. wants 50 percent:* Murdoch interview, September 19, 2007.

387  *Final negotiations:* Interviews with Murdoch, News Corp. executives, family members, Dow Jones executives, and advisors.

388  *Final phone call:* Andrew Steginsky, May 23, 2008.

BIBLIOGRAPHY

## BOOKS

Amann, Joseph Minton, and Tom Breuer. *Fair & Balanced, My Ass! An Unbridled Look at the Bizarre Reality of Fox News*. New York: Nation Books, 2007.

Auletta, Ken. *The Highwaymen: Warriors of the Information Superhighway*. New York: Random House, 1997.

Barry, Paul. *The Rise and Rise of Kerry Packer*. Sydney: Bantam, 1993.

Belfield, Richard, Christopher Hird, and Sharon Kelly. *Murdoch: The Decline of an Empire*. London: Macdonald, 1991.

Blibb, Porter. *Ted Turner: It Ain't as Easy as It Looks*. Boulder, Colo.: Johnson Books, 1993.

Block, Alex Ben. *Outfoxed: Marvin Davis, Barry Diller, Rupert Murdoch, Joan Rivers, and the Inside Story of America's Fourth Television Network*. New York: St. Martin's Press, 1990.

Bower, Tom. *Maxwell: The Final Verdict*. London: HarperCollins, 1996.

———. *Outrageous Fortune: The Rise and Ruin of Conrad and Lady Black*. New York: HarperCollins, 2006.

———. *Conrad and Lady Black*. London: Harper Perennial, 2007.

Britain, Ian. *Once an Australian: Journeys with Barry Humphries, Clive James, Germaine Greer and Robert Hughes*. Oxford: Oxford University Press, 1997.

Brivati, Brian. *Lord Goodman*. London: Richard Cohen Books, 1999.

Bruck, Connie. *The Predators' Ball: The Junk-Bond Raiders and the Man Who Staked Them*. New York: American Lawyer, 1988.

———. *Master of the Game: Steve Ross and the Creation of Time Warner*. New York: Penguin, 1994.

Campbell, Alastair. *The Blair Years: The Alastair Campbell Diaries*. New York: Alfred A. Knopf, 2007.

Chenoweth, Neil. *Rupert Murdoch: The Untold Story of the World's Greatest Media Wizard*. New York: Crown Business, 2001.

Chester, Lewis, and Jonathan Fenby. *The Fall of the House of Beaverbrook*. London: Andre Deutsch, 1979.

Chippindale, Peter, and Chris Horrie. *Stick It Up Your Punter! The Rise and Fall of the Sun*. London: Heinemann, 1990.

Coleridge, Nicholas. *Paper Tigers: The Latest, Greatest Newspaper Tycoons and How They Won the World*. London: Heinemann, 1993.

Cudlipp, Hugh. *Publish and Be Damned! The Astonishing Story of the Daily Mirror*. London: Andrew Dakers, 1953.

Curtis, Sarah, ed. *The Journals of Woodrow Wyatt*. 2 vols. London: Macmillan, 1998–99.

Davis, L. J. *The Billionaire Shell Game: How Cable Baron John Malone and Assorted Corporate Titans Invented a Future Nobody Wanted*. New York: Doubleday, 1998.

Dean, Brenda. *Hot Mettle: SOGAT, Murdoch and Me*. London: Politico's, 2007.

Dover, Bruce. *Rupert's Adventures in China: How Murdoch Lost a Fortune and Found a Wife*. Edinburgh: Mainstream Publishing, 2008.

Dyke, Greg. *Inside Story*. London: HarperCollins, 2004.

Edwards, Ruth Dudley. *Newspapermen: Hugh Cudlipp, Cecil Harmsworth King and the Glory Days of Fleet Street*. London: Secker and Warburg, 2003.

Evans, Harold. *Good Times, Bad Times*. New York: Atheneum, 1983.

Felsenthal, Carol. *Power, Privilege and the Post: The Katharine Graham Story*. New York: Seven Stories Press, 1999.

Fitzsimons, Peter. *The Rugby War*. Sydney: Harper Sports, 1996.

Frost, David. *David Frost: An Autobiography,* Part 1: *From Congregations to Audiences*. London: HarperCollins, 1993.

Fyffe, Hamilton. *Northcliffe: An Intimate Biography*. Whitefish, Montana: Kessinger Publishing, 2005.

Giles, Frank. *Sundry Times*. London: John Murray, 1986.

Goodman, Arnold. *Tell Them I'm on My Way*. London: Chapmans, 1993.

Grade, Michael. *It Seemed Like a Good Idea at the Time*. London: Macmillan, 1999.

Greenwall, Harry J. *Northcliffe: Napoleon of Fleet Street*. London: Allan Wingate, 1957.

Hack, Richard. *Clash of the Titans: How the Unbridled Ambition of Ted Turner and Rupert Murdoch Has Created Global Empires That Control What We Read and Watch.* Los Angeles: New Millennium Press, 2003.

Harrison, Bridget. *Tabloid Love: Looking for Mr. Right in All the Wrong Places.* New York: Da Capo Press, 2006.

Hentoff, Nat. *Speaking Freely: A Memoir.* New York: Alfred A. Knopf, 1997.

Hewat, Tim. *Golden Fleeces II: The Murdoch Years at Boonoke.* Sydney: Bay Books, 1987.

Holden, Anthony. *Big Deal: A Year as a Professional Poker Player.* New York: Viking, 2001.

Horrie, Chris. *Tabloid Nation: From the Birth of the* Daily Mirror *to the Death of the Tabloid.* London: Andre Deutsch, 2003.

Horsman, Mathew. *Sky High.* London: Orion, 1997.

Hughes, Robert. *The Fatal Shore: The Epic of Australia's Founding.* New York: Alfred A. Knopf, 1987.

Humphries, Barry. *More Please.* London: Penguin, 1992.

Hussey, Marmaduke. *Chance Governs All.* London: Macmillan, 2001.

Inglis, K. S. *The Stuart Case.* Melbourne: Melbourne University Press, 1961.

James, Clive. *Unreliable Memoirs.* London: Picador, 1981.

———. *As of This Writing: The Essential Essays, 1968–2002.* New York: Norton, 2003.

Jenkins, Simon. *The Market for Glory: Fleet Street Ownership in the 20th Century.* London: Faber and Faber, 1986.

———. *Thatcher and Sons: A Revolution in Three Acts.* New York: Penguin, 2007.

Keating, Stephen. *Cutthroat: High Stakes and Killer Moves on the Electronic Frontier.* Boulder, Colo.: Johnson Books, 1999.

Kiernan, Thomas. *Citizen Murdoch.* New York: Dodd, Mead, 1986.

Knightley, Phillip. *A Hack's Progress.* London: Vintage, 1998.

———. *The First Casualty: The War Correspondent as Hero and Myth-Maker from the Crimea to Iraq.* Baltimore: Johns Hopkins University Press, 2004.

Landes, David. *Dynasties: Fortunes and Misfortunes of the World's Great Family Businesses.* New York: Viking, 2006.

Langley, Andrew. *Rupert Murdoch.* Heinemann Profiles. Oxford: Heinemann Library, 2001.

Leapman, Michael. *Barefaced Cheek: The Apotheosis of Rupert Murdoch.* London: Hodder and Stoughton, 1983.

Lunn, Hugh. *Working for Rupert.* London: Hodder, 2001.

MacArthur, Brian. *Eddy Shah: Today and the Newspaper Revolution.* London: David and Charles, 1988.

Mahler, Jonathan. *The Bronx Is Burning: 1977, Baseball, Politics, and the Battle for the Soul of a City*. New York: Picador, 2005.

Marr, Andrew. *My Trade: A Short History of British Journalism*. London: Pan Books, 2003.

Monks, John. *Elisabeth Murdoch: Two Lives*. Australia: Macmillan, 1994.

Morgan, Piers. *The Insider: The Private Diaries of a Scandalous Decade*. London: Ebury Press, 2005.

———. *Don't You Know Who I Am?* London: Ebury Press, 2007.

Motavalli, John. *Bamboozled at the Revolution: How Big Media Lost Billions in the Battle for the Internet*. New York: Viking, 2002.

Munster, George. *Rupert Murdoch: A Paper Prince*. Victoria: Viking, 1985.

Murdoch, Anna. *In Her Own Image*. New York: William Morrow, 1985.

———. *Family Business*. New York: William Morrow, 1988.

Neil, Andrew. *Full Disclosure*. London: Macmillan, 1996.

Nissenson, Marilyn. *The Lady Upstairs: Dorothy Schiff and the New York Post*. New York: St. Martin's Press, 2007.

Paige, Bruce. *The Murdoch Archipelago*. London: Pocket Books, 2004.

Porter, Henry. *Lies, Damned Lies and Some Exclusives: Fleet Street Exposed*. London: Hogarth Press, 1984.

Rohm, Wendy Goldman. *The Murdoch Mission: The Digital Transformation of a Media Empire*. New York: John Wiley and Sons, 2001.

Shawcross, William. *Rupert Murdoch*. New York: Simon and Schuster, 1992.

Taylor, A. J. P. *Beaverbrook*. London: Hamish Hamilton, 1972.

Tifft, Susan, and Alex Jones. *The Patriarch: The Rise and Fall of the Bingham Dynasty*. New York: Summit Books, 1991.

———. *The Trust*. New York: Little, Brown, 1999.

Tofel, Richard. *Restless Genius: Barney Kilgore and the Invention of Modern Journalism*. Forthcoming.

Tucille, Jerome. *Rupert Murdoch: Creator of a Worldwide Media Empire*. London: Piatkus, 1990.

Watkins, Alan. *A Short Walk down Fleet Street: From Beaverbrook to Boycott*. London: Duckworth, 2000.

Wendt, Lloyd. *The Wall Street Journal: The Story of Dow Jones and the Nation's Business Newspaper*. New York: Rand McNally, 1982.

Wheatcroft, Geoffrey. *The Strange Death of Tory England*. London: Penguin, 2005.

Wintour, Charles. *The Rise and Fall of Fleet Street*. London: Hutchison, 1989.

Wyatt, Petronella. *Father, Dear Father: Life with Woodrow Wyatt*. London: Hutchinson, 1999.

Wyatt, Woodrow. *Confessions of An Optimist*. London: Collins, 1985.

Young, Hugo. *One of Us*. London: Macmillan, 1991.

Younger, R. M. *Keith Murdoch: Founder of a Media Empire*. Sydney: HarperCollins, 2003.

## PERIODICALS

Baker, Marina. "Life on the Couch with Freud." *Punch*, May 24, 1997, 32–35.

Baker, Russ. "Murdoch's Mean Machine: How Rupert Uses His Vast Media Power to Help Himself and Hammer His Foes." *Columbia Journalism Review*, May/June 1998, 51–56.

Burton, Tony. "Literary Lions at War." *Daily Mail*, Oct. 16, 1992, 22.

Carmody, Deirdre. "Tina Brown Accused of Misusing *New Yorker*." *New York Times*, Oct. 15, 1992, C15.

Dowling, Robert, and Paula Parisi. "Dialogue: Rupert Murdoch." *Hollywood Reporter*, Nov. 14, 2005.

Faith, Nicholas. "Lord Catto." *The Independent on Sunday*, Sept. 22, 2001.

"The Full Monty." *Punch*, Sept. 25, 1998, 8–11.

Griffen-Foley, Bridget. "The Fairfax, Murdoch and Packer Dynasties in Twentieth Century Australia." *Media History* 8, 1 (2002): 89–102.

Hagerty, Bill. "'I don't do it for the money'—Rupert Murdoch." *British Journalism Review* 10:4 (1999).

Harris, John. "The Odd Couple." *Guardian Weekend*, Nov. 3, 2007, 33–42.

Henderson, Gerard. "Digger Biography Not Dirty Enough for Some." *Sydney Morning Herald*, Nov. 10, 1992, 13.

"How Young Murdoch Hits the Right Note." *Punch*, Oct. 9, 1998, 16–17.

Le Carré, John. "The Letter She Wouldn't Print." Oct. 26, 1992: 72.

McVicar, John. "Murdoch's Big Balls-Up." *Punch*, Nov. 6, 1998, 6–7.

Morries, Merrie. "Murdoch Book Eschews Tabloid Gossip." *Washington Times*, March 8, 1993, D1.

Picardie, Ruth. "Feuds Corner: William Shawcross v. Francis Wheen." *Guardian*, Nov. 17, 1992: 4.

Prince, Dominic. "Dial M for Murdoch." *Punch*, Feb. 21, 1997, 12–15.

"Rupert Laid Bare." *Economist*, Mar. 20, 1999.

Shawcross, William. "Does It Make Sense to Hate Murdoch?" *Evening Standard*, Sept. 8, 1992, 9.

Silvester, Christopher. "Rupert Murdoch: The Sequel." *Spy*, May 1988, 97–104.

Streitfeld, David, and Charles Trueheart. "The Tiff of the Town: *New Yorker* Draws Le Carré's Fire." *Washington Post*, Oct. 15, 1992, C1.

Sullivan, Andrew. "A Press Lord Without a Rosebud." Review of *Murdoch* by William Shawcross. *New York Times*, Jan. 17, 1993.

Townsend, Philip. "Dishing the Dirt on Rupert." *Punch*, Aug. 14, 1998, 23–26.

Wheen, Francis. "Licentious Prude, Written in Wind and Water." Review of *Rupert Murdoch: Ringmaster of the Information Service* by William Shawcross. *Literary Review*, Sept. 1992, 4–6.

# INDEX